News in a Digital Age

Custom Edition for University of Arizona

Taken from:

Journalism: Who, What, When, Where, Why and How
by James Glen Stovall

New New Media, Second Edition
by Paul Levinson

The Media of Mass Communication, Eleventh Edition
by John Vivian

Cover Art: Courtesy of Photodisc, EyeWire/Getty Images.

Taken/Excerpts taken from:

Journalism: Who, What, When, Where, Why and How
by James Glen Stovall
Copyright © 2005 by Pearson Education, Inc.
Published by Allyn & Bacon
Boston, Massachusetts 02116

New New Media, Second Edition
by Paul Levinson
Copyright © 2013, 2009 by Paul Levinson
Published by Penguin Academics and Pearson Education, Inc.
Upper Saddle River, New Jersey 07458

The Media of Mass Communication, Eleventh Edition
by John Vivian
Copyright © 2013, 2011, 2009, 2008 by Pearson Education, Inc.
Upper Saddle River, New Jersey 07458

This special edition published in cooperation with Pearson Learning Solutions.

Pearson Learning Solutions, 501 Boylston Street, Suite 900, Boston, MA 02116
A Pearson Education Company
www.pearsoned.com

Printed in the United States of America

1 2 3 4 5 6 7 8 9 10 V3NL 17 16 15 14 13

000200010271786514

TS

ISBN 10: 1-269-41577-8
ISBN 13: 978-1-269-41577-4

Contents

Chapters 1–7 taken from *Journalism: Who, What, When, Where, Why and How* by James Glen Stovall.

Chapter 3

Law and the Journalist   42

Chapter 8 taken from *The Media of Mass Communication*, Eleventh Edition by John Vivian.

Chapter 9 taken from *Journalism: Who, What, When, Where, Why and How* by James Glen Stovall.

Chapter 9

Ethical Practices   178

Chapters 10–15 taken from *New New Media*, Second Edition by Paul Levinson.

Chapter 10

Youtube   193

Chapter 11

Blogging   **219**

Chapter 12

Twitter   260

Chapter 13

Wikipedia   274

Chapter 14

Politics and New New Media   292

Chapter 15

The Dark Side of New New Media   305

Chapter One

News and Society

Key Concepts and Terms

1. News is the major product of journalism; news is information that journalists believe is important or interesting for their audiences.

2. Open society: a society in which information is exchanged with no or relatively little interference from the government or other organizations that control the norms of society.

3. News values: characteristics of information that make an event or subject news; they include timeliness, conflict, impact, currency, prominence, proximity, and unusualness.

4. News is one of the main ways in which a society examines itself; that examination provides an important means by which the society can find solutions to its problems.

5. News helps individuals in society make decisions about their lives and actions.

6. Watchdog: the term given to the news media as an independent observer of other parts of society (government, business, educational institutions, etc.) to see that they are doing their jobs properly.

7. Bias: beliefs, attitudes, and points of view that prevent journalists from evaluating and presenting information in the fair and accurate manner expected by the audience.

8. News organizations have an obligation to present information to their audiences and to keep channels of communication in society open. They also have the added burden of maintaining their own economic health in a capitalist economic system.

Vignette

The morning of September 11, 2001, was cool and clear in western Pennsylvania where CNN reporter David Mattingly was vacationing. His wife's family lives in that part of the country and Mattingly, one of CNN's top environmental reporters, always likes to get a feel for the outdoors wherever he is. He and his brother-in-law were about to set out on a fishing trip to Canada when the news came.

His wife's aunt called and told them to turn on the television. Something was happening that was too significant to be ignored, even for a long-anticipated vacation. Planes had crashed into the World Trade Center towers in New York City. Another plane had crashed into the Pentagon in Washington, DC.

Then the local news broke in and said a fourth plane—United Airlines Flight 93—had crashed in Pennsylvania. It was not clear then if it was connected to the other crashes.

Mattingly called his editor in Atlanta but could not get through. The lines were jammed, and all the editors were trying to get people to New York and Washington. He then called a friend in another part of the building and had that person walk into the newsroom and tell his editors that he was trying to get in touch. Shortly after that, Mattingly was in his car driving toward Shanksville, the small town near the crash site.

"During times like this, it's hard to be a reporter first," he said. "I had been affected personally by what had happened in New York, as were many other people, and it was hard to separate my emotions."

Mattingly was one of the first national reporters on the scene. He was allowed into the media area that the police had set up, but he was still about 200 yards from the crash site. That site was over a ridge and not visible to the reporters.

Using his wife's cell phone, Mattingly called Atlanta and was soon on the air with live reports. CNN had dispatched a satellite truck and camera crew from Detroit, and it took several hours for them to arrive. Mattingly went on the air live that evening sometime between 7 and 8 P.M. By then he had ridden on in a police van to view the crash.

"I had seen airplane crashes before," he said, "but this was different. There was no identifiable part of the plane that you could see."

Mattingly continued to send live reports for the next eight hours, finally leaving the scene at about 3 A.M. He found the nearest motel and checked in, exhausted but unable to sleep. He then realized it was September 12, his birthday.

That event was not the first, nor the last, big story that Mattingly has covered for CNN. He was on the scene when the U.S. Supreme Court decided the presidential election in 2000, and he was in Houston covering the trial of Andrea Yates, the woman who killed her five children. In 2003 he was part of the CNN team that covered the investigation into the murder of Laci Peterson, a woman eight months pregnant when she disappeared just before Christmas. Her husband was later charged with the murder.

News is all around us, permeating our lives. Whether it is the extraordinary events of September 11, 2001, or everyday occurrences such as the weather (see Everybody Talks about the Weather, p. 9), news is an integral part of our modern existence.

News is the major function of journalism. News is information that helps us expand our lives and order the society in which we live. Our experience with the weather is something we can share with others, but it is made richer and more meaningful when it is supplemented by the information and experiences we have with journalism.

This chapter outlines and explains some of the aspects of news. As we explore the concept of news, keep in mind a few basic points:

- **News is a construct of journalism.**   That is, news is what journalism and journalists say it is. News does not happen naturally. News is not just information. There is lots of information around us; some of it qualifies as news, but most does not.

- **News relies on the experiences of the audience to be effective.**   Journalists assume that we can understand what they are telling us about because we can relate our own experience to what they are saying. Most people gather lots of experiences as they go through their daily routines. These experiences are important to the way in which we process and interpret the news that journalists produce for us.

- **The more open a society is, the better the news process works.**   When information is freely available, journalists find it easier to obtain, interpret, and process. News consumers have more journalistic sources that they can go to for information. America has created a relatively open society, although the pressures to close off information are constant. The events of September 11, 2001, have renewed efforts, particularly by the U.S. government, to restrict information. Such efforts and restrictions should be viewed very skeptically, even when they are called for in the name of "national security."

News Values

What makes an event or topic news in the eyes of the journalist? The same thing could happen to two people in two different places, and one would be a news story and the other would not. For instance, if you were involved in a minor automobile accident in which there were no injuries, the incident probably would not appear in your local newspaper. If the president were involved in that same type of accident, it would probably be the first story on all the nightly newscasts.

FIGURE 1.1   All Kinds of Weather Even disastrous floods such as the Red River flood in 1997 (pictured here) affect relatively few people directly. Yet they become part of our shared experience through the process of journalism and the mechanism of news. (Photo credit: Federal Emergency Management Agency)

The separation of events into "news" and "not news" categories is a function of what we call news values. These are concepts that help us decide what a mass media audience is or should be interested in. There are millions of "events" that occur in our society every day. Those few events editors and news directors select as news have at least one of the characteristics discussed here.

Impact

Events that change people's lives are classified as news. Although the event itself might involve only a few people, the consequences may be wide-ranging. For example, if Congress passes a bill to raise taxes or if a researcher discovers a cure for a form of cancer, both actions will affect large numbers of people. They have impact, and they would be considered news.

Timeliness

Timeliness is a value common to almost all news stories. It refers to the recency of an event. Without the element of timeliness, most events cannot be considered news. For example, a trial that occurred last year is not news; a trial that is going on right now may be news. How much time has to elapse before an event can no longer be considered news? No single answer to that question applies to every case. Most events that are more than a day to a day-and-a-half old are not thought to be news. (Look in today's newspaper and see if you can find a news story about an event that occurred more than two days ago.)

Prominence

Prominent people, sometimes even when they are doing trivial things, make news. The president of the United States is a prime example. Whenever he takes a trip—even for purely personal and private reasons—his movements are covered in great detail by the news media. The president is a prominent and important person. Anything he does is likely to have an impact on the country, and people are very interested in his actions. The president is not the only example of a prominent person who often makes news. Movie stars, famous politicians, advocates of social causes—all of these people make news simply because they are very well known.

FIGURE 1.2   Prominence as a News Value The president of the United States is the ultimate example of the news value of prominence. Just about anything the president says or does is newsworthy, whether he is playing a game of golf or making a major speech, as shown here just after the 2003 State of the Union address. (Photo credit: White House photos)

Proximity

Events occurring close to home are more likely to be news than the same events that occur elsewhere. For example, a car wreck killing two people that happens on a road in your home county is more likely to be reported in the local news media than the same kind of wreck that occurs 1,000 miles away. We are interested in the things that happen around us. If we know a place where something goes on, we are more likely to have a feeling for it and for the people involved.

Conflict

When people disagree, when they fight, when they have arguments—that's news, particularly if one of the other news values, such as prominence, is involved. Conflict is one of the journalist's favorite news values because it generally ensures there is an interesting story to write. One of the reasons trial stories are so popular with newspaper readers and television viewers is that the central drama involves conflict—two competing forces, each vying to defeat the other.

The Bizarre or Unusual

A rare event is sometimes considered news. There is an adage in journalism that goes, "When a dog bites a man, that's not news; when a man bites a dog, now that's news." These events, though they may have relatively little importance or involve obscure people, are interesting to readers and enliven a publication. For example, it's not news when someone's driver's license is revoked (unless that someone is a prominent person); it is news, however, when a state department of transportation revokes the license of a person called "the worst driver in the state" because he had twenty-two accidents in the last two years.

Currency

Issues that have current interest often have news value, and events surrounding those issues can sometimes be considered news. For example, a panel discussion of doctors may be held in your community. Normally, such a discussion might not provoke much interest from journalists. If the discussion topic were the latest cancer-fighting drugs, the news value of the event would change, and there would likely be a number of newspaper, radio, and television journalists covering it. Issues that have the value of currency come and go, but there are always many such issues being discussed by the public.

Beyond these basic news values, however, are many other factors that affect the daily news menu that is presented to you as a news consumer. One is the limited ability of a news organization to gather, process, and present news. Every broadcast organization is limited by time. There is only so much time in which news can be aired. Even twenty-four-hour news operations, such as Cable News Network or MSNBC, are limited by the number of hours in a day.

And, of course, twenty-four hours is not devoted to news. Much of this time is given over to promotions and advertising. In fact, on local news broadcasts, the amount of time available for local news is very small; when the time for ads, weather, and sports is subtracted from a thirty-minute newscast, there is usually only about seven or eight minutes left for local news. Sometimes a significant portion of that time is used up by chatting among the anchors.

Newspapers and magazines are limited by the amount of pages or space they have in which to place the news. In newspaper jargon, this space is called the "news hole." Except for special and important news events, a newspaper will not automatically add pages just because there is more news than anticipated. The amount of space available for news depends on the amount of advertising the newspaper ad staff has been able to sell, and most newspapers determine how large they will be by some formula based on advertising. For many newspapers, the ratio is about 50 percent news and 50 percent advertising, but in some it can be 40:60 (news to advertising) or even 30:70.

News web sites go a long way toward overcoming the limits of time and space that bedevil print and broadcast news organizations. Time is not a factor in presentation of news on the Web, and space is virtually unlimited. Far more information can be presented on the Web than in newspapers or on a news broadcast.

But news web sites run into another limitation that plagues all news organizations—limited staff. Any news organization can employ only a certain number of people to remain economically viable, and those people can gather, write, and edit only a limited number of stories each day. Consequently, there are significant events or topics in a community that may not receive the coverage they deserve because news organizations simply do not have enough people.

Why News Matters

News, essentially, is what journalists say it is, as we have seen in the previous section. But why does it matter? What is so important about news, and why should anyone who is not involved with journalism care?

Quote 1.1

WILLIAM BERKELEY

On the absence of printing and free schools

I thank God we have no free schools or printing, and I hope that we shall not have these for a hundred years. For learning has brought disobediences and heresy and sects into the world; and printing has divulged them and libels against the government. God keep us from both.

Sir William Berkeley was governor of the colony of Virginia from 1642 to 1652 and from 1660 until his death in 1677.

News performs specific and important functions for society. The contributions that news makes to our society can be classified into three categories: information, entertainment, and persuasion. These are not mutually exclusive. Rather, they are intertwined and sometimes difficult to separate in real life.

The information function of news is the most obvious and most important. News tells a society or community about itself. It helps to define and explain ourselves to ourselves. At one level, it simply gives us an awareness that there are people, places, and events that are beyond our personal experience. One psychological tendency that we have is to define the world in relationship only to ourselves and our experiences. News helps us step beyond ourselves to broaden our outlook and experience. Beyond the psychological aspects, news gives us a daily set of information that tells us about the world in which we are living.

That awareness can help us make decisions about our lives. Take the example of the weather. Many of us have made decisions about what to wear or whether to carry an umbrella based on the morning weather report. Sometimes we have made decisions about travel because we knew a storm was coming or one had just passed, knocking down trees that might block roadways. We have changed our schedules because of the news, making sure that we arrived on time for a concert or located ourselves in front of a television at the time we wanted to watch a baseball game.

Sometimes the news media are given too much credit for helping us make decisions. Some people believe that they manipulate us into making decisions on how to act or whom to vote for because of news reports we see or read. Advertising, particularly, is thought to have this magical power: We see an ad for something, and we go out and buy it. Decisions about what to buy or whom to vote for are much more complex than that, and the news media are not the only factors that help people make these decisions.

EVERYBODY TALKS ABOUT THE WEATHER

Everybody talks about the weather. When we meet a stranger or when we don't know what else to talk about with a friend, we can talk about the weather.

The topic offers many points of discussion. It's been too wet or dry. It's been too hot or cold. A cold front is moving in. It's about to get really hot. We wonder when the next hurricane, tornado, flood, or snowstorm will hit, and in the area when seasons change, we wonder what the winter, summer, or fall foliage will be like.

The weather is a shared experience, something that we all have in common. It changes constantly, so there is always something to talk about.

But beyond limited personal experience, what do we know about the weather? Probably not much. We know that in most places it is hot in the summer and cold in the winter, but we don't know how hot or cold it is. We know that we have had a lot (or a little) rain this spring, but we don't know exactly how much or how this year compares to what is normal. We know what the sky looks like right now, but we don't know if it will rain this afternoon or tomorrow. And if a major weather-related event occurs in another part of the nation, we don't have a clue about that.

Except through journalism and the news process.

They do contribute to a person's decision-making process, however, and the extent of this contribution is a source of continuing and important debate in our society.

News and the news media help us to organize and prioritize the world around us. By giving us certain types of information, news helps us orient our thinking about the world. It tells us what others think is important, thereby allowing us to decide if we want to accept or reject those priorities. Politics, economics, religion, personal awareness, and social interaction are areas of our lives that mean a great deal to us. News gives us information in each of these areas that aids us in knowing what we should think about and how we should assess the things that happen to us and to those around us.

News also gives us information about the issues that provide continuing debate and discussion about our society. Because we are a modern society—and a relatively free and open one—we believe that there should be a public discussion about any number of issues. The news media help select those issues, a process that scholars have called "agenda setting," give us information about those issues, and even provide a forum in which people can be heard.

FIGURE 1.3   News in Times of National Crisis In times of national crisis, news becomes particularly important to people. Whether it is a world war (this photo shows people standing in Times Square watching a news ticker give information about the Allied invasion of Europe) or a terrorist attack, news allows us to share the same information and reach a common understanding about current events. (Photo credit: Library of Congress)

The second major function of news is entertainment. This function is not a frivolous one; it is meaningful to us personally and has important implications for society. Much of the news we receive does not affect us personally. We do not necessarily need to know it in terms of how we order our lives or because of the decisions we have to make. Rather, much of the news is merely interesting.

But it is also distracting in a very positive sense. News, as we have said earlier, takes us beyond ourselves. It allows us to experience many people and events vicariously—experiences we would not have if it weren't for the news media. Those experiences are valuable and enriching. They deepen our lives and our thinking. This kind of news also gives us information that we can use for relating and interacting with others.

The entertainment function of news has been a matter of debate among journalists for many years. Some journalists and news shows have taken this function beyond what is considered to be standard journalistic practices and have thereby—in the minds of some—distorted the information being presented. One of the words for this is *sensationalism* (another term more recently used has been *infotainment*), which means that lurid aspects of the news are emphasized merely because those aspects will appeal to people and build an audience for the news program or publication. Supermarket tabloids and slickly produced, celebrity-emphasizing news shows are constantly under fire from journalists in more traditional organizations for practicing this kind of journalism.

The persuasion function of the news is the most subtle of the three functions but its importance is enormous. As we discussed earlier, news helps us make decisions about our personal and civic lives. It helps us to understand the world in which we live and order the experiences and events that occur in our realm. News aids in shaping our outlook. News can also help us decide what is important, what we will think about, and what we will discuss.

As such, many social critics have argued, the information we get from the news media helps to maintain social order. Some have even gone so far as to argue that news helps to control society by letting us know what is proper to think about and what is not. A crude example of this was the reaction of the news media and the public in the days and weeks after the events of September 11, 2001. During that time, much was said about the goodness of America, and a good deal of information about the nation's problems and the shortcomings of its leadership went unreported. Much negative information about the Muslim religion and people who adhere to that faith was presented by the news media. For a time, it became appropriate for many Americans not of that faith to think and speak negatively about it. This was just one instance in which the news media reflected and reinforced the social order.

Some people tend to see this persuasive function of the news as a great conspiracy whereby the masses of people are knowingly and openly controlled. That would mean that a significant number of people inside the profession of journalism are there for motives other than the accurate presentation of news and information. That is not the case. Rather, journalists too are citizens of society and have internalized the values that all of us share. They have an interest in maintaining the social order. But, like others, they also have an interest in raising questions about that order when necessary.

News and the Social Order

News is an integral part of modern society. It is particularly important to the functioning of various aspects of society. The following is a review of how news covers and affects some of the most important parts of our public life. This review is not comprehensive in its view of all aspects of society, but it does provide some examples as to how news works.

Politics is probably 90 percent talk and 10 percent action, as it should be. Much of politics is about ideas, attitudes, and beliefs. It is about presenting points of view and arguing those points, with some people attacking and others defending. It is about persuasion, discussion, and compromise. True, many politicians and political operatives

FIGURE 1.4   The Last Laugh for Harry Truman Tensions are always near the surface between presidents and the press. In 1948 President Harry S Truman surprised just about everyone on Election Day by beating Republican Thomas Dewey. The *Chicago Tribune,* which had vociferously opposed Truman, printed an early edition based on some first returns and ran the headline "Dewey Defeats Truman." Later in November, when Truman was traveling from Independence, Missouri, to Washington, DC, he stopped in St. Louis, and someone handed him an edition of the paper. Truman held it up and produced one of the great presidential images of modern American politics. (Photo credit: Associated Press Wide World Photos)

hold rallies from place to place, shake hands, and appear in many attention-getting situations. As legislators, they also propose and enact laws. If they are in the executive branch of government, they are in charge of putting laws into effect. But the main job of politics is to select and mold the ideas that hold us together as a civic society.

Much of daily journalism is devoted to the coverage of politics and the political arena. How we govern ourselves says a great deal about our society and in many ways determines the kind of life that we will lead. News coverage of this area of our society allows us to survey and record the way in which our governing philosophy is operationalized on a day-to-day basis. Journalism gives us information about who is running for election, what ideas they are presenting, and how they are conducting their campaigns.

One of the main jobs of news and the news media in the realm of politics is to serve as a "watchdog" on government and governmental officials. This role evolved from the development of journalism in the nineteenth century (see Chapter 5) when newspapers and magazines launched crusades against corruption and mismanagement of public funds. Many of these crusades also revealed problems with society, such as child labor, which the government had ignored and needed to be addressed. Journalism acted as an independent voice in the political system that could bring such problems to light and suggest reforms. The news media maintain that role today, sometimes with dramatic results such as in the Watergate scandal of the early 1970s.

A related role for news in the political arena is that of a conduit of public opinion. News not only tells us what the government is doing but also informs governmental officials about the public's reactions and concerns. By their selection of issues to spotlight and their approach to the information concerning these issues, the media also help to mold public opinion.

The news media's participation in the political system is far from perfect and is under constant criticism even from within the profession of journalism. In today's era of twenty-four-hour television news and always-on Internet availability, one of the major complaints about the media is that there is more opinion than information. In other words, ironically, there is not enough news. News organizations find it easier and cheaper to produce talk shows and opinion forums than news programs that present substantive information. This condition has led to another criticism that many people level at the news media—fragmentation. With so many people expressing so many opinions, the political system is becoming increasingly fragmented. Many political organizations, political parties in particular, have lost their ability to gather and coalesce opinions into concrete plans of action. This fragmentation has led to a shortened attention span on the part of the politicians and the public that focuses on short-term problems rather than long-term issues.

Another area of society in which news plays an important role is the economic arena. News provides consumers with important information to use in making choices, from deciding what toothpaste to buy to selecting investments for their money. News helps young people decide where to go to college and what career they should pursue. Just about every economic decision we make is influenced by the information we receive from journalism.

TEDDY ROOSEVELT AND THE "BULLY PULPIT"

Teddy Roosevelt called it a "bully pulpit," and he made it so.

Roosevelt ascended to the presidency in 1901 after the assassination of William McKinley in Buffalo, New York. Roosevelt was just 42 years old, the youngest man ever to hold the office. He was unlike anyone who had ever occupied the White House, particularly the faceless personalities who had been in office for the previous 40 years since the death of Abraham Lincoln.

Roosevelt loved a good argument. He did not mind controversy. And he loved the press, particularly reporters. They, in turn, loved him.

Roosevelt was always "good copy" for journalists. Despite childhood ailments of bad eyesight and asthma, Roosevelt was an energetic outdoorsman. He rode horses, went camping, explored the wilderness, and hunted wild game. With Roosevelt, there was always something interesting to write about. He was an environmentalist and scientist. He was also a historian and author of more than thirty books.

His bear-hunting exploits attached his name to America's all-time favorite toy— the Teddy bear.

Roosevelt relished making speeches. He had a high-pitched voice that pierced the inattention of an audience and made them sit up and listen. He waved his arms and pounded his fist.

He had much to debate. During his presidency, he championed legislation that reigned in railroads, established federal government inspection of meat, provided great consumer protection, and built the Panama Canal. He set aside vast stretches of land as national forests, parks, and monuments.

One of his enduring legacies is the lasting effect he had on politics, particularly the presidency. The force of his personality turned it into the white-hot center of American politics. Everything that Roosevelt did called attention to himself, and that was just the way he liked it.

Journalism also performs something of the same watchdog role on the economic system that it does on the political system. Many news organizations, both print and broadcast, have people on staff whose job is to be a consumer advocate. They not only help solve individual problems for consumers, but they also uncover corruption and unfair business practices. As in the political arena, many people criticize the news media for not being aggressive enough in bringing these practices to light. These critics point to the fact that news organizations are dependent on the advertising revenue they receive from the businesses they are covering. Consequently, for instance, a small-town newspaper that runs two pages of advertising from a giant chain department store is unlikely to write about how the chain forces its employees to work extra hours for less than appropriate overtime pay. Some media organizations do fall victim to this kind of pressure, but many editors and publishers have fought against it, even when it has cost them advertising income.

The legal system is another area of society in which news plays an important role. Adherence to the law is one of the basic operating principles of people in a civil society. In many nations of the world, there is no tradition of trust in the law or faith in those in power to administer the laws fairly. Those societies are open to civil strife and even civil war. Americans do have a basic faith in the law and a tradition of respecting those who administer it, but this faith must be constantly tended and renewed. News coverage of the system is a major way in which the law and the legal system can be seen to be working properly.

Ours has become an increasingly litigious society. That is, more people are looking to the courts to solve their problems, and more organizations and individuals are asking the courts to protect their property and their rights. Part of this increase in legal activity stems from the growing number of lawyers graduating from law school and going into practice. But part of it also stems from the increasing attention the news media—in a variety of forms—are giving to the legal system. Several high-profile trials, such as the O. J. Simpson murder trial in the mid-1990s, have stimulated this attention. But the news media have also found that trials are relatively easy to cover. They are confined to a single location and the participants are often readily available for interviews. They also provide the drama of conflict, a major news value (see discussion earlier in this chapter), and they usually have a definite conclusion, such as a verdict. Consequently, news consumers are inundated with trial coverage not only by daily journalism but also by television programs on cable channels such as Arts and Entertainment, The Learning Channel, and the Discovery Channel. CourtTV, another cable channel, devotes itself entirely to coverage of trials and has a substantial web site that supplements this coverage (www.courttv.com).

Despite the many positive aspects of this massive attention to the court system by the news media, critics make some valid points. One is that the trials that receive the most coverage are those involving celebrities or those whom the media have made into celebrities. Another criticism is that news coverage of trials is more likely to be entertaining than educational. Yet another criticism is that news coverage of high-profile trials does not give the public an accurate picture of how the legal system really works. Finally, critics point out that the news media's emphasis on criminal trials ignores a vast and important part of the legal system—civil litigation. Civil trials often have more long-term impact on the public because they formulate and refine public policy in many areas but, compared to criminal proceedings, they are virtually ignored.

A final area of society in which news plays a particularly important role is sports. Some people dismiss sports as being unimportant and meaningless. Those sentiments pointedly ignore the massive amount of time, money, and interest humans the world over give to sports. Newspapers have sports sections that are often larger than news sections. Local television news broadcasts devote a substantial amount of time to sports coverage. A number of cable channels carry nothing but sports events and news and commentary about sports. Our educational system is involved with sports at every level and, at the collegiate level, sports creates a major revenue stream for any

What Do You Think?

THE JOURNALIST'S DILEMMA

Even in an age of increasing interactivity, journalists have an uncertain relationship with their audiences. One of the enduring questions, often unstated, in newsrooms every day is, "Should we give audiences what they need—hard news and information, what's important, what has long-term effects on their lives—or should we give them what they want—sensationalism, celebrity, rumor, and opinion?"

Serious critics of the profession in every journalistic generation conclude that journalism has an inclination toward the latter—sensationalism, celebrity, and rumor.

The current generation of journalism is no different. Consider this:

Tim Rutten, media critic for the *Los Angeles Times,* noted in a column at the end of 2003 that Slobodan Milosevic had been on trial for two years. Milosevic had been president of Yugoslavia and is the first head of state to stand trial for war crimes. He has been charged with sixty-six counts

of involvement in atrocities in Croatia, Bosnia, and Kosovo, and his trial was taking place at the World Court in the Netherlands.

From January 1, 2000, to the end of 2003, Rutten found, the *New York Times* had printed 120 stories on the case. The *Washington Post* had printed 41 reports, and his own newspaper, the *Los Angeles Times,* had carried 58 stories.

Compare that with the coverage given to basketball star Kobe Bryant, charged with rape, and pop superstar Michael Jackson, charged with child molestation.

During 2003, the *New York Times* ran 113 stories on the Kobe Bryant case, the *Washington Post* 107 stories, and the *Los Angeles Times* 450 stories. The charges against Michael Jackson, which did not surface until the fall of 2003, produced 58 stories in the *New York Times,* 58 stories in the *Washington Post,* and 87 stories in the *Los Angeles Times.*

The charges against Bryant and Jackson are serious, but do they compare with the vast atrocities attributed to Milosevic? Many people, unfortunately, are charged with rape and child molestation, but how many people get charged with crimes against humanity?

It might be an easy conclusion to draw that news organizations should pay more attention to Milosevic than Bryant or Jackson, but before doing that, ask yourself this:

Whose trial would you rather read about (or hear about on television)—Slobodan Milosevic or Kobe Bryant and Michael Jackson?

institution. Professional athletes are among the highest-paid individuals in the world. Many city and state budgets devote millions of dollars to building and maintaining sports facilities, from Little League baseball fields to major league sports stadiums. Interest in sports—and news coverage of sports—is so pervasive that even those who claim not to be interested in it have trouble ignoring it or knowing something about the people involved in it.

FIGURE 1.5   **The Thrill of Victory** Sports is of great interest to many people, and it takes a great deal of the news media's time and attention. That attention is heightened when a major sports events such as the Olympics takes place. (Pictured here, U.S. athletes march into Olympic Stadium in Sydney, Australia, for the opening of the 2000 games.) (Photo credit: Department of Defense)

Two generations ago, news coverage of sports concentrated on sports events and ignored most of the other aspects of sports. Today, however, more attention is devoted to the salaries of athletes and the financial health of sports franchises than to the performance of the team. Such coverage reveals that athletes are not the individual role models that we idealize and that colleges and universities are not the paragons of virtue that academicians would like to claim. To cover news of sports takes more than knowledge of the game. It demands a wide range of understanding the rules of operations, economics, and even psychology.

Critics of news coverage of sports point out that the news media confer celebrity status on those athletes who are not ready or able to handle it. Another telling criticism, especially at a local level, is that news coverage of local teams is often favorable and forgiving rather than accurate and revealing because the audience of local fans demands that kind of coverage. Finally, critics point to the fact that with sports the news media is part of a system that encourages spectatorship rather than participation in sports and, consequently, gives it the wrong priority within our society.

Pressures on Journalists

Journalists meet many challenges in gathering, processing, and distributing the news. The most daunting is the sheer difficulty in doing the job, as we discuss throughout this book. Finding information, conceptualizing news stories, writing and editing copy, and then broadcasting or getting words into print or posted on a web site—none of these is an easy task.

A PASSPORT, A KEYBOARD, AND A PAYCHECK

Garrett Lane

Why study journalism? There is a noble reply. A free press is among our most cherished rights and remains critical to our democratic way of life. But there is another implication in the question. What about the lives of those who practice journalism? In other words, why should you study journalism and become a journalist?

I love being a journalist. I love press passes and scoops and deadlines and proofreaders' marks. I've been a working journalist for nearly eight years, and I still get excited every time I see my byline. I think you should study journalism and become a journalist, too. Here's why.

A journalist's life is a good one. It's a passport to a career, awash in options, full of open doors. You will be hard-pressed to imagine a more portable or versatile job. Pick a spot on the globe. Something's happening there, and journalists are writing about it. And it's not just the daily news flash. Journalists cover everything—French cuisine, Spanish soap operas, Italian red wines, Caribbean fly-fishing, American rockabilly music. Some journalists even write about the work of other journalists. How's that for flexibility?

Journalism offers you the rarest of perks: getting paid to do whatever makes you happy. You want to live in Michigan and restore vintage automobiles? Follow the professional surfing tour from beach to beach? Trek through rain forests?

Journalists I know get paid to do all of those things. A journalism degree is a blank check. You can live anywhere, do most anything—your personal interests will only make you a better journalist.

And this world needs better journalists. We need good information to conduct our daily doings. We need it to buy groceries, understand foreign policy, and go on vacation. In my observation, if three or more people take up an activity, it's probably a story. Other people will want to know about it, why it happened, and what it means. And that's what journalists do—they make information make sense.

Clear communication remains a commodity. Technology offers us an astonishing variety of outlets. We can speak across distances and cultures with increasing ease. But these fine channels are useless unless someone collects, analyzes, and organizes the messages we send. I encourage you to study journalism because it is noble and essential. And I encourage you to become a journalist because of the life you will lead.

Garrett Lane is online editor of Southern Accents *magazine, a national shelter publication that embraces a regional lifestyle. His professional experience includes work in print and online journalism as a reporter, illustrator, editor, instructor, and designer.*

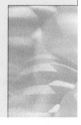

But journalists face difficulties in addition to the routine procedures of their job. These difficulties often prevent them from doing the job that they would like to do in giving their audience information.

One difficulty is their own bias or point of view. Journalists are supposed to be fair in presenting information, and some use the word *objective* to describe how journalists are supposed to approach their job. But no matter how well trained or experienced journalists are, they remain human beings who have feelings and ways of interpreting experiences that are different from other people. Journalists can never be completely objective or unbiased in presenting the news, and both they and their audiences should acknowledge this.

Another difficulty that journalists face in presenting the news is the very human trait of making mistakes. Journalists get things wrong, no matter how careful they are and no matter how strict the editing procedures are. Sometimes sources give them incorrect information. Sometimes they do not understand the information they have. Sometimes information gets tangled up in the editing process. Sometimes the point of view they have prevents them from seeing or understanding the event or topic they are covering. Most journalists and news organizations work very hard to keep errors to a minimum, and most of the time both are successful. But errors do occur, and when they do, the credibility of journalists and news organizations is damaged.

Journalists are also constantly confronted with the possibility of a "blame the messenger" syndrome. Journalists must deliver bad or uncomfortable news. That's their job. But the audience to whom they give this news is not always appreciative of their efforts. During the Vietnam War in the late 1960s, a lone journalist, Seymour Hersh, uncovered information that indicated U.S. servicemen had killed a village full of old men, women, and children. Exactly what happened in My Lai is still a matter of dispute, but whatever it was, the facts did not reflect well on the United States. Many people did not want to know this and blamed Hersh and other journalists for bringing it to light. They were called unpatriotic and un-American because they told people things they would rather not hear.

The Job of the Journalist

Journalists decide what is news, and in doing so they make many important decisions about what a society says to itself, how it explains itself, what social order is established and maintained, and how the problems and shortcomings of that society are revealed. In addition to doing all of these things, journalists also have certain responsibilities to their own profession:

- They must maintain the standards of their profession as well as the customs and conventions of the journalistic culture. These conventions include gathering news and information, editing it for their medium, and distributing it in ways that meet standards of fairness and accuracy.

- Journalists have the responsibility of maintaining the economic health of their news organizations. Because these organizations are not government sponsored

FIGURE 1.6 Always the News No matter what the political or economic situation—war or peace, boom or bust—people will always need to know the news, and they will always depend on journalists and the news organizations for which they work to provide it to them. They are willing to pay for that news, but they want it to be accurate and fair. (Photo credit: Library of Congress)

or supported (except in very rare instances), they must make enough profit to continue operation and to have the resources to practice the kind of journalism that is expected and necessary for society.

■ Finally, journalists are charged with fostering and promoting the idea of an open society in which information flows freely, people can think and speak creatively, and a variety of points of view about all topics is tolerated.

The chief tool that the journalist uses to do all of these things is news.

QUESTIONS FOR DISCUSSION

1. How much do you use the news to make decisions about your life? What types of decisions do you make based on the news you read or hear?

2. The author makes a number of statements in this chapter and elsewhere about how important the news is to society. Do you agree?
3. The author talks about a "blame the messenger" syndrome that sometimes occurs when the news media have to deliver bad news. How often do you think that happens? Can you think of any specific instances of it happening?
4. Do you think the news media pay too much attention to sports? Is this the news media's fault, or are they just giving the audience what it wants?

RELATED WEB SITES

Civic Journalism Interest Group, www.has.vcu.edu/civic-journalism

Committee of Concerned Journalists, www.journalism.org

Community Journalism Project, www.rtndf.org/resources/cj.shtml

Newseum, www.newseum.org

Pew Center for Civic Journalism, www.pewcenter.org

PJNet: Public Journalism Network, www.pjnet.org

The Readership Institute, www.readership.org

Web Credibility Project (Stanford University), www.webcredibility.org

"With the People," www.pewcenter.org/doingcj/pubs/pubs_toolbox.html

READINGS AND REFERENCES

Clark, R. P. (1994). *The American conversation and the language of journalism.* Poynter Paper No. 5, St. Petersburg: Poynter Institute.

Cohn, V., Cope, L., & Winsten, J. (2001). *News & numbers.* Ames, IA: Iowa State University Press.

Dennis, E. E., & Pease, E. C. (Eds.). (1997). *The media in black and white.* Rutgers, NJ: Transaction Books.

Fallows, J. (1995). *Breaking the news: How the media undermine American democracy.* New York: Pantheon.

Fry, D. (Ed.). (1985). *Believing the news.* St. Petersburg: Poynter Institute for Media Studies.

Gutierrez, F., Wilson, C., & Chao, L. (2003). *Racism, sexism, and the media: The rise of class communication in multicultural America.* Thousand Oaks, CA: Sage Publications.

Hohenberg, J. (1995). *Foreign correspondence: The great reporters and their times* (2nd ed.). Syracuse, NY: Syracuse University Press.

Klaidman, S., & Beauchampn T. L. (1987). *The virtuous journalist.* New York: Oxford University Press.

McGowan, W. (2001). *Coloring the news.* San Francisco: Encounter Books.

Meyer, P. (2002). *Precision journalism* (4th ed.). Lanham, MD: Rowman & Littlefield Publishers.

Reeves, R. (1999). *What the people know: Freedom of the press.* Cambridge, MA: Harvard University Press.

Chapter Two

2

Beginnings of Journalism

Key Concepts and Terms

1. Individuals and groups have always needed to communicate new information and the latest news to each other; consequently, journalism is a part of any society, ancient or modern.

2. Journalism in any age depends on the technology available to gather and disseminate information.

3. Writing makes information easier to convey than simply speaking; writing also creates a permanent record, something that establishes a history and a basis for a society.

4. *Acta Diurna:* a daily publication of political and society news begun during the reign of Julius Caesar in 59 B.C.

5. *Moveable type:* individual pieces of type that can be reused for different printing jobs. The concept of moveable type was the key to the invention of the printing press around 1450.

6. Printing was only one of the factors that brought Western civilization out of the Dark

Ages. Other factors included an increase in literacy and easier means of dissemination (such as the development of safer travel routes).

7. *Censorship:* prevention by governmental or religious authorities of dissemination of information they believed threatening to their position.

8. Benjamin Franklin was the great journalistic innovator of the eighteenth century; he pioneered the development of newspapers throughout the American colonies by investing in start-up papers, creating news services among newspapers, and promoting a light and entertaining style of writing.

9. Modern journalism, with its emphasis on fair and accurate presentation of information, did not exist during the 1790s, the first decade of the American Constitutional republic. Instead, it was the age of partisanship when newspapers presented political points of view rather than information.

When we look back through the history of journalism, we see the same themes recurring.

Journalism is at the mercy of technology, for example. Certainly we no longer write on parchment with a quill, but rest assured that medieval scribes would have used electronic computers and photocopying machines had they the chance. Journalists use what's available to do the best job with the least effort.

Journalism is equally at the mercy of its financial base. The economics of publishing have changed over time, but journalism has never been free or cheap. Gathering, understanding, and distributing information takes enormous effort and usually substantial investment.

Journalists write for an audience. They keep a sharp eye on their readers, on who needs information, and on who is willing to pay for it. That audience has changed over the centuries, just like technology and the financial base of publishing have changed. But journalism is always a form of communication and, thus, requires people who write and people who read.

The history of journalism is also characterized by the steady development and acceptance of professional practices. Our medieval scribe took great pains to make his illuminated manuscript beautiful, and today the best journalists take equal pride in investigating an event and choosing just the right words to report it. Excellence never goes out of style.

These themes and others will be traced through Chapters 3–5 and 7.

Where Does Journalism Begin?

Most of our attention for Chapters 4 and 5 will be on the written forms of communication that humans developed from the earliest known civilizations. But journalism itself is a prewriting concept. Oral and verbal communication was the first way in which humans communicated, and it continues to be an important means of communication today. As humans formed tribes and societies, they needed to exchange information about themselves and about the world around them. They did so orally.

But oral communication was inadequate for any society that grew more sophisticated. As hunting decreased and agriculture increased, societies grew more stable; workloads shifted and divisions of labor became more complex. Trading of goods and services meant that records had to be kept.

One of the earliest civilizations that we know about is that of the Sumerians, who populated the area of the Tigris and Euphrates rivers (present-day Iraq, Iran, Kuwait, and Saudi Arabia) about three thousand years before the birth of Christ. The Sumerians built a fascinating society in which writing played a vital role. The Sumerians developed a system of writing that used a standardized set of symbols and designs. This system did not evolve into a full alphabet as we think of it today, but it did allow Sumerians to scratch symbols into moistened clay so that they could keep records and know what others had written. (The Sumerians even developed some literature, stories about their people and past that included a tale about the world being flooded. This story appeared long before Jewish society was formed, and the story of Noah and the great flood was known.)

The remarkable thing about the Sumerians was not their system of writing but their system of printing. When multiple copies of an important mark were required, such as the designation of ownership, Sumerians first produced a stamp that they could press into soft clay. The stamp resembled the letters of a letterpress that came into use nearly five thousand years later.

But the Sumerians went beyond the stamp. At some point in their history, they developed cylinders that could be engraved with a number of symbols. These cylinders were small, about the size of an index finger. They could be easily transported and were used to spread information and ideas about the Sumerians beyond the immediate area. The idea of a rolling cylinder to "print" information was revived several thousand years later and is the way in which most of our printed information comes to us, but for the Sumerians (who did not have paper) cylinder "printing" was a simple idea that made life easier.

Writing, as crude as it was for the Sumerians, did for them what writing has always done for any individual or society that used it. It made information easier to convey, and it made the conveyance of that information more accurate. It also gave the information a permanence that extended the reach, and even the life, of the person who created it. Writing helped the individual Sumerians connect with each other and with those beyond their borders and their time. We know a great deal about the Sumerians today, five thousand years after their people dispersed and their buildings crumbled, because they wrote things down.

But was this journalism? Not in the modern sense possibly, but in the broadest sense, it was because the information was timely and what people needed and wanted. They needed information to operate their daily lives, and they needed the stories that helped them make sense of their world. These were basic needs, and journalism helped fulfill them.

Each civilization that succeeded the Sumerians developed their own means of communication and ways of exchanging information and making it permanent. The Chinese found ways to make paperlike substances on which to record their information; they also invented something very close to the nineteenth- and twentieth-century processes of printing. In addition, Chinese emperors instituted a postal system that enabled information to flow in from all parts of their vast holdings. Egyptians worked on a system of writing and, like the Sumerians, came close to creating a standardized alphabet. That achievement was finally accomplished by the Phoenicians (or so some historians believe); it was a system of symbols representing the sounds of speech. The Greeks took the alphabet from the Phoenicians or other peoples in the Orient and used it to articulate the information and ideas of a highly sophisticated society.

Greece, of course, had a far-flung empire that needed channels of communication to keep it together. Writing was a necessary but insufficient means for doing this. The Greeks had to send information quickly over long distances, and although sailing ships would do for this purpose in some instances, they did not always have the speed the times and situations demanded. Consequently, the Greeks put together a telegraph system with a series of signal fires and earthenware jars that would adjusted in a prearranged way to send messages quickly over great distances.* Several hundred years before the birth of Christ, Rome followed Greece in its role as the dominant world power. The Roman system of rule, both at home and outside of Italy, was more complex and sophisticated than any other the world had seen, and it depended on timely information. It is in Rome that we begin to see the first inklings of what we would recognize as journalism. Rome had inherited and developed its own system of writing that closely resembles the one we use today. A Roman citizen (and many within the empire who were not citizens) had a good chance of being literate. Citizenship required some degree of participation—at least to the extent that one was expected to understand the rights and responsibilities of citizenship—and that participation, to a greater or lesser degree, required current information.

FIGURE 2.1   Caesar Augustus A brilliant leader and organizer, Caesar Augustus understood the value of information and the importance of communicating with all parts of the Roman Empire. He built roads and established a postal system with regular deliveries. He also encouraged reading and the trading of books throughout the empire.

Rome, then, developed what many people believe is the first daily newspaper devoted to public and political affairs. The *Acta Diurna,* begun by Julius Caesar in 59 B.C., was an official daily account of political news and acts from the Senate. Its content went beyond governmental affairs, however. *Acta* contained information about events within the city of Rome, tidbits about famous people, news about executions, fires, and other calamities, and even news about the weather. The *Acta* was printed and posted around the city, read avidly, and remained a vital part of Roman life for many decades.

Augustus, who followed Julius as ruler of Rome, maintained and extended the system of roads and highways for which the Romans were justly famous. He put this system to good use by commissioning a postal system with a regular delivery schedule to make sure that Roman edicts and propaganda were spread to all parts of the empire.

Few of Augustus's successors could match his genius and innovation in governing the empire, and some were downright destructive. By the fifth century A.D., the empire was crumbling, beset by internal strife and by hoards of European tribes that the emperors had not been able to subdue. When the empire dissipated in 476 with the fall of Rome, Europe was plunged into several centuries when many of the progressive ideas the Romans had about communication and journalism were forgotten or abandoned. The Catholic Church became the dominant power, and for much of the next millennia it showed little inclination to encourage intellectual breakthroughs.

*For a detailed description of this system, see Jackson P. Hershell, "The Ancient Telegraph: War and Literacy," in *Communication Arts in the Ancient World*, Eric Havelock et. al., eds. (New York: Midpoint Trade Books, 1978) 82–87.

Most of the societies of Europe returned to reliance on an oral tradition. Writing was centered mainly in monasteries where book copying was a major activity. Books, which had replaced rolled manuscripts, were valued possessions, but any ideas about their mass production that might have followed from the Romans seem to have been lost. Instead, monks were put to the painstaking work of hand copying manuscripts.

The lack of development of Roman ideas of printing and mass communication was just one of several factors in the medieval environment that impeded intellectual progress. Travel was often dangerous, so commerce outside local areas was scarce. Literacy rates dropped, and people seemed to have little need for information. The Church maintained its position as the sole intermediary between the people and their Supreme Being. Despite all of these factors, some individuals, particularly monks and priests, continued to record events and develop ideas within their private journals and among select groups of contemporaries.

By A.D. 1400 this closed system was collapsing. Universities had sprung up around Europe, and students had taken over the tedious business of copying manuscripts. Order was returning to the major highways, and commerce was growing. A new spirit of inquiry about the world and humankind's place in it was forming. People wanted to know about themselves and about others. The time was right for a breakthrough, and that breakthrough occurred. It was technological, and it changed almost everything.

The Printing Press

No one knows who first had the combination of ideas that resulted in the modern printing process or who invented the first printing press. Some of those ideas had been around for a long time. The process of making a mold with raised or lowered letters or symbols had been developed by the Sumerians, as we have seen earlier in this chapter. The idea of a machine that could bring down a weight heavy enough to make an impression had also been around for a long time; such machines had been used for centuries to "press" the juice out of grapes to make wine. The idea of ink, a by-product of grapes and other natural substances, was also centuries old. Paper, too, had been developed by the Chinese and had been in use by Western civilizations for centuries.

But before the fifteenth century, none of these ideas or processes was enough to make printing as we know it feasible. The process was too cumbersome and expensive to make it worthwhile. Making the mold that would be used to print the page was the stumbling block. Unless the same mold could be used many times, it wasn't worth it.

The key idea that broke through this logjam was *moveable type*. Around 1450, someone thought about dividing the page mold into individual pieces. Each piece would contain one letter. Make enough of these pieces, organize them in different boxes, tie together the pieces you need to make a page, print however many copies you want, untie the pieces of type, and put them back in their boxes. The next day you could do the same thing but make a different page. And you could do the same thing the next day.

Suddenly, the winepress, the paper, and the ink made sense. You could print pages and do it efficiently. You could tell thousands of people what you knew or what you were thinking. You might even be able to make some money.

Johann Gutenberg is the name we generally associate with the invention of moveable type. Gutenberg was a printer in Mainz, Germany, around the middle part of the 1400s, and we know very little about him. He is connected with moveable type through some court documents (he was being sued by his partner), but it is not clear that he had the idea of moveable type first. About this time (around 1456), a set of Bibles—the first items that we know of printed with moveable type—appeared, and tradition has attached Gutenberg's name to them.

But who invented moveable type is not as important as what happened next. Everything began to change—including the way in which we saw the world.

Moveable type meant fast, efficient production of printed material. What had been very expensive was now very inexpensive and relatively easy to produce. It also ensured original duplication. That is, the last copy would be the same as the first. This was a problem with the hand copying of manuscripts that had gone on for centuries. You could never be sure what mistakes the hand copyist was making. With printing, no such mistakes occurred.

For printing to work—that is, for it to be effective in disseminating information—other things had to be in place, of course. For one, there needed to be supplies, particularly ink and paper. Paper was a problem because the process for making it cheaply was evolving. Yet, as any child who has ever owned a papermaking kit knows, there are lots of ways of making paper and lots of ingredients you can use.

Distribution was another problem. Getting what you had printed out of the printer's shop and into the hands of those you wanted to communicate with was no small chore. No post offices or delivery services existed at the time, so the distribution problem had to be solved by the individuals who had commissioned the printing. It was solved in a variety of ways, but it was expensive and cumbersome.

Finally, there needed to be a market for the printed material, and that required literacy, first, and then a need for information. Europe at this time was emerging from its medieval period. More people were taking part in commerce and learning to read. Universities were encouraging inquiry and the transmission of knowledge. Information was becoming more necessary for sustaining a good life. The world into which the modern printing process was born was changing.

Still, it was the solution to the technology problem—how to print quickly and efficiently—that was the engine that drove these other changes. With that problem solved, people could now concentrate on the message and the audience.

Dangerous Information

In 1517 Martin Luther, a German priest who had been questioning the teaching and practices of the Catholic Church for some years, nailed a piece of paper to the door of the university church in Wittenburg. The paper contained his "Ninety-five Theses," a bill of particulars that Luther had compiled against the Church. The door served as something of a public bulletin board, and Luther's paper resided there along with other notices that people had posted.

Luther's statement might have remained there, noticed only by those who passed by the door, but Luther took an additional step. He had copies printed and sent to all of the major cities in the country. Over the next three years, more copies were printed, and everyone who was anyone had read it and had an opinion about it. Through a combination of printing and word of mouth, Luther sparked the first great Reformation, and it changed the course of human history.

The advent of printing and the growth of literacy throughout Western Europe, as well as Luther's ideas about how the Church should operate, were part of a larger shift as to how human beings saw themselves. Before this period, the Scriptures were not considered terribly important in the development of a Christian life. Relatively few people read the Bible. It was not readily available even to those who might be literate. What was important in the religious life was what the priest and the Church said. How they interpreted the Scriptures was important; for individual laypeople to interpret for themselves was almost unheard of.

Luther, among many others at the time, had a different idea. He argued that individuals should read and interpret scripture for themselves, that God could speak to laypersons, and that they could choose a religious path that was correct for them.

And what was happening inside the Church was also happening in other aspects of people lives. Individuals were beginning to realize that they need not depend on others to make decisions about their lives. In their religious, political, and professional lives, they could decide things for themselves, based on their own acquisition of information. In addition, they could also speak for themselves if they felt that they had something to say.

These changes took root as more printed material appeared. Their effects were not always immediate, but they were profound. Religious, political, and social leaders could no longer rule with near absolute power because, try as they might they could not control the flow of information as they once had. They found they had to be more sensitive to something we know today as "public opinion."

Information, as well as being dangerous, became a valuable commodity. In the sixteenth century, as trade among cities and nations increased, merchants needed information on possible markets for their products. States were also developing identities and rivalries, and political news took on added importance. Those who produced information, from Bibles to gossipy tidbits, saw the possibility of making a profit on their product. They lacked a model, however, because there were no established newspapers or newsletters. Several forms of information dissemination sprang to life, including the broadside (a single sheet usually devoted to a single topic); the news pamphlet (a four-page booklet about a single subject); the newsletter (usually published by the government for disseminating an official version or interpretation of events); and the canto (a regularly published newsletter in Holland that was a precursor to what we now know as newspapers).

Possibly the first newspaper in the modern sense appeared in Oxford, England, in 1655. Published twice a week, the *Oxford Gazette* was produced by Henry Muddiman. Although it had news and information, it did little more than give the government's version of things. The paper was published in Oxford because much of the government had relocated there to avoid the plague. In 1666, with the government back in London, the paper moved to the capital city and became the *London Gazette* and continued its adherence to the government's point of view.

The first daily publication devoted to news and information came just after the turn of the century and may have had a woman, briefly, as its editor. The *Daily Courant* first appeared in 1702 under the editorship of "E. Mallett," probably Elizabeth Mallett. She lasted only a couple of weeks, however, and the paper was sold to Samuel Buckley, who continued with it for more than 30 years. The *Daily Courant* was real journalism, though in a crude form. It contained news and opinion, datelines, and an attempt at fair presentation of information.

Journalism was brand new to the people who were practicing it and the people who were consuming it. There were no rules and few precedents. People involved with publications were well aware that governments not long before then had executed heretics, many of whom had published information displeasing to the government and the established church. There was little to prevent an autocratic ruler from turning on some would-be journalist who stepped out of line. Various systems of licensing and censorship were put into place in every country in Europe, and printers often labored under the heavy yoke of government control.

Yet, ultimately these systems could not withstand the tendency of people to exchange information and opinions that did not meet with official approval. The European Enlightenment period of the 1680s put emphasis on the worth of the individuals, and philosopher John Locke argued eloquently that various opinions should be tolerated even when they did not conform to the government's interpretation. These ideas paved the way for believing that an independent press could exist and also be an asset to society.

The New World

The Reformation, Renaissance, and Enlightenment movements of the sixteenth and seventeenth centuries in Europe produced a feeling that people should look beyond themselves and their national borders. This feeling was enhanced by the possibility that profits could be made from the new worlds being "discovered" by European explorers. Consequently, the move by European governments to colonize various parts of the globe was economic. These lands, including America, might contain products that would appeal to domestic markets. They would also provide new markets for products produced domestically.

Beyond the economics, however, lay other ideas that drove colonization. The promise of land for land-starved Europe was one such idea. Being able to break out of the economic, social, and geographic confines of Europe appealed to many creative people as an opportunity not to be missed. America was especially rich in land, and as travelers returned, they brought fabulous tales of the abundance of soil and space.

The idea of refuge was another of the great appeals of the colonies. Groups who felt oppressed by governments or societies, who did not believe they could follow their religious and social beliefs in a corrupted Europe, and who simply wished to attempt living in a different way with different rules saw America as an ideal place.

Finally, the political idea of extending the reach and power of a nation by building colonies was a powerful one that appealed to many European monarchs. Colonies amounted to prestige, and every king or queen was tempted by that.

No nation was more aggressive or had more staying power in its colonization efforts than England. The English extended themselves to almost every part of the globe, and what became the British Empire dwarfed the ancient efforts of Rome and Greece to conquer the world. The jewel of that empire, however, was America.

America's land, abundance, and accessibility offered golden economic opportunities to which the English freely availed themselves. Beginning in the early 1600s, groups and individuals poured across the Atlantic Ocean with the notion of making money and starting a new life.

These people brought with them much of the world they left, including a civil and political society that was growing more mercantile and more convinced that a person's religious, political, and social beliefs were his own. This sense of tolerance was not mature—some things and people just were not allowed—but it was growing. In this society that these "Americans" were building, the free flow of information was necessary and natural. People had to know what was going on. They had to know about themselves and about the world outside their own experience. And they needed this information without interference from the government.

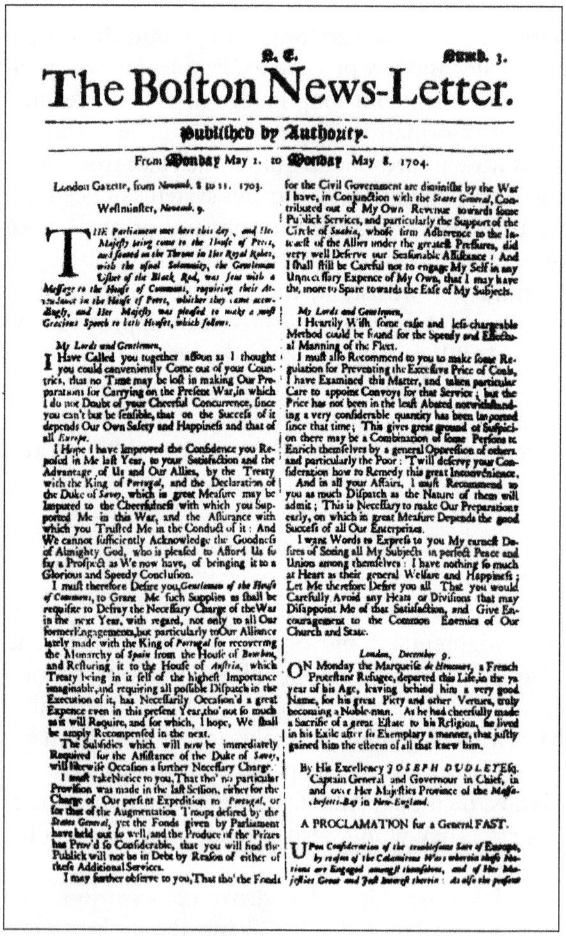

Journalism in this world grew, as it had in Europe, by fits and starts. Early colonists often did not bring with them the tools necessary for printing and did not manufacture it once they arrived. The technology had to be imported if it was to be put to use. The same systems of licensing that burdened printers in Europe also weighed down their American counterparts. At first, printing information was not especially necessary because

FIGURE 2.2 *Boston News-Letter* This first successful newspaper in America was about the size of a sheet of letterhead, but it contained news that was useful to its readers. John Campbell, its publisher, had the approval of the royal governor. Campbell was also Boston's postmaster, which gave his rather dull newspaper a decided edge.

colonies were so small. The church and the tavern, the two most prominent meeting places for people in the colonies, could suffice as the major channels of information. By the late 1600s with the colonies growing in population and sophistication, something more than public meetings was needed.

The first newspaper in America appeared in 1690 in Boston. It was published by Benjamin Harris, a man who had gained experience and jail time for his journalistic efforts in England. Harris's paper, *Public Occurrences Both Foreign and Domestic,* was planned as a weekly and had an official royal license, but it was closed down after just one issue. Two items in it were deemed offensive: one about native Americans that seemed to criticize the government and the other about the French king having an affair with his daughter-in-law that some thought salacious. It would be more than a decade before another newspaper with planned regularity appeared in the colonies.

That occurred when the *Boston News-Letter* was published by John Campbell in 1704. Campbell, the Boston postmaster, had been producing a handwritten newsletter for several years for distribution throughout the colonies. He found this burdensome, however, and turned to a printing press in 1704. The *Boston News-Letter* carried both news and advertising, something of an innovation for the time. Advertising, of course, has information that people consider newsworthy, and it also provides a source of revenue for the publication. Much of the news in Campbell's paper was foreign (people did not need to have local news in their papers since they were likely to know that anyway) and lifted from other newspapers (a common practice that continued long after this publication).

During the next two decades, several other men and women in Boston took an interest in starting a publication. Among them were James and Ann Franklin, who with backing from other prominent figures in the community, started the *New England Courant.* The paper was notable for its editorializing and particularly its anti-Puritan stance. Franklin eventually turned his editorial guns on the government itself and became so irritating that he was jailed at one point.

James Franklin was a notable figure in the early stages of American journalism because of his bold practices, but he is overshadowed by a far more prominent member of his family, his younger brother Benjamin, whose exploits in many fields, including science and politics, are well known. Benjamin, however, was first and foremost a printer, and his ideas and creativity made him the dominant figure in journalism in America in the 1700s.

Benjamin Franklin

No individual of the 1700s contributed more to the development of journalism than Benjamin Franklin. But Franklin did not consider himself a journalist. He was, rather, a printer. In those days printers could be editors and publishers of their own publications, but they might also print the publications of others. Franklin was proud of his vocation, so much so that it was the only one listed on his tombstone: "The Body of Benjamin Franklin, Printer (like the cover of an old Book, its contents worn out, and stript of its lettering and gildings) lies here, food for worms. Yet the work itself shall not be lost, for it will, as he believed, appear once more in a new and more beautiful edition, corrected and amended by its Author."

Franklin's self-composed epitaph shows the humor with which he approached both life and death. Fittingly, it was with humor that he entered journalism in 1722.

Franklin was apprenticed as a boy to his brother James's print shop, and there he learned the technical aspects of the trade. He also learned the power of words, being an avid reader, particularly of the works of English journalists Joseph Addison and Richard Steele, editors of the lively magazine the *Spectator*. The young Franklin could not help but notice the controversies in which his brother was involving himself, and at age 16 he decided to enter the fray. He wrote a series of articles under the pseudonym of "Silence Dogood," posing as a middle-aged woman and poking fun at the characters and controversies of the day. These weekly articles were lively and well written, showing a style and wit that Franklin had learned from reading Addison and Steele. Despite not knowing who the author was, his brother printed them. After about six months, Franklin confessed to his brother, who then stopped printing the articles.

Franklin never got along with his brother, and as soon as he could, he left his apprenticeship and left Boston for good. He went to Philadelphia where he set himself up as a printer and in 1728 took over the failing *Pennsylvania Gazette*. Franklin turned that publication into a lively and interesting newspaper, something that was informative and which people looked forward to reading. He brought to the newspaper business the same sense of spirit and innovation that he showed in his many other pursuits. He also made money. He was so successful that he was able to retire from the business at age 42 and devote himself to his many other interests, including invention, science, and politics. Franklin died in 1790 as one of the most famous people in the world, renowned for giving the world an understanding of electricity and a new nation called the United States of America.

FIGURE 2.3 **Benjamin Franklin** No one had a more profound effect on life and politics in the eighteenth century than Benjamin Franklin. His journalistic accomplishments were many, including the beginning of American magazine journalism and the publishing of the first non-English newspaper in the colonies, the *Philadelphia Zeitung*. (Photo credit: United States Senate)

As his epitaph indicates, Franklin always thought of himself as a printer and, along with that, a newspaperman. His contributions to the profession were enormous. They included a newspaper formula of news and advertising that satisfied and influenced readers. Franklin established a network of printers throughout the colonies by giving them the capital to begin their businesses and then sharing in their profits. These printers also shared some of the same editorial matter, thus creating a sense of unity among the scattered colonies. Franklin also pioneered a style of writing that broke away from the dull heavy-handedness that was normal for his time. His writing was short and lively, and one of the things we remember about him most today are his pithy sayings: "Early to bed, early to rise, makes a man healthy, wealthy and wise"; "A penny saved is a penny earned."

Most importantly, however, Franklin articulated the growing sense that people should be able to think, speak, and write freely. His famous editorial, "Apology for Printers," is still cited as an excellent defense for freedom of the press: "Printers are educated in the belief that when men differ in opinion, both sides ought equally to have the advantage of being heard by the public; and that when Truth and Error have fair play, the former is always an overmatch for the latter."

Due in part to Franklin but also to growing population and economic activity, the number of newspapers and circulation sizes grew during the 1700s. The growth was slow, hampered by governmental interference and lack of capital, equipment, and supplies, but the ideas and energy from which journalism springs were building. By the 1760s, American journalism was still toddling but was ready to fully participate in the political turmoils that lay ahead. Independence from England was an idea that some had advocated for decades. By 1765, it needed only a spark, and the king and Parliament in London obligingly provided one.

The Fire of Revolution

Taxes are necessary for the operation of a government, but few things spark more political opposition than taxes. This was true as much in the 1700s as it is today. And it was taxes—specifically the Stamp Act of 1765—that pushed many Americans from loyalty to the king to believing in independence.

The Stamp Act was imposed by Parliament at the end of a period of war when the British government needed money. Because part of the purpose of those wars was to secure the American colonies, the London lawmakers believed that Americans should foot at least part of the bill and that they might even be grateful to do so. They were wrong.

The provisions of the Stamp Act were particularly onerous. It required all legal papers, newspapers, and books to be printed on paper that carried a special stamp showing that a tax had been paid. Those who imposed the law not only misread the potential for opposition that the law would invoke but also aimed the law at those people who might be most dangerous in their opposition—lawyers, printers, and other members of the middle class who might deal with such documents. Printers were especially hard hit and, consequently, stridently vocal in their opposition.

London had handed radicals clamoring for revolution a nearly perfect issue. Even those sympathetic with the king found the Stamp Act difficult, if not impossible, to defend. The act was repealed in 1766, but the independence faction of America's political life never let it be forgotten. They did not need to. Every time Parliament attempted to impose another tax on the colonies, the perfidy of the Stamp Act could

WOMEN IN EIGHTEENTH-CENTURY JOURNALISM

No area of public or professional life in the eighteenth century offered women much of an opportunity. Journalism, unfortunately, was just as restrictive as any other area. Still, a few women managed to enter the profession and make significant contributions to it. Here are two examples:

Possibly the most prominent eighteenth-century female journalist was Elizabeth Timothy, publisher of the *South Carolina Gazette* in mid-century. Timothy was part of a French Huguenot family who immigrated to Philadelphia in 1731. Her husband, Louis, got to know Benjamin Franklin, who was looking for an editor of a German-language newspaper he wanted to start.

Louis Timothy published a couple of issues of the newspaper for Franklin, but then it turned out that Franklin needed an editor for a newspaper in Charleston that he had helped finance. He sent Timothy to take over the paper. Franklin's contract with publishers such as Timothy called for Franklin to finance the operation and receive a part of the profits for six years.

Timothy died in 1738, a year before his contract with Franklin was up. That's when Elizabeth Timothy took over. The publisher of the paper was listed as Peter Timothy, their son, but he was only 13

The first official printed copy of the Declaration of Independence. Mary Katherine Goddard's name appears at the bottom of the page.

years old at the time. It was Elizabeth who ran the operation, and she later received praise from Franklin for her good business practices. Timothy published the paper until her son turned 21 years old. She turned the paper over to him and opened a stationery shop next door to the newspaper printing office. She died in 1757.

Another prominent woman journalist was Mary Katherine Goddard, an experienced printer and publisher. Goddard had run printing operations in Rhode Island and Philadelphia. In 1774 she took charge of the *Maryland Journal* in Baltimore and ran it for her brother William until 1783. She supported the patriot cause, printed the first account of the Battle of Bunker Hill in Boston in 1775, and the next year was the printer chosen by Congress to print the first official copy of the Declaration of Independence.

In addition to her printing duties, she became Baltimore's post-mistress in 1775 and remained in that job until 1789. After that she ran a bookstore in Baltimore for twenty years.

be recalled. By the 1770s, the argument over taxation had become more generalized with the radicals arguing that Parliament had no right to tax the colonies because America had no representation in Parliament. Because Parliament would never agree to having representatives from the colonies within its midst, the representation argument proved potent for the radicals.

All of these arguments were made in the newspapers of the nation by men such as Samuel Adams of Boston writing for the *Boston Gazette* and Thomas Paine, who wrote for various publications and often published his own works. Paine's simple style and short memorable sentences ("These are the times that try men's souls") lent power to his arguments. Once the fighting had begun, Paine was most effective in articulating the cause, and George Washington at one point ordered Paine's *American Crisis* pamphlet to be read to the men of his army as a boost to their morale.

Despite the drumbeating of the radicals and the fumbling of Parliament, Americans were not of one mind about independence. A number of prominent newspapers were published by men who did not believe that the colonies should separate themselves from the Crown. Most notable among them was James Rivington, editor of the *New York Gazetteer*. Rivington was an open, friendly man who became more conservative as others become more radical. At first, his newspaper printed opinions on all sides of the issue of independence, but he moved steadily to the king's side and eventually even changed the name of the paper to the *New York Royal Gazetteer*.

Neither side believed in freedom of the press, particularly for the opposition. Printers could find themselves in trouble with a mob if they said the wrong thing in their publications. Rivington, one of the few to call for tolerance in the early stages of the debate, was arrested and forced to sign a loyalty oath by the continental army. Once released he continued publishing Tory opinions, and his printing office was destroyed. The same type of thing happened to printers on the other side of the issue.

JAMES RIVINGTON AND THE TORY PRESS

Historians are still unsure of where the American public stood in the 1770s with regard to independence, but the public debate was dominated by those who favored separation from England. In the 1770s, it was hard to imagine a newspaper sympathetic to the colonies' remaining a part of Britain to stay in business. That was particularly so for the man who was the most prominent Tory-leaning editor, James Rivington.

Rivington was a charming, roguish bon vivant who had made a fortune in England as a bookseller and then had lost it gambling. He came to America and established a printing shop first in Philadelphia and later in New York. In 1773, seeing a good business opportunity for an informative, well-written newspaper, Rivington started the *New York Gazetteer*.

Rivington himself supported the British, but he opened his columns to those on the other side. The paper was hugely successful, reaching a circulation of 3,600 copies, but his editorial stands made many enemies during those fractious times. The separatists were not interested in a balanced debate. They demanded conversion to their point of view. Those who refused could be the objects of violence.

That's what happened to Rivington. In 1775 a mob destroyed his print shop and press. Rivington was apprehended and forced into signing a loyalty oath to the patriot cause. Once released, however, Rivington reverted to his old allegiance. Again, a mob attacked his offices, and Rivington fled to England. He returned a short time later to New York with the title of King's Printer for New York.

In truth, however, Rivington did not seem to have much enthusiasm for either side. In 1781, when the tide was turning toward the patriot cause, Rivington supplied George Washington with important information about the British. After New York was occupied by the American army, Rivington stayed in the city and took the British coat of arms off his door. His business, however, did not flourish, and he spent the rest of his life in relative poverty.

He became the object of much ridicule, including a sharp epigram from editor Phillip Freneau, who wrote "Rivington's Last Will and Testament." Part of it read:

Provided, however, and
    nevertheless,
That whatever estate I enjoy
    and possess
At the time of my death
    (if it be not then sold)
Shall remain to the Tories,
    to have and to hold.

News of the war effort spread fitfully throughout the colonies. The profession of journalism still had not progressed to the point of having reporters follow an army and write a summary of events. No system of news coverage had been developed that could supply information to printers or keep the public informed. Eyewitness accounts were used whenever they were available; second- and third-hand reports were more the norm. Each side touted its victories and downplayed its defeats. Many newspapers found the war difficult to deal with because of the shortage of equipment and supplies that it created, and some papers ceased publication altogether.

While the war itself was hard on the press, the debates that led up to it showed the power of newspapers to lead public opinion. Those lessons were learned and remembered as the new nation began to define itself.

BALTIMORE, December 30.

CONGRESS received the following Intelligence from the Council of Safety, as coming from "an Officer of distinction in the Army."

Head Quarters, Newtown, Bucks county, Dec. 27.

IT was determined some days ago, that our army should pass over to Jersey at three different places and attack the enemy, accordingly about 2,500 men and 20 brass field pieces with his Excellency General Washington at their head, and Major General Sullivan and General Green in command of two divisions passed over on the night of Christmas, and about three o'Clock A. M. were on their march by two ruts towards Trenton—The night was sleety and cold and the roads slippery, that it was day break when we were two miles from Trenton, but happily the enemy were not apprized of our design, and our advance party were on their guards at half a mile from town where General Sullivan and General Green's divisions soon came into the same road.

Their guard gave our advance party several smart fires as we drove them, but we soon got two field pieces at play and several others in a small time, and one of our columns pushing down on the right while the other advanced on the left into the town. The enemy confisting of about 1500 Heffians under Col. Rohl formed and made some smart fires from their musquetry and 6 field pieces, but our people prefsed from every quarter and drove them from their cannon—They retired towards a field behind a piece of woods up the creek from Trenton and formed in two bodies, which I expected would have brought on a smart action from our troops who had formed very near them, but at that instant as I came in full view of them from the back of the woods with his Excellency General Washington, an officer informed him that one party had grounded their arms and furrendered prisoners—The other soon followed their example except a part which had got off in the hazy weather towards Princeton; their light horse made off on our first approach—Too much praise cannot be given to the officers and men of every regiment, who feemed to vie with each other, and by their active

spirited behaviour, they soon put an honorable issue to this glorious day.

You may rejoice and be exceeding glad at this intelligence of our succefs, which I hope and believe will prevent the enemy from paffing the river.

We took three standards, 6 fine brafs cannon and near 1000 stand of arms. They muft have had about 20 or 30 killed.

"I was immediately sent off with the prisoners to M'Conkey's ferry, and have got about seven hundred and fifty safe in town and a few miles from here, on this fide the ferry, viz. one Lieutenant Colonel, two Majors, four Captains, seven Lieutenants, and eight Enfigns. We left Col. Rohl, the Commandant, wounded, on his parole, and several other officers and wounded men at Trenton. We loft but two of our men that I can hear of, a few wounded, and one brave officer, Capt. Wafhington, who affifted in fecuring their artillery, fhot in in both hands. Indeed every officer and private behaved well, and it was a fortunate day to our arms, which I the more rejoice at, having an active part in it. The fuccefs of this day will greatly animate our friends, and add frefh courage to our new army, which, when formed, will be fufficient to fecure us from the depredations or infults of our enemy.

"Gen. Ewing's divifion could not pafs at Trenton for the ice, which alfo impeded Gen. Cadwalader paffing over with all his cannon and the militia, though part of his troops were over, and if the whole could have paffed, we fhould have fwept the coaft to Philadelphia.

Publifhed by order of Congrefs.

CHARLES THOMSON, Sec'ry.

BALTIMORE: Printed by JOHN DUNLAP.

FIGURE 2.4 Baltimore Broadside The broadside took on many forms, but it was usually a single sheet printed for a specific purpose. This broadside, printed in Baltimore on December 30, 1776, was the first announcement of the news of the American revolutionary forces' victory over the British at Trenton. The victory came after George Washington had ordered his men to cross the icy Delaware River on Christmas night. (Photo credit: Library of Congress)

Partisanship

With the war over in 1783 and independence won, the political landscape in America shifted. The major question that had occupied public discussion for more than two decades—whether or not the colonies would remain as part of the British

Empire—had been settled, but another one quickly took its place: Just what kind of a government and political system would the new nation have? The chief focus was on what kind of power the national and the state governments would exercise. The first government the states tried was the Articles of Confederation that left the federal government weak and the states with almost complete discretionary power. It did not work, and people on all sides knew that something else would have to be worked out.

Delegates from every state met in Philadelphia during the summer of 1787 to do just that. Under the leadership of people such as George Washington and James Madison, they worked out a Constitution that, while it did not answer every question, satisfied them enough to present it to the public. The delegates agreed that if nine of the thirteen states approved the Constitution, it would go into effect. Debates on the document occurred on a state-by-state basis, and for a time, the outcome was in some doubt. When the Constitution appeared to be failing, three of its chief proponents—James Madison, Alexander Hamilton, and John Jay—collaborated on a series of essays that was published in newspapers throughout the nation. These essays, later known as the Federalist Papers, were a high-minded articulation of the ideas the framers of the Constitution had about how it would work. (The Federalist Papers are still referred to regularly today when debates about the meaning of the Constitution come up.) Those essays represented the high point of journalism during this period.

What followed the institution of the new form of government and the election of Washington as president, however, was an era of partisanship and political infighting that would be shocking even to us today. Federalists were a loose coalition of those who felt the central government should be strong and should be able to enforce laws on the states. Nominally, they were led by George Washington, but Washington tried at all times to eschew partisanship. In reality, the Federalists were led by Alexander Hamilton and John Adams, the nation's first vice president. The Anti-Federalists (again, a very loose coalition) sought to preserve state prerogatives as much as possible; they were led by men such as Thomas Jefferson and James Madison.

More than at any other time in the nation's history, these coalitions (later to develop into political parties) exercised direct control over "their" newspapers. Newspaper editors saw themselves as the leading spokespersons for a political faction, and they did what they could to advance that faction's point of view. What these editors said about the opposing faction became increasingly bold and bitter. There were no rules and precedents for civil political debate. Opponents of a faction could be accused of all sorts of personal and social indiscretions and political highjinks. Even George Washington did not escape the battering ram of the opposition's newspapers.

Politicians even resorted to political appointments to keep "their" editors publishing. Accepting a government job, just as a postmastership or a clerk's appointment in a federal department, was nothing unusual for an editor or publisher. Each side used the power that it had to make sure that its point of view was heard, and editors had no scruples about any of this. John Fenno, editor of the *Gazette of the United States*, sided with the Federalists and got the printing contracts from the

U.S. Department of Treasury headed by Alexander Hamilton. Phillip Freneau, who published the *National Intelligencer* and spoke for the Anti-Federalists, received an appointment as a translator for the U.S. Department of State where Thomas Jefferson was in charge.

Vigorous debate is one thing, but the political discussions in the newspapers of the 1790s often degenerated into dialogues of disrespect and personal abuse. The new nation, through its newspapers, was learning to talk to itself, but the level and tone of discussion were as yet unsatisfactory. The low point of the period came not from the press but from the government. In 1798, with John Adams as president and Federalists in control of the legislature, Congress enacted the Alien and Sedition Acts. These laws made it a crime "to cause or procure to be written, printed, uttered or published . . . any false, scandalous, and malicious writing against the government of the United States or either house of Congress of the United States or the President of the United States. . . ." A number of prosecutions of Republican editors occurred under the law, but the danger of these laws to the political society that the nation was attempting to build was apparent. Though the Federalists were in power at the time, their hold on power was slipping, and the Alien and Sedition Acts have been viewed by some as a desperate attempt to maintain itself. The law expired after two years when Thomas Jefferson had assumed the presidency.

Newspapers experienced rapid growth through the 1790s. The decade began with about 91 newspapers and ended with about 234 in operation. Circulation sizes also grew. Equipment and supplies were somewhat easier to obtain. Literacy rates were high (as they had been all during the latter part of the century), and people were increasingly interested in what was happening with their new government.

Despite the extreme partisanship, some professional journalistic practices that were the precursors of what we would expect today began to emerge. Regular news coverage of the proceedings of Congress was a staple for many of these newspapers. While local news was still in short supply, newspapers shifted their outlook from foreign to domestic news. This change was helped by a law that allowed newspapers to send copies copies free to each other via the postal system. Newspapers would freely lift information from other papers for their own use.

But the major characteristic of any newspaper of the day was partisanship. A paper was expected to take sides in almost any dispute and to be a strong advocate for its faction. That partisanship would continue through the first two decades of the 1800s, but it abated because the Federalists had lost their leadership (John Adams had retired, and Alexander Hamilton had been killed in a duel) and their ability to attract a large number of adherents. No new faction or party had risen to take the place of the Federalists.

This era of partisanship ended on an important technological note for newspapers. The flatbed press, which had been a staple of printing since the days of Gutenberg, was replaced by the cylinder press. It required that single sheets be fed into it and pressed against a bed of type. The idea of the cylinder press had been around (as we saw earlier in this chapter) since the days of the Sumerians, but in the

1820s R. Hoe and Company of New York introduced a press with large cylinders that greatly increased the speed with which the press could produce copies of the paper. That kind of speed would be necessary for what was ahead for American journalism.

QUESTIONS FOR DISCUSSION

1. The author makes the point that Roman rulers had to control their empire from the city of Rome. The federal government in Washington, DC, has to do the same thing. Can you see any parallels as to how this happens?
2. Many people have called the printing press the greatest invention of human beings. Do you agree? Can you think of any other invention that might rival it? (You might revisit this question after referring to Chapter 4.)
3. Why would people in authority have seen the printing press as a threat? What did they do about it?
4. Europeans began colonizing America in the early 1600s, but it was nearly a century before newspapers appeared. Why did it take so long? List and discuss all the reasons you can think of.
5. George Washington is a revered figure in American history today, but when he was president, he came in for blistering criticism from some of the newspapers of the day. Go to a book about Washington or a web site that might tell you some of the things these papers said. Compare them to some of the things that are said about politicians today.

RELATED WEB SITES

AEJMC History Division, www.utc.edu/~aejhist

American Journalism Historians Association, www.ajha.org

American Women's History: Journalism, www.mtsu.edu/~kmiddlet

Jhistory Home Page, www.h-net.msu.edu/~jhistory

Media History Project, http://mediahistory.umn.edu

United States Newspaper Project, www.neh.gov/projects/usnp.html

Women's History: Journalism, www.distinguishedwomen.com/subject/journ.html

READINGS AND REFERENCES

Blanchard, M. A. (Ed.). (1998). *History of the mass media in the United States, an encyclopedia.* Chicago: Fitzroy Dearborn Publishers.

Bliss, E. (1991). *Now the news: The story of broadcast journalism.* New York: Columbia University Press.

Briggs, A., & Burke, P. (2001). *A social history of the media from Gutenberg to the Internet.* Malden, MA: Blackwell.

Copeland, D. A. (2000). *Debating the issues in colonial newspapers.* Westport, CT: Greenwood Press.

Crowley, D. J., & Heyer, P. (2003). *Communication in history.* Boston: Allyn and Bacon.

Folkerts, J., & Teeter, D. L. Jr. (1997). *Voices of a nation: A history of mass media in the United States.* Boston: Allyn and Bacon.

Hartsock, J. C. (2000). *A history of American literary journalism: The emergence of a modern narrative form.* Amherst, MA: University of Massachusetts Press.

Hollis, D. W. (1995). *The media in America.* Santa Barbara, CA: ABC-CLIO, Inc.

Horan, J. D. (1955). *Mathew Brady: Historian with a camera.* New York: Bonanza.

Hudson, F. (2000). *Journalism in the United States from 1690–1872.* New York: Routledge.

Nord, D. P. (2001). *Communities of journalism: A history of American newspapers and their readers.* Urbana: University of Illinois Press.

Rafferty, A. M. (2000). *American journalism 1690–1904.* New York: Routledge.

Sloan, W. D. (1991). *Perspectives on mass communication history.* Hillsdale, NJ: Lawrence Erlbaum.

Sloan, W. D., & Parcell, L. M. (Eds.). (2002). *American journalism: History, principles, practices.* Jefferson, NC: McFarland & Company.

Sloan, W. D., Stovall, J. G., & Startt, J. D. (1999). *The media in America: A history* (4th ed.). Northport, AL: Vision.

Startt, J. D., & Sloan, W. D. (1994). *The significance of the media in American history.* Northport, AL: Vision Press.

Ward, H. H. (1997). *Mainsteams of American media history.* Boston: Allyn & Bacon.

Williams, J. H. (1999). *The significance of the printed word in early America: Colonists' thoughts on the role of the press.* Westport, CT: Greenwood Press.

Chapter Three

Law and the Journalist

1. The First Amendment to the U.S. Constitution guarantees the nation a right to free speech and to a free press; it is the central legal element that allows journalism to operate and develop in this country.

2. Prior restraint: the power of the government to stop dissemination of information that the news media have acquired; except in a few rare instances, prior restraint does not occur in the United States.

3. American society generally operates as an open society; that is, we expect information to be available and we assume the right to distribute information.

4. One of the major legal restraints on news organizations is libel, the damage done to a person's reputation by the publication of false information.

5. *New York Times v. Sullivan:* this 1964 decision by the Supreme Court gave the news media an extra measure of protection from being sued for libel by public officials.

6. Actual malice: the standard of proof that was established by the *New York Times v. Sullivan* decision; a public official or public figure has to prove that a news organization showed "reckless disregard" for the truth to win a libel case.

7. Copyrights and trademarks protect intellectual property from unauthorized use.

8. The right of privacy is not guaranteed by the U.S. Constitution, but most courts recognize this right, and news organizations have to consider the right of privacy for individuals in making some editorial decisions.

9. News coverage of trials presents a problem for the news media and the legal system because of the feeling that too much publicity may prevent someone from getting a fair trial.

Vignette

When the Cherry Sisters decided to take their act on the road, they were simply trying to survive. They did not realize they would be making legal history.

The sisters—Addie, Effie, Jessie, and Lizzie—were left alone on the family farm near Marion, Iowa, in 1888 when their father died. A fifth sister, Ella, stayed on the farm, but the others decided to put together a vaudeville act that they hoped would get them at least to Chicago, where they planned to see the World's Fair and look for a long-lost brother.

Their act, consisting of songs and a variety of dramatic readings, was awful. It premiered before a local crowd that was apparently too polite to boo or express any displeasure. That did not stop other audiences, who booed and threw things. The sisters kept performing, apparently believing the crowd noise amounted to approval. Even when the crowds threw things on stage, the sisters seemed to think this was just part of what happened in the theater of the time.

Everywhere the Cherry Sisters went, the crowds got bigger and bigger. They were so awful that they had become a phenomenon. The sisters offered newspaper critics new opportunities to write vicious reviews, and the critics rarely passed up the opportunities. The sisters could not understand the reviewers. After all, they were drawing big crowds.

When the Cedar Rapids Gazette wrote, "If some indefinable instinct of modesty could not have warned them that they were acting the part of monkeys, it does seem like the overshoes thrown at them would convey the idea," the sisters sued the city editor for libel. They dropped the suit, and showing a bit of humor agreed to perform before a mock court on stage. That stunt generated even more publicity, and the sisters were invited to New York to play on Broadway in 1896. This they did, performing before crowds of as many as four thousand people. The critics continued to blast away.

Two years later, Billy Hamilton, editor of the Odebolt Chronicle in Iowa, saw the act and described it for his readers in a particularly devastating way: "The mouths of their rancid features opened like caverns, and sounds like the wailing of damned souls issued therefrom." His review was reprinted in the Des Moines Leader, and this time the sisters sued for $15,000. The sisters lost their suit and appealed to the Iowa Supreme Court, which ruled against the sisters in a 1901 decision. The court wrote:

> One who goes upon the stage to exhibit himself to the public, or who gives any kind of a performance to which the public is invited, may be freely criticised. He may be held up to ridicule, and entire freedom of expression is guaranteed dramatic critics, provided they are not actuated by malice or evil purpose in what they write. Fitting strictures,

sarcasm or ridicule, even, may be used, if based on facts, without liability, in the absence of malice or wicked purpose. The comments, however, must be based on truth, or on what in good faith and upon probable cause is believed to be true, and the matter must be pertinent to the conduct that is made the subject of criticism.

Without meaning to, the Cherry Sisters had established an important legal principle: the right to comment and criticize. That right is not unlimited, as we will see in this chapter, but the court's decision became a precedent that offers an important protection for journalists.

Corruption in Minneapolis

A quarter of a century later, in the middle of the Roaring Twenties, freedom of expression got another legal boost. Minneapolis today has a mild, even bland, reputation as a city. In 1927, however, as a major stopover for the route of illegal whiskey coming from Canada during the height of the Prohibition era, Minneapolis was a center for scandal and corruption. The mayor and much of the police force were on the take, bought by the bootleggers who were trying to get booze to Chicago, St. Louis, and points south.

Jay Near and his friend, Howard Guilford, did not like what they saw. Neither of them were paragons of virtue; they were opinionated and bigoted, openly disparaging ethnic groups they did not like. But they also felt they had a right to expose what public officials were doing to their city, so they started a publication called the *Saturday Press*. They told their readers that the city government was essentially mob

Quote 3.1

JAMES J. KILPATRICK

On individual liberty

The idea of individual liberty lies at the very heart of the American dream. In a very real sense, it is our national religion, and like other religions it is fearfully difficult to practice. It is not easy to be a good Christian, a good Jew. The tenets of faith are demanding. Many persons find it impossible to believe deeply—really, truly, to believe—in matters of doctrine. But as professing members of a church they have an obligation to try. So it is with freedom. Do we really believe in it? Really, deeply, believe in it? Do we believe in freedom sufficiently to tolerate the expression of political opinions we find intolerable? We must try.

James J. Kilpatrick is a columnist and former editor of the Richmond News-Leader.

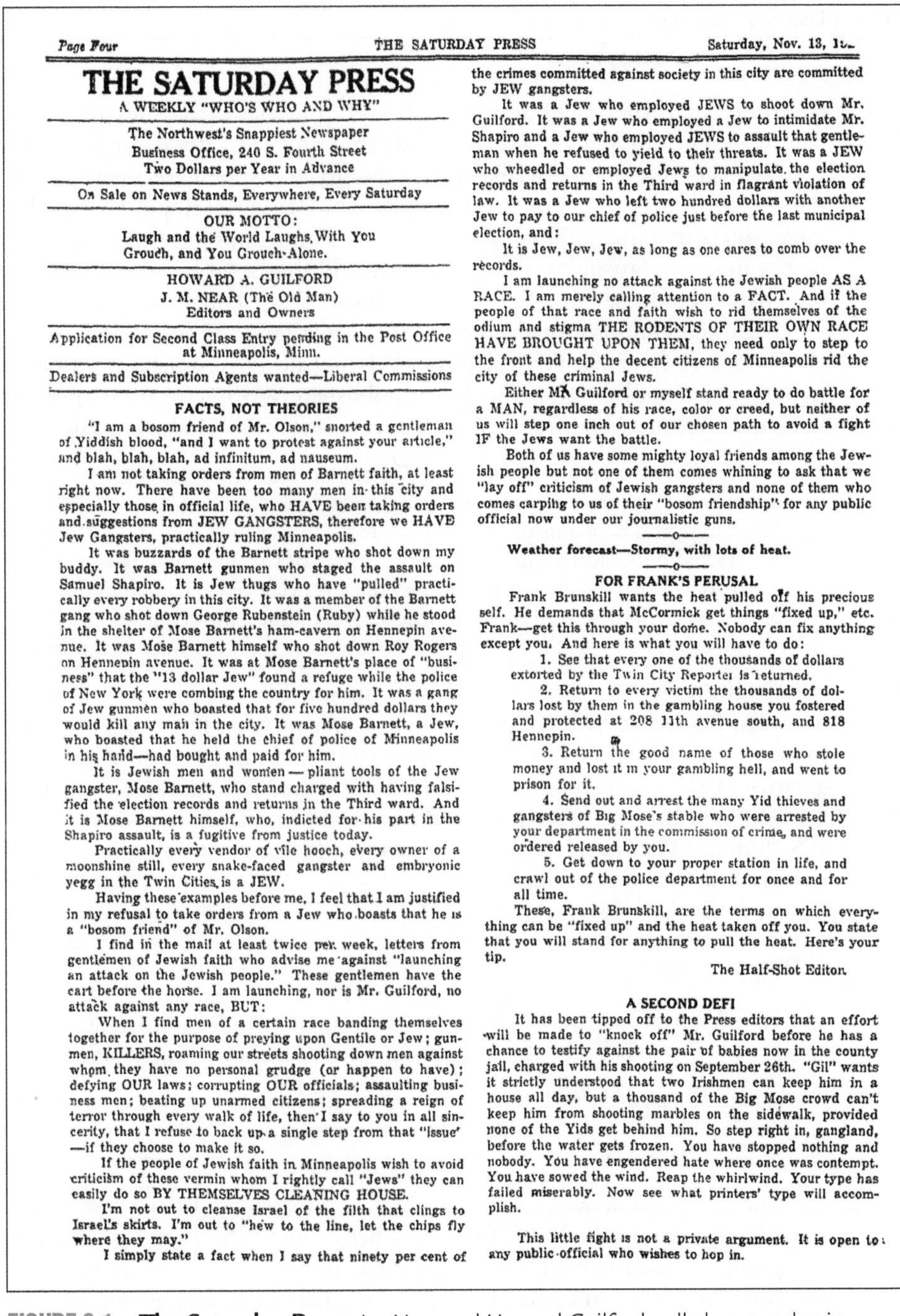

THE SATURDAY PRESS
A WEEKLY "WHO'S WHO AND WHY"

The Northwest's Snappiest Newspaper
Business Office, 240 S. Fourth Street
Two Dollars per Year in Advance

On Sale on News Stands, Everywhere, Every Saturday

OUR MOTTO:
Laugh and the World Laughs With You
Grouch, and You Grouch-Alone.

HOWARD A. GUILFORD
J. M. NEAR (The Old Man)
Editors and Owners

Application for Second Class Entry pending in the Post Office at Minneapolis, Minn.

Dealers and Subscription Agents wanted—Liberal Commissions

FACTS, NOT THEORIES

"I am a bosom friend of Mr. Olson," snorted a gentleman of Yiddish blood, "and I want to protest against your article," and blah, blah, blah, ad infinitum, ad nauseum.

I am not taking orders from men of Barnett faith, at least right now. There have been too many men in this city and especially those in official life, who HAVE been taking orders and suggestions from JEW GANGSTERS, therefore we HAVE Jew Gangsters, practically ruling Minneapolis.

It was buzzards of the Barnett stripe who shot down my buddy. It was Barnett gunmen who staged the assault on Samuel Shapiro. It is Jew thugs who have "pulled" practically every robbery in this city. It was a member of the Barnett gang who shot down George Rubenstein (Ruby) while he stood in the shelter of Mose Barnett's ham-cavern on Hennepin avenue. It was Mose Barnett himself who shot down Roy Rogers on Hennepin avenue. It was at Mose Barnett's place of "business" that the "13 dollar Jew" found a refuge while the police of New York were combing the country for him. It was a gang of Jew gunmen who boasted that for five hundred dollars they would kill any man in the city. It was Mose Barnett, a Jew, who boasted that he held the chief of police of Minneapolis in his hand—had bought and paid for him.

It is Jewish men and women — pliant tools of the Jew gangster, Mose Barnett, who stand charged with having falsified the election records and returns in the Third ward. And it is Mose Barnett himself, who, indicted for his part in the Shapiro assault, is a fugitive from justice today.

Practically every vendor of vile hooch, every owner of a moonshine still, every snake-faced gangster and embryonic yegg in the Twin Cities is a JEW.

Having recited these examples before me, I feel that I am justified in my refusal to take orders from a Jew who boasts that he is a "bosom friend" of Mr. Olson.

I find in the mail at least twice per week, letters from gentlemen of Jewish faith who advise me against "launching an attack on the Jewish people." These gentlemen have the cart before the horse. I am launching, nor is Mr. Guilford, no attack against any race, BUT:

When I find men of a certain race banding themselves together for the purpose of preying upon Gentile or Jew; gunmen, KILLERS, roaming our streets shooting down men against whom they have no personal grudge (or happen to have); defying OUR officials; assaulting business men; beating up unarmed citizens; spreading a reign of terror through every walk of life, then I say to you in all sincerity, that I refuse to back up a single step from that "issue" —if they choose to make it so.

If the people of Jewish faith in Minneapolis wish to avoid criticism of these vermin whom I rightly call "Jews" they can easily do so BY THEMSELVES CLEANING HOUSE.

I'm not out to cleanse Israel of the filth that clings to Israel's skirts. I'm out to "hew to the line, let the chips fly where they may."

I simply state a fact when I say that ninety per cent of the crimes committed against society in this city are committed by JEW gangsters.

It was a Jew who employed Mr. Guilford. It was a Jew who employed a Jew to intimidate Mr. Shapiro and a Jew who employed JEWS to assault that gentleman when he refused to yield to their threats. It was a JEW who wheedled or employed Jews to manipulate the election records and returns in the Third ward in flagrant violation of law. It was a Jew who left two hundred dollars with another Jew to pay to our chief of police just before the last municipal election, and:

It is Jew, Jew, Jew, as long as one cares to comb over the records.

I am launching no attack against the Jewish people AS A RACE. I am merely calling attention to a FACT. And if the people of that race and faith wish to rid themselves of the odium and stigma THE RODENTS OF THEIR OWN RACE HAVE BROUGHT UPON THEM, they need only to step to the front and help the decent citizens of Minneapolis rid the city of these criminal Jews.

Either Mr. Guilford or myself stand ready to do battle for a MAN, regardless of his race, color or creed, but neither of us will step one inch out of our chosen path to avoid a fight IF the Jews want the battle.

Both of us have some mighty loyal friends among the Jewish people but not one of them comes whining to ask that we "lay off" criticism of Jewish gangsters and none of them who comes carping to us of their "bosom friendship" for any public official now under our journalistic guns.

—o—

Weather forecast—Stormy, with lots of heat.

—o—

FOR FRANK'S PERUSAL

Frank Brunskill wants the heat pulled off his precious self. He demands that McCormick get things "fixed up," etc. Frank—get this through your dome. Nobody can fix anything except you. And here is what you will have to do:

1. See that every one of the thousands of dollars extorted by the Twin City Reporter is returned.

2. Return to every victim the thousands of dollars lost by them in the gambling house you fostered and protected at 208 11th avenue south, and 818 Hennepin.

3. Return the good name of those who stole money and lost it in your gambling hell, and went to prison for it.

4. Send out and arrest the many Yid thieves and gangsters of Big Mose's stable who were arrested by your department in the commission of crime, and were ordered released by you.

5. Get down to your proper station in life, and crawl out of the police department for once and for all time.

These, Frank Brunskill, are the terms on which everything can be "fixed up" and the heat taken off you. You state that you will stand for anything to pull the heat. Here's your tip.

The Half-Shot Editor.

A SECOND DEFI

It has been tipped off to the Press editors that an effort will be made to "knock off" Mr. Guilford before he has a chance to testify against the pair of babies now in the county jail, charged with his shooting on September 26th. "Gil" wants it strictly understood that two Irishmen can keep him in a house all day, but a thousand of the Big Mose crowd can't keep him from shooting marbles on the sidewalk, provided none of the Yids get behind him. So step right in, gangland, before the water gets frozen. You have stopped nothing and nobody. You have engendered hate where once was contempt. You have sowed the wind. Reap the whirlwind. Your type has failed miserably. Now see what printers' type will accomplish.

This little fight is not a private argument. It is open to any public official who wishes to hop in.

FIGURE 3.1 The Saturday Press Jay Near and Howard Guilford pulled no punches in fighting what they saw as corruption in Minneapolis, as this issue of the *Saturday Press* of 1927 demonstrates. Although many city officials of the time were corrupt, the two journalists went beyond exposing their corruption and disparaged their ethnicity. Despite this, the courts ruled that public officials could not use the city's nuisance laws to shut down the publication.

controlled, and they gave details. Just days after the first issue appeared (and was confiscated by city police), Guilford was shot and critically wounded by mobsters.

Near stepped up his crusade against the city as his friend recuperated. He targeted the mayor, the police chief, and even the county prosecutor. His weekly exposés increasingly irritated public officials for two months until they decided to use a Minnesota nuisance law against him. The law said that a "scandalous and defamatory" publication could be banned, and the publishers prevented from publishing.

Near and Guilford fought the banning order, and the case worked its way to the U.S. Supreme Court, which ruled in 1931 that no government at any level had the right to stop a publication before it was published. Writing for the majority in the case known as *Near v. Minnesota,* Chief Justice Charles Evans Hughes said:

> Public officers, whose character and conduct remain open to debate and free discussion in the press, find their remedies for false accusations in actions under libel laws providing for redress and punishment, and not in proceedings to restrain the publications of newspapers and periodicals. The fact that the liberty of the press may be abused by miscreant purveyors of scandal does not make any the less necessary the immunity of the press from previous restraint in dealing with official misconduct. Subsequent punishment for such abuses as may exist is the appropriate remedy, consistent with constitutional privilege.

Guilford recovered, but he and Near did not get to enjoy much of their legal victory. The *Saturday Press* continued for a couple of years but could not make enough money to sustain itself. Guilford quit in 1934 and ran for mayor but was killed by gangsters before his campaign got started. Near died two years later of natural causes.

The case they generated has had important implications. For the first time, the U.S. Supreme Court said that governments could not censor publications. They could not exercise "prior restraint."

Legal Precedents

The First Amendment to the U.S. Constitution gives people in America the legal right to speak and write what they think. It also gives citizens other important rights. It states:

> Congress shall make no law respecting an establishment of religion, or prohibiting the free exercise thereof; or abridging the freedom of speech, or of the press; or the right of the people peaceably to assemble, and to petition the government for a redress of grievances.

The amendment was added to the Constitution in 1791, four years after the republic was established and 140 years before the U.S. Supreme Court had issued its opinion in *Near v. Minnesota.* The First Amendment had been in place for more than one hundred years when the case of the Cherry Sisters, giving writers the right to comment and criticize on public affairs, was decided.

So what's going on here? Why did it take the courts more than a century to grant these rights? Did people have these rights before the Courts' decisions?

The answer to the last question is yes. From the nation's beginnings, people spoke and wrote freely, particularly about public subjects that merited comment and criticism. George Washington was treated very badly by his critics in the press, as has been every president since then. Throughout the nineteenth century, politicians and public corruption were the constant targets of newspapers and magazines. Unpopular causes such as abolition, women's suffrage, prohibition, unionism, anarchy, and the like were strongly advocated both by mainstream media and specialized publications devoted to a particular cause. Was prior restraint ever imposed on these publications by public officials?

Occasionally, it was, but the instances of prior restraint were relatively few and isolated. On the whole, however, the nineteenth century saw a free flow of information and ideas. Although those who participated in these public conversations may not have thought they were doing so as a First Amendment right, they certainly acted within the bounds and spirit of the First Amendment. The American public in the nineteenth century became used to an open and free conversation. They did not so much believe in it or advocate it as they practiced it. And that tells something important about legal cases and precedents.

A Court decision such as *Near v. Minnesota,* rather than granting new rights, will often confirm what has already become standard practice. In that particular case, the U.S. Supreme Court struck down a state law that got in the way of the commonly accepted exercise of First Amendment rights. In the case of the Cherry Sisters, the Iowa Supreme Court simply said that public criticism did not constitute libel, which is still an active and important legal concept, as we will see later in this chapter. The Court recognized that criticism of public figures and public officials was part of the way in which our social and political system works. Libel laws should not get in the way.

In these two cases, the Courts made the right decision in defending and expanding the freedoms granted by the First Amendment. Courts are not always so wise, however. Sometimes they hand down unwise or ill-considered decisions that restrict the liberties of the people to speak and to have access to information and ideas. State legislatures and the U.S. Congress also pass imprudent laws that they hope will fix a particular problem but that wind up attempting to restrict how people communicate with one another. Our system of laws and legal precedents is an imperfect one. Our hope is that all of us will be informed citizens who understand the value of the full freedoms granted by the First Amendment and who will actively oppose any restrictions on them.

The First Amendment

The First Amendment to the U.S. Constitution grants us five important rights:

- Freedom to hold religious beliefs and worship as we see fit; the government is prohibited from establishing an official religion.
- Freedom of speech.
- Freedom of the press; publications may generally publish what they wish without the permission of the government and without any prior restraint.
- Freedom to assemble peaceably; the government cannot prohibit people from getting together to talk about whatever is on their minds, as long as they are peaceful.

THE STATE OF THE FIRST AMENDMENT

The First Amendment Center, an arm of the Freedom Forum Foundation, conducts a national survey each year to see how Americans feel about the freedoms guaranteed by the First Amendment. The following are some of the key findings of the 2003 survey:

■ About 60 percent of respondents indicated overall support for First Amendment freedoms, whereas 34 percent said the First Amendment goes too far.

■ 52 percent said media ownership by fewer corporations has meant a decreased number of viewpoints available to the public; 53 percent said the quality of information also has suffered.

■ Almost eight in ten respondents said owners exert substantial influence over news organizations' newsgathering and reporting decisions. Only 4 percent said they believed there is no tampering with story selection or play.

■ 54 percent favored maintaining limits on how many radio, television, and newspaper outlets may be owned by a single company, but 50 percent opposed any increased regulation.

■ 65 percent favored the policy of "embedding" U.S. journalists into individual combat units; 68 percent said the news media did an excellent or good job in covering the war in Iraq.

■ 48 percent said they believe Americans have too little access to information about the federal government's efforts to combat terrorism—up from 40 percent last year.

■ About 55 percent of those surveyed opposed a constitutional amendment to ban flag-burning, up from 51 percent in 2002.

■ Freedom to petition the government; that is, we can tell our lawmakers and public officials what we think, and we can ask them to change things if we disagree with what they are doing.

In the realms of journalism, the First Amendment is the most important legal document on the books. Its two parts about speech and the press constitute the basic tenet of journalism—that people can exchange information and ideas. The First Amendment provides the sturdiest protection that journalists have against assaults by those who disagree with what they are saying or reporting. Many subsequent laws and court decisions that have outlined the specific freedoms that journalists have are based on an interpretation of this section of the Constitution.

But the First Amendment is more than just a legal document. It essentially lays out the most important principles of public life in America and in some sense provides a description of how life in America is supposed to work. The man most responsible for the First Amendment was James Madison, a Virginia congressman when the Constitution was ratified. Madison had been a leader at the convention in Philadelphia that wrote the Constitution in 1787, and he argued forcefully and brilliantly for its ratification in the months afterward. He later became the fourth president of the United States.

The vision that Madison forms for America in the First Amendment and in his other writing is one based on the free flow of information. Madison, like many of his contemporaries among the Founding Fathers, believed in a "marketplace of ideas," a concept made popular at the time by philosophers John Milton, John Stuart Mill, and others. They felt that the best ideas for society could be found only through a system that allowed many voices to participate and contribute. In 1791, the year the First Amendment was added to the Constitution, Madison wrote, "Whatever facilitates a general intercourse of sentiments, as good roads, domestic commerce, a free press, and particularly a circulation of newspapers through the entire body of the people—is favorable to liberty."

But none of the framers of the Constitution, as far as we know, believed that speech and the press should be completely unfettered. Although there have been some absolutists—people who argued that no restrictions should be placed on these freedoms—in the history of America, most people have been convinced that reasonable restraints in limited areas of the law are good for society. Those areas that have the most to do with journalism are libel, copyright, and to some extent privacy.

Defamation

A person's reputation, his or her "good name," is not only socially important but legally valuable. To harm that reputation is to commit defamation. The concept of defamation comes from English common law with the idea that someone who damages the reputation of another person should be held responsible and should have to pay for those damages. There are two types of defamation: libel, or written defamation; and slander, spoken defamation. Some people use the term *libel* to cover both libel and defamation. Libel is one of the most important legal considerations for a journalist.

Legally, the concept of libel is limited. State laws have libel clauses, but they are rarely very specific about what constitutes libel. That has been left to courts and juries to decide. As we saw with the case of the Cherry Sisters at the beginning of this chapter, libel is not just negative comments or criticism. Saying something bad about a person is not necessarily to harm that person's reputation.

So what does constitute libel? Libel actions most often have been brought and won in four areas: comments about someone's political beliefs (such as calling someone a Nazi or a terrorist); saying that someone has a physical illness (such as AIDS) or a mental disease (calling somebody "crazy"); disparaging someone's business practices or professional conduct; saying that someone is a criminal. In any of these areas, libelous words will cause people to be shunned or thought less of and might endanger their ability to earn a living or advance in their profession. We should note here that libel laws protect not only individuals but also businesses and organizations. Saying that a bank cannot meet its obligations, for instance, might cause people to withdraw their money or keep people from doing business with the bank. The bank itself can sue for libel.

The person or organization that brings a libel suit has to prove five things for the court: publication, identification, defamation, fault, and damages. Libel has to involve at least three people: the person who is libeled, the person who says or prints the libel, and a third person who reads or sees it. A libelous statement in a newspaper has obviously been published, but a libelous statement about someone that you put into an email and send to a third person has also been published.

The person who brings a libel suit must also prove that he or she has been identified as the person who has been libeled. Using someone's name in a libelous context obviously identifies that person, but there are other ways to identify someone. For instance, to say that the Smyth County High School basketball team "is full of drug dealers" might be enough identification for a member of that team to bring a libel suit. Or let's say a story appears in the newspaper about a person being convicted of a crime, but mistakenly a picture along with the story is of the wrong person. Even though the person's name was not used, the person could claim that the picture identifies him as being a criminal. Identification is not always as straightforward as it appears.

Proving defamation is usually the key part of the libel suit. As mentioned earlier, a person must show that his or her reputation was harmed by the publication by making people hate or shun him or her or by diminishing that person's ability to make a living.

Fault is an important concept that will be discussed more fully momentarily. A libel plaintiff (the person bringing the libel suit) must prove that the defendant (the person being sued) was responsible for the publication and was, in legal terms, "negligent." For most potential plaintiffs who are private citizens, this means proving that a publisher was careless and did not take the proper precautions; that is, they did not exercise the proper reporting and editing procedures.

Finally, the plaintiff must prove that he or she has been damaged by the libelous statements. Sometimes libel plaintiffs can show actual dollar amounts in loss of business, but this is not always possible or necessary. Sometimes they must simply demonstrate that people think less of them because of what was published or broadcast. Interestingly, some people have reputations so heinous that they cannot be libeled. Take, for instance, a person who has been convicted of killing a child. It would be difficult to imagine that anyone could say or print anything that would damage that person's reputation further.

Defenses against Libel Suits

Libel is a civil, not a criminal, offense. English and American law once had provisions for criminal libel—and people could go to jail for committing such a libel—but those provisions have mostly been rescinded by state legislatures. In a civil action, the plaintiff must prove to a court (and often a jury) that he or she has been libeled, but the defendant can also use "affirmative defenses" against libel. That is, even if the plaintiff can prove all five things discussed in the previous section, a defendant still may not be guilty because of affirmative defenses. These defenses include statute of limitations, truth, qualified privilege, and constitutional privilege.

Many civil and some criminal laws have a statute of limitations; that is, a suit may not be filed after a certain time has passed. This time period varies from state to state but is usually one or two years. So, in many states, if a libelous statement is more than two years old, a plaintiff may not file a suit to recover damages.

Truth is one of the strongest defenses against libel. The nature of libel is that it is a false statement. To prove that a statement is true is to take away this essential ingredient. Truth, however, can sometimes be difficult to prove. A journalist using truth as a defense must have solid evidence such as documents or credible witnesses to back up a claim.

Journalists may also claim "qualified privilege" as a defense against libel. Journalists are charged with reporting and disseminating the news. Sometimes that can include information that is potentially libelous. For instance, a prosecutor may accuse an innocent person of a crime. The journalist has the right to report that accusation without fear of being open to a libel suit. Journalists, as always, need to be careful about what they report, particularly when it contains this kind of information, but they should not censor themselves for fear of being sued. Courts have tended to understand and be sympathetic to the reporting process.

The defense of constitutional privilege grows out of a case the United States Supreme Court decided in 1964 called *New York Times v. Sullivan.* L. B. Sullivan was the police commissioner in Montgomery and sued the *Times* for information it had printed about how he handled a civil rights demonstration. The Supreme Court used that case to give the news media a strong layer of protection against suits by public officials. The Court said that a public official had to prove "actual malice" on the part of the publisher of the libel. The Court defined actual malice as either knowing something was false or having "reckless disregard" of the truth in the way the information about a person was handled. In other words, a public official would have to prove that the journalist knew what the truth was and deliberately said or wrote something else or that the methods the journalist used were so shoddy that the journalist had reckless disregard for the truth. The Court's intent was to stop public officials from using libel suits to stifle criticism and debate on public issues. The actual malice standard made it almost impossible for a public official to win a libel suit. Later the Court took another case and expanded this burden of proof to people it labeled "public figures." These would be famous people who are not public officials, people such as movie stars and athletes. Again, the Court intended that discussion of issues and personalities not be burdened by the threat of libel suits. This is called the constitutional privilege defense because the Court used the First Amendment as the basis for formulating this defense.

Who is a public official? And who is a public figure? Courts have tended to say that anyone employed by any level of government in a position of responsibility is a public official. That would include everyone from the president of the United States

Quote 3.2

WILLIAM BRENNAN

On the principle underlying the First Amendment

If there is a bedrock principle underlying the First Amendment, it is that the government may not prohibit the expression of an idea simply because society finds the idea itself offensive or disagreeable.

William Brennan was a U.S. Supreme Court justice and author of the New York Times v. Sullivan *decision.*

to the local high school principal. Defining a public figure is an ongoing debate. Some people such as Michael Jordan and Jennifer Lopez are certainly public figures, but there are many questions about others. Courts have tended to look at whether or not someone voluntarily injects themselves into a public discussion or situation; those who do so are public figures.

DEVELOPING THE CONCEPT OF THE PUBLIC FIGURE

When the Supreme Court decided the *New York Times v. Sullivan* case in 1964, it gave extra protection to the media against libel suits by public officials. The Court was seeking to encourage vigorous debate and discussion on issues of the day. But vigorous debate often involves more than public officials. Three years after the *Sullivan* decision, the Court expanded the actual malice standard of proof to include public figures.

It took two major college

University of Alabama football coach Paul "Bear" Bryant

football coaches and a retired Army general to make this happen. In the fall of 1962, Alabama's football team shellacked Georgia, 35–0. The next year, the *Saturday Evening Post* published an article about how the head coaches, Paul "Bear" Bryant of Alabama and Wally Butts of Georgia, colluded to fix the game. The article, "The Story of a College Football Fix," alleged that Butts had called Bryant during the week before the game and outlined the offensive and defensive plays the Bulldogs planned to run during the game. Butts sued the *Post* and won a $3 million judgment, which was reduced to $460,000 by an appeals court.

In a separate incident earlier in 1962, the Associated Press reported that retired Army Gen. Edwin Walker had encouraged people to riot when the first black student attempted to enroll at the University of Mississippi. Walker sued the AP in Texas and won a judgment of $800,000.

Both cases came to the Supreme Court at the same time, and as it occasionally does, the Court combined the cases into one decision.

The Court ruled that even though none of the plaintiffs in either of the cases held public office, they were "public figures"; that is, they were people involved in important issues of interest to the public. Therefore, if they were going to sue for libel, they had to prove actual malice, just as public officials had to prove it.

The Supreme Court did not define precisely who a "public figure" is, and courts have been struggling with the concept ever since. In 2003, for example, a U.S. Court of Appeals panel ruled that a former Navy lieutenant was a "limited purpose" public figure.

Cary Lohrenz was one of the first women trained to fly combat aircraft for the U.S. Navy in the early 1990s. In 1996 she sued the Center for Military Readiness, the *Washington Times,* and the *San Diego Union* for alleging that she was a substandard pilot. The appeals court said that her position as one of the first women to fly combat aircraft made her a public figure and that she had to prove actual malice.

You can read the full decisions in these cases on the Web at the following addresses: *Curtis v. Butts* (www.bc.edu/bc_org/avp/cas/comm/free_speech/curtis.html); *Lohrenz v. Donnelly* (http://fsnews.findlaw.com/cases/dc/025294a.html).

Copyright and Trademarks

Another area in which the freedom to write and publish is not unlimited is that of copyright and trademarks, which are part of a larger area of law known as intellectual property. People who create what we might term generally as *intellectual property*—books, musical works, art, sculpture, articles, poems, and so on—have some protection in the way that those works are used by others. If you write a poem, that poem is yours (at least for a limited amount of time), and no one else can reprint that poem without your permission.

Copyright protection does not extend to some things, however. Facts cannot be copyrighted. Let's say you are the only writer covering your high school basketball game, and you write a story about it for the high school paper. Another publication can take the facts that you have described (the details of the game, the score, etc.) and use them in its description of the game. That publication, however, cannot use your account of the game. The expression of facts can be copyrighted, but the facts themselves cannot. Ideas are the same way. Ideas cannot be copyrighted, but the expression of those ideas can. For instance, you can paint a picture of a tree, and that painting will be copyrighted. Others can paint a picture of the same tree. That's not against the law, as long as they do not use your painting.

Copyright protection is limited in two important ways. One is that it does not last forever. Currently, copyrights last for the life of the creator, plus seventy years. If the copyright is owned by a corporation, then copyright lasts longer, but it does not last forever. At some point, all creative works become part of the "public domain"; that is, everyone owns them. Consequently, the works of William Shakespeare, for instance, are in the public domain, and Shakespeare can be quoted at length without anyone's permission.

The other way in which copyright protection is limited is through the concept of fair use. This concept has been developed to encourage the dissemination of ideas and information without either putting a great burden on the user or infringing on the rights of the creator of the work. Fair use means that in certain limited circumstances, a copyrighted work—or more likely, some portion of it—may be used without the permission of the holder of the copyright. In considering what is fair use, courts have looked at four factors:

- the nature of the copyrighted material—how much effort it took to produce it;
- the nature of the use—for instance, material used in an educational setting for educational purposes is more likely to be thought of as fair use;
- the extent of the use—how much of the copyrighted material is used, whether just a few words or a whole passage;
- commercial infringement—most importantly, how much does the use hurt the commercial value of the work?

Unless material is being used in a very limited way, you should always get permission to use copyrighted material. Holders of copyright can be very aggressive about enforcing their copyrights, and the unauthorized user of a copyrighted work can be fined substantially. Many people in education believe that they can use any material in any way they wish, and it will be considered fair use. That is not the case. Educators are bound by copyright laws as much as anyone else.

A final important point: Material on the Internet has as much copyright protection as anything else. Some people believe that whatever is on a web site is in the public domain, but that is not the case. Just because material is easy to access does not mean that it does not have copyright protection.

Trademarks offer special protection for the commercial use of words, phrases, and symbols, and journalists need to be careful about how they use them. Many companies go to great lengths to protect their trademarks because that is how the public identifies their products. What if, for example, a shoe company named Nuke started using the Nike swoosh on its shoes? Consumers might become confused about what product to buy, and Nike, which holds a trademark on the swoosh, might be hurt by that.

Journalists generally do not run into much of a problem in using trademarks in what they right or print. If a newspaper used the Nike swoosh to illustrate a story about the company, that would probably be considered fair use because it would not be infringing on the commercial aspects of the swoosh or confusing consumers with it. But journalists should be careful about certain words they use that designate particular products. For example, *Xerox* is the name of a company, not a verb that means "photocopy." It should be capitalized and not used as a verb.

Privacy

Privacy is another area of the law that journalists need to be aware of, although it does not affect journalists as much as people think. The right of privacy is not a clearly established legal concept. In fact, some argue that because the U.S. Constitution says nothing about privacy, it should have no legal standing. Courts and some laws do protect certain aspects of a person's life, but these protections have more to do with advertising and commerce than they do with the publication of information about a person.

Essentially, the news media are allowed to publish almost anything about a person as long as it is true. They do not need a person's permission to publish anything about that person. How they get such information is often the important legal question. Journalists may not trespass on people's property, they may not steal information, and they may be in some trouble if they take information—particularly medical information—that state and federal laws try to protect. Otherwise, however, journalists are free to print and broadcast what they know. They are free to describe and photograph what they can see, even if what they see is on private property. For example, if someone is in a house but the window and curtains are open, a photographer standing in the street can take a picture of that person. No invasion of privacy has taken place.

Within the realm of journalism, privacy is more of a social and civil restraint than a legal one. Journalists may not choose to publish private facts about a person because they do not feel that it would be appropriate or necessary. Still, journalists should take some care in this area because in some situations the publication of private facts can be the basis for a legal action.

What Do You Think?   3.1

WHAT WOULD YOU DO?

Student editors at Wooster High School filed suit against their principal and school district in January 2003, accusing them of violating their First Amendment rights when the district confiscated 4,500 copies of the school's newspaper.

The newspaper contained a story saying athletes at the school and the daughter of one of the school board members were at a party where they drank alcohol.

The editors said the story is correct.

The principal and school officials said it's possible that some of the students were misquoted and that the article is potentially libelous.

A Coolidge High student in Washington, DC, had his video camera confiscated by school administrators in March 2003. He was shooting video of chained school doors, which at other schools had been found to be in violation of fire codes.

The student was working for a local television news program that was doing a story on conditions at the school. He said he had permission from school officials to bring the camera to the school, but after they saw what he was doing, they asked him to put it away.

He did so, but later they took it away from him and threatened him with a twenty-five-day suspension.

You can read about other First Amendment issues and situations at the web site of the Student Law Press Center (splc.org).

Legal Protections for Journalists

As we have noted throughout this chapter, very few laws restrict the work of journalists or the ability of news organizations to publish or broadcast what they know. In fact, there are a number of laws and legal precedents that protect journalists and assist them in their work. The most important, of course, is the First Amendment, which we discussed earlier in this chapter. Beyond that, courts and legislatures have recognized that the work of journalists is important enough that it needs some legal assistance.

One of the most important of these protections has been alluded to in our discussion of libel laws. That is the concept known as privilege, which means that a journalist should be given some leeway, that is sometimes not granted to others to do the job of reporting, writing, and editing. They are often able to go into areas from which the general public is restricted, such as crime scenes and disaster areas. Courtrooms reserve seats for reporters and make special accommodations for them to cover high-profile trials. Public officials plan for their presence because they are seen as agents of the public and disseminate valuable information.

Beyond these amenities, newsgathering itself is given some protection by the law and by courts. In some cases, journalists are protected from a lawsuit if they can demonstrate that they followed standard journalistic procedures or if they showed themselves to be "neutral reporters."

One of the most important areas in which journalists have received legal protection is that of confidential sources. Police investigators, prosecutors, and judges, in the course of their own duties, sometimes want to know what people journalists have talked with. There have been many instances in which they have tried to force journalists into revealing those sources. Journalists take seriously pledges they have given to sources to keep their identities confidential, and they usually resent others who try to intrude on their newsgathering procedures. To protect journalists from these intrusions, most states have laws that protect journalists from having to reveal anonymous sources. These laws have given journalists some, but not absolute, protection. As a result, legal officials usually try to avoid these confrontations with journalists.

Another area in which there are laws that help journalists has to do with meetings of public bodies, such as city councils and school boards, and with documents and records produced by all levels of government. Most states have laws that force governmental bodies to have public meetings and that mandate that most governmental records be open to the public. At the federal level, the U.S. government operates under the Freedom of Information Act, which allows citizens to make a formal request for records and documents. These laws are set up to help citizens, not just journalists, find out what their government is doing, but they are most often used by journalists in the reporting process. Unfortunately, many government officials at all levels spend a good deal of time ignoring or trying to get around these laws, believing they have no responsibility to the public for their actions or simply trying to cover up actions of which the public would not approve.

Free Press–Fair Trial

In 1954, the pregnant wife of Sam Sheppard, a prominent physician in Cleveland, Ohio, was murdered in her home in one of the city's better neighborhoods. The doctor was at home at the time and claimed that a one-armed intruder had broken in and injured him as well as killing his wife. Some evidence pointed to the doctor as the killer, but the police appeared slow to make an arrest. The *Cleveland Press* began an editorial campaign that criticized the police and called for the arrest of the doctor.

When Dr. Sheppard was arrested and charged, the newspaper's editors made no secret of their belief that he was guilty. Other news organizations in Cleveland joined in beating the editorial drums against the doctor. Sheppard's trial was conducted in a circus atmosphere that the judge did little to control. Sheppard was convicted, but he appealed, arguing that he did not receive a fair trial because of the negative comments in the city's newspapers. The Supreme Court agreed. It set aside Sheppard's conviction, criticized many aspects of how the investigation and trial were conducted, and had these words about the press coverage of the case:

> The massive, pervasive and prejudicial publicity attending petitioner's prosecution prevented him from receiving a fair trial consistent with the Due Process Clause of the 14th Amendment.

The U.S. Constitution guarantees citizens a speedy and fair trial if they are accused of a crime. That guarantee, some believe, is jeopardized by the First Amendment, the guarantee of a free press. Publicity about the accusation, the argument goes, will prejudice potential jurors and prevent the person accused from getting a fair trial.

The Sheppard trial was not an isolated incident, as we well know. (Dr. Sheppard, by the way, was tried again and found not guilty. His story inspired the television series *The Fugitive* and later the movie.) The news is constantly filled with stories about people accused of crimes. When the accused is famous or when the crime is unusual, news coverage can become massive, even overwhelming. People discuss the trial and even form opinions about the guilt or innocence of the accused.

Should the First Amendment be suspended whenever someone is accused of a crime? Should reporters not be allowed to write about anything connected with a trial until the courtroom proceedings begin? Although these ideas have been discussed, they are usually thought to be too radical or simply unworkable. In fact, they are dangerous. The judicial system is like any other part of government. People need to have confidence that it is working correctly, and the only way that confidence can be generated is if people are able to see how it works. The judicial system is also open to corruption, just as every other part of government is, and the press needs to serve its watchdog function in this area.

But what about the rights of the accused? In the glare of publicity, can the accused be assured of getting a fair trial? While the debate continues, all of those involved—prosecutors, defense attorneys, investigators, judges, and journalists—have generally tried to be sensitive to the legal fact that a person accused of a crime is innocent until proven guilty. Judges particularly have developed rules for judicial proceedings that reduce the circus atmosphere surrounding hearings and trials. They have used a number of standard legal options, such as gag orders for lawyers and witnesses and changing the location of a trial, to ensure that potential jurors will have an open mind about the charges against a person.

Quote 3.3

KURT VONNEGUT

On the First Amendment

The First Amendment reads more like a dream than a law, and no other nation, so far as I know, has been crazy enough to include such a dream among its fundamental legal documents. I defend it because it has been so successful for two centuries in preserving our freedom and increasing our vitality, knowing that all arguments in support of it are certain to sound absurd.

Kurt Vonnegut is a novelist whose books include Cat's Cradle *and* Slaughterhouse Five.

The free press–fair trial debate continues, however, and flares up every time a crime generates sustained coverage by the news media. Because both a "fair trial" and a "free press" are subjective concepts, there is unlikely to be any solution that will end this controversy.

Constant Vigilance

Journalists operate with great but not total legal freedom in the United States. Because of the way the First Amendment to the U.S. Constitution has been used by the public and the news media and reinforced by legislatures and interpreted by the courts, journalists are free to gather information and disseminate that information without the burden of prior restraint. This freedom is never completely secure. Journalists and the general public should always be on guard against efforts to restrict it, no matter how good the reasons are for wanting to do so.

QUESTIONS FOR DISCUSSION

1. Read the portion of this chapter that deals with how Americans feel about the First Amendment. What do you think about the responses to this survey? What would be your responses if you were asked questions like these?
2. Should privacy laws be stronger? If so, what should they protect?
3. What the reviewer said about the Cherry Sisters in the opening of this chapter was pretty vicious. Did the court make the right decision in this case? What if the sisters had been your relatives—how would you feel about the case then?
4. Do you feel that we should oppose all laws that might restrict First Amendment freedoms?

RELATED WEB SITES

First Amendment Center, www.fac.org

First Amendment Handbook, www.rcfp.org/handbook/viewpage.cgi

Media Watch, www.pbs.org/newshour/media

Minnesota News Council, www.mtn.org/~newscncl

Student Press Law Center, www.splc.org

READINGS AND REFERENCES

Bunker, M. (1996). *Justice and the media: Reconciling fair trials and a free press.* Mahwah, NJ: Lawrence Erlbaum and Associates.

Bunker, M. (2001) *Critiquing free speech: First amendment theory and the challenge of interdisciplinarity.* Mahwah, NJ: Lawrence Erlbaum and Associates.

Dennis, E., Gillmor, D. E., & Glasser, T. (Eds.). (1989). *Media freedom a* Westport, CT: Greenwood Press.

Gilmer, D., Barron, J. A., Simon, T., & Terry, H. (1996). *Fundamentals o, communication law*. St. Paul, MN: West.

Middleton, K., Chamberlain, B., & Lee, W. E. (2003). *The law of public communication*. Boston: Allyn and Bacon.

Chapter Four

Journalism Comes of Age

Key Concepts and Terms

1. The nineteenth century was a time of enormous change in the lives of Americans. One element of that change was the speed at which they were able to communicate. Another was the development of photography, which opened up a visual world of communication that had never before existed.

2. Journalism changed its very nature during the nineteenth century. Newspapers went from being organs of opinion to organs of information, and their audiences expanded to include more Americans than ever.

3. Journalism of the nineteenth century is often defined by the personalities who dominated the field—people such as James Gordon Bennett and Horace Greeley and, later in the century, Joseph Pulitzer and William Randolph Hearst.

4. Penny press: inexpensive newspapers (which often sold for a penny) that first appeared in the 1830s and that appealed to a large audience with stories of crime, human interest, and sports.

5. Abolition: the term used for the movement to abolish slavery; the fight over abolition was the great political issue of the first part of the nineteenth century affecting everything in political life, including journalism.

6. By the middle of the century, magazines had found their form and audience.

7. Photography was invented in 1839, and although it would be many years before photographs could be easily mass produced, photography began to change the way journalism was practiced by the mid-1800s.

8. The Civil War, 1861–1865, demonstrated profoundly the value of news to American news organizations and to their audiences.

Vignette

Many people who lived through a good part of the twentieth century have pronounced it the century of change. Certainly, knowledge expanded at an enormous rate during those years, and the technological changes were vast. We will be discussing some of those in Chapter 7. People who comment about all of the changes in the twentieth century sometimes imply that nothing like that had ever happened before.

Actually, it had. Profound changes in human activity and outlook occurred as well during the nineteenth century. Many of those changes set the stage for what we experienced in the twentieth century and will experience in the current century.

Imagine a young man born in 1815 in a mountainous county in western Virginia who lives until he is 80 years old. The president at the time he is born is James Madison, one of the founding fathers of the nation and the man chiefly responsible for the United States Constitution. The young man's father likely moved to that county years before and settled there to build a self-sufficient farm on which he could raise his family. He probably never traveled more than twenty miles from home after he settled there, and the young man did not travel outside the county either.

The young man could read, and books and newspapers were available to him. But the newspapers he read had news from faraway places, such as Washington, DC, New York, Boston, and even London, and the events the news stories referred to were weeks or even months old. Growing up, the boy would have no clear idea what these places looked like, how people in cities such as these lived, or how they dressed and spoke.

Closer to home, the boy wore clothes made for him by his mother, possibly from cloth purchased at a local store but just as likely from homespun wool made from sheep raised on the farm. Very little in the house was manufactured. Tools and household goods were handmade. Heat came from wood fireplaces, and oil lamps provided some light to pierce the darkness after sundown.

Once during the boy's childhood, a traveling artist came through the area and painted several small portraits of some of the people living there. The wealthier people had larger portraits. The artist was paid by some in cash and by others with what goods they made on their farms.

Travelers and occasionally relatives would come by, talking about the opportunities and the land—the unlimited quantities of land—that existed west of the mountains. The United States now owned most of the land west of the Mississippi River, a river so vast that the boy could not imagine it, and these travelers were headed there, convinced their future was there. Of course, they always talked politics. John Quincy Adams had stolen the election of 1824, they said; Andrew Jackson was a man of the people. Later they began to talk about how the federal government should leave the states alone to do as they pleased, especially on the question of slavery. Not many people owned slaves around the area where the boy grew up.

The young boy inherited his father's farm when he grew up. He married and had several children, some of whom survived their childhood and some of whom did not. He had once dreamed of moving west, but the family and the farm kept him there.

By the time he died at age 80 in 1895, the world had changed profoundly from his boyhood. The great public event of his life was the Civil War; two of his sons had fought for the Union, and one had been wounded. The area in which he lived was part of the state of Virginia at the beginning of the war but had seceded to form the state of West Virginia. Many people in the county now worked in the coal mines, which was difficult and dangerous work, and were thinking about joining a workers' organization called a union. When times were good, people had more cash than he had ever seen, but there also had been some bad times when some people just couldn't make ends meet.

The man had had his first picture taken by a traveling photographer sometime in the 1850s. It looked just like him; his wife kept it in the back of the family Bible. His picture was taken a couple of other times, too. Several years before his death, the man had traveled to Charleston, West Virginia, where some of his grandchildren and great-grandchildren lived. There he had seen electric lights, indoor plumbing, and large factories that manufactured all sorts of things. He had also read the newspaper published there; it contained news about local people and events that had occurred the day before. It even had news from Washington and Europe that did not seem very old. One of his great-grandchildren said that a friend of hers had a telephone in her house. She even took him by the house, a sprawling Victorian mansion that seemed larger than his farm. She said her friend's father was rich and had made his money in coal mines and railroads.

At the man's funeral, the men talked politics—something about reform and populism. People said one of these days, the rich would no longer be in control.

Change and More Change

The events of the life of the man just described intersect with many of the changes that occurred in communication and journalism in the nineteenth century. Those changes established the basis for the journalism that we know and practice today. In this chapter and the next, we will discuss how those changes occurred and the people who were responsible for them.

Here are some of the most important developments in journalism in the nineteenth century:

- Journalists of the nineteenth century developed many of the modern customs and conventions of journalism. Particularly important is the definition of news and news events. Journalists began to give regular and systematic coverage to politics, which changed politics profoundly, and they began to cover other parts of society that had never received attention (such as business news) or simply had not existed (such as organized sporting events).

- Technical innovations occurred throughout the century that opened up new opportunities for journalism. The two most important were the speed at which information could be transmitted and the invention and development of photography.

- Audiences for journalism expanded. In the 1700s journalism consumers were intellectuals and those interested in politics, but in the next century, journalists discovered that people were interested in all parts of society. America was still a nation of newspaper readers, but in the nineteenth century there were many more people and many more readers.

- Journalism, and particularly newspapers, became big business. Money was to be made by those bright enough or lucky enough to satisfy an audience, and some people made huge fortunes. Advertising became a vital part of the journalism formula; merchants and manufacturers needed the nation's newspapers to sell their products and were willing to pay for space there.

- Newspapers changed from partisan voices to businesses with editorial opinions. Journalists were no longer always linked to a political faction. News coverage took on a neutral tone, and journalists developed a sense of being independent observers of an event. Some newspapers claimed to represent their readers rather than a set of politicians.

- Still, journalism in the nineteenth century was never very far from politics. The great issues of the era were sectionalism, slavery, and the government's activities in the business environment, and newspapers had plenty to say about all of these things.

- The nineteenth century was an era of great personalities in journalism. A few people exercised profound influence on the profession and its practices.

- The century also witnessed a new and expanded role for women in the profession. Women were certainly present in the journalistic world before the 1900s, but they were often anonymous. The 1900s saw women act as reporters and editors, proudly exhibiting their names and gender. By the end of the century, they were still restricted in what they could do within the profession, but the progress they had made to that point was extraordinary.

- Finally, the nineteenth century saw the rise of a new medium, the magazine. Its purpose and content were different from the newspaper, but its usefulness to an audience was unmistakable.

The Penny Press

The idea of a cheap newspaper, paid for at the time of purchase and not by subscription, was phenomenally successful and changed journalism profoundly in the 1830s, but it was no sure thing. A number of entrepreneurs had the idea—in fact, it had already been tried successfully in London—but getting the formula right was not simple. The idea was that in a large city such as New York with a population that most newspapers had ignored, a newspaper could be sold on the streets for a penny. A penny wasn't much. Heretofore, a newspaper's revenue came mainly through subscriptions and party contributions. Subscribers were notoriously unreliable about paying, and party officials kept the editor under their yoke.

An early failure was that of Horace Greeley, who later enjoyed great success with penny newspapers. He copublished the *Morning Post* with Horatio David Sheppard, but their planning was ill-starred. They produced their first issue on January 1, 1833, a holiday rather than a workday when the streets were likely to be full. In addition, a snowstorm had fallen on New York the night before, so what street traffic there might have been was blocked. The paper had not been advertised, so no one had been given an opportunity to subscribe. The paper never recovered from the initial setbacks and was soon out of business.

Benjamin Day, like Greeley, another struggling job printer, also wanted to produce a cheap paper, but he saw the failure that Greeley had experienced and was reluctant. He had financial backers willing to try, however, so in September 1833, he brought out the *New York Sun*. The paper was a combination of news, shipping notices, and police items, as well as poetry and short stories; a third of the four-page issue was advertising. For a penny, it was a bargain.

That was the verdict of the public. Newsboys sold enough copies of the paper each day to keep it going and to quickly turn a profit for its owners. The *Sun* deemphasized politics and concentrated on human interests and on stories about the people who bought it. By 1838, it was selling about 34,000 copies a day, enough for Day to sell it for about $38,000. The *Sun* had started a trend in newspapering, but it was left to another publisher to see how far that trend could be pushed.

James Gordon Bennett and the *New York Herald*

James Gordon Bennett had a big idea. He wanted to publish a newspaper that would change the world, a newspaper that would be "the great organ and pivot of government, society, commerce, finance, religion and all human civilization." While his *New York Herald* fell somewhat short of that lofty goal, it did change journalism in ways that are still being felt many decades later.

Bennett was another of the entrepreneurs who saw the possibilities of the cheap newspaper. But his vision went beyond just making money—though make money he did. Bennett sought to decalcify the language that journalists used. The *New York Herald,* begun in 1835, used words of the street rather than words of the parlor— "legs" rather than "limbs," "petticoats and pantaloons" rather than "inexpressibles." That was shocking to middle- and upper-class New York, but Bennett knew that his audience was elsewhere. He declared his political independence and freely criticized the government, financial institutions, and organized religion. His reporters covered crime news in detail, talking about battered women and shocking murders.

His reporters and editors produced copy that was easy to read and understand by avoiding clichés and vague phrases.

Possibly Bennett's most important contribution to the definition of news was timeliness. Bennett realized that news was a perishable product. The faster it could be produced and distributed, the better it was. He also realized that people would prefer the newspaper that published information first, and he was determined for the *Herald* always to be first with the newspapers. Other editors had been willing to wait for two weeks for a report from Washington about what was happening in Congress. Bennett was not. He went to extraordinary lengths to get information into the *Herald* faster than other newspapers. Then he advertised the fact, making other papers seem like slackers. Who would buy the *Sun* when the *Herald* had the latest news?

Bennett's fellow publishers hated him. They hated him because of the *Herald*'s shocking content. They hated him because the *Herald* consistently beat them in news coverage. They hated him because he was so personally arrogant. In 1840, they organized what become known as the Moral War against him and his newspaper. They tried to persuade businesses to withdraw their advertising from the *Herald*. They tried to convince hotels to ban the *Herald*, and they called those who read the *Herald* immoral and antireligious. One editor even physically attacked Bennett in the street.

The Moral War did have some effect on curbing some of the rhetorical excesses in the *Herald*. The *Herald* lost circulation, and Bennett toned down some of the language to get it back, but his general journalistic fervor was unabated. He continued his quest always to have the news first. He tried to get news in every conceivable way, it seems. When steamships cut travel time to and from Europe from six weeks to less than three weeks, Bennett hired boats to meet the ships and get the news before the steamships came into port. Other newspapers did the same thing. Bennett at one time had people meeting ships in Boston and then sending him the news by carrier pigeon. Again other newspapers did the same thing. Then Bennett extended his carrier pigeon line to Halifax, Nova Scotia, to get news even faster. At that point, other papers hired sharpshooters to try to down the pigeons in flight. (Most of the pigeons survived.)

Jim Stovall

FIGURE 4.1 **James Gordon Bennett** James Gordon Bennett was ambitious and brilliant. He wanted to be remembered simply for his name, which he hoped would come to represent "one of the great benefactors of the human race." Bennett understood the essential nature of news—timeliness— and he always made every effort to get the latest news into his newspaper, the *New York Herald*.

These attempts to get news first were soon overcome by one of the nineteenth century's most important inventions, the telegraph. The first telegraph line was established between Washington and Baltimore. Bennett exploited the telegraph and tried to maintain a monopoly, but other newspapers banded together to form the precursor to today's Associated Press. Still, the competition among New York newspapers to get news first was fierce, and that aspect of journalism has remained to the present day.

Bennett introduced other basic concepts into the world of journalism. One of the most important was his attention to women and "women's news." In 1855 Bennett hired Jane Cunningham Croly, known to her readers as "Jennie June," who wrote about society, fashion, and beauty. She later left the *Herald* and wrote the first nationally syndicated column for women, founded the Women's Press Club of New York City, and in 1889 became the first woman appointed to teach journalism at the college level. Bennett demanded that advertising be as fresh as the paper's news. He stopped the practice of running the same ad again and again for months; he decreed that no advertisement could be run for more than two weeks and by 1848 was demanding that ads be changed every day.

By 1850 organized sporting clubs were forming in metropolitan areas in New York, and a new game—baseball—was becoming popular. Bennett's *Herald* produced some of the first sports writing in American journalism and gave regular coverage to the competition of these athletic clubs. He started a "personals" classified advertising column. When the occasion demanded it, he gave entire pages over to illustration rather than type, beginning the concept of visual journalism. Bennett also set up a series of foreign correspondents in most of the major cities in Europe, and he hired stringer correspondents throughout the nation and in Canada and Mexico. Those in Mexico became especially important when the Mexican War broke out in 1846.

The Mexican War freed the territory of Texas from the control of Mexico and ultimately gave the United States much of what is referred to as the Southwest today. Bennett and the *Herald* not only had their correspondents, but Bennett had also worked out an agreement with George W. Kendall, a cofounder of the *New Orleans Picayune,* to share information. Kendall was with General Zachary Taylor for much of the action and set up a series of riders to get the news back to Vera Cruz or another port in Mexico. From there ships would take the information to New Orleans. Then a set of 60 riders sped the information to Richmond, Virginia, which was then the southern tip of the telegraph system. Despite all these efforts, it still took about two weeks for northern readers to get news of the war. Still, covering the war taught reporters and editors much about getting information and this lesson would be useful for the next big conflict to come, the American Civil War.

Sectionalism, Slavery, and Abolition

The U.S. Constitution resolved many questions and conflicts about the American political system when it was adopted in 1789, but it did not solve the most fractious question: what powers would the federal government, and through it the people of a different region, have to impose their will on a state or region? The question

FIGURE 4.2 **Sports Coverage** One of the great innovations that James Gordon Bennett made was an emphasis on sports coverage. Sports was becoming a more organized activity in social life in America, and the new game of baseball was taking hold. Some form of the game had been played since the 1820s, and many trace its origins back to the English game of rounders. Contrary to the image that many have of the beginnings of baseball, it was not a game that was played in bucolic fields. It was a city game, and the first real baseball was played by teams fielded by social clubs in the major cities, particularly New York and Boston. Even today, major league baseball teams have the word *club* in their official name as a connection to the beginnings of organized baseball.

specifically revolved around the issue of slavery. As states were added to the Union in the early days of the republic, careful attention was paid to keep a numerical balance in Congress between those states that allowed slavery and those that did not. The hope was that the vexing question of slavery would somehow work itself out at some point in the near future.

It did not. Instead, by 1820 it seemed that slavery was as much entrenched in the South as it had been fifty years before. Many who had hoped for an end to slavery felt frustrated and betrayed. The South, they felt, had argued for years that it should be left alone to find its own solution to this problem. The solution it seemed to be finding was to grow more dependent on the slave economy.

SAMUEL F. B. MORSE: WHAT HATH GOD WROUGHT!

Samuel F. B. Morse was not a journalist, but he had as much to do with changing the profession in the nineteenth century as any American. Morse was a remarkable man, possessing a keen, inquiring, and inventive mind and the ability to inspire the same qualities in others.

Morse is most famous for the Morse code, a system of long and short clicks that enabled the telegraph to become a life-changing communication device in the 1840s. Morse did more than invent the code, however. He was instrumental in the invention of the telegraph itself.

Morse became fascinated by electricity while a student at Yale in the early part of the century, but he and others could see little practical use for it. Instead, Morse decided to become a painter and gained fame as one of the finest portrait artists in the country. He even studied for a time in Paris, where he met Louis Daguerre, the inventor of an early process that produced photographs called daguerreotypes.

When Morse returned to the United States, he advanced the cause of photography by encouraging others to pursue it. One of those he encouraged and trained was Matthew Brady.

What continued to fascinate Morse, however, was electricity and the idea that it could be used, somehow, to transmit messages over long distances. In 1837 Morse applied for a patent on a telegraph machine and sought financial backers to help him build a telegraph system. Few people could see the value of it, and Morse lived in poverty for several years trying to perfect his system and raise money.

Morse managed to secure some funds from Congress in the 1840s— enough to place telegraph poles from Baltimore to Washington, DC. In May 1844, he sat in the U.S. Capitol Building in Washington, DC, and tapped out a message that was received almost instantly in Baltimore. The message read, "What hath God wrought!"

What Morse had wrought was a revolution in communication. Never had people been able to send messages so far so fast. Within two years, telegraph lines stretched from Washington to Buffalo, New York, and Boston, Massachusetts. By 1853, every state east of the Mississippi except Florida was connected.

Morse became a wealthy man and remained an active businessman and public figure for many years. He died at the age of 80 in 1872. His home, Locus Grove, near Poughkeepsie, New York, is a national landmark (www.morse historicsite.org) and many of his papers are housed in the Library of Congress (http://memory.loc.gov/ ammem/atthtml/mrshome.html).

Antislavery societies began to spring up in many parts of the North and upper South. These societies had as their goal the end of slavery in the United States. Some wanted it immediately; others gradually. Some wanted free Negroes sent back to Africa; others wanted them to have full citizenship. Occasionally, there was a call for slaves to rise up in violent revolt against their masters. More frequently, members of these societies sought to help slaves escape, often to Canada where they would not be deported.

No one in the South who owned slaves or who believed in a slave-based economy viewed these antislavery societies as benign. Even those societies and groups that called for a gradual end to slavery with compensation to slave owners for their losses were seen as a threat, not just to an economic system but also to a way of life and sometimes to life itself. What many slave owners feared most was a slave revolt, and they felt that any sentiments expressed about freeing the slaves might spark such a revolt. Even to discuss the possibility of abolition was to encourage such danger, and slaveholders and sympathizers could not abide that.

Abolitionist societies gained added potency when they began to publish their own newspapers. The first such paper was the *Manumission Intelligencer,* published by Elijah Embree in the east Tennessee mountain town of Jonesborough in 1819. His publication was followed by many others, a few of which became highly influential and gained fame for their editors. The best of these early publications was the *Genius of Universal Emancipation,* first published in 1821 by Benjamin Lundy. The paper was begun in Boston but later moved to Baltimore in search of more support. The *Genius of Universal Emancipation* suffered from the same ailments that plagued subsequent abolitionist papers—too few subscribers and too little money. And even among people who might be sympathetic to the abolitionist cause, there was a feeling that the moral certainty of the editors made discussion of the issue difficult and any compromise solution impossible.

Still, editors like Lundy were morally certain and said so many times in many ways. Lundy was an early voice for emancipation, but in the late 1820s, he took on a partner who would become the greatest abolitionist editor of them all, William Lloyd Garrison. His writing shockingly powerful, Garrison advocated immediate freedom for all slaves; he also thought black people were equal in every way to whites and wanted them to have full citizenship.

FIGURE 4.3   William Lloyd Garrison No one in the 1840s and 1850s possessed a stronger voice in favor of emancipation than William Lloyd Garrison, editor of *The Liberator.* He was considered the ultimate extremist on the issue because he argued that slaves were human beings, in no way inferior to whites. He not only wanted emancipation but also full rights of citizenship, including suffrage. Most strong proponents of emancipation were unwilling to go that far.

Such sentiments proved unpalatable for most citizens of the North and South. Garrison spent some time in jail because he could not pay a libel judgment against him. The article in question concerned the owner of a slave ship whom he equated with "highway robbers and murderers." When he was released, he left Lundy to begin his own newspaper. On January 1, 1831, *The Liberator* was born in Boston, and because of Garrison's commitment and style, the paper had a wide reach. Its circulation never passed 600, but

Garrison's consistency in articulating his point of view made abolition a priority issue and framed many of the lines of the debate.

Garrison's advocacy did not include violence. He did not encourage slave revolts or white-led movements to free slaves. Still, his voice was so strong in favor of his cause that many felt he did not have to explicitly advocate revolution. The Georgia legislature offered $4,000 for the arrest of Garrison, and elsewhere in the South his newspaper was banned. He was attacked by a mob in Boston, and even fellow journalists often failed to protect his right to speak and write what he thought.

Garrison's fervor, though not his style and impact, were matched by others during the decades long debate over sectionalism and slavery. Being an abolitionist advocate could be dangerous. Elijah Lovejoy, an editor in St. Louis, Missouri, criticized a local judge for his leniency toward a mob that committed a racial murder, and he was told to get out of town. He moved his press across the Mississippi River to Alton, Illinois, and continued editorializing against slavery. Mobs twice charged his office and threw his printing press in the river. When he started again for the third time in 1837, the mob descended on his office and killed him.

Another powerful voice in the antislavery movement was that of Frederick Douglass, a former slave, who was editor of the *North Star* (later merged under the name *Frederick Douglass's Paper*). Douglass's paper spoke to a free black readership, urging them to improve themselves but also describing the restrictions they faced in a white-dominated society. Douglass was more than just an editor, however. He was a powerful speaker and a shrewd organizer and was easily the most famous black man of his time.

Among the mainstream press, the most ardent advocate of abolition was Horace Greeley, editor of the *New York Tribune*. Greeley held many radical political views. Not only was he staunchly antislavery, but also for a time he advocated socialism, and the *Tribune* carried a number of articles by the London-based Karl Marx. Greeley advocated prohibition (laws against selling alcohol), labor unions, and westward expansion. He was against capital punishment. Greeley was a powerful voice in favor of the election of Abraham Lincoln and was himself a losing presidential candidate in 1872.

Greeley's genius, however, was not the causes that he espoused but the personality that he imbued in the *Tribune*. He instituted many innovations to

FIGURE 4.4   Horace Greeley One of the most interesting characters of the nineteenth century, Horace Greeley advocated abolition, socialism (for a time), Republicanism, and westward expansion. He had a great talent for making his newspaper, the *New York Tribune*, interesting to read—so much so that loyal subscribers came to consider it a necessity. Greeley refused to print accounts of sensational trials, theater, or reports from police courts, and the *Tribune* became known as the "Great Moral Organ."

the journalistic world, including hiring the first woman to work regularly as a reporter and foreign correspondent. His weekly *Tribune* circulated throughout the nation, and one journalism historian of the period wrote that many people considered their Bible, Shakespeare, and the *Tribune* as the "three necessities of spiritual life."

Proslavery advocates generally did not establish newspapers specifically to advance their cause. They could count on the established press, particularly in the South. Newspapers there defended the institution in a variety of ways, and they had no trouble in pointing out the excesses of abolitionists or the damage they were doing to a way of life that many found comfortable and preferable to an increasingly industrialized North. As voices on both sides of the issue became increasingly shrill, a few southern editors were known as "fire-eaters," extremists who said that the South should secede from the union.

One such editor was Robert Barnwell Rhett of the *Charleston Mercury*. As early as 1837, he was writing that the South could no longer count on the federal government to protect its institutions or economy and that it might have to go its own way. Rhett came to believe in the future of an independent South so much that he envisioned a southern nation that would control its own economy and stretch from the Atlantic to the Pacific. When the South did secede in 1861, Rhett's was the first signature on the new constitution.

The Growth of Magazines

American readers wanted more than news and politics, however, and the nineteenth century saw the development of a different medium that would add to the culture that was American society. That medium was the magazine. Magazines had been in existence in some form since the early 1700s, but in these early years it was hard to distinguish between a magazine and a newspaper. Even then though, magazine editors sought to include in their publications poetry, literature, and commentary that readers would not necessarily find in newspapers. Magazines, though they might contain political content, were not part of the political environment in the same way that newspapers were. The high partisan years of the early republic (see Chapter 2) helped draw this distinction more clearly.

During the 1830s, with newspapers emphasizing news and politics—and, above all, speed—magazines became even more distinctive. They were published weekly or monthly, and their time frames for presenting information were much longer. Also distinguishing them from newspapers was the fact that many magazines appealed to special interests of the audience. There were publications that were solely concerned with fashion, literature, and scientific discovery.

In the early years of magazine publishing, editors struggled to find supplies and to find original editorial matter that was worth printing. They also had many problems with distribution because of the unreliability of the postal system. As the republic grew, these problems abated, and by the 1830s printing technology had advanced to make producing a magazine far easier. The postal system, too, had improved so that editors and readers could be confident that subscriptions would be filled.

Editorial content worthy of publication was still a problem, but the growing awareness of American writers of the country's assets and distinctiveness gave rise to an American genre of literature. Writers such as William Cullen Bryant, Nathaniel Hawthorne, James Fenimore Cooper, and Ralph Waldo Emerson were beginning to find their voices, and the magazine offered them the perfect outlet for their work. Edgar Allen Poe was another of America's foremost writers who worked to perfect the short story form, a form ideally suited to the periodical. Poe, whom many credit for inventing the mystery story, was editor for a short time of the *Southern Literary Messenger* published in Richmond, Virginia.

Many Americans, too, particularly in the middle and upper classes, were developing a reading habit, and they craved material that would satisfy this demand and help them pass the time. Americans also sought to educate themselves, developing a philosophy that the acquisition of knowledge could have not just moral benefits but economic benefits as well. Magazines offered them a chance to slow down lives that seemed to be accelerating at a dizzying pace. They could spend an evening reading a magazine to one another and discussing its contents.

Some of the most successful of the early genre magazines were those directed toward women. For more than eight years (1828–1836), Sara Josepha Hale published her *Ladies' Magazine* in Boston; it was a magazine filled with fashion news and helpful domestic advice. It was followed by the most successful of the early women's magazines, *Gody's Lady's Book,* published out of Philadelphia by Louis Gody. This magazine had huge appeal and gained a subscription list of an astonishing 40,000 by 1850.

The invention of photography indirectly affected magazines and helped make them more distinctive. The halftone process by which photographs could be integrated into the printing of publications had not been invented yet, so magazines and newspapers could not easily use photos. Photographs opened a world of possibilities for journalists, however. With photography, viewers for the first time could see faraway people and places, things they had never seen before. The technology of photography could bring these pictures into existence relatively quickly.

Photographs, which could not be used directly, gave rise to a realistic genre of illustration that had never been known before. Illustrators could look at photographs rather than having to go out and see the real-life objects. They could arrange those objects in various ways. Magazines soon developed several processes for using photographs to create illustrations that would be used in the printing of publication. One such process was to simply trace a photograph onto a smooth block of wood. Engravers would then chisel out the negative space of the photo—that is, the space where no ink should form. Once the chiseling was done, the block could be tied into the matrix along with the other type on a page so that a printing mold could be made. Wood engravers worked at this process mostly anonymously; they rarely received credit for their labors. Yet they produced thousands of extraordinarily detailed and beautiful illustrations that today are considered some of the period's best artwork.

General interest magaiznes, such as *Harper's Magazine* and *Frank Leslie's Illustrated Newspaper,* used large numbers of illustrations on their pages, and these and other publications were constantly working to improve the process. Because

PHOTOGRAPHING THE RICH AND FAMOUS

Less than a decade after it was invented in Europe in 1839, photography became the rage in America. A number of Americans studied the process, and a few decided that money could be made from it. One of those was Matthew Brady.

Brady opened a photographic studio in New York City in 1844. He took advantage of the universal curiosity about the photographic process by inviting every famous person who came to the city to his studio to have his or her picture taken. The result of Brady's promotion is a remarkable collection of pictures of the glitterati of the mid-nineteenth century. It also made Brady the most famous photographer in America.

Brady's most important photograph was taken in 1860 when Abraham Lincoln came to town. Lincoln had been prominently mentioned as a presidential candidate of the young and growing Republican Party. He had left Illinois to complete a speaking tour in the Northeast,

and in February he was scheduled to address an audience at the Cooper Institute. On the day of the address, Lincoln went to Brady's studio at 359 Broadway. The photograph Brady took was widely used by engravers during the next few months, so that most of the nation knew what Lincoln looked like.

The speech that Lincoln gave that evening was his most famous to date. Speaking on the issue of slavery and its threat to the nation, Lincoln established himself as a serious presidential possibility in front of a Northeastern audience. Lincoln later said, "Brady and the Cooper Institute made me president."

Brady's name today is associated with the many photographs he and his associates took during the Civil War. But we would have known about him anyway because before 1861 he had already been photographing the rich and famous.

magazines did not have to be produced on a daily basis, printers and engravers had more time than their counterparts on newspapers. The use of illustrations was another factor that made magazines distinctive.

Highly detailed illustrations had another effect on magazines and their readers, too. People did not have to read—or even know how to read—to view an illustration and to be entertained and informed about it. Most people in America at that time did know how to read, of course, but photography and illustration provided another means of presenting information that did not depend on type or literacy. It allowed people to form pictures in their heads about the world around them. That effect was one of the most important of the nineteenth century.

The Civil War

The period of war between the southern states and the rest of the country during 1861 to 1865 was the nation's most traumatic moment. It was also the nineteenth century's most dramatic and important news event. As all wars do, the Civil War called on every part of society to respond, sometimes in new and creative ways. American journalism did just that. Speed in gathering information and visual presentation of information—the two technical and content factors that had been developed before the war—had opportunities to develop more fully because of the demands of the conflict.

The war did not just suddenly happen, of course. The debates that led up to it had been going on for decades, and the discussions and events surrounding the issue of slavery in the 1850s had been particularly intense. Events such as the *Dred Scott* decision (in which the Supreme Court said that slaves could not be citizens and that Congress could not ban slavery from any territory); the fight over the Kansas territory; John Brown's raid on the military post at Harper's Ferry, Virginia; and Brown's subsequent trial and hanging were written about at length by the newspapers and magazines of the day and followed closely by the reading public. Abraham Lincoln's election as president in 1860 was the final blow for many proslavery advocates and secessionists. Although Lincoln denied that he had any plans to end slavery, Southerners could see that the rest of the country was demanding that the debate be put to rest, and the only means for doing that ultimately was abolition.

Among southern newspapers, there was little variance in opinion. Social pressures made almost all of them proslavery and eventually prosecessionist. A newspaper in the South simply could not survive—and, indeed, its editor and offices were in danger—if it took any other position. Northern newspaper opinion was more divided. Many newspapers said the Union could not be divided, and the South would have to be forced to return. Others, including the abolitionist Horace Greeley at one point, favored letting the South separate peacefully from the Union. Still others counseled both sides to continue negotiation so that conflict could be avoided.

It was too late for that. Early in 1861 the secessionist movement caught fire, and there seemed to be little anyone could do about that. South Carolinians demanded that the U.S. Army withdraw from its fortifications at Ft. Sumter in April, and when the commander refused, the Confederates of South Carolina opened fire. The war had begun.

In one sense, the nation was prepared for the demands that people would have for information about the conflict. The national telegraph system had grown from one line between Washington, DC, and Baltimore in the mid-1840s to more than 50,000 miles worth of lines in 1861. No war had ever been fought before during which information could be transmitted so quickly. That fact alone meant that this would be a profoundly different conflict, particularly for the news media.

In another sense, the newspapers—especially the larger newspapers in the larger northern cities—were prepared for the conflict. They had been refining their definition of news for three decades, and they had been honing their abilities to gather and process information quickly. This war promised to give them the opportunity to put all of their skills to use and also to gain readers and advertisers in the process. James Gordon Bennett's *New York Herald* claimed to have put sixty reporters into its war coverage, and other newspapers and magazines made similar commitments.

Despite these preparations, just about everything about the coverage of this war was new. There were few models or precedents to say how reporters should behave, where they should be, or even what they should be covering. The major battles, of course, were news items of greatest importance, but strategy and movement of armies turned out to be tremendously significant in this war. Some commanders welcomed reporters, hoping for favorable press reports to enhance their political standing in Washington and back home. Most generals, however, came to view reporters as a nuisance at best and even as a danger to their army. Reporters wrote about where the army was, what they were preparing for, and how many troops were available. Their newspapers sometimes printed maps tracing the army's movements—information that could be made readily available to the enemy. Reporters also pointed out flaws in command or strategy, sometimes relying on disgruntled junior officers or even more disgruntled enlisted men. Generals felt as though they had enough problems without having to deal with meddlesome reporters.

The tensions of this uneasy relationship produced the first modern methods of censorship of the news media by the armed forces. It is one of the many legacies of the Civil War to journalism that continues to this day. The war also proved how ineffective censorship could be in stopping a reporter determined to get information to his news organization. The war departments in Washington and Richmond, the Confederate capital, as well as the generals in the field, tried to limit what reporters saw and wrote. The simplest way to do this was to deny and limit their access to the telegraph lines; military censors would often read and delete information they felt put troops at risk. They also deleted material that made the army look bad, including on more than one occasion news of the army's defeat or retreat.

In one such instance, Henry Villard of the *New York Tribune* witnessed the battle of Fredericksburg in December 1863 and realized how badly the Union army had been beaten. He slipped off to Washington, DC, to try to scoop his fellow correspondents on a spectacular story only to be frustrated by Army censors who would not allow it to be transmitted. Villard then hired a special messenger to get his graphically told article to New York, but he ran up against another frustration. The *Tribune* would not print it; instead it ran a tepid account of the battle that did not inform readers of its true nature or conclusion. The pro-Republican *Tribune* was reluctant

FIGURE 4.5 **Newspaper Vendors** People back home were anxious to get news of the war, but so were the soldiers. They often had very little idea of where they were or where they were going. That's why newspaper carts such as the one pictured here were part of the entourage that followed the army, particularly in Virginia where Union forces were massed. (Photo credit: Library of Congress)

to tell its audience and the rest of the world that the Union forces had suffered yet another defeat. That year had not gone well for the Union or the Republicans, who had suffered a number of losses in the midterm elections in November. News of yet another defeat might tip public opinion against continuing the fight.

But the information Villard had was sought by at least one Republican— Abraham Lincoln. The president, desperate for details of the battle, asked Villard to come to the White House and describe to him what the reporter had seen. Villard, not wanting to be the one to give bad news to the president, tried to put the best face on what had happened, but he finally blurted out that this had been the Union's worst defeat of the war. Despite the efforts of Army censors and some Republican politicians and editors, word filtered out over the few days after the battle that the Union army had been completely repulsed, and Lincoln had yet another political crisis on his hands.

Such was the complex and conflicting nature of the work of correspondents who covered the war and those who tried to manage information about it. What correspondents saw and heard was important, but the way they interpreted this information was also important. Nor was it always easy to arrive at a conclusion. Sometimes the outcome of a battle was unclear. Even in the case of Fredericksburg, some correspondents had trouble in the early hours after the battle deciding if it was a victory or defeat for the Union. Few correspondents had any experience with the military or in covering a military campaign. Reporters for newspapers from the Confederacy faced all of the same difficulties of their northern counterparts but often with fewer resources. They too were subjected to censorship and to the difficulties of interpreting what they saw. Still, all of those involved realized that information had consequences whether it informed the enemy of troop movements or influenced public opinion.

And information was what the public demanded. The appetite for war news—even when the news was not good—was insatiable. One reason was that so many people were personally involved. Whenever word got out that a major battle was underway, crowds would gather at the newspaper office to get the latest information, even before it was in print. One of the things that people sought was the casualty list. They wanted to know who had been wounded or killed or who was missing. All too often, the name of a relative was on that list.

News correspondents were not the only ones who were providing up-to-the-minute information about the war. Americans were growing accustomed to seeing pictures of the places, people, and events that were in the news, and the Civil War accelerated the development of this form. Frank Leslie, publisher of *Frank Leslie's Illustrated Newspaper,* claimed to have put eighty artists to covering the war, and no one has been able to figure out how many others there were. (Some were actually members of the army who sent sketches to their favorite publications.) Illustrators who were in the war zone lived a lonely, dangerous, and nomadic existence. They traveled from place to place and army to army, hoping to find interesting subjects to depict. The most interesting subject, of course, was a battle, and the artist tried to position himself so he could see the action—something that took some skill and a good bit of luck.

Illustrators often did little more than outline sketches that they sent to the home office. There, in-house artists would fill in many of the details, based on their imaginations and on their own experiences. Once these illustrations were completed, they were given to engravers who cut these images into a block of wood. The process was speeded up by making a drawing on the wood's surface and then cutting the wood into two or three parts so that more than one engraver could work on the picture at the same time. When the engravers were finished, printers would tie the blocks back together so they could become part of the page mold. The final product of this multistep process was often inaccurate in many of its details, especially by today's standards, but they did give readers some visual idea of what the war was like.

One of the most famous illustrators was Alfred Waud, who worked for *Harper's Magazine* and who was a favorite of many of the Union soldiers. Not only did he produce excellent illustrations, but he was also good fun to be with. Many of his drawings, and those of his brother William, who worked for *Leslie's,* are now owned by the Library of Congress. The war also gave a start to two other artists who achieved later fame: Thomas Nast, the most prominent political cartoonist of the nineteenth century, and Winslow Homer, the pioneering turn-of-the-century watercolorist. Homer was a field artist who specialized in depicting camp life in the army.

FIGURE 4.6   **Startling Pictures** Matthew Brady and his assistants, including Alexander Gardner who took this picture, did not flinch at capturing the realities of battle. This photo of dead Union soldiers was taken just after the battle of Gettysburg in 1863 near the famous Little Round Top. These men were the ones that Abraham Lincoln referred to in his Gettysburg Address: "The brave men, living and dead, who struggled here have consecrated it far above our poor power to add or detract." (Photo credit: Library of Congress)

Photography is another medium that received a boost by the intense interest in the war. Photographs of the war could not be widely published in a timely manner, but those that were produced generated much attention and wide audiences. Matthew Brady is the name most often associated with Civil War photography, and his ideas and vision created an enduring legacy both for himself and for the nation's historical record. Brady had set up studios in New York and Washington, DC, in the 1840s, and by the time the war began, just about every famous person of the day had been to see him to have a photographic portrait taken. (Abraham Lincoln himself credited a Brady photograph with helping him win the presidency in 1860.)

Brady realized the opportunity that the war presented to enhance photography and also to make money. He received an official endorsement of his efforts from the war department (but not much else) and invested some $100,000 in equipment and people. He put numerous assistants into the field; they traveled in their "what-is-it" wagons, and their presence often sent a message to the common soldier that a battle was about to occur.

Despite the efforts of Brady and others, the technology that would allow newspapers and magazines to easily use their work had not developed yet. Printers still had to make woodcuts for the illustrations they used. Photographs were helpful certainly. A good photograph could be traced in detail, and the drawing would have a dramatic and lifelike appearance in a publication, but it was still missing many of the details that viewers could see in the photo. But even had the technology been available to reproduce photographs directly, they might have been rejected by both editors and readers. Many of the battlefield photos taken by Brady and his assistants were brutally honest, showing dead bodies and the awful physical destruction to landscapes and buildings that the war imposed. Illustrators were more likely to romanticize the war and sanitize its setting, thus making it more palatable for readers of the time.

The End of the War and Its Aftermath

The Union's vast resources and its willingness to pay a high price to preserve the United States finally overwhelmed the South, and General Robert E. Lee surrendered the Confederate Army at Appomattox Courthouse in central Virginia in April 1864. Most journalists believed the news would subside for a while, but there was one more great story of the period to be covered. Shortly after the surrender, Abraham Lincoln was assassinated while attending a production at Ford's Theater in Washington. He was the second president to die in office (William Henry Harrison had died in 1840, less than a month after being sworn in) and the first to be assassinated.

Celebrations of the war's end ceased and mourning for the slain president (at least in the northern states) began. The president's body was carried on a long, slow train back to Springfield, Illinois, and at every stop along the way newspapers did their best to outdo one another with their text and illustrations. The story continued as the assassin was captured and killed and as his conspirators were rounded up, tried, and executed.

By then, the great debate about how to deal with the southern states had begun in Congress, and the new president, Andrew Johnson, was having difficulty in exercising his influence. Those difficulties would eventually escalate into an impeachment of the president and a trial in the U.S. Senate, the first such trial in the history of the republic.

In other words, the fighting had stopped, but the news had not. Americans had become accustomed to news and to finding out about important events within a few days, if not a few hours, after they had occurred even in distant places. They expected their newspapers to give them that information, and they were far less interested in what the newspaper's editorial stance or party affiliation was. They were also accustomed to "seeing" the news, that is, to having pictures and illustrations that would give them visual information about those events.

In less than two generations Americans had gone from being citizens of localities to citizens of a vast nation. Part of that transition occurred because of the shared experience of the national debate over slavery and the war that concluded it. That transition continued, in great part, because of the shared information that newspapers and magazines were providing to all parts of the country. These trends would continue throughout the remainder of the century.

QUESTIONS FOR DISCUSSION

1. The chapter describes the invention of photography as making a profound change in the lives of people. Do you agree? What would it have been like before there was photography?
2. Of all the people mentioned in this chapter and Chapter 2, who had the most effect on the history of journalism?
3. Why is speed so important in the practice of journalism?
4. Why do you think magazines came into their own in the middle of the 1800s? What need were they fulfilling that newspapers were not?

RELATED WEB SITES

American Journalism Historians Association, www.ajha.org

American Women's History: Journalism, www.mtsu.edu/~kmiddlet/history/women /wh-jour.html

Black Journalists History Project (Maynard Institute), www.maynardije.org/programs/ history/index

Center for History and New Media, http://chnm.gmu.edu

Encyclopaedia of USA History: Journalists, www.spartacus.schoolnet.co.uk/USA journalists.htm

Jhistory Home Page, www.h-net.msu.edu/~jhistory

Journalism: Antebellum and Civil War America, www.uncp.edu/home/canada/work/allam/ 17841865/history/journal.htm

Media History Monographs, www.scripps.ohiou.edu/mediahistory

Media History Project, http://mediahistory.umn.edu

Media on Stamps, www.spacetoday.org/Stamps/Stamps.html

Soldiers Without Swords: The Black Press, www.pbs.org/blackpress

United States Newspaper Project, www.neh.gov/projects/usnp.html

READINGS AND REFERENCES

Beasley, M. H., & Gibbons, S. (1993). *Taking their place: A documentary history of women and journalism.* Washington, DC: American University Press.

Blanchard, M. A. (Ed.). (1998). *History of the mass media in the United States, an encyclopedia*. Chicago: Fitzroy Dearborn Publishers.

Brennen, B., & Hardt, H. (Eds.). (1999). *Picturing the past: Media, history and photography*. Champaign, IL: University of Illinois Press.

Briggs, A., & Burke, P. (2001). *A social history of the media from Gutenberg to the Internet*. Malden, MA: Blackwell.

Danky, J. P., et al. (Eds.). (1999). *African-American newspapers and periodicals: A national bibliography*. Cambridge, MA: Harvard University Press.

Fedler, F. (2000). *Lessons from the past: Journalists' lives and work, 1850–1950*. Prospect Heights, IL: Waveland Press, Inc.

Folkerts, J., & Teeter, D. L. Jr. (1997). *Voices of a nation: A history of mass media in the United States*. Boston: Allyn and Bacon.

Hudson, F. (2000). *Journalism in the United States from 1690–1872*. New York: Routledge.

Hutton, F., & Reid, B. S. (Eds.). (1996). *Outsiders in 19th-century press history*. Bowling Green: Bowling Green State University Press.

Mindich, D. T. Z. (1998). *Just the facts: How objectivity came to define American journalism*. New York: New York University Press.

Perry, J. M. (2000). *A bohemian brigade: The Civil War correspondents*. New York: John Wiley & Sons, Inc.

Pride, A. S., & C. Wilson, C. C. (1997). *A history of the Black Press*. Washington, DC: Howard University Press.

Rable, G. (2002). *Fredericksburg! Fredericksburg!* Chapel Hill, NC: University of North Carolina Press.

Rafferty, A. M. (2000). *American journalism 1690–1904*. New York: Routledge.

Sachsman, D. B., et al. (Eds.). (2000). *The Civil War and the press*. New Brunswick, NJ: Transaction Publishers.

Sloan, W. D. (1991). *Perspectives on mass communication history*. Hillsdale, NJ: Lawrence Erlbaum.

Sloan, W. D., & Parcell, L. M. (Eds.). (2002). *American journalism: History, principles, practices*. Jefferson, NC: McFarland & Company.

Sloan, W. D., Stovall, J. G., & Startt, J. D. (1999). *The media in America: A history* (4th ed.). Northport, AL: Vision.

Streitmatter, R. (1997). *Mightier than the sword: How the news media have shaped American history*. Boulder, CO: Westview Press.

Wolseley, R. E. (1995). *Black achievers in American journalism*. Nashville: James C. Winston Publishing.

Woodhull, N. J., & Snyder, R. W. (Eds.). (1998). *Defining moments in journalism*. New Brunswick, NJ: Transaction Publishers.

5

New Realities, New Journalism

Key Concepts and Terms

1. The Civil War began the consolidation of America into one nation, which continued with the industrialization that followed in the decades after the war. Journalism played a vital role in this consolidation and changed because of it.

2. During this period, newspapers as the major mass medium grew into corporate giants with high profitability.

3. Joseph Pulitzer: owner of the *New York World,* a newspaper known for its crusades and lively writing.

4. William Randolph Hearst: owner of the *New York Herald;* Hearst was a flamboyant personality who used the news columns of his newspapers to push his own issues, including war with Spain over Cuba.

5. Frank Leslie: published *Frank Leslie's Illustrated Newspaper,* which during the Civil War printed thousands of illustrations and drawings about news events of the day; when Frank Leslie died in 1880, his wife took over the publication (and changed her name to

"Frank Leslie") and ran it successfully for more than twenty years.

6. Mergenthaler: a typesetting machine that greatly speeded up the process of producing newspapers and magazines; named for Ottmar Mergenthaler, its developer.

7. Brand names: names given to products that were distributed nationally; newspapers offered an advertising venue that helped vault products from local to national sales and distribution.

8. Yellow journalism: a type of journalism that emphasizes sensationalism and distorts the accuracy and meaning of subjects and events that are covered; the major period of yellow journalism was the late 1890s and its chief practitioners were Joseph Pulitzer and William Randolph Hearst.

9. Watchdog press: the concept that journalism should be an independent observer of society, particularly government, and should point out its ills.

Vignette

The experience of the Civil War divided Americans, but in its aftermath, ironically, they found great unity. In fact, in 1865 for the first time in the nation's history, many people thought of themselves as Americans rather than Missourians, Pennsylvanians, or New Yorkers. (It took longer for most people in the South to accept this idea.) They had fought over a big idea—a nation, in the words of Abraham Lincoln, "conceived in liberty and dedicated to the proposition that all men are created equal." They had made enormous sacrifices. Lincoln himself, killed by an assassin just as the war ended in April 1865, had been lost to this idea.

During the fifty years after the war, America devoted itself to putting the nation back together and to building an enormous industrial engine. The nineteenth century had already seen enormous changes. Remember at the beginning of the previous chapter we described a young man born on a western Virginia farm in 1815. By 1865 he is 50 years old. Like his father, he is still a farmer, but he has experienced many changes in the world he inhabits. His farm is now in the state of West Virginia. Two of his sons fought in the Union Army during the Civil War; both saw action in battle and one was wounded. A third son, the youngest, has stayed with him on the farm and is likely to take over farming when his father gets too old to work. The other sons have come home from the war, but they show no interest in remaining on the farm. One wants to move to Charleston, the state capital, and get a job with the railroad. The other wants to head west, maybe California, he says.

Our farmer has seen all the changes he wants to see in his life. When he was growing up, an itinerant artist came into the area and painted small portraits of his parents. Just before the war, someone called a "photographer" came by and took a picture of him and his family. His newspaper now has news that is just a few days old, rather than three or four weeks old like when he was a boy. His wife subscribes to a "magazine," something he does not see much use for but she seems to enjoy it.

Change? He's seen enough of that. He would just as soon things stayed the way they are.

They won't, of course. By the time of his death in 1890, he will experience many more changes in his personal and economic life. The growing industries of America will demand a source of energy, and much of that energy will be found just below his farm in the coal mines. He will receive the sad news that his son— the one who migrated west—has died, and that news will come by telegraph. Almost despite himself, he will become more aware of the news of the nation and the world because there will be so much more news and information than he has ever experienced.

A Profession Matures

Journalism experienced many changes in its technology, economics, audience, and methods during the latter part of the nineteenth century, but the history of the profession can best be understood during this period with the concept of maturity. During the decades before the Civil War, journalism seemed to be finding itself, figuring out what it was. After 1865, many of these basic questions seemed to have been answered.

Growth, as much as change, is what we will be concentrating on in this chapter:

- Newspapers grew into giant, profit-making industries. The number of newspapers increased, as did circulation sizes. Advertising became a much more important part of the revenues of a newspaper.

- Journalists developed more sophisticated ideas about gathering and reporting the news. They obtained a better understanding of accuracy and accurately presenting information. The Civil War had taught them that the way they interpreted information could have great impact on their audiences, and they grew more sensitive as to how this power was used.

- Technological changes allowed presses to increase in size and capacity. Slowly newspapers developed a method of using photographs directly rather than converting them to woodcuts. The nation's telegraph and transportation system speeded up the flow of information to all parts of the nation. By the end of the century, journalists were using devices such as the telephone and the typewriter to help them gather and process information.

- The idea of the press as an independent voice, and as a watchdog over government and industry, developed during this period. That newspapers and magazines would speak "for" rather than "to" their audiences was a concept that grew slowly, but grow it did.

- As in the decades before the Civil War, journalism was dominated by a few outsized personalities. But these men were different. They had a broader outlook and understood many of the changes in society that were taking place. They were determined to have a hand in those changes through their newspapers and magazines. And they were determined to make money.

- Journalism opened its doors somewhat more widely to women than it had during the period before the Civil War. Women were still prevented from achieving their full potential as editors and publishers within the profession, but some were given opportunities as reporters that they had never had before, and a few women took full advantage of these opportunities.

The growth of journalism paralleled the growth and development of society during this Industrial Age. Indeed, journalism contributed to that growth, so that inside the home and inside the workplace, the world became very different during the two generations after the Civil War.

A Generation of Growth

Just as it had grown during the 1830s and 1840s, journalism experienced another spurt of growth in the decades after the Civil War. There was certainly room to grow. The western territories between Kansas and California presented Americans with some of the same opportunities that Europeans in the 1600s had seen in America itself. Indeed, descendents of those same Europeans who had looked but not immigrated looked again. This time many of them got on the boat. America's external borders, for the most part, were open. Internal borders did not exist. The land seemed to be limitless and the resources abundant.

As people moved west, they gathered into communities and demanded the benefits of nineteenth-century civilization. (The cowboy, the gunslinger, and the "wild West" existed but were only a small part of the movement that was taking place.) They wanted their own sources of information; they wanted newspapers. William Nelson moved to Kansas City, Missouri, in 1880 and founded the *Kansas City Star*. His was not the only newspaper in town, but his was the cheapest. It sold for two cents a copy, as opposed to the five cents that the others cost. Nelson made it a point to emphasize good news coverage and a dedication to making Kansas City a better place to live. Within three years, the *Star* had a circulation of 10,000, and by the end of the decade that figure had tripled.

Nelson's story was repeated in many places large and small. Charles Dana bought the *New York Sun,* the first of the penny newspapers, in 1868 when it lagged far behind many of the other newspapers in the city. Its circulation was less than 50,000, but in eight years he too had tripled the circulation. Nelson was a shrewd businessman; Dana was an editor who emphasized lively and interesting writing. Each found a different road to success.

These two examples are indicative of what was happening everywhere. The number of daily newspapers in the nation grew from fewer than 500 in 1860 to more than 2,000 in 1910. From 1860 to 1880, circulation of daily newspapers increased from 1.4 million copies to 3.5 million copies. The nation's population grew during this period but not at such an accelerated rate. People were simply demanding more newspapers.

One of the reasons for this demand was the increase in literacy that occurred during this time. Public school systems became more common, and the one thing that children did, even if they attended school for only a short time, was learn to read. By 1900, about three-fourths of all adults were fully literate. Another reason for the growth was that the price of newspapers generally decreased. Changes in technology made the newspaper less expensive to produce, and the increase in advertising that newspapers experienced lessened their dependence on circulation revenue.

A change had also occurred in the outlook of Americans. Service in the army during the Civil War had given a large number of Americans the opportunity to travel to a different part of America. This movement continued after the war, made possible by the growth of passenger railroads. Before the war, the West was populated by wagon trains and people traveled from place to place by stagecoach. Both were immensely difficult means of travel. The railroad, with its relative comfort and affordable prices,

FIGURE 5.1   Newspapers in the West Newspapers quickly found a ready audience of readers in western towns like Broken Bow, Nebraska, where this 1886 photograph of the *Nebraska Statesman* was taken. (Photo credit: Library of Congress)

made traveling long distances a reasonable idea. With that broader outlook came the demand for more information about more places, and newspapers and magazines stepped forward to meet that demand.

An Age of Personalities

More than any other time in the history of journalism, the Industrial Age was dominated by the great personalities who populated the field and by the work and the examples they produced. The pre–Civil War era had James Gordon Bennett, William Cullen Bryant, and Horace Greeley, but within a decade after the war's end, these men had died. (Horace Greeley, ever the most eccentric personality of the age, won the Democratic presidential nomination in 1872 and lost to Ulysses S. Grant in the general election; he died shortly after the votes were counted.) These men were replaced by a second generation of modern editors, who established their own tone of journalism and who set the stage for an even more forceful set of personalities that ended the century.

FIGURE 5.2   Charles Dana The editor of the *New York Sun,* Charles Dana grew up in the era of the penny press, but when he purchased the paper in 1868, he emphasized a clear, condensed form of writing that readers immediately took to. Dana tagged President Rutherford B. Hayes as "his fraudulency Mr. Hayes" because Hayes got into office after a dispute over how the votes were counted.

Chief among this second generation was Charles Dana, editor of the *New York Sun.* Dana's success in reviving the *Sun* and increasing its circulation was noted in the previous section. Dana emphasized good writing and hired people who could produce it. Possibly the most famous editorial ever to appear in a newspaper was written by Francis Church, one of the *Sun*'s editorial writers under Dana's direction. A young woman wrote to the paper one Christmas asking if there really was a Santa Claus, saying that she had heard from others that Santa Claus did not exist. Church gave her the famous answer: "Yes, Virginia, there is a Santa Claus. . . ."

Like his father, James Gordon Bennett Jr. was no paragon of virtue. In fact, he grew up spoiled and profligate. By one estimate, Bennett spent $30 million of the $50 million that the *New York Herald* was worth in his lifetime. Still, Bennett was like his father in that he understood the value of news and discerned what his readers wanted. One thing they wanted was adventure, and when the *Herald* had the opportunity to give it to them, it did. The paper sent reporter Harold Stanley on a months-long search for the missionary David Livingstone—a search that ended with Stanley greeting Livingstone with the famous line: "Dr. Livingstone, I presume." All during the son's editorship, the *Herald* continued to produce high circulation figures and high profits.

E. L. Godkin's publications never achieved the circulation numbers of the *New York Sun* or the *Herald,* but no one could deny his influence. Editor of both the *Nation* magazine and the *New York Evening Post,* Godkin emphasized editorials and opinion over news. He had little interest in appealing to the masses of readers. Rather, he was interested in developing ideas that would improve and advance society. The opinions he formed and the editorials he wrote were closely reasoned and discomfiting to the comfortable. The story is told of Godkin that a subscriber to the *Evening Post* was once asked if she minded living alone in the country. No, she replied. When the newspaper carrier threw the *Evening Post* in her front lawn, "it just lay there and growled."

All of these editors, however, were overshadowed by two of journalism history's most dominant personalities: Joseph Pulitzer and William Randolph Hearst. Each appeared on the New York journalism scene after learning their trade elsewhere,

YES, VIRGINIA, THERE IS A SANTA CLAUS

The editorial that follows is one of the most famous in the history of journalism. It appeared in the *New York Sun* in 1897 and has been reprinted widely ever since. The editorial was written by Francis Church, a former reporter who had covered the Civil War for the *New York Times.*

We take pleasure in answering thus prominently the communication below, expressing at the same time our great gratification that its faithful author is numbered among the friends of *The Sun*:

Dear Editor—
I am 8 years old. Some of my little friends say there is no Santa Claus. Papa says, "If you see it in *The Sun,* it's so." Please tell me the truth, is there a Santa Claus?

Virginia O'Hanlon

Virginia, your little friends are wrong. They have been affected by the skepticism of a skeptical age. They do not believe except they see. They think that nothing can be which is not comprehensible by their little minds. All minds, Virginia, whether they be men's or children's, are little. In this great universe of ours, man is a mere insect, an ant, in his intellect as compared with the boundless world about him, as measured by the intelligence capable of grasping the whole of truth and knowledge.

Yes, Virginia, there is a Santa Claus. He exists as certainly as love and generosity and devotion exist, and you know that they abound and give to your life its highest beauty and joy. Alas! how dreary would be the world if there were no Santa Claus! It would be as dreary as if there were no Virginias. There would be no childlike faith then, no poetry, no romance to make tolerable this existence. We should have no enjoyment, except in sense and sight. The external light with which childhood fills the world would be extinguished.

Not believe in Santa Claus! You might as well not believe in fairies. You might get your papa to hire men to watch in all the chimneys on Christmas Eve to catch Santa Claus, but even if you did not see Santa Claus coming down, what would that prove? Nobody sees Santa Claus, but that is no sign that there is no Santa Claus. The most real things in the world are those that neither children nor men can see. Did you ever see fairies dancing on the lawn? Of course not, but that's no proof that they are not there. Nobody can conceive or imagine all the wonders there are unseen and unseeable in the world.

You tear apart the baby's rattle and see what makes the noise inside, but there is a veil covering the unseen world which not the strongest man, nor even the united strength of all the strongest men that ever lived could tear apart. Only faith, poetry, love, romance, can push aside that curtain and view and picture the supernal beauty and glory beyond. Is it all real? Ah, Virginia, in all this world there is nothing else real and abiding.

No Santa Claus! Thank God! he lives and lives forever. A thousand years from now, Virginia, nay 10 times 10,000 years from now, he will continue to make glad the heart of childhood.

Pulitzer in St. Louis and Hearst in San Francisco. Pulitzer came to New York in 1883, a dozen years before Hearst arrived, and he quickly established himself as a man with ideas, frenetic energy, and skill in selecting the very best people to work for him.

In St. Louis, Pulitzer had distinguished himself and his newspaper, the *Post-Dispatch,* by exposing and crusading against local corruption. His newspaper, he declared, would be an independent voice opposing "all frauds and shams wherever and whatever they are." He carried that same purpose to New York when he purchased the *New York World*. He promised more and better news coverage, and part of that coverage included massive and detailed illustrations. His newspaper gave people something to look at as well as something to read. A year after coming to New York, he installed a photoengraving plant in the newspaper to use the latest technology available in building illustrations. Within ten years every other newspaper in the city had done the same thing.

Pulitzer continued his crusades against corruption, particularly against prostitution, which became one of the newspaper's favorite topics. Pulitzer also engaged the *World* in a number of civic projects, including the raising of $200,000 from readers to pay for the base of the Statue of Liberty. An immigrant himself, Pulitzer was sympathetic to the growing immigrant population in New York City, and those people constituted a substantial part of the newspaper's readership. Within two years of his arrival in New York, the *World*'s circulation had passed 200,000 and led every other newspaper in the city. It was also producing huge profits for its owner.

Pulitzer himself, however, was becoming less able to enjoy those profits. He suffered from an increasing loss of sight and a nervous disorder that made him extremely sensitive to noise, and his condition was so bad that he was unable to work in the *World*'s building, even though the publisher's office was at the pinnacle of one of the tallest structures in New York at the time. By 1890 Pulitzer had to escape to his yacht and communicate with his editors by memo and messenger from there.

Despite his infirmities, no newspaper editor in New York could match Pulitzer's ideas and his drive until William Randolph Hearst showed up as the owner of the *New York Journal* in 1895. Hearst wanted to outdo Pulitzer by adopting Pulitzer's ideas and taking them beyond what Pulitzer had conceived.

Hearst was a flamboyant character who had grown up in California as the son of a rich mine owner. His father owned the *San Francisco Examiner,* and Hearst—after being kicked out of Harvard—asked his father to let him run it. His father refused, and Hearst went to New York and got a job on Pulitzer's *World.* There he got a close look at Pulitzer's methods of running a newspaper and increasing circulation. He was determined to do

FIGURE 5.3 Joseph Pulitzer Joseph Pulitzer was undoubtedly one of the leading editors of the day, but he managed to achieve journalistic immortality by endowing in his will a set of awards that became known as the Pulitzer prize, the highest award in journalism. Though a great editor himself, Pulitzer fell victim to the competition of the yellow journalism era.

the same in San Francisco. His chance came when his father was appointed to the U.S. Senate. The young Hearst (he was 24 at the time) took over the paper in 1887, spent boatloads of his father's money, engaged in Pulitzer-like editorial crusades, and increased circulation. By 1890 the newspaper was making a profit, and Hearst was ready to take on New York. He got his chance in 1895 when the *New York Journal,* a newspaper once owned by Pulitzer's brother, came up for sale. He bought it for $180,000.

Hearst did not have time to build a staff that would challenge Pulitzer, so he bought one—Pulitzer's. He hired away the entire staff of the *Sunday World,* including R. F. Outcault, the artist who drew the popular comic strip, "The Yellow Kid." (Pulitzer simply retained another artist to draw the comic strip, so both the *Journal* and the *World* had comic strips called "The Yellow Kid.") After that coup, Hearst made repeated attempts to hire individuals from the daily staff of the *World.* Often he was successful. His biggest catch was Arthur Brisbane, one of Pulitzer's top editors, who left to work for Hearst in 1897.

Hearst's raid on the *World*'s staff was an open declaration of war, and the two newspapers fought a journalistic hand-to-hand combat for several years after that. Each touted its own scoops and campaigns with huge pictures and illustrations and bold, blaring headlines. Each pointed out the misdeeds and mistakes of the other. Each declared itself the keeper of the public good and the voice of the people. They did so sometimes at the cost of perspective and even accuracy. Hearst had enormous personal resources inherited from his family. Pulitzer had made a fortune from his newspaper, but the war in which he was engaged eventually depleted that fortune.

The Hearst–Pulitzer competition pulled in many other newspapers to the conventions of using large illustrations and bold headlines to trumpet their own triumphs. But no two papers did it as well as the *Journal* and the *World,* and the late 1890s has been tabbed by historians as the age of yellow journalism (named after the comic strip "The Yellow Kid," as we will explain later). The apex of the yellow journalism period came in 1898 when, egged on particularly by Hearst's *Journal,* America declared war on Spain because of its treatment of Cuba. When tensions were building, Hearst, Pulitzer, and others sent an army of correspondents to Cuba to cover the conflict. One of those was artist Frederic Remington, who at one point wired Hearst: "Everything is quiet here. There is no trouble. There will be no war." Hearst replied in a return wire: "Please remain. You furnish the pictures and I'll furnish the war." Soon thereafter, the American battleship USS *Maine* was blown up in Havana harbor, and with very little evidence, the newspapers blamed the Spanish and beat the drums for war. Congress and President William McKinley eventually went along. Hearst even sailed his own yacht into the battle zone. Both Pulitzer and Hearst spent many thousands of dollars on war coverage, but it paid off at least temporarily. On its best day during the short conflict, the *Journal* sold slightly more than 1 million copies.

While Pulitzer and Hearst were shouting at each other, one other personality was making his presence felt in New York, and his work would continue to influence journalism long after his death. His name was Adolph Ochs. Ochs was born in Knoxville, Tennessee, and learned the printer's trade at a newspaper there. After failed attempts at running his own newspaper, he acquired the *Chattanooga Times* in

FIGURE 5.4 **The War Hearst Wanted** William Randolph Hearst had beat the drum steadily in his *New York Journal* for the United States to go to war with Spain over Cuba. The pretext for that war came when the USS *Maine* exploded in Havana harbor. With no real evidence, Hearst blamed Spain, and the United States soon declared war.

1878 and made it a modest success. He had misread the possibilities of Chattanooga as a resort town, however, and accumulated massive debts over the next two decades. He left Chattanooga for New York in 1896 where he purchased the faltering *New York Times* for $75,000.

While Hearst continued to out-Pulitzer Pulitzer, Ochs was equally determined to be different from them both. He refused to engage the *New York Times* in the large headlines, bold illustrations, and thunder-and-lightning journalism of the *Journal* and the *World*. Ochs developed for the *Times* a calm, reasonable voice that gave the readers "All the News That's Fit to Print." Ochs appealed to the respectable and reasonable side of the readers. After two years, Ochs made another move that was a huge gamble in the circulation-dependent world of newspapers. He cut the price of his paper from two cents to one cent. (The *Journal* and *World* were also selling at two cents a copy at the time.) Circulation increased dramatically, and by 1900 Ochs had taken the paper from less than 10,000 copies a day to more than 80,000 copies.

The straightforward reporting of the *Times* won it a great deal of respect among an increasing number of New Yorkers who were tired of the sensationalism of the other newspapers in the city. The *Times* emerged from this era with a reputation for accuracy and objectivity, and Ochs made sure that reputation continued. His descendents continue to operate the vast publishing empire that is the *New York Times* while most other newspapers in New York City that were published at the beginning of the century have failed to survive.

Advancing Technology

Journalism's post–Civil War period witnessed a number of advances in technology that would aid its development and improvement. One such advance involved new techniques in making paper. Paper was an expensive product, and its cost and scarcity had frustrated publishers who were looking to increase the circulation of their newspapers and magazines. Paper was made of a combination of wood pulp and rags or cloth or other substantive material. New ways of making paper, using only wood pulp, promised to make the production of paper easier and cheaper, and by 1870 those techniques, perfected in Europe, had arrived in America. Paper production rose, and costs decreased, allowing newspapers to go all out in increasing their circulation.

Typesetting was another technology that improved greatly after the war, although in this area improvements were a long time in coming. Since the days of Gutenberg, type had been set by hand, letter by letter. Each metal letter would be picked up out of its own section of a giant case and placed into a matrix that formed the words and the lines of type. It was slow, laborious work and took a great deal of skill and practice. A machine that would automatically cast a line of type was finally developed by a German immigrant, Ottmar Mergenthaler, in 1890, greatly speeding the process of the newspaper's "backshop." Merganthaler Linotype machines were large units with the ability to melt and mold a line of type; they soon became a major part of a newspaper's operation and remained so until the 1970s.

Printing presses were also objects of the attention of inventors and innovators. Rotary presses were the great breakthrough in printing technology of the nineteenth century, but there were other innovations that allowed presses to run faster and more efficiently. The use of electricity for power became more widespread during the latter

FIGURE 5.5 **Newspaper Illustration** During the last two decades of the nineteenth century, technology made reproducing photos and illustrations much easier for newspapers, and the journalism of the age took full advantage of it. Newspapers hired excellent artists and gave them an extraordinary amount of space with which to work. The illustrations, such as those pictured here concerning the 1906 murder of a prominent New York architect, were not only meant to grab the attention of the reader but also to add a dimension of information that the reader could visualize.

part of the century. Presses grew bigger and faster in concert with the demand for more copies of the publication. Newspapers sought in every way they could to reduce the printing time so they could speed up getting the news to their readers. In addition to speed, these new presses allowed for the use of "spot" color. Spot color is use of a single color other than black on the page. One of the first uses of spot color was the placement of yellow inside a comic strip called "Hogan's Alley" in Pulitzer's *New York World*. The strip was dubbed "The Yellow Kid," which later became its official name and eventually became the nickname for the genre of journalism practiced by Pulitzer and Hearst.

Improvements in the process for reproducing pictures took place and typesetting and printing techniques advanced. The idea of converting a photograph to a series of dots that would serve as a code for where ink should and should not be had been around for some time, and by the 1870s, innovators were making strides to adapt it to the printing process. As they did this, the laborious process of making woodcuts was replaced, and the skill that went with this process gradually died out. By 1890 most of the major publications were using some type of photoengraving. Photos, of course, gave more accurate illustrations and in many ways could be more dramatic. Clear photographs of subjects in motion were rare, and color photography was yet to come, but journalistic publications in the 1890s looked far different than they did in the 1870s.

None of these technical advances represented the dramatic breakthrough that the invention of photography or the rotary press meant to journalism. Each played a part, however, in making journalism a little more professional and better able to serve the reader. They allowed newspapers to be larger and carry more content that would appeal to a broader readership and be produced more quickly. Taken together, new advances made the newspaper industry more accessible and efficient and increased the ability of owners to make a profit. As the industry grew and became more profitable, more people were involved at every level, especially as reporters and editors. Their world, too, was changing.

Reporters and Reporting

In the late nineteenth century prohibition, the idea of outlawing alcohol, had replaced abolition as the great moral issue of the day. Women's suffrage, which advocated giving women the right to vote, sprang from a sense that women could do many of the jobs that men did in the workplace and that women already had major responsibility for life at home. Many suffragettes, though by no means all, were prohibitionists, and some suffrage groups made prohibition a part of their state goals.

The prominence of women in these social movements was an indication that women were beginning to break away from the domestic roles that they had fulfilled for generations. Despite the prejudices and customs that continued to restrict them throughout the nineteenth century, women pushed the door ajar in many fields of endeavor. More were obtaining education, and women were becoming doctors, lawyers, and even politicians. They also became more prominent in the field of journalism.

YELLOW JOURNALISM

The competition for readers between Joseph Pulitzer's *New York World* and William Randolph Hearst's *New York Herald* spun out of control in the 1890s with each man trying to outdo the other on almost a daily basis. The type of journalism they practiced became known as *yellow journalism,* a term that still has meaning more than a century later.

The name actually comes from one of the first successful comic strips, the Yellow Kid. The strip was originated by R. F. Outcault, an illustrator for the *World,* who managed to capture working-class life in New York City with great sympathy and humor. Pulitzer used his advanced printing technology to shade the strip in yellow and, thus, the name.

Hearst knew how popular the comic strip was and eventually hired Outcault away to work for the *Herald,* where he continued to draw the strip. Pulitzer simply hired someone else to draw the strip for the *World,* and for a time both newspapers boasted of having a Yellow Kid comic strip.

But yellow journalism was not about comic strips. It came to symbolize sensationalism in presenting the news. Printing technology in the late 1800s allowed newspaper publishers to print large headlines and massive illustrations. Both Pulitzer and Hearst took full advantage to gain their readers' attention.

The result was blowing insignificant stories out of proportion, putting down articles and crusades mounted by the competition, and often turning the coverage of public policies into personal vendettas. The excesses of yellow journalism were intrusive journalists, inaccurate reporting, and even falsified stories and interviews.

More seriously, yellow journalism could result in bad public policy. Many believe that the United States would not have gone to war with Spain in 1898 had not the *World* and especially the *Herald* made such an issue out of what was occurring in Cuba.

And just as seriously, the period of yellow journalism taught journalism something about the importance of credibility. Eventually, many of the readers of both the *Herald* and the *World* turned to other newspapers—most notably the *New York Times*—because they simply did not trust what the papers were saying.

A good deal of journalism was being directed at women, not only in daily newspapers but particularly in magazines. Publications, such as *Woman's Home Journal* and *Ladies Home Journal,* tried to serve the domestic interests of women. This was where women journalists had the most natural entry. Among the most prominent women editors of the day was Mary Booth, who edited *Harper's Bazaar,* a fashion magazine, for more than twenty years. Others, such as suffragettes Susan B. Anthony and Elizabeth Cady Stanton, edited magazines devoted to their cause.

In daily journalism, the most notable woman of the age was Nellie Bly (née Elizabeth Cochrane), whom Pulitzer hired to work for the *New York World*. Bly was an adventuress and woman of uncommon courage; she feigned insanity so she could be committed to the notorious Blackwell Island insane asylum. There she found poor food, unhealthy conditions, and general abuse of patients, all of which she wrote about in a blistering exposé. Bly later gained more fame when she attempted to travel around the world in less than eighty days. Bly's feats have been dismissed as "stunt journalism," and there was certainly a sensational aspect to what she did. But she also proved that women could master the rigors of journalism just as men could.

"STUNT" JOURNALIST NELLIE BLY

The table reached the length of the room and was uncovered and uninviting. Long benches without backs were put for the patients to sit on, and over these they had to crawl in order to face the table. Placed close together all along the table were large dressing-bowls fixed with a pinkish looking stuff which the patients called tea. By each bowl was laid a piece of bread, cut thick and buttered. A small saucer containing five prunes accompanied the bread. One fat woman made a rush, and jerking up several saucers from those around her emptied their contents into her own saucer. Then while holding on to her own bowl she lifted up another and drained its contents at one gulp. This she did to a second bowl in shorter time than it takes to tell it. Indeed I was so amused at her successful grabbings that when I looked at my own share the woman opposite, without so much as by your leave, grabbed my bread and left me without any. Another patient, seeing this, kindly offered me hers, but I declined with thanks and turned to the nurse and asked for more. As she flung a thick piece down on the table she made some remark about the fact that if I forgot where my home was I had not forgotten how to eat. I tried the bread, but the butter was so horrible that I could not eat it.

Critics called it "stunt journalism," and some of it was, but the words that Elizabeth Cochrane,

a.k.a. Nellie Bly, wrote for the *New York World* after spending ten days in New York's notorious insane asylum are still powerful today.

And they changed lives. Cochrane's exposé of the asylum sparked outrage and increased funding and needed reforms.

Cochrane was one of a number of "girl reporters" hired by the publishers of the time to pump up circulation and outdo one another. Unlike many of them, Cochrane took her job seriously and wrote about people, situations, and conditions that needed attention. In 1894 she went to Chicago to cover the Pullman railroad strike and was the only reporter to tell the side of the striking workers. Her writing, as always, was vivid, descriptive, and powerful.

Still, she was not above a stunt or two. In 1889, she circled the globe in seventy-two days (in a race against the mythical record of the Jules Verne novel, *Around the World in Eighty Days*), writing dispatches from every place she landed. The *World* gave her much space and ink (see the illustration).

Bly married an industrialist in the mid-1890s and lived quietly for about ten years. When her husband died, she resumed her public life and was writing for the *New York Journal* in 1922 when she died at the age of 58.

Another important woman journalist was Ida B. Wells, an African American who, against very long odds, edited the *Free Speech and Headlight* in Memphis, Tennessee. She put her life in danger with a campaign against lynching and a penchant for public oratory. After the turn of the century, a movement of reform journalism to expose ills in society so that they could be corrected was undertaken by a number of national magazines. One of the first of these "muckrakers," as President Theodore Roosevelt called them, was Ida Tarbell, who began a biographical series on John D. Rockefeller for *McClure's Magazine*. The series turned into an exposé of the corruption of Rockefeller's company, Standard Oil. It told how the company had systematically tried to destroy its competition and create a favorable environment for itself, even to the point of contracting with more than one hundred Ohio newspapers to run editorials and news favorable to the company.

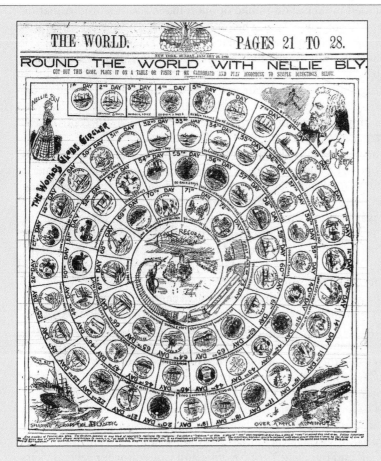

Nellie Bly's round-the-world trip was played for all it was worth by Joseph Pulitzer's *New York World.*

One of the highest-ranking women in the field was Mrs. Frank Leslie, whose husband had founded *Frank Leslie's Illustrated Newspaper,* one of the leading journals in reporting the Civil War. Frank Leslie died in 1880, and Mrs. Leslie took over the publication and ran it successfully for more than twenty years. She was a high-profile society character who changed her own name to Frank Leslie after her husband died.

Although women were more prominent in journalism than many have assumed, the accomplishments of Booth, Bly, Wells, Tarbell, and Leslie did not signal a general opening of the profession to women. Few women could count on building a career in journalism or advancing to an editorship. On most newspapers, if there were any women at all, they were restricted to clerical or proofreading duties or confined to writing for women's sections. Most of the journalistic work was done by men.

That work had changed with the times. Reporters and editors had achieved more status, and their assumed influence on public opinion made sources of information more cooperative. The "beat" system in which one reporter covered the same area day after day—something that had been in place to some extent since the days of the penny press—was now fully functional, and reporters were able to develop an expertise on their subjects. They were also becoming more dependent on their sources and, thus, making more efforts to be accurate in the information they presented. Journalism was still a long way from developing a full-fledged code of ethics, however. Hoaxes still occasionally appeared in print, and reporters used sly, deceptive, and unsavory methods to get information.

Journalists had new tools to use in their work. Possibly the most important was the advent of electric power to light the inside of buildings and to power machinery. Electricity was cheaper than oil-burning lamps and allowed journalists to extend their work well into the evening. Although much of the journalistic copy was written by hand, the typewriter was beginning to appear in a number of newspaper offices. Using a typewriter greatly increased how fast an article could be written. Telephones also aided reporters in obvious ways. A source could be called instead of seen personally. Reporters could call in a story rather than having to travel back to the newspaper office or find an intracity telegraph. And when traveling did occur, reporters had more choices than horse-drawn carriages. If they were nimble enough, they could hop on a bicycle and speed to the scene of the news. In some cities reporters could take street-cars, and if they had to travel any distance at all, they most often could take a train.

Journalism even developed something of a star system in this era. Reporters began getting bylines, often using their real names, for the first time, and many were free to display distinctive styles of writing. Reporters sometimes made themselves part of the story, as did Henry Stanley in his search for David Livingstone. A few notable reporters developed a style of humor and satire that made them famous. Samuel Clemens first used the name of Mark Twain in his dispatches from Carson City, Nevada, to the *Territorial Enterprise* in Virginia City in 1862. Twain went on to write for the *San Francisco Morning Call* and the *New York Tribune* and was editor for several years of the *Buffalo Express,* all experiences that contributed to his becoming America's chief man of letters late in the century.

The brightest light in the reportorial star system was Richard Harding Davis, whose drop-dead handsome looks were as charmed as his journalistic career. He paid a great deal of attention to his clothes and his demeanor, developing a devil-may-care swagger that many people, especially women, found irresistible. Davis sought adventure where he could find it and seemed to love covering war. He was the chief correspondent for William Randolph Hearst's *New York Journal* during the Spanish-American War (a war that Hearst had a great deal to do with). His writing was full of on-the-scene description, such as the following:

> They (the Americans) had no glittering bayonets, they were not massed in regular array. There were a few men in advance, bunched together, and creeping up a steep, sunny hill, the tops of which roared and flashed with flame. The men held their guns pressed across their breasts and stepped heavily as they climbed. Behind these first few, spreading out

FIGURE 5.6   Newspaper Humorists The latter part of the nineteenth century produced a number of outstanding and well-remembered newspaper humorists. Chief among them is Mark Twain (seated, second from right), but others (beginning at left) include David Ross Locke, whose pen name was Petroleum V. Nasby and was one of the era's great political satirists; Finley Peter Dunne, who often viewed the world as Martin Dooley, an Irish immigrant and saloonkeeper; Ambrose Bierce, a San Francisco journalist who was bitter and caustic in his observations; George Peck, a Wisconsin publisher who created the mischievous Peck's Bad Boy; and Edgar Wilson (Bill) Nye, a Westerner who came to New York and viewed what he saw with a simple but amazingly funny point of view.

like a fan, were single lines of men, slipping and scrambling in the smooth grass, moving forward with difficulty, as though they were wading waist-high through water, moving slowly, carefully, with strenuous effort. It was much more wonderful than any swinging charge could have been. They walked to greet death at every step, many of them, as they advanced, sinking suddenly or pitching forward and disappearing in the high grass, but the others waded on, stubbornly, forming a thin blue line that kept creeping higher and higher up the hill. It was as inevitable as the rising tide. (Lubow p. 186)

Davis' fellow journalist with the *Journal* in Cuba was artist Frederick Remington. His precise and economic drawings of the people participating in the war added immensely to the information that the readers of the *Journal* received. His work increased his fame and added to the value of the artwork that he later produced.

Change in Advertising

During the decades after the Civil War, America experienced a period of phenomenal economic growth. Although there were panics and depressions along the way, generally more people had more money and goods than ever before. The harnessing of electrical energy and the innovations in machinery turned life at home and in the workplace upside down. Mass production of goods meant that things were cheaper to buy and easier to acquire. America was becoming a consumer society.

A vital part of the consumer society is information. Manufacturers must know what goods and services people need; they must know where the markets are for those goods and services; and they must have a way of reaching those audiences and asking, or persuading, them to buy the products. Consumers also need information. They must learn what is available, how it can be obtained, and how much it will cost.

Before the Civil War, much of this economic activity took place on a local level. Goods were made locally and sold locally. After the war, however, manufacturers began to conceive of regional, national, and even international markets for their goods. Manufacturers developed "brand names" for the products they produced and began to foster brand loyalties. At the local level, one-product stores began to give way to "department" stories that carried a wide variety of goods produced locally and elsewhere. A transportation system in the form of trains was being built so that goods made in New York could be shipped to California and vice versa at a relatively low cost. But there needed to be an information system, and newspapers often provided the first step in that system.

Consequently, advertising became an increasingly important part of the newspaper after the Civil War. And as one manufacturer advertised, others who produced the same types of good had to advertise also in order to stay competitive. An established newspaper was assumed to have a ready audience that would be a good market for many products. Newspapers were in a perfect position to accept the money that advertisers were trying to give them. Advertising revenue became a growing part of a newspaper's revenue, often allowing newspapers to reduce their subscription prices and, thus, increase circulation. Increased circulation meant larger markets for advertisers and, consequently, higher advertising rates. It was a win-win-win situation for newspapers, and many newspaper owners and their families became fabulously wealthy during this time. By 1900, more than half of the revenue of the average newspaper was coming from advertising, a huge change from fifty years earlier.

There were side effects, however. One was that advertisers, because they spent so much money on the newspaper, sometimes believed they had the right to control the newspaper's editorial content. Honest publishers, editors, and reporters fought off these attempts and ultimately established in journalism a clear line between news and advertising.

Another effect of the increase in advertising was to help newspapers sever their last ties to political parties and organizations. At the beginning of the century, a newspaper's existence usually depended on the financial support of a political faction. If an editor fell out with the faction, that probably meant the newspaper would cease publication. By the end of the century, newspapers were big businesses. Editorially,

FIGURE 5.7   Bigger Newspapers, Bigger Buildings As newspapers grew in size and circulation, they needed bigger buildings to occupy. The age of "skyscrapers" was dawning. In the late 1800s, that meant multistoried buildings. Most major newspaper offices had a grand edifice to show off their prosperity.

they might (and probably did) support a political party or faction, but the politicians no longer controlled what they printed; nor could they wreak vengeance on them for straying from the party fold.

The Watchdog Press

Newspaper crusades against public corruption were nothing new to the nineteenth century. From the time newspapers have existed, they have carried on the fight for what editors considered the public good and have sought to expose those who were dishonest or who violated a trust.

Before the advent of the penny press in the 1830s, such campaigns were likely to be generated by political motives as much as a concern for the general welfare. One political faction sought to expose the nefarious dealings of its rival and did this through the newspapers that it published. As newspapers became more independent from their political ties, these campaigns became more credible and, in some cases, effective.

Newspaper publishers had more than the public good on their agendas when they undertook such campaigns, of course. These campaigns could provoke marvelous circulation gains for the newspaper. They could establish the credibility of the paper

FIGURE 5.8 Thomas Nast, Cartoonist Thomas Nast began his journalistic career as a field artist during the Civil War. He remained with *Harper's Magazine* after the war and became American journalism's best-known cartoonist. He aimed a sharp pen at the Boss Tweed ring in New York City and was instrumental in drawing attention to the ring's perfidy. (Photo credit: Library of Congress)

with whole groups of people. Both Pulitzer and Hearst understood this perfectly and used such campaigns to their great advantage. Other newspapers and magazines did the same thing. The most famous public scandal of the age was that of the Tweed Ring in New York City in the years just after the war. Political boss William Marcy Tweed controlled the city government of New York and all of the contracts that it issued. In 1870, the *New York Times* received a series of documents that showed how many public officials were stealing money from the city by accepting bribes and payoffs. Along with *Harper's Weekly*, the *Times* campaigned against the ring's practices and finally got Tweed and many of his cronies thrown out of office and thrown into jail.

What made the newspaper campaigns of this age different was not only the lack of political ties of the newspaper but also the emphasis on reporting and bringing facts to light. Documentary evidence as well as eyewitness reports became the basis on which these campaigns were built. Editors could no longer assert or imply wrongdoing. They had to present specifics and the evidence to back it up.

By doing this again and again throughout the late nineteenth and early twentieth centuries, the press established itself as the watchdog of government—the independent voice the public could rely on to see that the public was well served. The press, of course, did not always live up to this role, but entering the twentieth century, it had taken on that responsibility as a new age of journalism approached.

QUESTIONS FOR DISCUSSION

1. Does the treatment that newspapers gave to news during the Yellow Journalism period sound different from the way news is treated today? Why or why not?
2. During the latter part of the nineteenth century, a large number of immigrants entered the United States. How would this have affected newspapers and the journalism of the time?
3. Which of the technologies mentioned in this chapter had the most effect on the practice of journalism during this period? Make a list of the technologies and put them in order of those that had the most effect.
4. The author mentions several women who were prominent in journalism during the nineteenth century. Find out more about them and find some of the other women who were pioneers in the field. What obstacles did women have to overcome generally in society at the time to have careers and professional lives?

RELATED WEB SITES

AEJMC History Division, www.utc.edu/~aejhist

American Journalism Historians Association, www.ajha.org

American Women's History: Journalism, www.mtsu.edu/~kmiddlet/history/women/wh-jour.html

Associated Press 150th Anniversary, www.ap.org/anniversary/nhistory/index.html

Black Journalists History Project (Maynard Institute), www.maynardije.org/programs/history/index

Center for History and New Media, chnm.gmu.edu

Encyclopaedia of USA History: Journalists, www.spartacus.schoolnet.co.uk/USAjournalists.htm

Jhistory Home Page, www.h-net.msu.edu/~jhistory

Media History Monographs, www.scripps.ohiou.edu/mediahistory

Media History Project, http://mediahistory.umn.edu

Newseum, www.newseum.org

New York Times Company History, www.nytco.com/company-timeline.html

Women's History: Journalism, www.distinguishedwomen.com/subject/journ.html

Yellow Journalism, www.pbs.org/crucible/journalism.html

Yellow Journalism and the Spanish American War, http://tnt.turner.com/movies/tntoriginals/roughriders/jour.home.html

READINGS AND REFERENCES

Beasley, M. H., & Gibbons, S. (1993). *Taking their place: A documentary history of women and journalism.* Washington, DC: American University Press.

Blanchard, M. A. (Ed.). (1998). *History of the mass media in the United States, an encyclopedia.* Chicago: Fitzroy Dearborn Publishers.

Brennen, B., & Hardt, H. (Eds.). (1999). *Picturing the past: Media, history and photography.* Champaign, IL: University of Illinois Press.

Briggs, A., & Burke, P. (2001). *A social history of the media from Gutenberg to the Internet.* Malden, MA: Blackwell.

Danky, J. P., et al. (Eds.). (1999). *African-American newspapers and periodicals: A national bibliography.* Cambridge, MA: Harvard University Press.

Fedler, F. (2000). *Lessons from the past: Journalists' lives and work, 1850–1950.* Prospect Heights, IL: Waveland Press.

Folkerts, J., & Teeter, D. L. Jr. (1997). *Voices of a nation: A history of mass media in the United States.* Boston: Allyn and Bacon.

Hudson, F. (2000). *Journalism in the United States from 1690–1872.* New York: Routledge.

Hutton, F., & Reid, B. S. (Eds.). (1996). *Outsiders in 19th-Century press history.* Bowling Green: Bowling Green State University Press.

Lubow, A. (1992). *The reporter who would be king: A biography of Richard Harding Davis.* New York: Charles Scribner's Sons.

Mindich, D. T. Z. (1998). *Just the facts: How objectivity came to define American journalism.* New York: New York University Press.

Pride, A. S., & Wilson, C. C. (1997). *A history of the Black Press.* Washington, DC: Howard University Press.

Rafferty, A. M. (2000). *American journalism 1690–1904.* New York: Routledge.

Sachsman, D. B., et al. (Eds.). (2000). *The Civil War and the press.* New Brunswick, NJ: Transaction Publishers.

Sloan, W. D. (1991). *Perspectives on mass communication history.* Hillsdale, NJ: Lawrence Erlbaum.

Sloan, W. D., & Parcell, L. M. (Eds.). (2002). *American journalism: History, principles, practices*. Jefferson, NC: McFarland & Company.

Sloan, W. D., Stovall, J. G., & Startt, J. D. (1999). *The media in America: A history* (4th ed.). Northport, AL: Vision.

Streitmatter, R. (1994). *Raising her voice: African-American women journalists who changed history*. Lexington, KY: University of Kentucky Press.

Streitmatter, R. (1997). *Mightier than the sword: How the news media have shaped American history*. Boulder, CO: Westview Press.

Suggs, H. L. (Ed.). (1996). *The Black Press in the Middle West, 1865–1985*. Westport, CT: Greenwood Press.

Tifft, S. E., & Jones, A. S. (1999). *The trust: The private and powerful family behind the New York Times*. New York: Little Brown and Company.

Wolseley, R. E. (1995). *Black achievers in American journalism*. Nashville: James C. Winston Publishing.

Woodhull, N. J., & Snyder, R. W. (Eds.). (1998). *Defining moments in journalism*. New Brunswick, NJ: Transaction Publishers.

Chapter Six

Journalism: Present and Future

1. Journalism is a profession in which even the most basic questions, such as the nature of news and the process of gathering and disseminating it, are being examined and debated continuously.

2. Journalism is an open profession; anyone can be a journalist without undergoing any training or gaining any credentials.

3. Media organizations are generally in good financial health.

4. One of the things that makes the future uncertain for journalism is the presence of the World Wide Web; no one can see clearly how it might change the practice or nature of journalism.

5. Journalists today struggle with the question of how to remain relevant to their audiences.

6. Attracting bright and thoughtful young people into journalism is one of the great challenges of today's profession.

Vignette

By the end of 2003, just about everybody in America knew the name Jessica Lynch. Most people also knew something about her, but just what they knew probably depended on how closely they had been paying attention to the news.

Jessica Lynch—19 years old, West Virginian, blond, small (some described her as "waif-like"), photogenic—had been a private in the U.S. Army. Her unit had been assigned to Iraq for combat support. Less than two weeks into the war, her unit was ambushed in central Iraq, with some soldiers killed and others captured. During that time, British and American forces had been making steady progress toward the capital city of Baghdad, but Iraqi forces were not collapsing at the sight of the Westerners as some in the Bush administration had rosily predicted.

In the midst of the not-so-good news came the word on April 1, from the U.S. Army command, that Lynch had been rescued. Anonymous sources within the Army command leaked details of Lynch's ordeal: she had fought bravely when her unit was ambushed; she had been wounded, including a stab wound that indicated hand-to-hand combat; she had "not wanted to be taken alive." Here is what the Washington Post *wrote about her on April 3, two days after her rescue:*

> *Lynch, a 19-year-old supply clerk, continued firing at the Iraqis even after she sustained multiple gunshot wounds and watched several other soldiers in her unit die around her in fighting March 23, one official said. The ambush took place after a 507th convoy, supporting the advancing 3rd Infantry Division, took a wrong turn near the southern city of Nasiriyah.*
>
> *"She was fighting to the death," the official said.*

The details of her rescue seemed equally heroic. Under cover of darkness, a Special Operations unit of the Army entered the hospital where she was being treated and whisked her away on a stretcher. The unit did not meet any resistance, but it was under constant threat, according to the Army, and it was the skill and courage of the soldiers in the unit that got her out.

In the few days after her rescue, the story of her ambush, capture, and rescue grew. Fed by Army sources, newspapers described—or, in some cases, speculated—on her actions and circumstances. Her wounds, gunshot and stabbing, were described in more detail. Her fighting determination turned her into a Rambo-like warrior. Some stories said she had been mistreated and even tortured while in captivity. In stories about her rescue, Navy Seals (a Special Operations unit of the U.S. Navy) joined the Army unit that helped get her out.

Overnight Lynch became the new American hero—a silent symbol (Lynch had not spoken to anyone in the news media about what had happened to her) that America's newest generation of young people could produce soldiers worthy of American history.

But just as this was happening, information began to emerge that did not fit into the story that had been constructed. Prompted by questioning, reporters from the

British Broadcasting Company, the Washington Post *and other news organizations began to reexamine the whole Jessica Lynch story. Ultimately, they found that:*

- *Lynch had not been engaged in a gunfight with Iraqi forces. Her unit had gotten lost when it was ambushed, and her injuries occurred because the vehicle in which she was riding had overturned. She did not shoot her gun or kill any enemy soldiers.*
- *She had not been wounded or stabbed. She had suffered numerous broken bones and other injuries because of the accident.*
- *She had not been mistreated while in captivity. Quite the opposite, she had received good treatment.*
- *Some evidence emerged that indicated some Iraqis had tried to return her to American forces but were unsuccessful. Whatever the case, her rescue was considerably less dramatic and dangerous than had first been described. All Iraqi forces had left the hospital by the time U.S. forces came to get her.*

In late May, in its reprise of the Jessica Lynch story, the Chicago Tribune *concluded that it was "the story of how a modern war icon is made and perhaps how easily journalists with different agendas accepted contradictory self-serving versions of what happened to her." (Read a more detailed assessment of the Jessica Lynch story at Journalism.Org, www.journalism.org.) The* Tribune *was one of several news organizations that revisited the whole story.*

Even though they did, however, Jessica Lynch—whatever her heroine status— had become a celebrity. She returned to her West Virginia hometown in the summer, still recovering from her injuries, with a parade, massive media coverage, and television networks vying to sign her up for news exclusive interview shows. The cycles of her story had been rapid and confounding.

The profession of journalism remains in a state of constant flux, always seemingly confused about its present and unsure about its future. What does the Jessica Lynch episode tell us about the profession and how it is practiced? Maybe not much. The circumstances of combat are highly unusual. The United States was in full combat mode, and yet information was sparse and sometimes unreliable. The war was not going as predicted, and the frustration of armed forces and administration officials with what they perceived as the "mood swings" of the media were widely known. Their claims were that the war was going better than the new media were reporting. When the Jessica Lynch story first appeared, it may have sounded too good to be true, but it gave some relief to all involved, including a concerned public.

FIGURE 6.1 **Jessica Lynch Tells Her Story** Jessica Lynch, second from left, and author Rick Bragg, a former reporter for the *New York Times,* sign a copy of their book *I Am a Soldier Too, The Jessica Lynch Story* at the Wirt County High School in Elizabeth, West Virginia, Saturday, December 20, 2003. Jessica's father Greg Lynch, center rear, organizes and readies books to be autographed. Lynch was always careful not to take credit for actions in battle that were attributed to her in the early reports of capture. For a time, the book was on national bestseller lists. (Photo credit: AP Wide World Photos)

But maybe Jessica Lynch's story tells us a great deal about the news media. It was a good tale with appealing characters and interesting details. Many reporters gravitated to it. As they did, they fed off of each other's reports. They also placed themselves at the mercy of sources who were not willing to be identified. The information from these sources should have been treated with more suspicion, but the pressure to report something—sometimes anything at all—in the pressurized and competitive atmosphere of today's journalism tempts reporters to set aside those suspicions.

The state of the profession and where it is headed is far more complex a topic than can be exemplified for a single incident, even one with the twists and turns of the Jessica Lynch story. To get a handle on this topic, we need to examine a variety of aspects about the news media.

An Open Profession

Almost every generation of journalists in the twentieth century spent a good deal of time and effort debating the question of whether or not journalism is a profession.

Professions are occupations that require some level of education, testing, and even governmental licensing on the part of those who enter them. In addition, the profession itself may require some additional training throughout one's career. Professionals that we are likely to know most about are attorneys, medical doctors, accountants, and clergy. One aspect of a profession that some people find particularly appealing is that they usually have a structure to police themselves; that is, when a professional violates a rule or practice of the profession, other members of the profession may judge whether or not that person should answer for that behavior.

Should journalists also be part of a profession?

Some parts of becoming a professional have great appeal, particularly the aspects of education and training. Most believe that journalists should have a college education—if not a journalism degree then a liberal arts degree of some kind. They should also be trained in the rudiments of reporting, writing, and editing. This requirement would certainly relieve employers of the responsibilities of basic on-the-job training.

Another aspect of professionalism that appeals to many people is the self-policing of professionals. Good journalists are very aware of those who do not abide by professional standards and often feel embarrassed or tarnished by them. They are often frustrated because they would like to have some way of telling the public that journalism has its own way of separating good journalism from that which does not live up to the commonly accepted standards of the field. A formal policing mechanism would also offer members of the public a way to ask questions or make complaints about those in the field. Many who argue for such a process believe that it would enhance the credibility of journalists with the public.

Finally, making journalism into a profession would likely raise the pay for those who achieve professional status. Compensation, especially entry-level pay, is a continuing problem for journalists who feel that many news organizations do not pay them what they are worth or in relation to the profits the organization makes. Status as a professional, some feel, would help alleviate this situation.

Not everyone believes that making journalism into a profession is a good idea, however. In fact, there are many who are vehemently opposed to it. Most of those people oppose it on the grounds of the First Amendment and what it is supposed to guarantee to all citizens, not just journalists. The U.S. Constitution does not guarantee all citizens the right to practice law or medicine. The opportunity to do that may be available to most of us, but it is not a fundamental right. States grant that privilege to certain people only after they have done certain things (obtain a degree, pass a test, etc.).

The First Amendment, however, does grant to all citizens the right to speak and to write (see Chapter 3). No one has to go to school or pass a test. A person can simply do it whenever he or she chooses. In the same vein, a person who makes a living doing something else can research and write an article for a newsletter, newspaper, magazine, or web site. No formal training or certification from the government is required for that activity. Nor should there be. It is a right guaranteed by the First Amendment.

The rights guaranteed by the First Amendment (freedom of religion, speech, press, and assembly and the right to petition the government) continue to be in force no matter what a person does or how that person uses or misuses those rights. (Even people in jail convicted of vicious crimes still have First Amendment rights, even though they may be limited because of incarceration.) Although the government or some professional agency can tell lawyers that they can no longer practice law or doctors that they cannot practice medicine, no government or agency can tell people they can no longer write or speak. Consequently, a self-policing journalism profession would mean a fundamental alteration of the way that we exercise basic rights.

So, probably the best that journalism can do is to call itself an "open profession," available to anyone who wishes to join it. Although journalism has no formal and enforceable policing process, it does what few other fields of endeavor do: conduct open investigations of itself and discuss vigorously its failures and shortcomings. The progress of the Jessica Lynch story shows that news organizations are often willing to examine what they do, correct their errors, and attempt to revise procedures. (Another example of this is the *New York Times*–Jayson Blair fiasco.) These critiques and revisions are not always satisfactory to those involved or to outside critics, but the fact that they take place at all speaks well for the field.

Financial State of the Profession

Journalism is no simple matter, and assessing its health is a complex task. An overview of various aspects of journalism shows that the profession in the early twenty-first century is thriving in many ways. Still, there are many great questions about the future and some dark clouds looming on the horizon.

Economically, most news organizations report themselves to be in good shape as the century begins. The latter half of the twentieth century witnessed the death of a great many newspapers. The number of daily newspapers in the United States declined from nearly 2,000 in 1910 to less than 1,500 in 2001. Many of the newspapers that have gone out of existence were the weaker or smaller newspaper of a two-newspaper city and had been owned by the larger paper. Eventually, they were swallowed up by the larger paper, leaving the surviving newspaper in a monopoly position.

For most newspapers, being in such a position has been extremely profitable. Many newspapers have profit margins far above other businesses, and even with the advent of new technology, the likelihood of this monopoly position being challenged is small. A one-newspaper town will probably remain a one-newspaper town for the foreseeable future. The greatest possibility for those who would like to start a new newspaper is in suburban enclaves of growing cities. As a city grows, the ability of the large newspaper located in the downtown area to cover suburbs and neighborhoods diminishes. It is also less able to serve local retail advertisers efficiently. This situation gives an opening to those who might attempt to begin a newspaper based on local readership and local advertising. Still, start-up costs are high for such ventures, and success is not guaranteed.

Despite their high profits, established newspapers do not face a cloudless future. The number of newspaper readers has been flat for many years and has begun in the last years of the twentieth century to decline slightly. Young people particularly are not growing up as newspaper readers, and although in previous generations newspapers could count on them becoming readers as they became adults, it is no longer safe to make that assumption. Many young readers get their news from the Web, and experts expect that trend to continue and grow. Newspapers are beginning to wake up to this trend and to respond by investing in their web sites and gearing them to younger readers. That response, however, has been slow and has met mighty resistance from print-loving traditionalists within the industry. The financial health of newspapers in the next generation, then, is very much in question.

Television stations have also been high-profit organizations, but they too face serious questions about their audience. A local television station can no long guarantee a local and passive audience for an advertiser. Individual viewers have many choices, a clicker that allows them to switch channels quickly, and a recording system that enables viewers to watch programs at any time and to skip the commercials if they so choose. Local cable systems are also selling advertising that can be slotted into popular national cable networks (such as CNN, MSNBC, and ESPN). In addition, the Web is eroding the monopoly that television has had in delivering breaking news immediately.

The one thing local television stations can offer viewers is local news in a timely fashion. That news, including weather and traffic information, is difficult and expensive to gather. Many television journalists are discouraged about the willingness of local stations to invest in quality news coverage. Pay scales at many stations continue to be low in an effort to save money, and many people in television journalism fear that good people will be discouraged from entering the field.

Magazines also face an uncertain future, but individual magazines have always lived more precariously than other traditional media. Magazines that have a solid readership and advertising base and that continue to deliver useful and interesting content to their readers are likely to survive. The magazine format, despite the invasion of the Web, is still an easy format for readers to use and for advertisers to understand. Magazines, however, will have to find some way of coexisting with and using the Web to maintain their print products. They need to have their web sites and print edition complement and promote one another.

News web sites, by contrast, are beginning to find a means of operation that will generate profitable revenue. Audiences for such sites are growing, and web journalists are finding new ways to use the technology to market their news and the products of their advertisers. As the economy improves from its slump at the beginning of the century, the financial outlook for news sites has brightened, and many predict that they will be highly profitable in the future.

Areas of Concern, Optimism

As journalism enters a new century, it faces a number of challenges and opportunities. The major challenge of journalism is to improve both its practices and its product in an environment of increasing speed and competition. Specifically, the profession needs to address the following issues:

| FIGURE 6.2 | 25 Leading Media Companies |

RANK U.S.	MEDIA COMPANY	HEADQUARTERS	MEDIA REVENUE 2002*
1	AOL Time Warner	New York	$28,629
2	Viacom	New York	16,326
3	Comcast Corp.	Philadelphia	16,043
4	Walt Disney Co.	New York/Burbank	9,763
5	NBC-TV (General Electric Co.)	Fairfield, CT	7,390
6	Cox Enterprises	Atlanta	7,349
7	News Corp.	Sydney	6,645
8	DirecTV (General Motors Corp.)	El Segundo, CA	6,445
9	Clear Channel Communications	San Antonio, TX	5,851
10	Gannett Co.	McLean, VA	5,617
11	Advance Publications	Newark, NJ	5,420
12	Tribune Co.	Chicago	5,162
13	Charter Communications	St. Louis	4,566
14	EchoStar Communications Corp.	Littleton, CO	4,430
15	Hearst Corp.	New York	4,231
16	Adelphia Communications Corp.	Coudersport, PA	3,426
17	Cablevision Systems Corp.	Bethpage, NY	3,292
18	The New York Times Co.	New York	3,092
19	Knight Ridder	San Jose, CA	2,841
20	Bloomberg	New York	2,240
21	The Washington Post Co.	Washington	1,963
22	Primedia	New York	1,684
23	Dow Jones & Co.	New York	1,559
24	Belo	Dallas	1,428
25	E. W. Scripps Co.	Cincinnati	1,402

*Numbers represent millions of dollars.

Source: *Advertising Age,* Top Media Companies, 2002.

Bias

Journalists need to continue efforts to include more points of view in their reporting. The society they cover is increasingly diverse, not just ethnically but also in attitude and spirit. Journalists who continue to reflect the information and attitudes of traditional sources will miss a great deal of the stories they are asked to cover, and more seriously, they will lose touch with their audience. Journalists should learn to reach beyond their own attitudes and experience.

Errors/Credibility

Most journalists try to gather accurate information and present it in an accurate context. Even so, they make many mistakes—mistakes that could be avoided with greater care and experience. Consequently, publishers and managers should invest more in quality people and should do more to retain people who are experienced. They also need to encourage reporters and editors to take more time in gathering and producing their reports. Although competition will always be part of the journalistic culture, competitive attitudes should be dampened when it endangers accuracy and completeness.

Sensationalism/Relevance

In its "Statement of Shared Purpose," the Committee of Concerned Journalists and the Project for Excellence in Journalism (both can be found at the Journalism.org web site) have addressed this issue elegantly:

> Keeping news in proportion and not leaving important things out are also cornerstones of truthfulness. Journalism is a form of cartography: it creates a map for citizens to navigate society. Inflating events for sensation, neglecting others, stereotyping or being disproportionately negative all make a less reliable map. The map also should include news of all our communities, not just those with attractive demographics. This is best achieved by newsrooms with a diversity of backgrounds and perspectives. The map is only an analogy; proportion and comprehensiveness are subjective, yet their elusiveness does not lessen their significance.

Intrusiveness

Journalists should recognize and constantly remind themselves that what they do has real and sometimes lasting effects on people's lives. Journalists should approach their jobs not just with a sense of purpose but also with a sense of humanity. Although most working journalists are rarely as insensitive as they are portrayed in movies and television dramas, they do need to remind themselves that their work can disrupt the lives of people. News organizations should develop a culture that allows questions to arise about the effects of their reports on the people involved.

Recruitment, Training, and Retention

One of the ongoing problems of journalism is attracting and keeping good people. Journalism training is not usually a part of high school curriculum, in part because local media do not get involved with the schools and do not insist that it be included. Where high school journalism does exist, local news organizations often are not supportive of the efforts of teachers and students. In addition, many professional journalists are openly dismissive of collegiate journalistic training. They argue, with little evidence, that such training is not valuable and not worth supporting. Finally, journalism is known as a profession that wears people out. Young people who enter the field often leave after just a few years because of the difficulty of the work, the long hours, and the low compensation. The profession needs the benefits of more people with long-term experience, and news organizations should renew their commitment to keeping their best people, paying them generously, and offering them expanding opportunities.

Changing Technology, Changing Audience

In 2003 the A. C. Nielsen company, the most prominent of the television audience measurement services, reported that young men were spending less time watching television and more time going online or playing video games. In the November sweeps period, Nielsen said, young men (ages 18–34) watched 6 percent less television than previous sweeps periods; primetime watching among this group was down nearly 8 percent. Because advertising rates that television networks and stations charge are based on such ratings, the new figures were likely to cost television a lot of money. Young men are a prime audience for advertisers because they have a lot of money to spend.

Some television executives reacted with fury—against Nielsen. They blamed Nielsen for doing shoddy research and tried to poke holes in the findings, hoping to convince advertisers that DVDs, TiVo, video games, and the Web were not drawing this audience away from the traditional media. Their fury has been indicative of the way in which traditional media (newspapers and television) have reacted to the new technology that is available to the audience and how the audience is using it.

The fact is that we have become an online society. Media Audit, another audience analysis company, reported early in 2004 that the number of "heavy users" of the Internet had surpassed that of television and newspapers and was growing. More adults spent an hour a day online rather than with a newspaper, but more significantly, online time seems also to be drawing away from time spent with television.

Still another survey organization, The Harris Poll, found in late 2003 that two-thirds of adults were online at home, work, school, the library, or some other location. The increasing availability of fast broadband connections is making online information and activities available to more people.

All of these studies indicate that the audience for the mass media is shifting. These shifts are going to change the way journalists operate and the relationship that journalists have with their readers and viewers. Just what those changes will mean is by no means clear. Journalists will continue gathering information, processing it, and disseminating it to an audience. But finding that audience and interacting with it will be a challenge that no other generation of journalists has ever had to face.

Despite these problems and challenges, the future of journalism has many bright spots. Journalism is well on its way to developing a new medium, the Web, which has myriad possibilities for innovative and creative people. Journalism remains a vital

Most common online activies

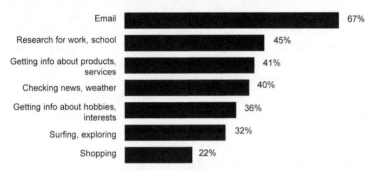

Based on a survey of 729 adults in the United States
conducted by The Harris Poll, Dec. 10-16, 2003.
www.harrisinteractive.com

FIGURE 6.3   Going Online—What People Do Study after study has
shown the number of people using the Web is growing. This graph, based
on research conducted by The Harris Poll, shows what people say are their
most common activities when they go online. The number of people who
seek news, weather, and other information is significant for journalists and
for the profession of journalism.

area of endeavor, one in which individuals and organizations can make a real difference in their communities and in society as a whole. Journalism can help improve the
lives of the people it serves. As long as it does that, it will remain a field that attracts
the best and brightest people of any generation.

QUESTIONS FOR DISCUSSION

1. The chapter lists several areas to which the field of journalism needs to pay attention. Can you think of others where the field might be having problems?
2. One area of concern for the future of journalism is the concentration of ownership. Many news organizations that were once independently owned are now
   part of conglomerate companies. What effect will that have on the profession?
3. How can journalists and news organizations connect more effectively with young
   people so that they become a reliable part of the news organization's audience?
4. Is journalism an attractive profession for you? Why or why not?

RELATED WEB SITES

Cyberjournalist, www.cyberjournalist.net

New Directions for News, www.newdirectionsfornews.com

NewsLab, www.newslab.org

Online Journalism Review, www.ojr.org

Poynter Institute, www.poynter.org

READINGS AND REFERENCES

Downie, L., & Kaiser, R. (2003). *The news about the news.* New York: Vintage Books.

Fallows, J. (1996). *Breaking the news: How the media undermine American democracy.* New York: Pantheon.

Fuller, J. (1997). *News values: Ideas for an information age.* Chicago: University of Chicago Press.

Kovach, B., & Rosenstiel, T. (2001). *The elements of journalism: What newspeople should know and the public should expect.* New York: Crown.

Jamieson, K. H., & Waldman, P. (2002). *The press effect: Politicians, journalists and the stories that shape the political world.* New York: Oxford Press.

Serrin, W. (Ed.). (2000). *The business of journalism.* New York: New Press.

Chapter Seven

Twentieth Century and Beyond

Key Concepts and Terms

1. The most profound change in journalism in the twentieth century came with the development of broadcasting—first radio and then television.

2. At the end of the twentieth century, a new medium—the Web—promised to render additional profound changes in the profession.

3. Radio brought news events to its audience immediately, often as they were happening; consequently, audiences were able to share a single experience.

4. The twentieth century was the era of the Big News Event—from the Scopes Monkey Trial in 1925 in Dayton, Tennessee, to World War II.

5. Muckrakers: journalists who looked deeply into the ills of society, such as the abuses of child labor and governmental corruption, and wrote long exposés; the term was coined by President Theodore Roosevelt.

6. Radio Act of 1927: established that the electromagnetic spectrum belongs to the public, and the U.S. government has the power to regulate it.

7. Newsmagazine: a type of publication pioneered by Henry Luce and Brittan Hadden, founders of *Time,* that summarized and wrote entertainingly about the events of the week.

8. Edward R. Murrow: the chief European correspondent for CBS radio during World War II; Murrow set the standard for broadcast news.

9. Television came of age as a news medium in the 1960s with its coverage of three major stories: the assassination of President John F. Kennedy, the civil rights movement, and the war in Vietnam.

10. Watergate: the name given to the scandals of the Nixon administration in the 1970s that eventually resulted in the resignation of Richard Nixon in 1974; Watergate, a watershed in American journalism, was a story pursued by two young reporters for the *Washington Post,* Robert Woodward and Carl Bernstein.

Vignette

It was a moment of high drama.

The king of England sat in a room alone, a microphone in front of him. Weeks of negotiation with politicians, emotional exchanges with family and friends, rumors whispered in public and shouted in the press—all of it had come to this. Edward VIII, who had been king for less than a year, had decided to abdicate.

By all accounts, people not only in England but all around the world loved him. They thought he was handsome, debonair, and more than competent enough to be the symbol of the nation. But his romance with an American divorcée had put everything about his future in doubt. When he made it known that he wanted to marry Wallis Simpson, politicians and church leaders told him he could not. As these debates were taking place in the latter half of 1936, Edward could say nothing publicly.

Finally, on December 11, 1936, after he had made his decision, he had his chance. Around the world, millions of people bent their ears to their radios to hear his crackling voice. The king was speaking to more people at one time than any human being in history had ever addressed. In the middle of his short speech, he delivered these famous lines:

"But you must believe me when I tell you that I have found it impossible to carry the heavy burden of responsibility and to discharge my duties as King as I would wish to do without the help and support of the woman I love."

It was a quintessential moment of the twentieth century. The world had come together. Millions of people in many parts of the globe knew the same thing at the same moment. The king of England had sacrificed his throne for "the woman I love." That moment, and many after it, was made possible by radio.

Radio and its successor, television, changed the way the world got its news. The speed achieved by the telegraph in the nineteenth century seemed slow compared to the light-speed of radio waves that came straight into the home.

But broadcasting had introduced an even more profound change. It was exemplified by the king's speech. One person could talk directly to millions of people at the same time. The contact could be instantaneous and, to some extent, personal. The newsmaker didn't need to go through the media. He or she could go directly to the audience.

That kind of communication would define the century and many of the news events it produced.

A Century of Technology

The twentieth century saw the birth and development of two new technologies that changed the form and practice of journalism. One was broadcasting at the beginning

Quote 7.1

BOB TROUT

On radio in the 1930s

It's no exaggeration to say that radio brought the whole country together, all at the same instant, everyone listening to the same things. And the country liked being tied together that way. In the morning people would say, "Did you hear that last night? Did you hear Hitler speaking again? What was he talking about? Did you hear them all cheering, 'Sieg Heil'? What did you think?" It was on the tip of everybody's tongue. People didn't quite see, just yet, exactly how overseas events were ever going to intimately affect their daily lives. But it was the greatest show they'd ever been offered.

Bob Trout was a longtime radio broadcaster for CBS News. He introduced the radio broadcasts of President Franklin Roosevelt and first referred to them as "fireside chats."

of the century, and the other was the Internet toward the end of the century. Each technology began modestly with its original inventors and innovators not imagining the extraordinary implications of what they were doing.

The century also witnessed the maturation of the "old media," newspapers, both as news organizations and as businesses. The number of newspapers grew for a short time as the century began but then declined. The circulation and revenue of the newspapers that were left increased so that newspapers became healthy, stable institutions, destined to survive unchanged in many ways for many decades. Magazines continued on a less stable path (as they had in the nineteenth century), appearing and often dying as trends and styles faded. The print media, particularly newspapers, set the standard for journalism and journalistic practices, but that position was challenged and overtaken by broadcasting as the century wore on.

One of the most important phenomena of the twentieth century was the development of the audience as an important consideration in the practice and economics of journalism. Audiences, of course, had always been important to journalism, but in the nineteenth century, they seemed willing to accept what the "great men" of journalism—Pulitzer, Hearst, Greeley, and Bennett—decided to give them. In the twentieth century, the "great men" faded, and the needs and desires of the audience increased in importance. Many media organizations pursued the mass audience, trying to gain the attention and adherence of as many people as possible. Toward the end of the century, the concept of the specialized audience became more sophisticated. This changing view of the audience had a great deal to do with advertising, of course. Those people, companies, and organizations that had products to sell were beginning to discover the mass audience and mass marketing. They made demands on the news organizations to deliver large audiences for their advertising, and the news organizations responded. Later in the century, marketing to specialized or segmented audiences became more efficient for some products and manufacturers. Media systems matured so that they could also deliver these audiences for the advertiser.

Finally, the twentieth century was the century of the Big News Event. The two costliest wars in human history, World War I (1914–1918) and World War II (1939–1945), occurred during the first half of the century. World War II ended with the explosion of the atom bomb, an event that altered the course of human history. The century was dotted with Big Events—the Scopes Monkey Trial, the Lindbergh kidnapping, the civil rights movement, the Kennedy assassination, the first landing on the moon, the war in Vietnam, the resignation of Richard Nixon, the trial of O. J. Simpson, and so on. Some of these events were truly profound, some merely interesting. Either way, they captured the attention of the news media at the time and, thus, captured the attention of media consumers. Journalists and news organizations geared themselves to covering the Big Event of the moment and also to the ever-present charges that their very presence was creating the news.

Thus, journalism changed and developed throughout the century. The technical changes that occurred in the field were important, but they were only the beginning.

The Decline of Newspapers

Newspapers both prospered and declined during the twentieth century. Their size grew and their content became broader and more sophisticated. Circulation numbers increased, and they cemented their place as a major civic and social force in their communities. Financially, they developed into one of the most profitable of all businesses, by the end of the century often boasting of more than a 20 percent profit margin (huge by most business standards).

But newspapers also declined in the twentieth century, and that decline began in the first two decades. Newspapers entered the 1900s slightly hung over, as it were, from some of the excesses of the late nineteenth century. The yellow journalism period, fueled by the New York giants, the *Herald* and the *World,* revealed newspapers as more interested in gaining attention than in delivering a quality product. Publishers, exemplified by William Randolph Hearst and Joseph Pulitzer, acted imperiously and spent money lavishly and sometimes foolishly. Many blamed newspapers for the Spanish-American War and the costs associated with America's fit of imperialism.

The real problem for newspapers, however, was that they had overreached their business potential. Journalism historian Frank Luther Mott called newspapers "leviathans" at this point in their history. They were large and ponderous and could not adapt to a changing market or audience. They had grown faster than the population, and at the beginning of the century, there were simply too many of them. The number of newspapers continued to grow in the first decade until there were about 2,200 daily newspapers in the country, but by the beginning of World War I, that number had receded. Advertisers had begun putting their money into the newspapers that had the largest circulations because they wanted to attract the largest audience for their products. Those larger newspapers could then buy out the smaller ones and either close them down or merge their operations. This decreased the competition to the point that the surviving newspaper had a monopoly—that is, it was the only newspaper available for readers and advertisers in an area. By 1920, there were more cities in the nation with single newspapers than with competing newspapers.

Magazines rather than newspapers provided what sparks there were to the profession of journalism during this period. A few magazines employed journalists and editors who were willing to face up to the effects of industrialization and unwilling to accept the niceties of the Gilded Age. Notable among these was S. S. McClure, who launched *McClure's Magazine* in 1893. The magazine became popular with its readers because of its well-written feature stories and its excellent illustration. One of its best writers was Ida Tarbell, who in 1902 finished a ground-breaking series innocuously titled "A History of the Standard Oil Company." It had taken her four years to research and write the series, which detailed the way in which John D. Rockefeller had attempted to destroy the company's competition in the oil business. The series eventually led to an investigation of the company and a lawsuit that broke the giant corporation into smaller companies.

Tarbell's colleague at *McClure's* was Lincoln Steffens, one of the best investigative reporters in the history of journalism. In 1902 he began a series of articles that looked at how many of the major cities in the United States were run. He found example after example of waste, fraud, theft, and corruption, and often he was able to get those perpetrating the frauds to talk to him about it. The work of Tarbell and Steffens inspired other magazine journalists to take hard looks at the government and industries around them. They were called "muckrakers," and their work energized a reform movement that changed much about American life and society. Many reform measures, such as the Pure Food and Drug Act of 1907, were passed because of the work of the muckrakers.

The reformist movement played itself out by the time Europe went to war in 1914. World War I was the result of a series of mistakes and miscalculations by Europe's heads of state, but once it had begun, no one could find a way out. Nor could anyone figure out exactly how to fight it. Generals on both sides had modern weapons but fought with eighteenth-century tactics. The result was enormous casualties and stalemate. Americans were glad to be out of it, but the British–French side seemed determined to get America involved. They encouraged correspondents from American newspapers to visit, and they made sure that the American press had their side of the story. British officials in particular did everything they could to play upon the affinity that Americans had for Great Britain. After Germany had committed a number of acts of aggression against the United States and President Woodrow Wilson asked Congress for a declaration of war in 1917, the American mainstream was fully supportive of Wilson and the war effort.

The major postwar development for newspapers was the introduction of the tabloid newspaper to American readers. The tabloid newspaper was half the size of a full-size newspaper and easier to handle, particularly for urban readers. The first major tabloid was the *New York Daily News,* begun in 1919 by Joseph Medill, grandson and namesake of the founder of the *Chicago Tribune*. Whereas most newspapers presented their information in a graphically subdued fashion with small headlines and relatively small pictures, the tabloid used large pictures and headlines to attract readers to its sensational mix of news that often involved crime, sports, and sex. In

FIGURE 7.1   Women in the Newsroom By 1910 when this photograph of the *Rocky Mountain News* newsroom in Denver, Colorado, was taken, women had, to some extent, taken their place beside men in journalism. Women writers and reporters were not plentiful, but they did exist and were showing that they could be every bit as effective as journalists as men. (Photo credit: Library of Congress)

the 1920s, Americans prospered economically and were distracted by new fashions and freedom for women, jazz, and sports, especially baseball, boxing, and horse racing. Tabloids fit perfectly into this era of "jazz journalism," as it came to be known, and by 1925 tabloid newspapers were found in most of the large cities in the country.

During these years, newspapers did not realize that their supremacy as the nation's major communication medium was about to end. Like the nation as a whole, they seemed prosperous and profitable. Despite the excesses of the tabloids, professional standards of reporting and writing had taken hold. Some of the great writers of the age—from Grantland Rice in the sports section to H. L. Mencken on the editorial page—could be found in the columns of the American press. But newspapers faced a challenge that they did not recognize—the advent of broadcasting.

The Development of Radio

The discovery of electromagnetic waves in the atmosphere and the harnessing of them for communication is one of the great achievements of mankind. The scientific and conceptual breakthroughs that were made in this area in the waning years of the nineteenth century laid the base for the structure of the life we live today.

Just who "invented" radio is a matter of some dispute among historians. Many people contributed to its development, beginning even before the Civil War with those who were interested in the properties of electronic telegraphy, or wireless telegraphs. Eventually those experiments and theories came to fruition with the work of Nathan Stubblefield, who broadcast speech and music from his home in Murray, Kentucky. Word of Stubblefield's success brought him great attention, and in 1904 he predicted that his invention would be used "for the general transmission of news of every description." At the same time, Italian Guglielmo Marconi was also figuring out how to get messages through the atmosphere. Marconi could see the commercial value of his work, and he conducted a number of public experiments in order to sell the idea to investors. In 1901 he sent wireless signals from England to Canada, demonstrating the possibility of transmitting messages across the ocean without cable.

But there were additional problems to be solved. Capturing and transmitting sound, not just telegraphic signals, was still difficult, and building devices that would receive those sounds conveniently had yet to be accomplished. Even before those problems had been overcome, radio proved its worth as a medium of news transmission during the *Titanic* disaster of 1912. The first reports of the disaster came from the radio signals of the ship *Carpathia,* which was about fifty miles from the *Titanic* when it sank. The enormous publicity given to the *Titanic*'s sinking helped focus attention on the value of wireless transmission, and later that year, Congress passed the Radio Act of 1912 that put the U.S. Department of Commerce in charge of licensing radio stations and assigning frequencies.

Experiments and innovations continued during the years of World War I, and by the end of the war, commercial companies were investing in this new technology. American Telephone and Telegraph manufactured and sold transmitters; General Electric and Westinghouse sold receiving sets. Radio Corporation of America (RCA) entered the fray as the sales agent collecting royalties on the patents that these devices used. The structure of broadcasting as we know it was beginning to form. In November 1920, radio station KDKA in Pittsburgh went on the air and broadcast the results of the presidential election that year. KDKA is widely acknowledged as the first radio station of the kind we listen to now, and it is still in operation today.

In the next few years, the popularity of radio exploded. In 1921, there were about 30 radio stations broadcasting with some regularity; by 1923 there were more than 600. Westinghouse had sold more than 600,000 receiving sets by that time. That number grew to 14 million by the end of the decade. Radio stations proliferated throughout the decade, with many entrepreneurs recognizing the value of radio as an advertising medium. A company could build a radio station simply to broadcast information about its products. Others conceived of the idea of selling time on their station to many companies that wanted to advertise. In just a few short years, radio was everywhere.

Even at this early stage, radio introduced a different kind of journalism to the world. Radio could take people to the scene of an event and could do so instantly. Audiences could hear the sounds of the event, rather than just reading about them.

FIGURE 7.2   Herbert Hoover and the Regulation of Radio As secretary of commerce under President Calvin Coolidge, Herbert Hoover recognized the importance and power of radio and was instrumental in overseeing some of the first regulations the U.S. government imposed. Hoover was elected president in 1928 but was defeated by Franklin Roosevelt in 1932. (Photo credit: Library of Congress)

In 1925, the small east Tennessee town of Dayton captured the world's attention by putting on trial a biology professor who had discussed the theory of evolution in his high school class. Such discussions were viewed as sacrilegious and were a violation of Tennessee law, and the trial was a clash of cultural forces represented by fundamentalist religion and science. The trial attracted two of the most famous figures of the day, defense lawyer Clarence Darrow and three-time presidential candidate William Jennings Bryant, who argued the case for the prosecution. The Scopes Monkey Trial, as it came to be known (after John Scopes, the biology teacher), also attracted the world's press. That press included WGN, a Chicago radio station that spent $1,000 to broadcast the weeklong trial. For the first time the entire nation could sit inside the courtroom of a sensational trial. Radio gave its audience an immediacy that it had never known before.

But there was a problem. The growth in the number of radio stations soon produced a babble rather than a coherent set of voices. The electromagnetic spectrum that can handle radio is limited. Radio signals travel for a limited geographic area, and within that area wavelengths can be used effectively by only one operator. The Radio Act of 1912 did not anticipate the problem of more than one operator in an area broadcasting over the same wavelength. That soon happened, and the result was interference on the part of the sounds and great irritation on the part of the listeners. The result of this babble and confusion was the Radio Act of 1927, an important piece of legislation that established a number of principles: that the electromagnetic spectrum belongs to the public; that the government has the power to regulate it; that broadcasting is an important service that should be equitably distributed; and that broadcasting is a form of speech that deserves First Amendment protection. The Radio Act of 1927 was followed by the Communication Act of 1934, which expanded the Federal Communications Commission (FCC) and gave it broad powers over the technical communication structure (telephone, telegraph, television, cables, etc.) in America.

With order imposed by the government, radio prospered. Even during the Depression years, radio audiences and advertising expanded. Networks used telephone lines to link local radio stations and provided programs and services that could be heard in every part of the nation. Music, drama, comedy, and variety show formats were developed to keep listeners entertained. Live performances were staged for the radio audience. Companies and products were identified with a show or a personality. Some politicians, the foremost being President Franklin Roosevelt, recognized the power of radio to communicate with the nation. Roosevelt used a series of radio broadcasts, called "fireside chats," to explain his ideas to America and rally support for his policies. Roosevelt's voice was clear, firm, and unmistakable. He spoke with assurance and with the power of radio installed a confidence in Americans when they desperately needed it.

Radio news was also developing its voice. One of the networks, the Columbia Broadcasting System, hired Lowell Thomas, a deep-throated writer and traveler, to be its news commentator in 1930. Many others followed, including personalities such as Dorothy Parker and Walter Winchell. Radio could use the ambient sounds of a news events to make listeners feel as if they were on the scene along with the correspondent.

The style of writing and presentation was different. Correspondents used short, simple sentences to deliver the information and describe action. They could use their voices to be low-keyed or emphatic. They could interview newsmakers and let their voices be heard.

Newspapers realized the threat that radio news was to their supremacy, and at first, most simply tried to ignore it, hoping it would go away. Radio did not go away, and newspapers became more aggressive. As cooperative owners of the Associated Press (AP), newspaper publishers refused to allow radio news departments to subscribe to the AP. An agreement in the mid-1930s between newspaper owners and radio networks designed a limit to the amount of "news" that radio stations could broadcast, but it did not limit "commentary." Radio continued to develop its news and information function through the guise of commentary. The power of radio as a news medium could not be suppressed, and after a few short years, all agreements with publishers had dissipated. By the end of the decade, with war raging in Europe, radio news was in full flower.

The brightest bloom of that flower was Edward R. Murrow. Born in North Carolina and raised in Washington state, Murrow was president of the National Student Federation when he graduated from college and convinced CBS to air a program called *A University of the Air*. Murrow

FIGURE 7.3 **Edward R. Murrow**
Edward R. Murrow became one of the most respected and revered of all news broadcasters because of the work he did in reporting the war in Europe in the 1930s and 1940s. He fostered a set of young correspondents, many of whom continued to have long careers in television and radio. (Photo credit: Library of Congress)

joined CBS in 1935 and two years later found himself in Europe covering the crisis that was enveloping the continent. When the Nazis marched into Vienna, Austria, in 1938, Murrow was there to describe Adolph Hitler's triumphal appearance: "Herr Hitler is now at the Imperial Hotel. Tomorrow, there is to be a big parade. . . . Please don't think that everyone in Vienna was out to greet Herr Hitler today. There is tragedy as well as rejoicing in this city tonight." The next year, Hitler invaded Poland, and Europe went to war. Murrow began his regular broadcasts with "This is London." Murrow had put together a team of reporters stationed in the major European capitals; many of them would achieve fame as writers and news reporters and commentators, but they would always be known as Murrow's Boys. CBS was not the only network to develop a news team, of course. The National Broadcasting Company had done the same thing, and other smaller networks had also put together news operations. As the world plunged into war, these teams went to work at home and abroad to bring the story of the world's biggest event into the offices and homes of radio listeners.

Time and Development of the Newsmagazine

Radio was not the only threat to the newspaper as the chief information medium for the nation. In 1923, college friends Henry Luce and Briton Hadden, graduates of Yale, produced an idea that had been stirring within them for some time. The nation was ready, they thought, for a weekly publication that would summarize news events. These summaries could be written in a livelier way than they appeared in newspapers. Because they were weekly, they could gather up events into a more coherent narrative. They could contain the point of the view of the writer, and they could be entertaining. The magazine that Luce and Hadden conceived was originally called *Facts;* that was soon changed to *Time.*

The first issue appeared on March 23, 1923. Hadden is credited with developing the peculiar writing style of *Time* (verbs before subjects, creative use of attribution, comments inserted straight into the news reports, etc.). Hadden and Luce gave their own twists to the news, and the magazine prospered. Hadden died in 1929, and Luce took over the business and built it into a publishing empire. In 1930 Luce began *Fortune* magazine, a publication aimed at covering the business world, a bold move at the beginning of the Depression.

But that was not Luce's boldest idea. That came six years later when the company published the first issue of *Life* magazine. *Life's* forte was pictures. Luce sensed that American journalism was ignoring an important dimension of its technology—photography. People wanted to see as well as read. *Life* gave them a chance to do just that. Its larger-than-average format and slick paper provided an ideal forum for the best photojournalism of the day. *Life* was an instant success, selling out the nearly 500,000 copies of the first issue it produced. It attracted millions of subscribers and the very best photojournalists available, including Margaret Bourke-White, Alfred Eisenstadt, and Robert Capa. The magazine spared no expense in putting photographers at the scene of an important story, and its editors were experts in selecting and cropping photos that emphasized all that was interesting and dramatic about the picture.

HENRY LUCE AND THE MARCH OF *TIME*

Henry Luce knew the value of news and information. And he knew how to give it to people in a way they wanted it.

Luce and his friend from Yale, Briton Hadden, had an idea in 1923 that people would like to get their news in a different form than the newspapers use. They wanted it brief, summed up and, if possible, entertaining. And rather than do it once a day, they would do it once a week. That would give the writers time to put information together and tell the story.

The original title of their magazine was *Facts;* it soon became *Time.*

The magazine was not an instant success, but it managed to survive and establish itself. The formula worked, and as more and more people learned about it, they signed up. Hadden died in 1929, and Luce took over the operation with expansion in mind. If *Time* worked for news, other magazines could work for other areas. His string of successes was phenomenal:

Fortune (1930)

Life (1936)

Sports Illustrated (1954)

And after Luce's death in 1967, Time, Inc. hit on yet another idea—*People* (1974), a celebration of celebrity.

No man has had such a successful magazine publishing career, and no company has been more influential than Time, Inc.

Luce's magazine empire produced its imitators. In 1933, two other newsmagazines came onto the scene that are still being published today: *Newsweek* and *U.S. News. Look* magazine was a more modest operation than *Life* but went after the same market. Magazines that combined news and pictures were the *Saturday Evening Post* and *Colliers.*

These publications were geared to bring Americans the biggest story of the century, World War II. By the time Pearl Harbor was bombed on December 7, 1941, Americans could hear the latest events on their radios, read the daily reports in their newspapers, catch up on the week's news in their newsmagazines and see the best and most dramatic pictures of the war in any of several national publications. They were inundated with information, and with their intimate involvement in the war, they could not get enough.

Television

The age of radio lasted less than three decades. Once World War II was finished, the world was about to get another medium that would go beyond radio. Television was coming, though its advent was delayed by first the war and then by the U.S. government. Those involved with radio were highly interested and gravitated to the new medium. Newspapers and magazines looked upon television with a mixture of fear and disdain. Nothing could ever replace print, they said. They were right, of course,

FIGURE 7.4   Attack on Pearl Harbor The Japanese attack on U.S. naval forces in Pearl Harbor, Hawaii (shown here is the USS *Shaw* exploding), plunged America into World War II, the greatest news story of the century. With radio, newsmagazines, and photomagazines, as well as newspapers, Americans had plenty of news sources at the beginning of the war. (Photo credit: National Archives)

but the electronic media of radio and television were destined to have a profound effect on print to revise, again, the whole concept of news.

Almost as soon as radio was formed, people began thinking in terms of pictures rather than just sound. The first demonstration of pictures being transmitted by electromagnetic waves occurred in 1927 in the laboratory of Philo Farnsworth in San Francisco. Farnsworth, an independent scientist, held many of the patents on the technology that would eventually produce television, and it was a dispute over these patents that delayed the introduction of television to the general public.

By the end of World War II there were six television stations in the United States. The number began to grow, but in 1948 the FCC stopped granting licenses in order to resolve some of the technical questions that various approaches to television had raised. Those questions were settled by 1952, and the prosperity of the times allowed television to boom. The FCC granted hundreds of new licenses over the next few years, and millions of television receivers were sold. The radio networks evolved into the television networks, and many of the stars and programs from radio became the stars and programs of early television. People who grew up imagining what the Lone Ranger and his faithful companion Tonto looked like when they heard the program on the radio could now see the pair as everyone else saw them.

Television news also brought many of its stars from radio, but the medium demanded something different, something that was much harder to acquire and edit—pictures, and moving pictures, at that. In 1948 CBS aired *Douglas Edwards and the News;* that was quickly followed by *John Cameron Swayze's Camel Caravan* on NBC. Both programs were fifteen minutes long, barely time enough to present a few short stories and pictures. But other news formats were developed. Edward R. Murrow and Fred Friendly produced an interview/documentary show called *See It Now.* Newsworthy interviews were often contained on entertainment shows such as the NBC's *Today Show,* hosted by Dave Garroway, and the late-night *Jack Paar Show.*

The network's nightly news programs spawned a generation of news super-stars—the anchors. Among them were Chet Huntley and David Brinkley at NBC, who were first teamed to do the coverage of the national political conventions in 1952. Every night, one was in Washington and the other in New York, as they read the news and introduced reports from around the world. Networks became more sophisticated about the way they presented their reports, and the technology improved so they could obtain film and video faster and could do live, on-the-scene reports. In the summer of 1963, the networks expanded their fifteen-minute news shows to thirty minutes.

Nothing, however, had prepared the nation for the four traumatic days in November of that year when President John F. Kennedy was assassinated. Kennedy was riding in an open car in a motorcade in downtown Dallas, Texas, when he was hit by bullets from a long-range rifle. The time was 12:30 p.m. Central time on Friday, November 22, and the networks cut into their normal programming immediately to make the announcement. They stayed on the air, broadcasting what little information they had. About an hour later, Kennedy was pronounced dead at Parkland Hospital. The network news anchors stayed on the air all afternoon and evening following the story—the inauguration of Lyndon Johnson on *Air Force One,* the return of Kennedy's body to Washington, the arrest of Lee Harvey Oswald as the chief suspect in the shooting, and so on. On Saturday, the networks ceased their normal programs for the next seventy-two hours while America watched. The live cameras were there on Sunday morning when Lee Harvey Oswald was being moved from the Dallas City Jail and Jack Ruby stepped in front of him and shot him at close range. Oswald died later that day. On Monday, the world was transfixed by the images of Kennedy's funeral and procession to Arlington Cemetery.

Those three days demonstrated the power of television to cover an event and hold an audience as never before. Newspapers, magazines, and radio played only supporting roles to television as Americans dealt with their shock, horror, and grief. Television proved itself able to provide both the pictures and the emotion of that tragic event.

FIGURE 7.5   **Television Tells the Civil Rights Story** Television news brought images such as this one—a 17-year-old civil rights demonstrator, defying an antiparade ordinance of Birmingham, Alabama, and being attacked by a police dog on May 3, 1963—into the living rooms of America. The civil rights movement was transformed from a local battle against segregation into a national moral issue. (Photo credit: AP Wide World Photos)

Newspapers: Clouded Stability and Prosperity

Despite the development of these new sources of information, newspapers continued to attract large audiences and to occupy the pinnacle of journalistic standards and integrity. Many of the people on television news programs had been former newspaper reporters. (Walter Cronkite, for instance, had once worked for the news service United Press International.)

By the 1960s, however, the strength of newspapers began to erode. Large cities were likely to have competing newspapers, but most newspapers operated as monopolies in their hometowns. Their profit margins remained high. But about 1960, overall newspaper circulation hit a plateau of slightly more than 60 million newspapers per day. That was disturbing because the population continued to grow. It meant that newspapers were being seen by a smaller and smaller percentage of the population.

That decrease was small and not life-threatening, but it has not abated during the past forty years.

Why the decline? In many ways newspapers had gotten better. During the 1960s, the technology of newspaper production changed, allowing them to be more innovative in their designs and freer to use pictures and illustrations. Newspaper writing improved as many editors allowed reporters more leeway in how they put together their stories. Journalism schools were coming into their own and graduating flocks of young journalists who were bringing a more sophisticated level of training into the newsroom. Computerization hit the newsroom in several waves, particularly in the 1970s and 1980s, allowing journalists more time and freedom to report and write their stories.

The slow demise of readership of newspapers has been attributed to many factors. Among them is the feeling that other media, especially television, are distracting people and taking away time that they would have once devoted to newspapers. Another reason that has been suggested for this decline is the content of newspapers themselves; that is, newspapers do not pay attention to events and subjects that many people are interested in, particularly young people. Some have even suggested that there is a general decline in literacy, or at least the value of literacy, and newspapers have suffered because of it. This suggestion is disputed by others who cite the fact that more books are being published, sold, and read than ever before. In surveys of how people spend their leisure time, respondents are likely to say "reading" more than any other activity.

Despite this decline in readership, newspapers remain a vital part of American life and the place where basic journalistic skills are most likely to be learned and practiced. Occasionally newspapers, because of their prominence and slower production schedules (compared to broadcasting and the Web), will lead the nation into news stories that other media avoid. One such instance was Watergate, the political scandal of the early 1970s that led to the resignation of Richard Nixon as president. In June 1972, five men broke into the Democratic Party headquarters in the Watergate building (thus, the name) in Washington, DC. They were found to have ties to the reelection campaign of Richard Nixon, and eventually it was discovered that Nixon himself had participated in a cover-up that kept investigators from properly investigating the crime. Two years after the break-in, Nixon had to resign as president.

The story had few visual angles so that its attraction for television journalists was not great. In the first months after the break-in, there were few major events associated with it because the Nixon administration had done such a good job in covering it up. The story was uncovered by two *Washington Post* reporters, Bob Woodward and Carl Bernstein, who spent months examining documents, interviewing people, and putting the story together. Their reporting eventually led to a Congressional investigation and the appointment of a special prosecutor by the U.S. Department of Justice. The actions of the *Washington Post* showed that newspapers could do what other media could not or would not; they could stay with an important story over a long period of time.

In addition to this strength, the continuing value of newspapers is their ability to report local news. No other news organization, including the largest television stations, can match the resources and effort that newspapers put into gathering and reporting local information. This kind of information is found nowhere else, and readers place great value on it. Consequently, despite declines in readership rates, newspapers are likely to continue to have a strong place in their communities.

Expanding Television with Cable

The decades of the 1950s and 1960s saw television stabilize into a local system of stations that was supported by three national networks. Those networks provided thirty-minute newscasts each evening, whereas the local stations usually put together an additional thirty minutes of news. Other news programs on both the national and local levels might be aired (as we discussed earlier in this chapter), but news constituted a relatively small but important part of a station's offering to its viewers. Television stations and national networks were assured of large audiences because the program offerings, both news and entertainment, were so limited.

Over-the-air broadcasting did not reach every area of the country, however. Even the most powerful local stations could not send a very strong signal outside of a metropolitan area. The way television reached nonurban viewers was through cable. A tall receiving tower would be set up in a small town to catch the television signals; those signals would then be relayed through a cable that ran into the homes of the residents. Local stations and networks were quite happy to have their audiences expanded in this way.

In the 1960s and 1970s, the United States launched a series of communication satellites that would orbit the earth in a way that made them "stationary" above one point on the earth. These satellites could send and receive signals and in many ways revolutionized the global transmission of information. One of the things these satellites allowed was the direct transmission of television signals. That is, a local television station could transmit its programming directly to a satellite; that satellite could then relay those signals to a receiving tower that could be a long way from the station itself.

One of the first people to understand the implications of this technology was Ted Turner, owner of WTBS, a struggling, independent (non-network-affiliated) station in Atlanta. Many people in Atlanta liked WTBS because it showed lots of old movies, something they could not get on the network-affiliated channels. Turner had the idea that viewers in other areas would also like to have that choice, and the availability of satellites gave him the means of offering it to them. He began offering his station to cable systems for a relatively small fee. WTBS became a "super-station," and Turner made a huge profit on his idea.

Other entrepreneurs saw other opportunities and possibilities in the satellite–cable technology. They realized that with cable, television sets were open to more channels than just those provided by the local stations. Religious broadcasters, for instance, found that people across the nation would view their programs. At the other end of the technology, cable systems in the late 1970s and early 1980s began to grow. Urban areas, which had heretofore never "needed" cable, became lucrative markets for cable

WATERGATE: A "THIRD-RATE BURGLARY" AND A PULITZER FOR TWO YOUNG REPORTERS

It was a story no one seemed to want to pursue.

Five burglars were caught breaking into the Democratic National Committee headquarters in the Watergate apartment building in Washington, DC, on June 17, 1972. Who were they? What were they doing there? Who sent them?

The questions begged for answers, but no one seemed to want to find them—no one except two young reporters for the *Washington Post*, Bob Woodward and Carl Bernstein. America was in the middle of a presidential election campaign. Republican Richard Nixon was seeking a second term and likely to swamp his Democratic opponent. Nixon's press secretary dismissed what happened at the Watergate as a "third-rate burglary."

But Woodward, Bernstein, and the *Post* would not be put off so easily. They began looking into the connections the burglars had with the White House and Nixon's reelection campaign organization. Their reporting took months. Some people would not talk; others gave them bits and pieces of

Senator Sam Ervin of North Carolina, chairman of the Senate Watergate Committee, questions a witness during the televised hearings.

E. Howard Hunt, one of the Watergate burglars, demonstrates to the Senate committee the bugs that the burglars were trying to place in the Democratic National Committee headquarters.

systems because those viewers too wanted expanded choices. Between 1970 and 1985, the number of cable subscribers grew from about 5 million to more than 35 million.

Turner's success with marketing his superstation led him into another area—news. Turner realized that what the networks and the local stations offered in terms of news was relatively meager, particularly compared to what viewers wanted. His idea was to have a cable station that would broadcast news twenty-four hours a day and would be worldwide in its scope and coverage. Many people scoffed at the idea, saying that it would be too expensive and that the viewership would be small. Turner ignored those critics and in 1980 launched Cable News Network (CNN).

The critics were right about the first criticism. It was very expensive. But they were wrong about the second. CNN was immediately picked up by many cable systems, and its audience ratings were substantial. People had never been able to turn

President Richard Nixon (right) and his wife Pat prepare to board a helicopter on the south lawn of the White House just after Nixon had said farewell to his staff. Nixon was in the process of resigning as president. Gerald Ford (left) is about to be inaugurated as the new president.

The reporters still would not quit. Even after Nixon began his second term, their stories kept appearing in the *Post*. Finally, in 1973 the U.S. Senate appointed a special committee to investigate what had happened on the night of the burglary and who was responsible for it. That committee held public hearings and heard the testimony of current and former White House aides about how Nixon's reelection campaign had been run. Eventually, one aide revealed that most of the conversations in the Oval Office had been taped.

A long judicial battle ensued, with Nixon trying to keep the tapes from the public. When the U.S. Supreme Court ordered him to turn the tapes over to a special prosecutor in the summer of 1974, Nixon made public the fact that he had participated in covering up the scandal. Later that week, on August 8, 1974, he became the first president to resign from office.

Woodward and Bernstein were widely credited with bringing that resignation about. They won a Pulitzer prize for their efforts, and their book, *All the President's Men,* which described in detail their dogged reporting efforts, was made into a movie starring Robert Redford and Dustin Hoffman.

information. While they were connecting these dots, Nixon was on his way to one of the biggest election victories in the history of the nation.

on their televisions and get news whenever they wanted it; they were always made to wait for scheduled newscasts. CNN had news any time they wanted it. And by gearing itself toward news and only news, CNN could cover live news events, from start to finish if necessary, without "breaking in" to normal programming. CNN paid top dollar to some of the most experienced television journalists in the business. When the Gulf War broke out in 1991, CNN had veteran war correspondent Peter Arnett in Baghdad, the capital city of Iraq, sending daily and sometimes hourly reports. Overall, it provided such thorough coverage of the war that when the fighting was over, most critics conceded that CNN had established itself as equal to the national news networks.

News has become a standard and substantial offering of cable television. A number of news operations have imitated CNN's twenty-four-hours-a-day, seven-days-a-week approach, so that cable viewers have many choices. In addition, news channels have been developed to deal with particular subjects, such as sports, and some large cities have their own twenty-four-hour news stations.

The Development of the Web

Just as the beginning of the twentieth century saw the development of the medium of radio, the end of the century saw the development of yet another medium—the World Wide Web. This medium, in the beginning, had little to do with journalism but a lot to do with news and information.

Two threads of creativity and problem solving—each as old as human intelligence—merged in the early 1990s to form the World Wide Web. Each thread had a tradition, a set of important personalities and contributors, and an approach. Each thread intersected and intertwined itself through the other in ways that ultimately helped to develop the communication system that we have today.

One thread was what we might call literary–scientific. The basic "problem" was the volume of human knowledge. The first half of the twentieth century witnessed a vast expansion of knowledge (information, ideas, technology), much of it wrought from a desire to win in warfare. At the end of World War II, Vannevar Bush, a scientist at the Massachusetts Institute of Technology, published a seminal article in the *Atlantic Monthly* on this problem.

> There is a growing mountain of research. But there is increased evidence that we are being bogged down today as specialization extends. The investigator is staggered by the findings and conclusions of thousands of other workers—conclusions which he cannot find time to grasp, much less to remember, as they appear. (Bush pp. 101–108)

Bush thought photography and compression might be the answer—taking pictures of documents and then reducing them so that a set of encyclopedias could fit into a matchbox. The cards on which these pictures would reside (microfiche) could then be read on some machine that would help the scientist in remembering the associations and threads of thinking. Bush's solution to the problem had some validity for a while, but it was his articulation of the problem itself and his ideas about sharing and linking that became important.

What Bush was beginning to envision was hypertext, a name later coined by Ted Nelson. In the 1960s Nelson conceived of a universe of documents, called a "docuverse," where documents would exist and be shared for a small fee. He called this docuverse Xanadu, the precursor of the World Wide Web that we know today.

The second thread was technological, and there were two "problems" that needed to be solved here. One was communicating over long distances, a problem that had existed from the time that individuals realized people lived beyond a day's walk. The other was a much more current problem. In the post–World War II nuclear age, the U.S. Department of Defense was fearful that a single, well-placed nuclear blast would eliminate the ability of the United States to communicate and defend itself. In the 1960s, the department's Advanced Research Project Agency (APRA) began developing an information distribution system that would not be knocked out with one blow.

The product of ARPA's work was a series of connected computers and computer networks called the Internet that was first instituted in 1969. Slowly and somewhat fitfully through the 1970s and 1980s, protocols for transferring information—email, online research tools and information, and even discussions groups—were formed.

In 1991, Tim Berners-Lee, a physicist working for a European research consortium in Switzerland, developed a hypertext system to allow people to share what they had through the Internet. It required a software program to be installed on an individual computer, and the information to be shared had to be formatted with a set of tags (hypertext markup language, or HTML). The browser that would allow all this to happen was called WorldWideWeb. More sophisticated browsers were later developed by others, but the name and the system that Berners-Lee donated to the world stuck (he has never made any money off his work).

The work of Berners-Lee and others took the Internet, previously confined to computer geeks and computer bulletin board users, and placed it into the hands of the general public. By the beginning of the twenty-first century, there were millions of web sites and web pages (collections of text and images) that represented individual people, organizations, companies, governments, and ideas. A survey by the U.S. Department of Commerce in September 2001 found that more than half the population was using the Internet, and the number of users was growing by about 2 million people per month. The Commerce Department report also said that 90 percent of children from ages 5 to 17 used computers, and 75 percent of 14- to 17-year-olds were on the Internet. In addition, 45 percent of the entire population used email (up from 35 percent in the previous year), and 36 percent used the Internet to search for product and service information, such as finding airline schedules and buying books online.

But after ten years, the Web has changed. The Web is certainly bigger, with more sites and more information. It is also technically easier to browse, or surf, and to find information. New design tools have made web sites easier to create and have allowed users increased ease in navigation. People who design and produce web sites have also become more sophisticated in presenting information and more adept at knowing why people visited a web site.

The web is now a "place," virtual though it may be, where people do things, and one of the chief web activities is getting information. People want airline schedules, recipes, Sunday school lessons, wedding registrations, the bestseller list, the latest prices on new computers—a wide variety of information that has one thing in common. It must be current.

That is why, above all else, the Web is a news medium.

People want news, and they want it immediately. Even when the information is not "breaking news," they expect the web sites they visit to be different whenever they show up. People rarely return to a web site if they keep seeing the same information. Web site producers quickly realized this, even though they may have begun their site with the idea that they could put it up and leave it alone. Web sites are not billboards. In order to maintain and increase their traffic, they must be changed often. The monster, as many webbies have found, must be fed.

This is, of course, what news organizations do, and this is one of the reasons the Web is so effective as a news medium. The development of Web journalism will allow, if not force, journalists to examine some basic questions about how we gather, process, and distribute information, and what our relationship with the audience is. The journalistic process itself is unlikely to shift dramatically as we enter this new medium. The culture of journalism is that we tell ourselves about ourselves; we try to do so with accuracy and grace and with the least harm, but we know that sometimes harm or discomfort will be the result.

How we do what we do is the question that is fascinating many web journalists in this era. The Web offers many possibilities and permutations on those possibilities, and anyone with energy, imagination, and a sense of adventure will enjoy the web environment for the next decade. New forms of storytelling and information presentation will be developed. Some will be discarded, and some will remain and mature. Watching and participating in this process will be fun.

The last question—the relationship of journalists with their audience—will probably be the most vexing and ultimately the most important one of all. How do we give the audience what it needs when there will be increased pressures to give the audience only what it wants? What kind of a dialogue should we develop with the audience, and when and how should the audience participate in the journalistic process? What standards of accountability will both journalists and the audience accept? Finally, how will web journalism achieve the ultimate goal of the journalist—to tell ourselves about ourselves in order to build a healthier community of people?

The journey of web journalism is just beginning.

QUESTIONS FOR DISCUSSION

1. What do you think are the three most important things that happened to journalism in the twentieth century? Be prepared to defend your answer with facts and logic.
2. Do you believe the World Wide Web will change journalism as much as the chapter predicts?
3. If you were going to publish a newspaper for your area (town, neighborhood, etc.), what would you do that is different from what your local newspaper is now doing? What kind of stories would you run that the local newspaper does not run?
4. Can you imagine a world without television? Some of your relatives may be old enough to remember what that was like. If so, it might be useful for you to have a discussion with them. What did people do with their time? Was radio a big deal? What kind of programs did they listen to?

RELATED WEB SITES

Center for History and New Media, http://chnm.gmu.edu

CNN 20th Anniversary Special Project, www.cnn.com/SPECIALS/2000/cnn20

Encyclopaedia of USA History: Journalists, www.spartacus.schoolnet.co.uk/USAjournalists. htm

Greensboro Sit-Ins: Media/Headlines, www.greensboro.com/sitins/media_headlines.htm

Image of the Journalist in Popular Culture, www.ijpc.org

Library of American Broadcasting, www.lib.umd.edu/UMCP/LAB

Media History Monographs, www.scripps.ohiou.edu/mediahistory

Media History Project, http://mediahistory.umn.edu

Media on Stamps, www.spacetoday.org/Stamps/Stamps.html

Milestones in Journalism Diversity (News Watch), http://newswatch.sfsu.edu/milestones

Museum of Broadcast Communications, www.museum.tv/index.shtml

Museum of Television and Radio, www.mtr.org

National Public Broadcasting Archives, www.lib.umd.edu/UMCP/NPBA/index.html

Newseum, www.newseum.org

New York Times Company History, www.nytco.com/company-timeline.html

Oral Histories Relating to Journalism History, www.elon.edu/dcopeland/ajha/oralhistory. htm

Poynter's "New Media Timeline," www.poynterextra.org/extra/Timeline/index.htm

Presstime: 20th Anniversary Issue, www.naa.org/presstime/9910/2019.html

Pulitzer Prize Photographs, www.newseum.org/pulitzer

Radio News, www.otr.com/news.html

Reporting Civil Rights, www.reportingcivilrights.org

Washington Post: 125th Anniversary, www.washingtonpost.com/wp-dyn/metro/specials /post125

What a Century! (CJR), www.cjr.org/year/99/1/century.asp

Women Come to the Front: Journalists, Photographers and Broadcasters During World War II, http://lcweb.loc.gov/exhibits/wcf/wcf0001.html

Women in Journalism Oral History Project, http://npc.press.org/wpforal/ohhome.htm

READINGS AND REFERENCES

Beasley, M. H., & Gibbons, S. (1993). *Taking their place: A documentary history of women and journalism.* Washington, DC: American University Press.

Blanchard, M. A. (Ed.). (1998). *History of the mass media in the United States, an encyclopedia.* Chicago: Fitzroy Dearborn Publishers.

Brennen, B., & Hardt, H. (Eds.). (1999). *Picturing the past: Media, history and photography.* Champaign, IL: University of Illinois Press.

Briggs, A., & Burke, P. (2001). *A social history of the media from Gutenberg to the Internet.* Malden, MA: Blackwell.

Bush, V. "As We May Think." Atlantic Monthly, July 1945, pp. 101–108.

Danky, J. P., et al. (Eds.). (1999). *African-American newspapers and periodicals: A national bibliography.* Cambridge, MA: Harvard University Press.

Fedler, F. (2000). *Lessons from the past: Journalists' lives and work, 1850–1950.* Prospect Heights, IL: Waveland Press.

Folkerts, J., & Teeter, D. L. Jr. (1997). *Voices of a nation: A history of mass media in the United States*. Boston: Allyn and Bacon.

Hudson, F. (2000). *Journalism in the United States from 1690–1872*. New York: Routledge.

Hutton, F., & Reid, B. S. (Eds.). (1996). *Outsiders in 19th-Century press history*. Bowling Green: Bowling Green State University Press.

Mindich, D. T. Z. (1998). *Just the facts: How objectivity came to define American journalism*. New York: New York University Press.

Pride, A. S., & Wilson, C. C. (1997). *A history of the Black Press*. Washington, DC: Howard University Press.

Rafferty, A. M. (2000). *American journalism 1690–1904*. New York: Routledge.

Sloan, W. D. (1991). *Perspectives on mass communication history*. Hillsdale, NJ: Lawrence Erlbaum.

Sloan, W. D., & Parcell, L. M. (Eds.). (2002) *American journalism: History, principles, practices*. Jefferson, NC: McFarland & Company.

Sloan, W. D., Stovall, J. G., & Startt, J. D. (1999). *The media in America: A history* (4th Ed.). Northport, AL: Vision.

Sorel, N. C. (1999). *The women who wrote the war*. New York: Arcade Publishing.

Streitmatter, R. (1994). *Raising her voice: African-American women journalists who changed history*. Lexington, KY: University of Kentucky Press.

Streitmatter, R. (1997). *Mightier than the sword: How the news media have shaped American history*. Boulder, CO: Westview Press.

Suggs, H. L. (Ed.). (1996). *The Black Press in the Middle West, 1865–1985*. Westport, CT: Greenwood Press.

Tifft, S. E., & Jones, A. S. (1999). *The trust: The private and powerful family behind the New York Times*. New York: Little Brown and Company.

Wolseley, R. E. (1995). *Black achievers in American journalism*. Nashville: James C. Winston Publishing.

Woodhull, N. J., & Snyder, R. W. (Eds.). (1998). *Defining moments in journalism*. New Brunswick, NJ: Transaction Publishers.

8

Mass Media
Effects

Key Concepts and Terms

1. Scholars today believe that the effects of mass communication generally are cumulative over time.

2. Mass messages are significant in helping children learn society's expectations.

3. Most of the effects of mass communication are difficult to measure and predict.

4. Mass communication binds large audiences culturally but also can reinforce cultural fragmentation.

5. Some notions about the effects of mass messages, including subliminal messages, have been overstated.

6. Scholars differ on whether media-depicted violence triggers aggressive behavior.

Vignette

The boy genius Orson Welles was on a roll. By 1938, at age 23, Welles' dramatic flair had landed him a network radio show, Mercury Theater on the Air, *at prime time on CBS on Sunday nights. The program featured adaptations of well-known literature. For their October 30th program, Welles and his colleagues decided on a scary 1898 British novel, H. G. Wells'* War of the Worlds.

Orson Welles opened with the voice of a wizened chronicler from some future time, intoning an unsettling monologue. That was followed by an innocuous weather forecast, then hotel dance music. Then the music was interrupted by a news bulletin. An astronomer reported several explosions on Mars, propelling something at enormous velocity toward Earth. The bulletin over, listeners were transported back to the hotel orchestra. After applause the orchestra started up again, only to be interrupted by a special announcement:

Seismologists had picked up an earthquake-like shock in New Jersey. Then it was one bulletin after another.

The story line accelerated. Giant Martians moved across the countryside spewing fatal gas. One at a time, reporters at remote sites vanished off the air. The Martians decimated the Army and were wading across the Hudson River. Amid sirens and other sounds of emergency, a reporter on a Manhattan rooftop described the monsters advancing through the streets. From his vantage point he described the Martians felling people by the thousands and moving in on him, the gas crossing Sixth Avenue, then Fifth Avenue, then 100 yards away, then 50 feet. Then silence.

War of the Worlds. Young Orson Welles scared the living daylights out of thousands of radio listeners with the 1938 radio drama War of the Worlds. Most of the fright was short-lived, though. All but the most naïve listeners quickly realized that Martians really had not had the time within a one-hour real-time drama to devastate the New Jersey militia en route to wading the Hudson River to destroy Manhattan.

To the surprise of Orson Welles and his crew, the drama triggered widespread mayhem. Neighbors gathered in streets all over the country, wet towels held to their faces to slow the gas. In Newark, New Jersey, people—many undressed—fled their apartments. Said a New York woman, "I never hugged my radio so closely....I held a crucifix in my hand and prayed while looking out my open window to get a faint whiff of gas so that I would know when to close my window and hermetically seal my room with waterproof cement or anything else I could get a hold of. My plan was to stay in the room and hope that I would not suffocate before the gas blew away."

Researchers estimate that one out of six people who heard the program, more than 1 million in all, suspended disbelief and braced for the worst. The effects were especially amazing considering that:

Orson Welles

His radio drama cast doubt on powerful effects theory

- *An announcer identified the program as fiction at four points.*

- *Almost 10 times as many people were tuned to a popular comedy show on another network.*

- *The program ran only one hour, an impossibly short time for the sequence that began with the blastoffs on Mars, included a major military battle in New Jersey and ended with New York's destruction.*

War of the Worlds

Novel that inspired a radio drama that became the test bed of the media's ability to instill panic

Unwittingly, Orson Welles and his Mercury Theater *crew had created an evening of infamy and raised questions about media effects to new intensity. In this chapter you will learn what scholars believe to be true about the effects of the mass media on individuals and society.*

Effects Theories

Study Preview   *Early mass communication scholars assumed that the mass media were so powerful that ideas and even ballot-box instructions could be inserted as if by hypodermic needle into the body politic. It's called the bullet theory. Doubts arose in the 1940s about whether the media were really that powerful, and scholars began shaping their research questions on the assumption that media effects are more modest. Most scholars now look to long-term, cumulative media effects.*

powerful effects theory

Theory that media have immediate, direct influence

Bullet Theory

The first generation of mass communication scholars thought the mass media had a profound, direct effect on people. Their idea, called **powerful**

Walter Lippmann
His *Public Opinion* assumed powerful media effects in 1920s

effects theory, drew heavily on social commentator **Walter Lippmann**'s influential 1922 book *Public Opinion.* Lippmann argued that we see the world not as it really is but as "pictures in our heads." The "pictures" of things we have not experienced personally, he said, are shaped by the mass media. The powerful impact that Lippmann ascribed to the media was a precursor to the powerful effects theory that evolved among scholars over the next few years.

Harold Lasswell
His mass communication model assumed powerful effects

Yale psychologist **Harold Lasswell,** who studied World War II propaganda, embodied the effects theory in his famous model of mass communication:

> *Who says what,*
> *In which channel,*
> *To whom,*
> *With what effect.*

At their extreme, powerful effects theory devotees assumed that the media could inject information, ideas and even propaganda into the public consciousness. The theory was explained in terms of a hypodermic needle model or **bullet model.** Early powerful effects scholars would agree that newspaper coverage and endorsements of political candidates decided elections.

bullet model
Another name for the overrated powerful effects theory

The early scholars did not see that the hypodermic metaphor was hopelessly simplistic. They assumed, wrongly, that individuals are passive and absorb uncritically and unconditionally whatever the media spew forth. The fact is that individuals read, hear and see the same things differently. Even if they did not, people are exposed to many, many media—hardly a single, monolithic voice. Also, there is skepticism among media consumers that is manifested at its extreme in the saying "You can't believe a thing you read in the paper." People are not mindless, uncritical blotters.

third-person effect
One person overestimating the effect of media messages on other people

A remnant of now-discredited perceptions that the media have powerful and immediate influence is called **third-person effect.** In short, the theory holds that people overestimate the impact of media messages on other people. Scholar **W. P. Davison** who came up with the concept, told a story about a community film board that censored some movies because they might harm people who watch them—even though the board members denied that they themselves were harmed by watching them. The theory can be reduced to this notion: "It's the other guy who can't handle it, not me."

W. P. Davison
Scholar who devised third-person effect theory

Davison's pioneering scholarship spawned many studies. Most of the conclusions can be boiled down to these:

- Fears about negative impact are often unwarranted.

- Blocking negative messages is often unwarranted.

Minimalist Effects Theory

Paul Lazarsfeld
Found voters are more influenced by other people than by mass media

minimalist effects theory
Theory that media effects are mostly indirect

two-step flow
Media affects individuals through opinion leaders

opinion leaders
Influential friends, acquaintances

multistep flow
Media affects individuals through complex interpersonal connections

agenda-setting
Media tell people what to think about, not what to think

status conferral
Media attention enhances attention given to people, subjects, issues

Maxwell McCombs and Don Shaw
Articulated agenda-setting theory

Scholarly enthusiasm for the hypodermic needle model dwindled after two massive studies of voter behavior, one in Erie County, Ohio, in 1940, and the other in Elmira, New York, in 1948. The studies, led by sociologist **Paul Lazarsfeld** of Columbia University, were the first rigorous tests of media effects on elections. Lazarsfeld's researchers went back to 600 people several times to discover how they developed their candidate preferences. Rather than citing particular newspapers, magazines or radio stations, as had been expected, these people generally mentioned friends and acquaintances. The media had hardly any direct effect. Clearly, the hypodermic needle model was off-base, and the powerful effects theory needed rethinking. From that rethinking emerged the **minimalist effects theory**, which includes:

Two-Step Flow Model.   Minimalist scholars devised the **two-step flow** model to show that voters are motivated less by the mass media than by people they know personally and respect. These people, called **opinion leaders,** include many clergy, teachers and neighborhood merchants, although it is impossible to list categorically all those who are opinion leaders. Not all clergy, for example, are influential, and opinion leaders are not necessarily in authority roles. The minimalist scholars' point is that personal contact is more important than media contact. The two-step flow model, which replaced the hypodermic needle model, shows that whatever effect the media have on the majority of the population is through opinion leaders. Later, as mass communication research became more sophisticated, the two-step model was expanded into a **multistep flow** model to capture the complex web of social relationships that affects individuals.

Status Conferral.   Minimalist scholars acknowledge that the media create prominence for issues and people by giving them coverage. Conversely, media neglect relegates issues and personalities to obscurity. Related to this **status conferral** phenomenon is **agenda-setting**. Professors **Maxwell McCombs** and **Don Shaw**, describing the agenda-setting phenomenon in 1972, said the media do not tell people *what to think* but tell them *what to think about*. This is a profound distinction. In covering a political campaign, explain McCombs and Shaw, the media choose which issues or topics to emphasize, thereby helping set the campaign's agenda. "This ability to affect cognitive change among individuals," say McCombs and Shaw, "is one of the most important aspects of the power of mass communication."

Narcoticizing Dysfunction.   Some minimalists claim that the media rarely energize people into action, such as getting them to go out to vote for a candidate. Rather, they say, the media lull people into passiv-

*narcoticizing
dysfunction*
People deceive
themselves into
believing they're
involved when
actually they're
only informed
ity. This effect, called **narcoticizing dysfunction,** is supported by studies
that find that many people are so overwhelmed by the volume of news
and information available to them that they tend to withdraw from involvement in public issues. Narcoticizing dysfunction occurs also when
people pick up a great deal of information from the media on a particular subject—poverty, for example—and believe that they are doing
something about a problem when they are really only smugly well-in-
formed. Intellectual involvement becomes a substitute for active involvement.

Cumulative Effects Theory

*Elisabeth
Noelle-Neumann*
Leading
cumulative
effects theorist
*cumulative
effects theory*
Theory that
media influence
is gradual over
time
In recent years some mass communication scholars have parted from the
minimalists and resurrected the powerful effects theory, although with a
twist that avoids the simplistic hypodermic needle model. German scholar
Elisabeth Noelle-Neumann, a leader of this school, concedes that the media
do not have powerful, immediate effects but argues that effects over time are
profound. Her **cumulative effects theory** notes that nobody can escape either
the media, which are ubiquitous, or the media's messages, which are driven
home with redundancy. To support her point, Noelle-Neumann cites multi-
media advertising campaigns that hammer away with the same message over
and over. There's no missing the point. Even in news reports there is a redundancy, with the media all focusing on the same events.

Noelle-Neumann's cumulative effects theory has troubling implications. She says that the media, despite surface appearances, work
against diverse, robust public consideration of issues. Noelle-Neumann
bases her observation on human psychology, which she says encourages
people who feel they hold majority viewpoints to speak out confidently.
Those views grow in credibility when they are carried by the media,
whether they really are dominant or not. Meanwhile, says Noelle-

Elisabeth Noelle-Neumann. Her spiral of silence
theory sees people with minority viewpoints being
discouraged into silence by louder majority views.
These majority views sometimes come into dominance
through media amplification. The more the dominance,
the less these views are subject to continuing review and
evaluation.

Neumann, people who perceive that they are in a minority are inclined to speak out less, perhaps not at all. The result is that dominant views can snowball through the media and become consensus views without being sufficiently challenged.

spiral of silence
Vocal majority
intimidates
others into
silence

To demonstrate her intriguing theory, Noelle-Neumann has devised the ominously labeled **spiral of silence** model, in which minority views are intimidated into silence and obscurity. Noelle-Neumann's model raises doubts about the libertarian concept of the media providing a marketplace in which conflicting ideas fight it out fairly, all receiving a full hearing.

APPLYING YOUR MEDIA LITERACY

- In our cultural folklore, the magic bullet theory of mass communication effects remains alive and well. Identify an example in your recent experience and assess it.

- What layers of complexity did Paul Lazarsfeld add to our understanding of the effects of mass communication?

- Cull your own experience for an example of the spiral-of-silence model and explain how it worked.

Lifestyle Effects

Study Preview   Mass media have a large role in initiating children into society. The socialization process is essential in perpetuating cultural values. For better or worse, mass media have accelerated socialization by giving youngsters access to information that adults kept to themselves in earlier generations. While the mass media affect lifestyles, they also reflect lifestyle changes that come about for reasons altogether unrelated to the mass media.

Socialization

Nobody is born knowing how to fit into society. This is learned through a process that begins at home. Children imitate their parents and brothers and sisters. From listening and observing, children learn values. Some behavior is applauded, some is scolded. Gradually this culturization and **socialization** process expands to include the influence of friends, neighbors, school and at some point the mass media.

socialization
Learning to fit
into society

In earlier times the role of the mass media came into effect in children's lives late because books, magazines and newspapers require reading skills that are learned in school. The media were only a modest part of early childhood socialization.

Today, however, television and the internet are omnipresent from the cradle. A young person turning 18 will have spent more time watching

MEDIA TIMELINE

Pre-1950

Mass Media Effects Milestones

Cathartic Theory
Aristotle dismissed notion that depictions of violence beget violence (350 B.C.)

Powerful Effects Theory
The media shape the pictures in our heads (1922)

Minimalist Effects Theory
Paul Lazarsfeld tested media effects on elections (1940s)

Pivotal Events

Aristotle saw depictions of violence positively.

- Greek Hellenistic period
- Right to vote for women (1920)
- Radio emerged as commercial medium (late 1920s)
- Great Depression (1930s)
- World War II (1941–1945)

1950–1969

Mass Media Effects Milestones

Bobo Doll Studies
Albert Bandura concluded media cause violence (1960)

Cognitive Dissonance
Media depictions cause overt racism to fade (1960s)

Cultural Imperialism
Herbert Schiller examined media's impact on indigenous cultures (1969)

Can mass media wipe out entire cultures?

Pivotal Events

- Television emerged as commercial medium (early 1950s)
- Vietnam war (1964–1975)
- Humans reached moon (1969)

1970–1979

Mass Media Effects Milestones

Agenda Setting
Maxwell McCombs and Don Shaw showed that media set agendas, not opinions (1972)

Cumulative Effects Theory
Elisabeth Noelle-Neumann theorized media effects (1973)

Pivotal Events

- Unabomber Ted Kaczynski mailed first bomb in 17-year spree (1978)

Media campaigns affect behavior. Smoking becoming less acceptable.

1980–1989

Mass Media Effects Milestones

Intergenerational Eavesdropping
Joshua Meyrowitz observed that television was eroding childhood innocence (1985)

What Causal Connection?
Scholar William McQuire: Studies flawed on violence causality (1986)

Pivotal Events

- Reagan presidency (1981–1989)
- U.S. invaded Grenada (1983)
- Meese Commission concluded that pornography has harmful effects, but report criticized as overstated and based on flimsy evidence (1969)
- U.S. invaded Panama (1989)
- George H.W. Bush presidency (1989–1993)

Can media trigger violence? For the unstable like Ted Bundy.

1990–1999

Pivotal Events

- Internet emerged as commercial medium (late 1990s)

Need evidence that audiences like to see violence? Check out an evening of prime-time television.

- Federal agents held Ruby Ridge family in Idaho siege.
- Clinton presidency (1993–2001)
- FBI destroyed Waco religious compound in siege (1993)
- Oklahoma City federal building bombing (1995)
- Dolly the sheep born after cloning from adult cell (1997)
- The movie *Titanic* (1997)
- Columbine High School massacre (1997)

2000–

Mass Media Effects Milestones

Offensive Mascots Debated
Nebraska *Journal Star* banned offensive sports mascots (2005)

Pivotal Events

- George W. Bush presidency (2001–2009)
- 9/11 terrorist attacks (2001)
- Iraq war (2003–2011)
- Hurricane Katrina (2005)
- Great Recession (2007–2009)
- Obama presidency (2009–)
- BP Gulf oil disaster (2010)

Campaign against media stereotyping included ridding athletics of racial mascots.

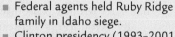

television than in any other activity except sleep. Television and the internet have displaced much of the socializing influence that once came from parents. *Sesame Street* imparts more information on the value of nutrition than does Mom's admonition to eat spinach.

By definition, socialization is **prosocial.** American children learn that motherhood, baseball and apple pie are valued; that buddies frown on tattling; that honesty is virtuous; and that hard work is rewarded. The stability of a society is ensured through the transmission of such values to the next generation.

prosocial
Socialization
perpetuates
positive values

Living Patterns

The mass media both reflect lifestyles and shape them. The advent of television in the mid-1950s, for example, kept people at home in their living rooms in the evening. Lodge memberships tumbled. Wednesday-night vespers became an anachronism of earlier times. Television supplanted crossroads taverns in rural areas for socializing and keeping up-to-date.

Media and lifestyle are intertwined. To find and keep audiences, media companies adjust their products according to the changes caused by other changes. Department stores, a phenomenon in the 1880s, put

Tobacco Warning. After 25 years of a government-required all-text health warning on cigarette packs, the U.S. Food and Drug Administration had planned to go graphic. The plan, to start in 2013, was for packs to carry gruesome depictions designed to steer young people away from tobacco. The labels in the proposed Smoking Can Kill You campaign were to be based on the premise that media campaigns can shape behavior. But the tobacco industry responded in 2011 by going to court against the labels. The industry claimed that the labels would coerce the companies to say things they don't want to say and thereby would infringe on their corporate rights of free speech.

shopping into the daily routine of housewives, giving rise to evening newspapers carrying store ads so that women could plan their next day's shopping expeditions. Newspapers previously were almost all in morning publication.

A century later, with the growing influx of women into full-time, out-of-the-house jobs, newspapers dropped their evening editions. Today almost all U.S. newspapers have only morning publication. Other societal changes also contributed to the demise of evening newspapers. In the old industrial economy, most jobs were 7 a.m. to 3 p.m., which allowed discretionary evening time to spend with a newspaper. With the emergence of a service economy, with 9 a.m. to 5 p.m. jobs coming into dominance, the market for evening newspapers withered. Television, as an alternative evening activity, also squeezed into the available time for people to read an evening paper.

Intergenerational Eavesdropping

The mass media, especially television, have eroded the boundaries between the generations, genders and other social institutions that people once respected. Once, adults whispered when they wanted to discuss certain subjects, like sex, when children were around. Today, children "eavesdrop" on all kinds of adult topics by seeing them depicted on television, in movies, and on YouTube. Though meant as a joke, these lines ring true today to many squirming parents:

> **Father to a friend:** My son and I had that father-and-son talk about the birds and the bees yesterday.
> **Friend:** Did you learn anything?

Joshua Meyrowitz
Noted that media have reduced generational and gender barriers

Joshua Meyrowitz, a communication scholar at the University of New Hampshire, brought the new socialization effects of intergenerational eavesdropping to wide attention with his 1985 book, *No Sense of Place.* In effect, the old socially recognized institution of childhood, which had been protected from "grown-up issues" like money, divorce and sex, has disappeared. From television sitcoms, kids learn that adults fight and goof up and sometimes are just plain silly. Kids have front-row seats to the world of adults from tabloid television to trashy reality shows.

Television also cracked other protected societal institutions, such as the "man's world." Through television many women enter the man's world of the locker room, the fishing trip and the workplace beyond the home. Older mass media, including books, had dealt with a diversity of topics and allowed people in on the "secrets" of other groups, but the ubiquity of television and the internet and the ease of access to them accelerated the breakdown of traditional institutional barriers.

APPLYING YOUR MEDIA LITERACY

■ Why is mass communication a growing issue in child development?

■ What examples can you offer of mass communication reflecting lifestyles? How about the opposite—lifestyles reflecting mass communication?

■ How has modern media content eroded the innocence of childhood?

Attitude Effects

Study Preview   When media messages rivet people's focus, public opinion can take new forms almost instantly. These quick cause-and-effect transformations are easily measured. More difficult to track are the effects of media messages on opinions and attitudes that shift over time—like customs and social conventions. Studies on role models and stereotype shifts seek to address these more elusive effects and how media messages can be manipulated to influence opinions and attitudes.

Influencing Opinion

How malleable are opinions? People, in fact, change their minds. In politics, the dominance of political parties shifts. Going into the 2008 election and again in 2012, polls found a growing disaffection with the Democratic and Republican parties. More people were calling themselves independents. Enthusiasm for products can spiral to success overnight and collapse just as fast. We know that people adjust their opinions, sometimes gradually, sometimes suddenly. Also, we know that media messages are important in these processes.

Some cause-and-effect is tracked easily. A horrendous event, like the unexpected Japanese attack on U.S. Navy facilities at Pearl Harbor in 1941, instantly transformed American public opinion. Before the attack, sentiment had been against armed resistance to Japanese and German expansionism. In an instant, a massive majority decided to go to war. In 2005 public confidence in the federal government bottomed with the failure to deal with the hurricane devastation in New Orleans and the Gulf coast. British Petroleum was gaining traction with its eco-friendly and green-theme "Beyond Petroleum" campaign until 2010 and its Gulf oil disaster. Such sudden shifts result from information carried by mass media, including statements from opinion leaders.

Causal explanations for gradual opinion shifts are elusive, although mass messages are a factor. What puts a company atop lists of most-admired brands? What makes the rest of the country view California as it does? Or New York? Or New Jersey? Many institutions, including state tourism agencies, budget millions of dollars to promote an image that they hope will be absorbed over time. One concentration of corporate image messages airs weekly on Sunday-morning television talk shows.

Scholars have puzzled for decades over how to measure the effects of media content on opinion. Except for major events that trigger sudden turnarounds, media effects on opinion are gradual.

Role Models

The extent of media influence on individuals may never be sorted out with any precision, in part because every individual is a distinct person and because media exposure varies from person to person. Even so, some media influence is undeniable. Consider the effect of entertainment idols as they come across through the media. Many individuals, especially young people casting about for an identity all their own, groom themselves in conformity with the latest heartthrob. This imitation, called **role modeling,** even includes speech mannerisms from whoever is hip at the moment. Let's not forget "yadda-yadda-yadda" from *Seinfeld.*

role modeling
Basis for imitative behavior

No matter how quirky, fashion fads are not terribly consequential, but serious questions can be raised about whether role modeling extends to behavior. Many people who produce media messages recognize their responsibility for role modeling. Whenever Batman and Robin leaped into their Batmobile in the campy 1960s television series, the camera always managed to show them fastening their seat belts. Many newspapers have a policy of mentioning in accident stories whether seat belts were in use. In the 1980s, as concern about AIDS mounted, moviemakers went out of their way to show condoms as a precaution in social situations. Now schoolyard bullying is portrayed less and less in a kids-will-be-kids spirit.

Angry Birds Everywhere. Well into 2011, more than 12 million video game players had bought the addictive touchscreen game Angry Birds from Apple's App Store. And Finnish game-maker Roxio was expanding to Android devices. Outpacing game sales, however, were Angry Bird toys, T-shirts and themed what-have-you. Eleven million items had been sold, not counting Halloween costumes that were the season's top-seller. And the Christmas sales were only beginning, A television series next? Movies? Roxio is working on those too.

MEDIA TOMORROW: CIA'S 'NINJA LIBRARIANS'

During the tumultuous Mideast unrest of 2011, the White House got a daily snapshot of the world built from tweets, Facebook updates, and traditional news media. The reports were prepared by the Open Source Center, a secretive agency of the CIA. Usually the reports ended up in President Barack Obama's daily intelligence briefings. The material answered questions from the president about threats and trouble spots.

The daily reports gave the president insight into world reaction to events like the Navy raid that killed Osama bin Laden and the end of the war in Iraq. Earlier the reports accurately predicted the regime-toppling uprising in Egypt. So too the reports predicted social media could be a Mideast game-changer.

Hardly anyone knew about the Open Source Center until the Associated Press was allowed inside late in 2011. That's when the world found out that the CIA analysts working at the OSC jokingly called themselves Ninja Librarians. The center's director, Doug Naquin, explained that a good open source officer was someone

with a master's degree in library science and knowledge of multiple languages. The most successful analysts were likened to the heroine of *The Girl With the Dragon Tattoo:* "A quirky,

Hero of the Revolution. Social media were a key vehicle to amass people for the revolution that toppled the Egyptian regime in the Arab Spring of 2011. Here an art student at the University of Helwan paints the Facebook logo on a mural commemorating the revolution. Facebook postings, as well as Twitter chatter, have proven revealing to U.S. policy-makers in assessing and predicting unrest around the world.

If role modeling can work for good purposes, such as promoting safety consciousness and disease prevention, it would seem that it could also have a negative effect. Some people linked the Columbine High School massacre in Littleton, Colorado, to a scene in the Leonardo DiCaprio movie *The Basketball Diaries*. In one scene, a student in a black trench coat executes fellow classmates. An outbreak of shootings followed other 1990s films that glorified thug life, including *New Jack City*, *Juice* and *Boyz N the Hood*.

Stereotypes

Close your eyes. Think "professor." What image forms in your mind? Before 1973 most people would have envisioned a harmless, absent-minded eccentric. Today, *The Nutty Professor* movie remake is a more likely image. Both the absent-minded and irreverent computer hacker who knows how to find stuff other people don't know exists."

The Open Source Center started examining social media after the Twitter-sphere rocked the Iranian regime during Iran's Green Revolution of 2009. By 2011 there were days when the center checked as many as 5 million tweets—almost an unimaginable quantity of messages. The center also checked out Facebook updates, newspaper articles, television news channels, local radio stations, internet chat rooms—anything to which people overseas had access and could contribute openly. The ninjas cast their net widely, tracking things as disparate as Chinese internet access and the mood on the street in Pakistan. The traffic ranged from angry tweets to thoughtful blogs.

After a Navy team killed bin Laden, the center gathered information from Twitter for a snapshot of world public opinion. Because tweets can't be tracked geographically, the analysts broke the information down by language. The majority of tweets in Chinese were negative. So were most of the tweets in Urdu, the language of Pakistan. The Ninja Librarians had become a proven and useful tool in assessing grassroots world opinion—and certainly quicker than traditional assessments from U.S. embassies around the world.

According to the AP, the CIA facility was set up in response to a recommendation by the 9/11 Commission. The identity of most employees is secret. So is the location.

The center's director, Doug Naquin, is the agency's public face. When AP reporter Kimberly Dozier asked him about his predictions for the next generation of social media. Naquin said it would probably be closed-loop, subscriber-only cell phone networks like those used by the Taliban terrorist organization to send messages among hundreds of followers. Those non-open source networks can be penetrated today only by technical eavesdropping by branches of U.S. intelligence, like the National Security Agency. But Naquin predicted his covert colleagues, the Ninja Librarians, will find ways to adapt. Just like the people they spy on do.

WHAT DO YOU THINK?

Is it proper for government agencies to eavesdrop on people using Twitter and Facebook?

What level of confidence would you place in the Open Source Center's daily snapshots of grassroots opinions in world trouble spots?

---

later nutty professor images are known as stereotypes. Both flow from the mass media. Although neither is an accurate generalization about professors, both have long-term impact.

stereotyping
Using broad strokes to facilitate storytelling

Stereotyping is a kind of shorthand that can facilitate communication. Putting a cowboy in a black hat allows a movie director to sidestep complex character exploration and move quickly into a story line because moviegoers hold a generalization about cowboys in black hats: They are the bad guys—a stereotype.

Newspaper editors pack lots of information into headlines by drawing on stereotypes held by readers. Consider the extra meanings implicit in headlines that refer to "Arab terrorists," a "Southern belle" or a "college jock." Stereotypes paint broad strokes that help create impact in media messages, but they are also a problem. A generalization, no matter how useful, is inaccurate. Not all Scots are tightfisted, nor are all Wall Street brokers crooked, nor are all college jocks dumb—not even a majority.

By using stereotypes, the mass media perpetuate them. With benign stereotypes there is no problem, but the media can perpetuate social injustice with stereotypes. In the late 1970s the U.S. Civil Rights Commission found that blacks on network television were portrayed disproportionately in immature, demeaning or comic roles. By using a stereotype, television was not only perpetuating false generalizations but also being racist. Worse, network thoughtlessness was robbing black people of strong role models.

Critics call for the media to become activists to revise demeaning stereotypes. Although often right-minded, such calls can interfere with accurate portrayals. Italian-Americans, for example, lobbied successfully against Mafia characters being identified as Italians. Exceptions like HBO's Soprano family remained ir-

MEDIA PEOPLE: STEREOTYPING ON FIELD AND COURT

To people who criticize mass media for trafficking in misleading stereotypes, Kathleen Rutledge is a hero. When she was editor of the Lincoln, Nebraska *Journal Star*, Rutledge banned references to sports mascots and nicknames that many American Indians consider insulting. Readers of the *Journal Star*, circulation 76,300, no longer read about the Washington Redskins, just Washington. The Cleveland Indians' mascot, Chief Wahoo, whose weird grin irked many Indians, doesn't appear in the newspaper either.

Rutledge's policy change rankled some readers. In 500-some letters and e-mail messages, readers accused the newspaper of abandoning tradition and succumbing to the leftist politically correct agenda. Leftist? Hardly, responded Rutledge, noting that the *Journal Star* endorsed the self-proclaimed "compassionate conservative" George Bush for president in 2000. More than anything, the political tinge of some critics bespoke blind emotional attachments to tradition.

Can school nicknames and mascots have ill effects? Jesse Steinfeldt, an Indiana University

Kathleen Rutledge.

psychology professor who has studied the issue, says that "a racially hostile education environment" can affect the self-esteem of Native American kids.

In 2005 the National Collegiate Athletic Association stepped up pressure on colleges to drop Indian nicknames. Eighteen schools were listed for using nicknames and imagery the NCAA considered "hostile or abusive." The University of North Dakota was blacklisted by the NCAA. The university resisted for years but eventually retired its Fighting Sioux nickname and logo on order of the State Board of Higher Education.

In Kewaunee, Wisconsin, it was retired teacher Marsha Beggs Brown who pushed for change. A new state law went into effect in 2010 to eliminate race-based nicknames, logos and mascots. Seeing the law being ignored locally, Brown filed a complaint about the Kewaunee High School Indians. In the small town of 2,700, some people sent Brown anonymous letters and made unpleasant phone calls. She was snubbed. A popular t-shirt read: "Once an Indian, Always an Indian." Brown was motivated by a respect ritants, however. In general, activists against stereotyping have succeeded. New sensitivities have set in.

Agenda-Setting and Status Conferral

Media attention lends a legitimacy to events, individuals and issues that does not extend to things that go uncovered. This conferring of status occurs through the media's role as agenda-setters. It puts everybody on the same wavelength, or at least a similar one, which contributes to social cohesion by focusing our collective attention on issues we can address together. Otherwise, each of us could be going in separate directions, which would make collective action difficult if not impossible.

Examples of how media attention spotlights certain issues abound. An especially poignant case occurred in 1998 when a gay University of Wyoming student,

At the Last Dance. After the University of Illinois mascot Chief Illiniwek danced for the last time during a Fighting Illini halftime, students Kelby Lanning and Alison Perle couldn't conceal their lament at the passing of an era. The university retired Chief Illiiniwek after 71 years, deciding that the Indian-derived mascot was a demeaning stereotype.

for all people: "There's just no refuting that these names harm children."

The Kewaunee school board asked the community for alternative names. Almost 200 ideas were submitted. In a community-wide vote, 1,400 ballots were cast to choose between the two finalists: River Bandits and Storm.

Not all Indian references are out, however. In Michigan the Mishicot Indians have granted permission to the Hannahville Potawatomi high school to use the name because the town is named for a chief from that tribe.

In Wisconsin in 2011, American Indian Cultural Support reported 45 schools still had mascots it considered offensive. Councilman Brandon Stevens of the Oneida Nation, the tribe closest to Kewaunee, sees an upside: "As long as there's debate, there's an avenue for education."

At Kewaunee High School it's now "Go Storm. Ride the Wind!"

WHAT DO YOU THINK?

Should sports teams be required to choose kinder, gentler mascots and nicknames so as not to offend?

Can a media ban on references to a controversial mascot be effective in reducing stereotyping?

Matthew Shepard, was savagely beaten, tied to a fence outside of town and left to die. It was tragic, more than gay-bashing in that it was outright murder, and coverage of the event moved gay rights higher on the national agenda. Coverage of the gruesome death was an example of the media agenda-setting and of status conferral.

APPLYING YOUR MEDIA LITERACY

- How frequently does mass communication trigger sudden and drastic changes in public opinion? Offer examples.

- From your experience, cite examples of role modeling on issues more consequential than fashion and fads.

- Although media-perpetuated stereotypes can be false, misleading and damaging, stereotypes are nonetheless essential in mass communication. Why?

- How does mass communication wield power through status conferral on some issues and neglect others?

Cultural Effects

Study Preview   *Mass media messages to large audiences can be culturally unifying, but media demassification, with messages aimed at narrower audiences, has had a role also in the fragmentation of society. On a global scale, media have imposed U.S. and Western values on the traditional values of other cultures. Even in countries with emerging media systems, the indigenous media continue to be influenced by media content from dominant cultures.*

Values

Mass media are factors in shaping and reflecting contemporary values with the immense quantity of content that they carry. Often overlooked is that media also allow generations to share experiences, thoughts and values over the centuries.

Historical Transmission.   Human beings have a compulsion to pass on the wisdom they have accumulated to future generations. There is a compulsion, too, to learn from the past. In olden times, people gathered around fires and in temples to hear storytellers. It was a ritual through which people learned the values that governed their community. This is a form of **historical transmission.**

historical transmission
Communication of cultural values to later generations

Five-thousand years ago the oral tradition was augmented when Middle Eastern traders devised an alphabet to keep track of inventories, transactions and rates of exchange. When paper was invented, clay tablets gave way to scrolls and eventually books, which became the primary vehicle for storytelling. Religious values were passed on in holy books. Military chronicles laid out the lessons of war. Literature provided lessons by exploring the nooks and crannies of the human condition.

Books remain a primary repository of our culture. For several centuries it has been between hard covers, in black ink on paper, that the experiences, lessons and wisdom of our forebears have been recorded for posterity. Other mass media today share in the preservation and transmission of our culture over time. Consider these archives:

- **Paley Center for Media** in New York, with 120,000 television and radio performances, productions, debuts and series.

- **Library for Communication and Graphic Arts** at Ohio State University, whose collection includes editorial cartoons.

- **Vanderbilt Television News Archive** in Nashville, Tennessee, with 900,000 items from network nightly news programs and also special coverage such as political conventions and space shots.

Contemporary Transmission.   The mass media also transmit values among contemporary communities and societies, sometimes causing changes that otherwise would not occur. This is known as **contemporary transmission.** Anthropologists have documented that mass communication can change society. When Edmund Carpenter introduced movies to an isolated New Guinea village, the men adjusted their clothing toward the Western style and even remodeled their houses. This phenomenon, which scholars call **diffusion of innovations,** occurs when ideas move through the mass media. Consider the following:

contemporary transmission
Communication of cultural values to different cultures

diffusion of innovations
Process through which news, ideas, values and information spread

- **American Revolution.** Colonists up and down the Atlantic seaboard took cues on what to think and how to act from newspaper reports on radical activities, mostly in Boston, in the decade before the Declaration of Independence. These included inflammatory articles against the 1765 Stamp Act and accounts of the Boston Tea Party in 1773.

- **Music, fashion and pop culture.** In modern-day pop culture, the cues come through the media, mostly from New York, Hollywood and Nashville.

- **Third World innovation.** The United Nations creates instructional films and radio programs to promote agricultural reform in less developed parts of the world. Overpopulated areas have been targets of birth control campaigns.

- **Demise of Main Street.** Small-town businesses are boarding up throughout the United States as rural people see advertisements from regional shopping malls, which are farther away but offer greater variety and lower prices than Main Street.

Scholars note that the mass media can be given too much credit for the diffusion of innovations. Diffusion almost always needs reinforcement through interpersonal communication. Also, the diffusion is hardly ever a one-shot hypodermic injection but a process that requires redundancy in messages over an extended period. The 1989 outburst for democracy in China did not happen because one Chinese person read Thomas Paine on a sunny afternoon, nor do rural people suddenly abandon their local Main Street for a Walmart 40 miles away. The diffusion of innovations typically involves three initial steps in which the mass media can be pivotal:

- **Awareness.** Individuals and groups learn about alternatives, new options and possibilities.
- **Interest.** Once aware, people need to have their interest further whetted.
- **Evaluation.** By considering the experience of other people, as relayed by the mass media, individuals evaluate whether they wish to adopt an innovation.

The adoption process has two additional steps in which the media play a small role: the trial stage, in which an innovation is given a try, and the final stage, in which the innovation is either adopted or rejected.

Cultural Imperialism

cultural imperialism
One culture's dominance over another

Nobody could provoke debate quite like Herbert Schiller, whether among his college students or in the whole society. He amassed evidence for a pivotal 1969 book, *Mass Communications and American Empire*. His argument: U.S. media companies were coming to dominate cultural life abroad. He called it **cultural imperialism.**

Herbert Schiller. Schiller sounded the alarm that Western culture, epitomized by Hollywood, was flooding the planet. The result, he said, was that traditions and values in other cultures were being drowned out. The phenomenon, called cultural imperialism, has been offset somewhat by the growth in media content originating in other countries and targeted at U.S. and other Western audiences.

Schiller sensitized readers to the implications of exporting movies and other U.S. media products. He also put leading media companies on notice that Mickey Mouse in Borneo, no matter how endearing, had untoward implications for the indigenous culture. U.S. corporate greed, he said, was undermining native cultures in developing countries. He described the process as insidious. People in developing countries found U.S. media products so slickly produced and packaged that, candy-like, they were irresistible no matter the destruction they were causing to the local traditions and values that were fading fast into oblivion.

Plenty of evidence supported Schiller's theory. In South Africa, robbers have taken to shouting, "Freeze," a word that had no root in either Afrikaans or other indigenous languages. The robbers had been watching too much American television. A teen fashion statement in India became dressing like *Baywatch* characters, a fashion hardly in subcontinent tradition. In India, too, television talk shows began an American-like probing into private lives. Said media observer Shailja Bajpai: "American television has loosened tongues, to say nothing of our morals."

Schiller's observations were a global recasting of populist-elitist arguments. Populists, whose mantra is "Let the people choose," called Schiller hysterical. These populists noted that Hollywood and other Western media products weren't being forced on anyone. People wanted the products. Some elitists countered that traditional values, many going back centuries, were like endangered species and needed protection against Western capitalistic instincts that were smothering them pell-mell. Elitists noted too that the Western media content that was most attractive abroad was hardly the best stuff. *Rambo* was a case in point at the time that Schiller was becoming a best-selling author with his ideas.

Post-Schiller Revisionism.   Schiller's ideas took firmer hold in the 1990s as major U.S. and European media companies extended their reach. MTV and ESPN turned themselves into global brands. The Murdoch empire was flying high as his SkyTV satellite serviced virtually all of Asia plus similar ventures in Europe and Latin America. Hollywood was firmly in place as a reigning international icon. The largest U.S. newspaper, *USA Today*, launched editions in Europe and Asia.

At the same time, cracks were appearing in Schiller's model. Homegrown television production powerhouses in Latin America, like TV Globo in Brazil and Televisa in Mexico, were pumping programs into the United States. In Asia and the Middle East, Western programming ideas were being adapted to local cultures. Countless variations of *American Idol*, for example, from a growing number of independent companies in the Middle East, went on the air in Arabic countries. Pokémon wasn't invented in America, nor was Hello Kitty. Manga comics from Japan have mushroomed into $180 million in U.S. sales, roughly a third of comic sales.

Too, Western media products are adapted to local cultures. Profanities are edited from movies exported to Malaysia. For India, Spider-Man switched his crotch-hugging tights for the traditional billowing Hindu dhoti. He also wears pointy sandals.

By the first decade of the 21st century, the idea of a monolithic Western culture displacing everything else on the globe needed rethinking. Yes, Hollywood was still big globally, but other players were emerging.

Transcultural Enrichment.   Turning the cultural imperialism model on its head has been the British-based Virgin Comics, a Johnny-come-lately to the comic book business. With London capital and Bangalore studios, comics with story lines from Indian religion and mythology have been launched in U.S. and other markets. Other themes were drawn from the epic Sanskrit poem *Ramayana.* Could this be called cultural counter-imperialism?

Adventurer-entrepreneur Richard Branson, who was one of the original masterminds behind Virgin Comics, now Liquid Comics, set his sights far beyond just another product on magazine racks. Aware that the sources for franchise movie series like *Superman, Batman, Spider-Man* and *X-Men* are nearing exhaustion, Branson looked to Indian mythology as a Next Big Thing. The comic *Sudhu*, about a Brit who discovers he was a Hindu holy man in a previous life, became a Virgin movie. John Woo, whose action films include *Reign of Assassin,* cocreated a China-themed story, *Seven Brothers*, for Virgin. Now a digital entertainment company, Liquid Comics uses numerous media platforms to offer films and graphic novels.

The Liquid Comics phenomenon is hardly isolated. Think Al-Jazeera, the Middle Eastern news channel that went global in 2006. Think the Chinese policy to become

Occupy Wall Street. When the loosely organized 99 Percenters began their demonstrations in 2011 against growing and concentrated wealth in the United States, they employed the media devices du jour to do their thing. One technique, in case of arrest, was a pre-programmed message to friends, family and perhaps an attorney that they had been arrested. The messages were sent from their GPS location before police could shut down their calls.

a global player in motion pictures. This can be seen as enriching. Scholar George Steiner has made the point that U.S. and European cultures are the richer for, not corrupted by, the continuing presence of Greek mythology from over 2,000 years ago. Sociologist Michael Tracey points to silent-movie comedian Charlie Chaplin, whose humor traveled well in other cultures: "Was it not Chaplin's real genius to strike some common chord, uniting the whole of humanity?"

APPLYING YOUR MEDIA LITERACY

- How does mass communication connect us to the past, as well as help us resolve diverse contemporary values?

- Can transcultural communication be enriching even if also imperialist? Why or why not?

Behavioral Effects

Study Preview   The overstated magic bullet theory on how mass communication affects people has been perpetuated by advertising. The message is "buy me" or "test me" either immediately or soon. Manipulative advertising can have behavioral effects, although some techniques, like subliminal messages, are overrated and dubious.

Motivational Messages

The 1940s marked the beginning of a confusing period about the effects of mass communication that remains with us. Early magic bullet theories, challenged by Lazarsfeld and others, were falling apart. Even so, as World War II progressed, people had a growing uneasiness about how media might be affecting them. Sinister possibilities were evident in the work of Joseph Goebbels, the minister of propaganda and public enlightenment in Nazi Germany. His mantra for using the media: Tell lies often enough and loudly enough, and they'll be believed. In the Pacific the Japanese beamed the infamous Tokyo Rose radio broadcasts to GIs to lower morale. Then during the Korean war in the early 1950s, a macabre fascination developed with so-called brainwashing techniques used on U.S. prisoners of war. In this same period, the work of Austrian psychiatrist **Sigmund Freud,** which emphasized hidden motivations and repressed sexual impulses, was being popularized in countless books and articles.

No wonder, considering this intellectual context, that advertising people in the 1950s looked to the social sciences to find new ways to woo customers. Among the advertising pioneers of this period was **Ernest Dichter,** who accepted Freud's claim that people act on motivations that they are

Sigmund Freud
Austrian psyciatrist who theorized that the human mind is unconsciously susceptible to suggestion

Ernest Dichter
Pioneered motivational research

MEDIA COUNTERPOINTS: MEDIA IN IMMIGRATION DEBATE

When Arizona Governor Jan Brewer met President Obama to discuss her state's controversial new immigration enforcement law in 2011, one of the protestors outside the White House snapped a photo and posted it on Twitter. Within minutes, the tweet was re-posted on the Illinois Coalition for Immigrant and Refugee Rights' own Twitter feed. Also effective in communicating the immigration cause, especially to people without internet access, has been a text messaging system run by the Reform Immigration for America campaign.

Social media also connect undocumented immigrant youth. They meet on Facebook and share their experiences, fears and hopes. At California State University, Fullerton, students started a Facebook group to protest the Arizona immigration enforcement bill. The group featured photos of members holding signs with the words, "Do I Look Like an Illegal?" The page started with five photos. Before the end of the year there were 1,600 members.

Activists claim that social media have allowed them to re-frame the immigration debate and put it into human terms—being able to see a face in a photo or a video has allowed people to identify with immigrants.

Media, however, have played a second and contradictory role in the U.S. immigration debate.

A report by the Brookings Institution, one of Washington's oldest think tanks, concluded that media make the search for compromise on immigration issues more difficult in Washington.

The report examined how both traditional media and social media covered immigration going back to 1980 with a focus on the extended policy debates. Those debates collapsed. Why?

The Brookings report pointed to three tendencies in media coverage:

- Immigration is a story that has developed gradually over a long period of time. In contrast, media coverage has been episodic. The spikes of coverage have conditioned the public and policymakers to think of immigration as a sudden event, often tinged with crisis.

- Although illegal immigrants have never been more than a third of the foreign-born population in the United States, the government's efforts to control illegal immigration have dominated news coverage. As a result, the public and policymakers associate the influx of foreign-born people with violations of the law, disruption of social norms, and government failures.

- Immigrants, policymakers and advocates have dominated the coverage, depriving the public of news about the labor market, employers and consumers, and the size and characteristics of immigrant flows—and overemphasized the role of government. Audiences with a negative attitude toward immigration who are deprived of this context can readily view immigrants as villains and themselves as victims. This leads to distrust of government.

---

motivational research

Seeks subconscious appeals that can be used in advertising

not aware of. Depth interviewing, Dichter felt, could reveal these motivations, which could then be exploited in advertising messages.

Dichter used his interviewing, called **motivational research,** for automotive clients. Rightly or wrongly, Dichter determined that the American male is loyal to his wife but fantasizes about having a mistress. Men, he noted, usually are the decision makers in purchasing a car. Then, in what seemed a quantum leap, Dichter equated sedans, which were what most people drove, with wives. Sedans were familiar, reliable. Convertibles, impractical for many people and also beyond their reach financially, were focusing on political process and gamesmanship rather than the substance of the issues. The media narrative has left the issue open to exploitation by extremists on both sides.

POINT
Media give voice to strongly felt and well-defined views at either end of the immigration policy spectrum.

COUNTERPOINT
Media tend to emphasize crime, crisis or controversy in covering immigration. This mischaracterizes a massive demographic event that has developed over decades and mostly through legal channels.

DEEPENING YOUR MEDIA LITERACY
Explore The Issue: Can you find an immigration story that explores issues instead of just reporting crime, crisis or controversy?

Dig Deeper: What issues do you think are missing from the media's coverage of immigration?

WHAT DO YOU THINK?
What kind of stories about immigration would you like to read? Do you think pundits add to the debate about immigration in the U.S.? Why hasn't new media done a better job than traditional media in coverage of the immigration debate in America?

The Power of Tweeting. Phone-snapped images of Lafayette Square protestors against immigration laws, near the White House, made the rounds quickly on Twitter. Similar protests with same message, "Do I Look Illegal," soon were mounted all around the country.

The Brookings report concluded that the media response to audience fragmentation and more competition for audience shares was to convey an air of crisis by pouncing on subjects, all with the goal of generating a surge in viewership. That, in turn, heightens public anxieties and impedes the development of consensus by

equated with mistresses—romantic, daring, glamorous. With these conclusions in hand, Dichter devised advertisements for a new kind of sedan without a center door pillar. The hardtop, as it was called, gave a convertible effect when the windows were down. The advertisements, dripping with sexual innuendo, clearly reflected Dichter's thinking: "You'll find something new to love every time you drive it." Although they were not as solid as sedans and tended to leak air and water, hardtops were popular among automobile buyers for the next 25 years.

Dichter's motivational research led to numerous campaigns that exploited sexual images. For Ronson lighters, the flame, in phallic form, was reproduced in extraordinary proportions. A campaign for Ajax cleanser, hardly a glamorous product, had a white knight charging through the street, ignoring law and regulation with a great phallic lance. Whether consumers were motivated by sexual imagery is hard to establish. Even so, many campaigns based on motivational research worked.

To some extent, mass communication can move people to action—at least, to sample a product. This, of course, is far short of brainwashing. Also, the effect is uneven—not everybody buys. And the effect can be short-lived if an advertised product fails to live up to expectations. Seen many pillarless sedans lately?

Jim Vicary
Made dubious subliminal advertising claims

subliminal message
Cannot be consciously perceived

Subliminal Messages

Some concern about mass communication as a hidden persuader was whacky. In 1957, for example, market researcher **Jim Vicary** that he had inserted messages like "Drink Coca-Cola" and "Eat Popcorn" into movies. The messages were flashed too fast to be recognized by the human eye, but, Vicary claimed, were nonetheless recognized by the brain. Prompted by the **subliminal message,** he claimed that people flocked mid-movie to the snack bar. Vicary had

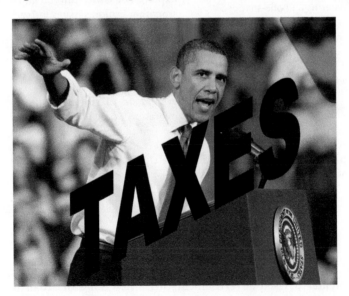

Flashed Message. Master political tactician Karl Rove knows how to get attention for his message. In a web ad opposing President Obama, 39 seconds into the ad, Rove flashed the word TAXES over the President's face for a split second. Rove knows there's no evidence that subliminal messages prompt people to action, but he knew too that reviving the discredited technique would prompt bloggers to pick up the ad and spread his anti-Obama message.

impressive numbers from his experiments, supposedly conducted at a New Jersey movie house. Coke sales increased 18 percent, popcorn almost 60 percent. Vicary's report stirred great interest, and also alarm, but researchers who tried to replicate his study found no evidence to support his claim.

subception
Receiving
subconscious
messages that
trigger behavior

Despite doubts about Vicary's claims, psychologists have identified a phenomenon they call **subception,** in which certain behavior sometimes seems to be triggered by messages perceived subliminally. Whether the effect works outside laboratory experiments and whether the effect is strong enough to prod a consumer to go out and buy are uncertain. Nevertheless, there remains a widespread belief among the general population that subliminal advertising works, and fortunes are being made by people who peddle various devices and systems with extravagant claims that they can control human behavior. Among these are the "hidden" messages in stores' sound systems that say shoplifting is not nice.

David Ogilvy, founder of the Ogilvy & Mather agency, once made fun of subliminal effects claims, pointing out the absurdity of "millions of suggestible consumers getting up from their armchairs and rushing like zombies through the traffic on their way to buy the product at the nearest store." The danger of "Go Taliban" being flashed during the *NBC Nightly News* is remote, and whether it would have any effect is dubious.

APPLYING YOUR MEDIA LITERACY

- What in the mid-20th century American experience contributed to the belief that mass communication can trigger radical changes in our behavior?
- Why does the fraudulent research of Jim Vicary persist as urban legend?

Media-Depicted Violence

Study Preview   Some individuals mimic the aggressive behavior they see in the media, but such incidents are exceptions. Some experts argue, in fact, that media-depicted violence actually reduces real-life aggressive behavior.

Learning About Violence

*observational
learning*
Theory that
people learn
behavior by
seeing it in real
life, in depictions

The mass media help to bring young people into society's mainstream by demonstrating dominant behaviors and norms. This prosocial process, called **observational learning,** turns dark, however, when children learn deviant behaviors from the media. In Manteca, California, two teenagers, one only 13, lay in wait for a friend's father in his own house and attacked him. They beat him with a fireplace poker, kicked him and stabbed him, and choked him to death with a dog chain. Then they poured salt in his wounds. Why the final act of violence—the salt in the wounds? The

13-year-old explained that he had seen it on television. While there is no question that people can learn about violent behavior from the media, a major issue of our time is whether the mass media are the cause of aberrant behavior.

Individuals on trial for criminal acts occasionally plead that "the media made me do it." That was the defense in a 1974 California case in which two young girls playing on a beach were raped with a beer bottle by four teenagers. The rapists told police they had picked up the idea from a television movie they had seen four days earlier. In the movie a young woman was raped with a broom handle, and in court the youths' attorneys blamed the movie. The judge, as is typical in such cases, threw out media-projected violence as an unacceptable scapegoating defense and held the young perpetrators responsible.

Although the courts have never accepted transfer of responsibility as legal defense, it is clear that violent behavior in the media can be imitated. Some experts, however, say that the negative effect of media-depicted violence is too often overstated and that media violence actually has a positive side.

Media Violence as Positive

Aristotle
Defended portrayals of violence

cathartic effect
People release violent inclinations by seeing them portrayed

Seymour Feshbach
Found evidence for media violence as a release

People who downplay the effect of media portrayals of blood, guts and violence often refer to a **cathartic effect.** This theory, which dates to ancient Greece and the philosopher **Aristotle,** suggests that watching violence allows individuals vicariously to release pent-up everyday frustration that might otherwise explode dangerously. By seeing violence, so goes the theory, people let off steam. Most advocates of the cathartic effect claim that individuals who see violent activity are stimulated to fantasy violence, which drains latent tendencies toward real-life violence.

In more recent times, scholar **Seymour Feshbach** has conducted studies that lend support to the cathartic effect theory. In one study, Feshbach lined up 625 junior-high school boys at seven California boarding schools and showed half of them a steady diet of violent television programs for six weeks. The other half were shown nonviolent fare. Every day during the study, teachers and supervisors reported on each boy's behavior in and out of class. Feshbach found no difference in aggressive behavior between the two groups. Further, there was a decline in aggression among boys who had been determined by personality tests to be more inclined toward aggressive behavior.

Opponents of the cathartic effect theory, who include both respected researchers and reflexive media bashers, were quick to point out flaws in Feshbach's research methods. Nonetheless, his conclusions carried a lot of influence because of the study's unprecedented massiveness—625 individuals. Also, the study was conducted in a real-life environment rather than in a laboratory, and there was a consistency in the findings.

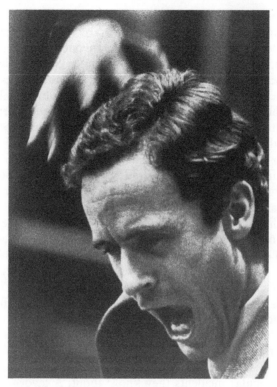

Scapegoating. On the eve of his execution, serial killer Ted Bundy claimed that his violence had been sparked by girlie magazines. Whatever the truth of Bundy's claim, scholars are divided about whether media depictions precipitate violent behavior. At one extreme is the view that media violence is a safety valve for people inclined to violence. At the other extreme is the aggressive stimulation theory that media violence causes real-life violence. The most prevalent thinking, to paraphrase a pioneer 1961 study on television and children, is that certain depictions under certain conditions may prompt violence in certain people.

Prodding Socially Positive Action

Besides the cathartic effect theory, an argument for showing violence is that it prompts people to engage in socially positive action. This happened after NBC aired *The Burning Bed*, a television movie about an abused woman who could not take any more and set fire to her sleeping husband. The night the movie was shown, battered-spouse centers nationwide were overwhelmed by calls from women who had been putting off doing something to extricate themselves from relationships with abusive mates.

On the negative side, one man set his estranged wife afire and explained that he was inspired by *The Burning Bed*. Another man who beat his wife senseless gave the same explanation.

aggressive stimulation
Theory that people are inspired to violence by media depictions

Media Violence as Negative

The preponderance of evidence is that media-depicted violence has the potential to cue real-life violence. However, the **aggressive stimulation** theory is often overstated. The fact is that few people act out media violence in their lives. For example, do you know anybody who saw a murder in a movie and went out afterward and murdered somebody? Yet you know many people who see murders in movies and *don't* kill anyone.

We need to be careful when we talk about aggressive stimulation. Note, for example, the qualifiers used by scholar Wayne Danielson in summing up the conclusion of the 1995–1997 National Television Violence Study: Viewing violence on television tends to increase violent behavior in viewers, more in some situations and less in others. Increased violence can be found only when the circumstances are right and a tendency to imitate what weakens an inner resistance against engaging in violent behavior.

The study concluded that children may be more susceptible than adults to copying media violence, but that too was far, far short of a universal causal statement.

Why, then, do many people believe that media violence begets real-life violence? Some early studies pointed to a causal link. These included the 1960 **Bobo doll studies** of **Albert Bandura,** who showed children a violent movie and then encouraged them to play with oversize, inflated dolls. Bandura concluded that kids who saw the film were more inclined to beat up the dolls than were other kids. Critics have challenged Bandura's methodology and said that he mistook childish playfulness for aggression. In short, Bandura and other aggressive-stimulation scholars have failed to prove their theory to the full satisfaction of other scholars.

When pressed, people who hold the aggressive-stimulation theory point to particular incidents they know about. A favorite is the claim by serial killer Ted Bundy that *Playboy* magazine had led him to stalk and kill women. Was Bundy telling the truth? We will never know. He offered the scapegoat explanation on his way to the execution chamber, which suggests that there may have been other motives. The Bundy case is anecdotal, and anecdotes cannot be extrapolated into general validity.

An alternative to aggressive stimulation theory is a theory that people whose feelings and general view of the world tend toward aggressiveness and violence are attracted to violence in movies, television and other media depictions of violence. This alternative theory holds that people who are violent are predisposed to violence, which is far short of saying that the media made them do it. This leads us to the **catalytic theory,** which sees media-depicted violence as having a contributing role in violent behavior, not a triggering one.

Catalytic Theory

Simplistic readings of both cathartic and aggressive stimulation effects research can yield extreme conclusions. A careful reading, however, points more to the media having a role in real-life violence but not necessarily triggering it and doing so only infrequently—and only if several nonmedia factors are also present. For example, evidence suggests that television and

Bobo doll studies
Kids seemed more violent after seeing violence in movies

Albert Bandura
Found that media violence stimulated aggression in children

catalytic theory
Media violence is among factors that sometimes contribute to real-life violence

movie violence, even in cartoons, is arousing and can excite some children to violence, especially hyperactive and easily excitable children. These children, like unstable adults, become wrapped up psychologically with the portrayals and are stirred to the point of acting out. However, this happens only when a combination of other influences is also present. Among these other influences are:

- **Whether violence portrayed in the media is rewarded.** In 1984 David Phillips of the University of California at San Diego found that the murder rate increases after publicized prizefights, in which the victor is rewarded, and decreases after publicized murder trials and executions, in which, of course, violence is punished.

- **Whether media exposure is heavy.** Researcher Monroe Lefkowitz studied upstate New York third-graders who watched a lot of media-depicted violence. Ten years later, Lefkowitz found that these individuals were rated by their peers as violent. This suggests cumulative, long-term media effects.

- **Whether a violent person fits other profiles.** Studies have found correlations between aggressive behavior and many variables besides viewing violence. These include income, education, intelligence and parental childrearing practices. This is not to say that any of these third variables cause violent behavior. The suggestion, rather, is that violence is far too complex to be explained by a single factor.

Most researchers note, too, that screen-triggered violence is increased if the aggression:

- **Is realistic and exciting,** like a chase or suspense sequence that sends adrenaline levels surging.

- **Succeeds in righting a wrong,** like helping an abused or ridiculed character get even.

- **Includes situations or characters** similar to those in the viewer's own experience.

All these things would prompt a scientist to call media violence a catalyst. Just as the presence of a certain element will allow other elements to react explosively but itself is not part of the explosion, the presence of media violence can be a factor in real-life violence but not be a cause by itself. This catalytic theory was articulated by scholars **Wilbur Schramm,** Jack Lyle and Edwin Parker, who investigated the effects of television on children and came up with this statement in their 1961 book *Television in the Lives of Our Children,* which has become a classic on the effects of media-depicted violence on individuals: "For *some* children under *some* conditions, *some* television is harmful. For *other* children under the same conditions, or for the same children under *other* conditions, it *may* be beneficial. For *most* children, un-

Wilbur Schramm
Concluded that television has minimal effect on children

der *most* conditions, *most* television is *probably* neither particularly harmful nor particularly beneficial."

Societally Debilitating Effects

George Gerbner
Speculated that
democracy is
endangered by
media violence

Media-depicted violence scares far more people than it inspires people to commit violence, and this, according to **George Gerbner,** a leading researcher on screen violence, leads some people to believe the world is more dangerous than it really is. Gerbner calculated that 1 in 10 television characters is involved in violence in any given week. In real life the chances are only about 1 in 100 per *year.* People who watch a lot of television, Gerbner found, see their own chances of being involved in violence nearer the distorted television level than their local crime statistics or even their own experience would suggest. It seems that television violence leads people to think they are in far greater real-life jeopardy than they really are.

The implications of Gerbner's findings go to the heart of a free and democratic society. With exaggerated fears about their safety, Gerbner said, people will demand greater police protection. They are also likelier, he said, to submit to established authority and even to accept police violence as a trade-off for their own security.

Media Violence and Youth

Nobody would argue that Jerry Springer's television talk show is a model of good taste and restraint. In fact, the conventional wisdom is that such shows do harm. But do they? Two scholars at the University of Pennsylvania, Stacy Davis and Marie-Louise Mares, conducted a careful study of 292 high-school students in North Carolina, some from a city and some from a rural area, and concluded from their data that some talk shows may offend people but that evidence is lacking that teenagers are desensitized to aberrant or tawdry behavior.

One issue was whether talk-show viewing desensitizes teenagers to tawdry behavior. The conventional wisdom, articulated by many politicians calling for television reform, is that teenagers are numbed by all the antisocial, deviant and treacherous figures on talk shows. Not so, said Davis and Mares: "Heavy talk-show viewers were no less likely than light viewers to believe that the victims of antisocial behavior had been wronged, to perceive that the victim had suffered, or to rate the antisocial behavior as immoral."

Do talk shows undercut society's values? According to Davis and Mares, Davis and Mares concluded that talk shows actually are conservative. Studio audiences, they noted, boo guests who flout social norms and cheer those who espouse mainstream vales and behavior. These shows actually are "cautionary tales," Davis and Mares said. The result is that teenagers end up with heightened perceptions about how certain behaviors come about and the seriousness the social issues are.

Tolerance of Violence

desensitizing theory
Tolerance of real-life violence grows because of media-depicted violence

An especially serious concern about media-depicted violence is that it has a numbing, callousing effect on people. This **desensitizing theory,** which is widely held, says not only that individuals are becoming hardened by media violence but also that society's tolerance for such antisocial behavior is increasing.

Media critics say that the media are responsible for this desensitization, but many media people, particularly movie and television directors, respond that it is the desensitization that has forced them to make the violence in their shows even more graphic. They explain that they have run out of alternatives to get the point across when the story line requires that the audience be repulsed.

Some movie critics, of course, find this explanation a little too convenient for gore-inclined moviemakers and television directors, but even directors who are not inclined to gratuitous violence feel that their options for stirring the audience have become scarcer. The critics respond that this is a chicken-or-egg question and that the media are in no position to use the desensitization theory to excuse including more and more violence in their products if they themselves contributed to the desensitization. And so the argument goes on about who is to blame.

Desensitization is apparent in news also. In 2004 the New York *Times,* traditionally cautious about gore, showed a photo of victims' corpses hanging from a bridge in war-torn Iraq. Only a few years earlier there had been an almost universal ban on showing the bodies of crime, accident and war victims in newspapers and on television newscasts. Photos of U.S. troops torturing Iraqi prisoners, integral in telling a horrible but important story, pushed back the earlier limits. No mainstream media showed the videotaped beheading of U.S. businessman Nick Berg by terrorists in Iraq, but millions of people found the gruesome sequence online. This desensitizing did not come suddenly with the Iraq war and its aftermath, but the war has clearly established new ground rules.

It is undeniable that violence has had a growing presence in the mass media, which makes even more poignant the fact that we know far less about media violence than we need to. What do we know? Various theories explain some phenomena, but the theories themselves do not dovetail. The desensitizing theory, for example, explains audience acceptance of more violence, but it hardly explains research findings that people who watch a lot of television actually have heightened anxiety about their personal safety. People fretting about their own safety are hardly desensitized.

Violence Studies

The mass media, especially television and movies that deal in fiction, depict a lot of violence. Studies have found as many as six violent acts per hour on prime-time network television. In and of itself, that may seem a lot, but a study at the University of California, Los Angeles, operating on the premise that the issue should not be how much violence is depicted but the context in which it occurs, came to a less startling conclusion: Slapstick comedic violence shouldn't be lumped with graphic homicide in counting depictions of violence. Nor should a violent storm.

Violence Assessment Monitoring Project
Conducted contextual nonviolence studies and found less serious media depictions than earlier thought

The UCLA research, called the **Violence Assessment Monitoring Project,** concluded in its first year that distressing human violence was much less prevalent than earlier studies had counted. Of 121 prime-time episodes, only 10 had frequent violence and only eight had occasional violence. This was after comedic violence and nonhuman violence, such as hurricanes, were screened out. The next year, 1996, found violence in only five prime-time shows—half the number of the year before. Also, most of the shows didn't survive the season. In 1998, the number was down to two series.

William McQuire
Found most media violence research flawed

The UCLA study added sophistication to Gerbner's counting acts of media-depicted violence but still didn't assess whether the violence affected people. In 1986 scholar **William McQuire** reviewed the literature on mediated violence and found that hardly any of the studies' evidence was statistically reliable. The exception was controlled laboratory studies, for which the statistics were more meaningful but did not indicate much causality.

APPLYING YOUR MEDIA LITERACY

■ Why do the courts refuse to excuse violent criminals who blame their behavior on media-depicted violence?

■ What variables contribute to a person's proneness for violence after an experience with media-depicted violence?

■ Recall someone from your experience whose media experience has led to an elevated and unwarranted concern for their personal safety. What can be done about this?

■ How can it be argued that media portrayals of deviant behavior discourage real-life deviance?

■ What difficulty do researchers have in measuring violent media content?

CHAPTER WRAPUP

Effects Theories (Pages 143–147)
Early mass communication scholars assumed that media messages had powerful and direct impacts on people. At an extreme, the bullet theory said the media could immediately affect behavior. Further scholarship found that the bullet theory was simplistic and vastly overstated the effects of mass

communication. This does not mean that the media are without effect but that the dynamics of the effects generally are gradual over time.

Lifestyle Effects (Pages 147–152)
In most of the world, mass media are integrated into people's lives from the cradle. In fact, media have a large role in initiating children into society by instilling cultural values. It is worth asking whether the media's role in childhood development is good, bad or neutral. The answer is not obvious. It can be said, however, that media reflect existing cultural values. This reflection, because values are in continuing flux, means that media content includes a rich mix of values. The mix includes traditional values as well as challenges to tradition.

Attitude Effects (Pages 152–158)
Mass messages bring information and opinions to large numbers of people, in effect setting an agenda and conferring status on issues. What is missed by the media generally doesn't get on the public radar. But what are the effects of media content on attitudes and opinions? Scholars know a lot about the effect of stereotypes, which, when repeated, can have a compounding effect. Also, there is a copycat factor, at least for superficial issues like fashion and style. Which celebrity haircut will be the rage tomorrow? On more significant issues, shifts in attitudes and opinions generally are gradual.

Cultural Effects (Pages 158–163)
Cultural values of dominant societies, as depicted in mass media content, have had unmistakable effects on developing societies. The extent of this so-called cultural imperialism can be debated, as can whether the effects are good, bad or nil. The export of dominant cultural values has been mitigated by the rise of indigenous media in developing countries, but there remains a lot of transcultural influence, some with content that imitates content from other countries and also the direct importation of content.

Behavioral Effects (Pages 163–167)
Advertising research has found ways to tap into consumer psyches, sometimes with tactics so subtle as to be unrecognized for what they are. Precise control on hidden persuasion, however, is impossible. The larger the audience, the more exponentially the degree of influence decreases. Even so, a mythology exists about the effect of hidden persuasion. The power of subliminal communication has never been demonstrated conclusively to be a trigger of behavior. This is not to say, however, that media content has no effect on behavior. Media depictions of unacceptable behavior, especially when widely publicized, can have a dampening effect on such behavior. Also, media campaigns that explicitly encourage certain behaviors, as in Ad Council public-service announcements, can have an impact, albeit one that is difficult to measure.

Media-Depicted Violence (Pages 167–174)
Media-depicted violence has been around forever. Read any Shakespeare lately? Despite anecdotal stories and testimony that "the media made me do it," scholars have come up empty in confirming the claim that media-depicted violence causes mentally healthy people to commit real-life violence. In fact, there is a line of reasoning dating to Aristotle

that says witnessing violence sways people away from committing violence. There are, however, people, including the mentally deranged, who are susceptible to what's called aggressive stimulation. Research goes both ways on whether children are moved to violence by seeing it. The classic study on the issue says some children may be affected some of the time in some circumstances. That hardly is a firm conclusion of a predictable causal effect.

THINKING CRITICALLY

1. Why has the bullet theory of mass communication effects lost support? What has replaced the bullet theory?
2. How is the role of mass messages in childhood development changing?
3. What are examples of the influence of mass communication on attitudes and opinions?
4. How has advertising perpetuated myths about the effects of mass communication?
5. What continues to fuel magic bullet theory beliefs about immediate, powerful effects of mass messages, including subliminal messages?
6. Identify and discuss different ideas about the effects of media-depicted violence.

MEDIA VOCABULARY

agenda-setting (Page 145)
aggressive stimulation (Page 169)
Bobo doll studies (Page 170)
bullet model (Page 144)
catalytic theory (Page 170)
cathartic effect (Page 168)
contemporary transmission (Page 159)
cultural imperialism (Page 160)
cumulative effects theory (Page 146)
desensitizing theory (Page 173)
diffusion of innovations (Page 159)
historical transmission (Page 158)
minimalist effects theory (Page 145)
motivational research (Page 164)
multistep flow (Page 145)
narcoticizing dysfunction (Page 146)
observational learning (Page 167)
opinion leaders (Page 145)
powerful effects theory (Page 143)
prosocial (Page 150)
role modeling (Page 153)
socialization (Page 147)
spiral of silence (Page 147)
stereotyping (Page 155)

subception (Page 167)
subliminal messages (Page 166)
third person effect (Page 144)
two-step flow (Page 145)

MEDIA SOURCES

Steven J. Kirsh. *Children, Adolescents, and Media Violence: A Critical Look at the Research,* 2nd edition. Sage, 2011. Kirsh, a child developmental psychologist, reviews research on the effects of media-related violence on children, including internet aggression, violent music, and teen suicide.

Catherine A. Luther, Carolyn Ringer Lepre and Naeemah Clark. *Diversity in U.S. Media.* Wiley-Blackwell, 2011. The authors, all scholars, examine the roots and evolution of how social groups are portrayed.

Dorothy G. Singer and Jerome L. Singer. *Handbook of Childen and the Media,* 2nd edition. Sage, 2011. The authors, both research psychologists, examine research on children's use of media, including smart phones, iPods, iPads, digital readers, social networks, and Skype, and the effects of cyber-bullying, sexting, and violent video games.

John Gosling. *Waging The War of the Worlds: A History of the 1938 Radio Broadcast and Resulting Panic.* McFarland, 2009. Includes original script. Gosling's almost life-long interest in the broadcast has led to a thorough review of the people behind the program and variations and translations in other countries

Cass R. Sunstein. *On Rumors. How Falsehoods Spread, Why We Believe Them, What Can Be Done.* Farrar, Straus & Giroux. 2009. Sunstein, a Harvard legal scholar, argues that internet communication has compounded the dangerous potency of rumors to undermine public confidence in political leadership and thus erode functioning democracy. Sunstein, an adviser to President Obama, offers examples, many political, in advancing his thesis.

Brenda R. Weber. *Makeover TV: Selfhood, Citizenship and Celebrity.* Duke University, 2009. Weber, a gender scholar, studied 2,000 television programs with self-reinvention themes for lessons on cultural desires and fears.

Lisa Blackman and Valerie Walkerdine. *Mass Hysteria: Critical Psychology and Media Studies.* Palgrave, 2001. Blackman and Walkerdine draw on numerous psychology theories to examine the relationship between psychology and the mass media.

Chapter Nine

Ethical Practices

1. As in most other professions, journalists find that there are few, if any, moral absolutes; even "tell the truth" is not something that can be strictly observed when telling the truth would do more harm than good.

2. Honesty is at the heart of the journalistic process; journalists should be honest not only about the information they present but also about their motivations.

3. Journalists should treat their audiences with respect.

4. The basic job of the journalist is to gather important and interesting information, put that information in a form acceptable to the medium for which the journalist works, and disseminate information to an audience.

5. One approach to journalistic ethics is to examine the loyalties that journalists have to their news organizations, their audiences, their professional colleagues, and themselves.

6. Plagiarism: using the work of another person and presenting it as your own without giving any credit.

7. Conflict of interest: a situation in which a journalist may have divided loyalties, a loyalty to the profession and a loyalty outside the profession; this conflict might prevent the journalist from presenting information honestly.

Vignette

On the afternoon of September 11, 2001, in the midst of a day of trauma, newspaper editors found that among the many pictures coming out of New York were shots of the World Trade Center before it collapsed with small black dots next to it. Those dots, while indistinct, were people who in desperation had jumped from the burning and falling towers. They were only a second or two away from death. The pictures were some of the most horrific of a horrific day. Editors across the country debated on where those pictures should be printed in the next day's edition of newspaper.

In order to investigate corruption in city and state government, the Chicago Sun-Times *secretly buys a downtown bar it names the Mirage. Reporters and editors run the bar and, thus, have to deal with inspectors and other officials governing such a business. They secretly record and photograph many of those officials taking bribes and payoffs rather than enforcing the legal regulations on the bar's owners. When the newspaper publishes a series detailing what has happened, a number of officials are indicted and eventually pay fines or go to jail.*

The committee that awards the Pulitzer prizes, the highest awards in journalism, decides not to give the award to the Sun-Times *because it used deception in getting the stories.*

A high school principal announces that students, when they leave campus in the afternoon, should not enter a convenience store just down the street from the school. He says the school has received complaints from the store's owners about all the students flooding in there in the afternoons. A couple of students on the school newspaper staff ask the owners of the store about these complaints, and they seem surprised. They say they have never complained to the principal about the school's students. In fact, they welcome the students in their store.

At the next meeting of the newspaper staff, the students debate whether or not they should write a story about this situation for the next edition of the newspaper.

Basketball star Kobe Bryant is accused of rape by a woman in Colorado. The accusation is shocking because Bryant has a reputation of quiet living and loyalty to his family. Bryant at first denies the accusation but later admits that he had sex with the woman. The sex, he says, was consensual. Most traditional news media organizations do not publish the names of rape victims or people who bring charges of rape. Because of Bryant's celebrity status, however, great attention is given to this charge, and the woman's name is broadcast over talk radio. She is identified on several nonnews web sites, where details about her life can also be found. Every time a story about the case occurs, professional journalists have to decide whether or not to use her name and must face questions about what good they are doing by withholding her name.

An investigation by the St. Paul Pioneer-Press *finds that several members of the University of Minnesota basketball team have received too much academic help from one of their tutors. The tutor has regularly written English themes and other papers for the students. The newspaper's investigation has also shown that the university has been investigating this situation but has not made it public or reported it to the National Collegiate Athletic Association, the organization that enforces rules concerning athletics in colleges and universities.*

The newspaper publishes the story on the day before the team is to play its first game of the NCAA tournament. Four of the team members are suspended, and the team—even though heavily favored—loses the game and is out of the tournament. Many readers become angry with the newspaper, and some even cancel their subscriptions.

A pitcher for the hometown baseball team is having a good day. A great day, as a matter of fact. He has a no-hitter going into the bottom of the eighth inning. With two outs, the hitter hits a ground ball to the right of the first baseman. The infielder dives for the ball, knocks it down and keeps it close by, but he can't pick it up to throw the runner out. The play is officially scored an error, and the pitcher's no-hitter stays intact. He finishes the game without giving up any other hits and, thus, has a no-hitter to his credit. While he is cheered wildly, many of the discerning baseball fans believe that the hitter should have been given a hit in the eighth inning. They think the official scorer made a mistake. The official scorer is a sportswriter for the local newspaper, and he is covering the game for his newspaper, but his story the next day does not mention that he made a controversial call.

A police reporter for a small-town newspaper goes through arrest reports at the city police station. She is putting together a list that the newspaper publishes regularly. The list does not include names, only that arrests were made and what the charges are. On one of the reports is a name she recognizes. It's the minister at her church, who was arrested and charged with soliciting a male prostitute. Several other arrests were made that same night with the same charge. All of the arrests were made late at night in a downtown park that, during the day, is popular with many people, including mothers who bring their children to play on the park's extensive playground equipment. It is obvious to the reporter that the police have conducted a raid on the late-night activities in the park. This is a real story, she thinks.

Be good. Do right.

What mother has not admonished her children with these simple commands?

Most of us have learned about morality and moral behavior at a very early age. It was one of the big jobs of our parents or whoever was raising us to teach us what is acceptable behavior in a civil society. Many of the rules of moral behavior stem from religious training, but even if religion was not involved, we still learned that there were some basic tenants that we needed to follow to be good citizens and good people. We learned, we thought, the difference between right and wrong.

But did we?

As we grew up, we began to realize that maybe we did not know the difference between right and wrong as well as we thought. Life was complicated because people we knew to be good sometimes did things with which we disagreed. We learned that we could not be completely honest at all times. We were told to eat our aunt's cookies and tell her they were good, even though they tasted like cardboard, because if we did not, she would get her feelings hurt. We were told that when our friends did something wrong, we should not tell on them because nobody liked a "tattler." The moral absolutes that we began learning as small children were chipped away by life's real situations.

At some point, we learned that "being good" was not as easy as it sounds and "doing right" was no simple thing after all.

The Good Journalist

Life's many moral dilemmas, large and small, are reflected in the practice of journalism, as the situations described at the beginning of this chapter demonstrate. Journalists do not have an easy time in deciding what the right thing to do is. They have certain principles to which they try to adhere, but like the rest of us have discovered these principles are rarely absolute or applicable in every situation. The human condition demands that they be refined and sometimes shaped to the situation at hand.

So journalists, like the rest of us (we hope), strive to do the right thing. Quite often they are put in uncomfortable situations in which they have to choose between two or more good or moral principles that they will follow. Sometimes they have to choose between two bad things and have to decide which action would be worse. Most journalists try to make these decisions based on a commonly accepted set of practices and overlapping principles that includes the following.

Honesty

Being honest lies at the heart of journalistic attitudes and practices. Journalists attempt to present information based on facts to an audience. They are also obligated in many instances to tell the audience the source of these facts so the audience can have some basis on which to judge the facts. So, the outcome of what a journalist does should be an honest outcome.

That outcome, however, has an additional obligation. Journalists must be honest about who they are and what they are doing. Journalists should identify themselves and should make sure that people around them understand who they are and how they work. If someone is going to be quoted in a news article, the journalist is required to make it clear that this is the case before the person has said very much. If the journalist promises a person that he or she will not be quoted or that the person's name will not be used in a news article, the journalist is obligated to keep that promise. Many journalists have done this at great personal cost, including spending time in jail when a judge ordered them to reveal the name of an anonymous source.

Professional Practice

Journalists are expected to follow professional standards in practices. Some of those practices were referred to in the previous paragraphs, such as making sure that people know who they are and keeping confidences when they are given.

Professional practices also include trying to approach reporting, writing, and editing without an attitude that would limit or slant news coverage of a subject or event. A reporter who personally opposes abortion, for instance, is still obligated to seek out those who may favor abortion if that is at all relevant to the story. Political, personal, or religious feelings should be set aside, as much as possible, when journalists are pursuing a story.

Journalists are particularly obligated to allow people who may be disadvantaged by a story to have their say. If a source accuses someone of anything negative—from criminal acts to bad attitudes to incompetence—the person against whom the accusation is made should have ample opportunity to answer those accusations. Reporters are expected to take extra steps in the reporting process to be sure that this occurs.

Another part of professional practice expects journalists to take credit only for the original material they produce. Journalists should not copy the work of others without giving proper and appropriate credit to the source. In the same manner, journalists and news organizations are expected to acknowledge and correct errors quickly and appropriately. They should not try to cover up or explain away their mistakes.

Respect

Journalists should respect their audiences, the people with whom they deal, and each other.

The concept of respect is covered to some extent in some of the situations that we have just discussed. Journalists should be open not only to the information that people have but also to their attitudes and points of view. They should be appropriately empathetic and sympathetic.

Journalists should understand how others see the news process and product. Many people regard journalists as intrusive, and they do not want to be in the news or subject to the attention of journalism. They are uncomfortable being in the limelight. For example, when Gerald Ford was president in the mid-1970s, his life was saved by a California man who saw that a woman was trying to shoot him. The man grabbed the gun from her. That act thrust the man onto the national spotlight and made him the subject of much investigation by reporters. Despite his pleas to be left alone, details about his life were found and published, including the facts that he was a homosexual and that he had a history of mental problems. After this information was made public, it was generally acknowledged that reporters had gone too far and should have respected the man's wishes.

Journalists are often accused of arrogance—essentially, of not having respect for others outside the profession. They are in a position to be arrogant for a number of reasons, the chief being that the First Amendment and other laws protect them from having to answer legally for most of what they do. For example, the fact that a person does not want his or her name published in the newspaper carries no legal weight. An editor can publish a name without consent, and the person has no recourse.

In addition to their legal position, the social and economic position of journalists can also spawn arrogance. Most daily newspapers in the country are monopolies; that

FIGURE 9.1 **Lunging into the Public Eye** Oliver "Billy" Sipple (left) dives toward a woman who had just taken a shot at President Gerald Ford on September 22, 1975, outside a San Francisco hotel. Sipple grabbed the gun, wrestled it away from her, and was later regarded as a hero. When Ford took three days to thank Sipple, the *San Francisco Chronicle* ran a story speculating that it was because he was a homosexual. Sipple, an ex-Marine, had kept his homosexuality from his family, but once the story was out, his father in Detroit never spoke to him again. Sipple sued the newspaper but the case was dismissed. Sipple lapsed into obesity and alcoholism and died alone in 1989.

is, they do not have any direct competition in their immediate area. Likewise, other media do not have to be directly responsive to individual complaints. Consequently, when people outside media organizations bring complaints or suggestions, they are not always satisfied with the response. Media professionals seem reluctant to admit mistakes or to acknowledge that there may be a point of view that is different from their own. For their part, media professionals often argue that theirs is a difficult job and that people outside the profession sometimes do not understand the procedures they must follow. Whatever the case, media people have a reputation of being unresponsive and disrespectful—a reputation that, justified or not, needs careful and constant attention.

An Approach to Ethical Behavior

Scholars and philosophers have attempted to outline many approaches to ethical behavior over the centuries, and some modern media scholars have tried to adapt these approaches to the profession of journalism. Such attempts have been occasionally interesting because the situations that journalists face involve substantive questions that many people find relevant. However, these approaches have often been ultimately dissatisfying. They are not easily applicable to the fast-paced world in which journalists work, where decisions to publish or not publish are made with few moments to spare and are often based on incomplete information.

In discussing ethical behavior, it is perhaps more productive to talk about the loyalties that journalists have to their audience, their organizations or employers, their profession, and themselves. These loyalties exert themselves simultaneously and usually harmoniously as the journalist works. Occasionally, however, these loyalties come into conflict, and the dilemma for journalists is choosing which loyalty is most important.

The basic job of journalists is to disseminate information to an audience. Journalists do not get paid, nor do news media organizations make money, by not gathering information or by withholding that information from the audience. Most journalists believe that their first duty is to their audience, and that duty is to give the audience as much information as possible. In most situations, the inclination of journalists will be to say as much as possible by finding an acceptable way to tell the audience what they know.

The information that journalists have should be properly vetted, of course. That is, it should be as full and as accurate as possible given proper journalistic procedures. The information should also be in a form that is appropriate for the medium and expected by the audience. Given that, however, disseminating information is the first duty of the journalist, and no journalist feels good about keeping information away from the audience.

Another strong loyalty that journalists feel is to their employer or news organization. Part of this loyalty stems from the fact that the news organization is providing their livelihood, and journalists—like anyone else—normally would not want to jeopardize the source of their income. But the sense of loyalty goes deeper than this. Journalists view their news organizations as the embodiment of the profession and understand the value of keeping it healthy. The news organization has rules and procedures that become the mode of practice for journalists who work there. Journalists who work for these organizations have accepted these procedures and are willing to abide by them at least for the term of their employment. Doing so is a way of preserving the stability of the profession and maintaining professional standards.

An additional element in the journalist's loyalty to the news organization is personal loyalty that develops among those who work together in an organization. Journalists who share their experiences (as well as work space, meals, and bits of information about their personal lives) often grow close to one another, help each other out, and defend each other against criticism from those outside the organization. Journalists may also develop personal loyalties to editors for whom they work. (None of this is unique to journalism, of course. Such personal loyalties can develop within any organization.)

What Do You Think? 9.1

LOYALTY TO WHAT?

The U.S. invasion of Iraq during the spring of 2003 provoked predictable reactions. Many people across the country favored the invasion and stood behind the Bush administration's decision to start the war. But many people opposed it just as strongly, and some even took to the streets. Almost every major city in the nation witnessed crowds in some prominent area, gathered to protest the war.

One of the largest demonstrations was in San Francisco. One of the people at that demonstration was Henry Norr, a technology columnist for the *San Francisco Chronicle*. He was there as a participant, not as a reporter. As a technology writer, Norr does not delve into many political issues.

Should he have been there?

The editors of the *Chronicle* did not think so, and they fired him. That set off a legal dispute that Norr and the *Chronicle* finally settled many months later. Details of the settlement were not disclosed, but Norr did not get his job back.

Should the newspaper's editors have fired him?

The paper's decision was defended by Dick Rogers, the *Chronicle*'s public editor, who argued that newspapers do not have a lot of credibility with the public and that they need to preserve what they have.

"If it were up to me, I'd take a cue from the Old West hotels that told gunslingers to check their weapons with the front desk clerk. Only the sign over the entrance to the *Chronicle* would read: 'Check your activism at the door.'"

But others argued that Norr had a First Amendment right to be a citizen, and the paper should encourage, not penalize, that. After all, the newspaper is produced under the auspices of the First Amendment. Beside, critics of the paper pointed out, Norr would have had the opinions he held whether or not he showed up at a public demonstration.

So what do you think? Should the newspaper have fired him?

And what about Norr? Should he have demonstrated knowing his newspaper's policies?

This description is not to say that all journalists are happy with their jobs or content with their organizations. Many journalists develop serious reservations about the approach their organizations take to covering the news and other journalistic methods. Even when that occurs, however, journalists understand the value of organizational loyalty and usually adhere to it in some form.

Loyalty to the profession is another means by which journalists work through ethical dilemmas. Most people who commit themselves to journalism believe that they are doing something good for society. They have accepted the norms and procedures that are the standard practice of journalism because these have been developed over a long period of time. Many of these procedures, customs, and expectations exercise great influence on the thinking and behavior of journalists.

Finally, the profession of journalism allows a good deal of latitude for journalists to be loyal to themselves and their beliefs and attitudes and moral framework. Journalists are expected to bring to the profession a sense of honesty, integrity, and morality that will govern their actions both as they are working in the profession and as they are conducting their personal business. The profession generally does not expect them to act against personal moral precepts.

Again, none of this should lead to the impression that everyone in the profession is a paragon of moral virtue. Journalists have all of the personal failings that other people in society exhibit. But however they may fail in their personal standards, they are expected to have a good idea of what they should do in order to act humanely and morally. This sense also serves as a guide to making ethical decisions.

Ethical Difficulties

Modern journalists are most likely to confront ethical dilemmas in a number of areas described in this section. In some, the choices are fairly clear as to what the profession expects, and journalists who violate these expectations simply make the wrong choices. In other areas, however, the choices are not so clear, and the choices journalists make are open to debate.

Falsifying Information

Journalists should not make things up. They should not create "facts" that do not exist. They should not put words into the mouths of people who did not say them. They should not extend assumptions into information unless that information can be independently verified. The first duty of the journalist is to present true and accurate information. Nothing about the profession, it would seem, should be clearer.

Yet the journalism of this new century has been filled with stories of reporters who simply made up information. One of the most prominent of those stories is that of Jayson Blair, a young man of obvious talent, who was identified by editors of the *New York Times* as an excellent reporter and writer and for many month was given excellent and important assignments. Blair, it seems, could always get information that other reporters could not discover. He could talk with people whom others could not find. Some editors did have doubts about his methods and abilities, but because he seemed to be favored by the top editors at the paper, these doubts were not explored.

Finally, in late April 2002, an editor of the *San Antonio Express-News* emailed the *Times* saying that information in one of Blair's stories was "disturbingly similar" to information that had appeared in his newspaper earlier in the month. That set off an investigation of Blair by the *Times* that resulted in his resignation and even the resignation of Howell Raines, the executive editor of the newspaper. Blair's deception and falsification might not be worth noting had it been an isolated incident, but the profession has been peppered with stories about reporters making up information or citing sources that turned out not to be verifiable. The fact is that violation of one of journalism's most basic tenants—presenting accurate information—is a continuing problem for the profession, and the reasons for it often mystify those who are steeped in professional principles.

Plagiarism

A related problem that haunts journalism is plagiarism— the copying of the work of another and presenting it as one's own. Jayson Blair had committed this sin against the profession, too, and that is how he was caught, but again, he is not the only one.

One of the fundamental procedures of journalism is that information is presented so that readers and viewers have an idea of its source. The basic assumption of this presentation is that the journalist has gathered the information, and what is not directly attributed is a product of the journalist's observation or experience. When journalists take the words and ideas of others and use them so they appear to be the creation of the journalist, that's plagiarism.

Plagiarism, like falsification, is a cardinal sin against the profession. Few people who get caught doing these deeds have much of a future in journalism. They cannot be trusted.

Conflicts of Interest

Less clear-cut for journalists than falsification or plagiarism is the area of conflict of interest. Journalists are supposed to be independent observers, working for a news organization and no one else. Some journalists take this sense of independence to extremes by not joining any social or civic organizations; a few even declare that they will not vote or participate in politics in any way.

Yet most journalists seek to balance their professional demands with the desire to be active and participating members of their communities. They join religious, social, civic, and even political organizations. Editors and publishers are actively sought after as members of civic and even commercial boards of directors. They have an expertise and community-wide view that few others have. Some editors have even been known to run for and hold public office (something that most in the profession would disapprove of).

So, how can journalists balance these conflicting loyalties—the loyalty to the profession and the loyalty to the desire to be a good citizen and a contributing part of the community?

Most journalists do this by trying to separate their personal activities from the organizations and events that they cover. For example, a journalist who is a member of a church that finds itself in the news would be expected not to have anything to do with the coverage of the story. Journalists are also expected to report (and get approval for) any employment they have outside of the news organization.

News organizations, of course, cannot monitor all of the activities of their reporters and editors, and they depend on their employees to be honest and forthright about what they do. Journalists are expected to inform their editors when situations arise in which there may be conflicts of interest. A journalist's loyalty to the news organization requires that he or she not put the organization in jeopardy or open the organization to criticism by allowing a conflict of interest to develop.

Another clear tenet of journalistic procedure is that reporters and editors should not accept compensation from any individual or organization for a news story other than the news organization they are working for. Journalists are rarely offered money to do a story, but they are offered many other types of gifts and gratuities. Theme parks and recreational destinations regularly give free travel and accommodations to travel writers. Movie theaters give tickets to reviewers. Promoters of sports events not only give sports writers tickets but also offer special accommodations during the event, such as certain rooms where food and drinks are free. Most news organizations have specific rules about what reporters can accept; sometimes it is an item or service that is less than $10 in value. That would preclude even being taken to lunch by someone with an interest in a story or the coverage of events. Even with the rules, however, news organizations have to rely on the honesty of the reporters to turn down such gifts or report them when they are made.

Privacy

Another area that creates ethical dilemmas for journalists is the privacy of individuals they cover. Although privacy does have some force as a legal concept (see Chapter 3), journalists generally do not get involved with the legalities of privacy. As long as journalists obtain information legally—that is, they do it without trespassing or stealing—they generally will suffer no legal consequences by publishing it.

But the human aspect of publishing information about people or even using their names does—and should—give journalists pause. As we mentioned earlier in this chapter, many people do not seek the limelight and are uncomfortable with having their names published or broadcast. They would prefer that they not be the objects of attention by journalists or the reading and viewing public. These people get caught up in news situations, and journalists, in order to do their jobs, must seek information from and about them.

When these situations are depicted in movies or television dramas, journalists are often depicted as rude, obnoxious, and unfeeling. The reality is usually quite different. Occasionally, journalists are persistent, but they often try to respect the wishes of those caught in news situations. They find there is little point in trying to persuade an unwilling source to talk or give information. Resourceful reporters know that there are many ways to get information, and harassing an individual is unnecessary and counterproductive.

Sometimes journalists face the decision of publishing very private or embarrassing information about an individual. The most publicized instances have concerned sexual activities of presidents or presidential candidates, but other instances of publishing private information pose dilemmas for journalists. Reporters and editors must decide if such information is relevant and necessary to present an accurate and fair picture of the people and events in a story. These decisions are easier when the people involved have thrust themselves before the public by running for public office or participating willingly in public debates.

Bias, Unfairness, Selective Reporting

When most people think about bias and the news media, they are likely thinking about some kind of political bias. For years the news media have been tagged as more "liberal" than their moderate or conservative audience, even though there is much evidence that conflicts with this perception. The more common and persistent problem with bias is not political, however, but what we might call "point-of-view" bias, and it does not have much to do with politics.

Every reporter approaches every story with a point of view, not necessarily political but one based on experience and inclinations. Journalistic procedure requires that reporters go through certain steps to gather information and talk to certain people. Usually these sources are experts or officials involved with the subject the reporter is covering. Which sources the reporter chooses or has the opportunity to interview will greatly influence the outcome of the story, more so than any political bias that the reporter has.

Reporters generally seek to include as many points of view about a controversial topic as they can in their stories. They try to get different versions of an event that they do not personally witness. They try to quote people as accurately as they can, even though most reporters do not have a good shorthand note-taking system. In doing all of these things, a reporter constantly exercises personal judgments about the information being gathered. The reporter has to make selections about what to use in a story and what to leave out. If an editor is particularly interested in a story, the editor's views about what is included will also come into play. Considerations of time and space—how close is the deadline, how much room is available for the story—are also influential in this selection process.

The outcome of this process is not always satisfactory to news consumers who are part of a story or vitally interested in it. They will complain that the story is biased, especially if it does not include their opinion or point of view. In a sense, they are correct. As reporters and editors select information—even as they select what stories and subjects they will cover—they are exhibiting a bias that leans toward their own inclinations about what is important and what their news organizations, given that they have limited resources, can do.

Journalists struggle with these dilemmas every day. The decisions they make are often ones of expediency given that they work under deadline pressure and in a competitive environment. Undoubtedly, they have their personal points of view about the events they cover, and sometimes those inclinations have a major influence on how stories are presented. But how could it be otherwise? Journalists are humans who attempt to achieve the status of objective observer but rarely succeed.

Persistent Problems

No matter how pure in heart or procedurally careful journalists are, they will never be able to avoid ethical dilemmas. The course of human events and activities makes conflicts and differing points of view inevitable. No system of moral behavior or ethical problem solving will provide the answers that journalists need to meet the day-to-day encounters with these conflicts.

Journalists must begin with a strong sense of personal honesty and integrity. They must understand the loyalties they are expected to exercise and must realize that sometimes journalistic procedures and conventions will bring those loyalties into conflict. They must be sensitive to their own points of view and try at every opportunity to rise above them, acting to advance not themselves but their profession and their audience.

In other words, as their mothers admonished them, they must be good and do right.

QUESTIONS FOR DISCUSSION

1. The chapter says that most journalists try to be ethical, but many people do not believe that. Some think that journalists have other agendas that they follow. What do you think? Do you have any experiences to relate in this regard?
2. Is plagiarism a problem for you or any of your colleagues? What is the nature of the problem? How is it different from the plagiarism difficulties that journalists face?
3. Select one of the situations described at the beginning of this chapter. What loyalties are involved? How do you think the situation should be resolved?
4. One fact of journalistic life that is hardly mentioned in this chapter is that of competition. Journalism is a highly competitive profession. How do you think this competition enters into ethical decision making?

RELATED WEB SITES

APME National Credibility Roundtables Project, www.apme-credibility.org

ASNE Ethics Codes Collection, www.asne.org/ideas/codes/codes.htm

Center for Religion, the Professions, and the Public, http://rpp.missouri.edu

Ethics Connection, www.scu.edu/SCU/Centers/Ethics

Ethics in Journalism, www.spj.org/ethics.asp

Ethics in Public Broadcasting, www.current.org/ethics

Ethics Matters, http://commfaculty.fullerton.edu/lester/writings/nppa.html

FAIR: Fairness and Accuracy in Reporting, www.fair.org

Global Journalism Ethics (World Press Institute), www.macalester.edu/~wpi/ethics.htm

Journal of Mass Media Ethics, http://jmme.byu.edu

Journalism Ethics Cases Online, www.journalism.indiana.edu/Ethics

OJR Section: Ethics, www.ojr.org/ojr/ethics

ONO: Organization of News Ombudsmen, www.newsombudsmen.org

Payne Awards for Ethics in Journalism, http://jcomm.uoregon.edu/departments/payneawards

Poynter Online's Ethics Journal, http://poynteronline.org/column.asp?id=53

Poynter Online's Ethics Resources, http://poynteronline.org/subject.asp?id=32

Poynter Online's Talk about Ethics, http://poynteronline.org/column.asp?id=36

RTNDA Code of Ethics, www.rtnda.org/ethics/coe.shtml

RTNDA Ethics Project and Coverage Guidelines, www.rtnda.org/ethics/fepcg.shtml

Web Resources for Studying Journalism Ethics, www2.hawaii.edu/~tbrislin/ethics/index.html

World Wide Codes of Conduct, www.presswise.org.uk/display_page.php?id=40

READINGS AND REFERENCES

Arant, D. (Ed.). (1999). *Perspectives: Ethics, issues and controversies in mass media.* St. Paul, MN: Coursewise Publishing.

Berkman, R. I., & Shumway, C. A. (2003). *Digital dilemmas: Ethical issues for online media professionals.* Ames, IA: Iowa State University Press.

Berry, D. (Ed.). (2000). *Ethics and media culture.* Woburn, MA: Focal Press.

Bertrand, C.-J. (2000). *Media ethics and accountability systems.* Piscataway, NJ: Transaction Publishers.

Bugeja, M. J. (1995). *Living ethics.* Boston: Allyn and Bacon.

Christians, C. G. (1993). *Good news.* New York: Oxford University Press.

Christians, C. G., et al. (2001). *Media ethics.* White Plains, NY: Longman Publishing Group.

Cohen, E. D., & Elliott, D. (Eds.). (1998). *Journalism ethics: A reference handbook.* Santa Barbara, CA: Abc-Clio.

Day, L. A. (2003). *Ethics in media communications* (4th ed.). Belmont, CA: Wadsworth.

Downie, L. Jr., & Kaiser, R. G. (2002). *The news about the news.* New York: Knopf.

Fallows, J. (1996). *Breaking the news: How the media undermine American democracy.* New York: Pantheon.

Fuller, J. (1996). *News values: Ideas for an information age.* Chicago: University of Chicago Press.

Goodwin, H. E., Smith, R. F., & Goodwin, G. (1999). *Groping for ethics in journalism.* Ames: Iowa State University Press.

Herbert, J. (2002). *Journalism and broadcast ethics.* Woburn, MA: Focal Press.

Iggers, J. (1998). *Good news, bad news: Journalism ethics and the public interest.* Boulder, CO: Westview Press.

Keeble, R. (2001). *Ethics for journalists.* New York: Routledge.

Knowlton, S. R. (1997). *Moral reasoning for journalists.* Westport, CT: Praeger.

Knowlton, S. R., & Parsons, P. R. (Eds.). (1995). *The journalist's moral compass.* Westport, CT: Praeger.

Kovach, B., & Rosenstiel, T. (2001). *The elements of journalism: What newspeople should know and the public should expect.* New York: Crown Publishers.

Leslie, L. Z. (2000). *Mass communication ethics: Decision making in postmodern culture.* Boston: Houghton Mifflin.

Lester, P. M. (1996). *Images that injure: Pictorial stereotypes in the media.* Westport, CT: Praeger.

Limburg, V. E. (1994). *Electronic media ethics.* Boston: Focal Press.

MacDonald, B., & Petheram, M. (1998). *Keyguide to information sources in media ethics.* London: Mansell Publishing.

Matelski, M. J. (1991). *TV news ethics.* Boston: Focal Press.

Patterson, P., & Wilkins, L. (2002). *Media ethics: Issues and cases.* Boston, MA: McGraw-Hill.

Pritchard, D. (Ed.). (2000). *Holding the media accountable: Citizens, ethics, and the law.* Bloomington: Indiana University Press.

Rosenstiel, T., & Mitchell, A. (2003). *Thinking clearly: Cases in journalistic decision-making.* New York: Columbia University Press.

Seib, P. (1994). *Campaigns and conscience: The ethics of political journalism.* Westport, CT: Praeger.

Seib, P., & Fitzpatrick, K. (1997). *Journalism ethics.* Fort Worth: Harcourt Brace.

Weaver, P. H. (1995). *News and the culture of lying: How journalism really works.* New York: The Free Press.

Chapter Ten

YouTube

If text is closest to the oldest permanent form of human communication—the oldest form, period, if we include the cave paintings in Altamira and Lascaux as a kind of picture writing, or etchings on 60,000-year-old ostrich eggs as a form of writing (Lloyd, 2010)—then audiovisual recordings are surely the newest.

Even though the ancient Alexandrians knew about persistence of vision—the characteristic of human perception that keeps images in our vision a split second after they are in front of our eyes, and makes motion pictures possible—motion pictures themselves did not become a mass medium until the 1890s. The first movies back then were voiceless. Talkies arrived in the late 1920s, around the same time television was invented, which did not begin to have a major impact until the late 1940s. But commercial television grew quickly—it still holds the record for fastest rate of growth for a medium in the United States—and was being watched in nearly 90 percent of American homes by the end of the 1950s. VCRs were introduced in the mid-1970s, and cable as an independent source of programming in the early 1980s. The history of audiovisual media prior to YouTube, in other words, only goes back fewer than a hundred fast-moving years.

YouTube was created in February 2005—the work of Chad Hurley, Steve Chen, and Jawed Karim, who had been colleagues at PayPal—and publicly debuted in November 2005. It has certainly thrived on clips from network and cable television, a striking partnership of old and new media. But its most unexpected and long-lasting impact has come from videos made by nonprofession-als, or, rather, by people who are not cable or network television producers. Its trademark, along with the YouTube logo, is "Broadcast Yourself."

Consider, for example, the story of Obama Girl—a YouTube and new new media classic, seen nearly 24 million times as of January 2012, generating videos seen more than 120 million times, and chosen by *Newsweek* as one of the top 10 memes of the decade.

"Obama Girl"

The story of Obama Girl begins in December 2006 on an old medium. *Saturday Night Live*, on NBC television, aired an hilarious skit originally titled "My Dick in a Box." Thanks to the FCC, however, NBC was afraid to broadcast the comical routine with its original wording. "My Dick" was replaced by "Special Treat."

But the singing and dancing with the original wording somehow made its way onto YouTube, where it attracted millions of viewers, likely more in the long run than had seen the bowdlerized skit on television. (Congress has unsuccessfully tried to impose language restrictions on the Internet, and although Bill Clinton actually signed the Communications Decency Act of 1996 into law, it was struck down by the Supreme Court.)

Enter Ben Relles, who, with singer/songwriter Leah Kauffman, had an idea for an answer or a response video to "My Dick in a Box": "My Box in a Box." Answer videos or video responses are a YouTube equivalent of text comments on Facebook, and they give new producers a good way to attract attention by literally appending the response video (if the original video owner approves) to a video that already enjoys a big audience, or large number of views. YouTube also has a thriving text comment section. Popular videos generate thousands of comments, in contrast to a handful of response videos.

"My Box in a Box" did not do nearly as well as the original "My Dick in a Box," which received more than 24 million views in the first six months it was on YouTube (see *Catch Up Lady*, 2007). "Box in a Box" has been taken down and put back up numerous times since then, so its statistics as of January 2012 of nearly 5 million views since its posting in December 2006 are not strictly comparable to "My Dick in a Box." But the numbers were more than enough to get Ben Relles and his team, BarelyPolitical.com, interested in YouTube as a medium to showcase their productions.

Fox's *24* started a new season ("Day Six") in January 2007. Relles and com-pany had an idea for a video, "I've Got a Crush on Jack Bauer" (the charismatic lead character on *24,* played by Kiefer Sutherland). That's the way Kauffman wrote the song. Barack Obama announced he was running for president in February 2007, and that gave Relles the idea that Obama would be an even more exciting object of a video crush than Bauer. Amber Lee Ettinger was brought in to act the smitten part, lip-synching Kauffman's voice. "I've Got a Crush on

Obama" was put up on YouTube in June 2007. It received more than 2.3 million views the first month (Sklar, 2007). Obama Girl became a popular icon. Further video with Obama Girl followed, as well as a bevy of similar or answer videos for other candidates in the 2008 presidential election, including Hillary Clinton and John McCain. When Ben Relles and Amber Lee Ettinger visited my "Intro to Communication and Media Studies" class at Fordham University in September 2007, there wasn't a person in my 120-student class who had not already seen or heard about Obama Girl (Levinson, 2007). Obama Girl returned to YouTube in 2012, with a parody video of "You're the One That I Want" (from *Grease)*, and a takeoff from *Glee,* in which she tells Obama that he'll have to work to win her vote this time (Hayes, 2012). "Glease" (Polipop, 2012) had 75,000 views within a week of its posting in February 2012.

Did Obama Girl have an impact on the 2008 election? Who would admit to voting for a candidate because of a saucy, funny video? But this much is clear: Obama did very well with the under-30-years-of-age voter—in the primaries and the general election—and this was precisely the group that did not go to the polls in the numbers needed by Democratic presidential candidate John Kerry in 2004, and the group that most watched Obama Girl on their computer screens in 2007. And the Obama Girl video went viral at a very early and therefore crucial time in the campaign, when many people were still first learning whatever they could about Barack Obama. The video, at the very least, showed Obama as someone cool, interesting, and attractive.

Linda Wertheimer reported on National Public Radio (June 24, 2008) that the number of voters under age 30 in the 2008 primaries and caucuses across America was two to three times greater than in 2004. Fifty-eight percent of these voters identified themselves as Democratic, and they voted for Obama over Clinton by 3-to-1 margins in states such as Georgia, which Obama won in the 2008 primaries, and 2-to-1 margins for Obama in states such as Pennsylvania, which Obama lost in the 2008 primaries.

The trend held through the November 2008 general election, in which at least 50 percent of 18- to 29-year-olds voted in America for the first time since 1972, and 66 percent of them voted for Obama, "up 12 percent from those who voted for John Kerry in 2004 and 18 percent from those who supported Al Gore in 2000" (Grimes, 2008; see also Dahl, 2008). As we will see in chapter 14, the 2008 "Obama campaign was able to leverage many types of new and social media" (Baird, 2008)— techniques that Republicans as well as Democrats had well mastered by 2012.

YouTube 2008 Presidential Primary Debates

The 2008 presidential campaigns also saw the debut of YouTube primary debates in 2007, in which questions for the candidates were submitted via YouTube video clips. CNN, under whose auspices the candidates assembled to answer the questions, selected the video clips, making these debates a little less than a breath of totally direct democracy, or an example of completely new new media in politics. But the origin of questions directly from American citizens was a significant improvement over questions asked by news commentators, presumably asking questions on our behalf. No doubt some of the questions were coached and perhaps even prepared by surrogates for the candidates. But even with such inevitable abuses, the YouTube debates marked an important step forward in the democratization of the debate and thus the election process.

What follows are my blog posts, entered immediately after the Democratic CNN-YouTube primary debate on July 23, 2007, and the Republican CNN-YouTube primary debate on November 28, 2007:

> The first YouTube/CNN Presidential Debate—this one with the Democrats—just concluded. I said I would wait until I saw it, to say how much of a revolution it was. Having seen it, I think it was revolutionary indeed—and, in fact, as much a leap forward in the debates and democracy as the first presidential debates on television in 1960.
>
> I don't ever recall seeing a debate in either party with such a refreshing, humorous, frank and incisive series of questions. The people asking the questions in the YouTube videos were far more on the money than any panel of experts.
>
> And the candidates rose to the occasion with honest and important answers.
>
> Barack Obama, when asked about whether he is a legitimate African-American candidate—given his access to power—quipped, "Ask the New York cabbies!" (African-Americans unfortunately have a tougher time getting a cab to stop for them and pick them up than Caucasian New Yorkers—I'm Caucasian, I've lived in New York all of my life, and maybe this problem has lessened a little, but it still exists.)
>
> Hillary Clinton, responding to a question about the election of Bush in 2000, responded that, actually, Bush was not elected president.
>
> John Edwards, on health care, gave an impassioned plea for the need for all Americans to have it—he did this even though he had exceeded his time, and Anderson Cooper was trying to cut him off.
>
> Joe Biden answered a YouTube question about gun control, asked by someone who was armed with an automatic weapon, which he called his "baby." Answered Biden: if that's your baby, you need help....
>
> And that's just a sampler.
>
> Even Anderson Cooper, who did seem to unfairly cut off the minor candidates—such as Mike Gravel—more than the major candidates, was in fine form tonight. The final questioner asked each candidate to cite something liked and disliked about the candidate to the left. Kucinich quipped that there was no one standing to his left on the stage (true). Cooper replied—we tried to find someone to your left but there was no one....
>
> There's nothing like the fresh air of democracy to energize a debate and give people clearer choices. There was concern, before the debate, about CNN exercising too much control in choosing the YouTube questions to be shown—I agree that CNN should not have selected the questions, but I don't see how the choices could have been any better.
>
> I'm looking forward to the Republican rendition of this fine experiment—which will become the norm—in September.

But on July 27 I added, with link to new blog post: "Republicans Now Thumb Noses at YouTube as Well as Evolution."

The last line was added because, as of July 27, 2007, only John McCain and Ron Paul had committed to a Republican primary CNN-YouTube debate in September 2007, so CNN was obliged to cancel it. The Republicans eventually did see the YouTube light, and their YouTube debate took place on CNN on November 28, 2007. I posted the following on my blog immediately after the debate:

> I didn't find tonight's Republican YouTube/CNN debate as refreshing and provocative as the first YouTube debate among the Democratic contenders for president a few months ago. Possibly the YouTube bloom is off the rose. More likely the questions weren't as humorous or provocative tonight as those received via YouTube for the Democrats.
>
> Otherwise, it was a good, punchy debate, which showed most of the candidates off to their best advantage. McCain, in particular, was more eloquent and forceful than usual in his support of the war and his denunciation of torture. Romney was on the receiving end of McCain's torture lecture—Romney falling back on his all-too-typical letting the experts decide—but Ron Paul had a fine moment in his cogent explanation, back to McCain, on the difference between being an isolationist and a noninterventionist (Ron Paul is the latter). And Ron Paul also spoke truth about why violence has decreased in southern Iraq—that it happened because the British left.
>
> But Romney was excellent in knocking down Giuliani's attack on Romney's alleged employment of illegal aliens—Romney reasonably replied that he contracted with a company to work on his home, he did not directly hire illegal aliens.
>
> I should note here, however, that although I admired Romney's rhetoric in this exchange—a rarity—I think most of the Republicans and many of the Democrats are making too big a deal about illegal aliens (not that terminology matters all that much, but I can't help thinking of people from outer space whenever I hear that phrase). One of America's greatest strengths has always been its openness to people from other countries and cultures.
>
> Huckabee was probably the best on stage about this issue, refusing to back down from his funding of education for children of illegal immigrants.
>
> Giuliani, other than the exchange with Romney on the employment of illegal immigrants, was pretty much on top of his game, and Fred Thompson was a little more animated than usual tonight, too.
>
> So where do we stand: Huckabee is personable and gaining in the polls and could conceivably pull an upset in Iowa. Even if he comes close, he could be a good running mate for Giuliani. I'd say it's too late for McCain and Thompson, whatever they do or say from now on. Romney is still Giuliani's major competition.
>
> And Ron Paul still has by far the best positions. He alone among the Republican candidates continues to speak the truth to authority about war. We'll soon find out how many votes this translates into in the primaries.

Huckabee went on to win in Iowa; McCain was not too late to win the Republican nomination; Ron Paul, in fact, did very poorly in actual primary voting—even though articles in favor of his candidacy were "Dugg up" to the front page of Digg every day in the primary campaigns, and phone-ins after presidential debates frequently declared him the winner.

Barack Obama did very well in new new media in 2008, and won not only the nomination but also the general presidential election. Part of the reason is that Obama also looked very good on the older medium of television.

Telegenic + YouTube = Cybergenic

Barack Obama was first described as "cybergenic" by Paul Saffo in June Saffo, 2008, an observation Mark Leibovich picked up in *The New York Times* in August Leibovich, 2008. The logic of the appellation is that just as FDR was a master of radio (see "Radio Heads" in Levinson, 1997, for more on FDR's—as well as Churchill's, Hitler's, and Stalin's—political wielding of radio), and JFK was a natural for television (in contrast to Nixon), so was Obama a perfect Internet candidate in 2008, especially in comparison to his opponent John McCain.

The historical analogies, however, are not completely apt. FDR and his advisers understood and harnessed the power of radio, whereas JFK merely looked better than Nixon on television. On the other hand, Kennedy and his advisers knew after the debates that he had performed well on TV—a majority of people who heard the debates on radio thought Nixon did better, in contrast to the majority of television viewers who liked Kennedy (see McLuhan, 1964, p. 261)—and televised press conferences became a hallmark of his administration. Indeed, JFK's press conferences are still the high watermark for élan and style of a president talking to the media, though historians may conclude that Obama and Ronald Reagan came close.

But, more important, the designation of Obama as cybergenic, in contrast to telegenic, misses the crucial role that looking and sounding good on television plays in making a candidate cybergenic.

In fact, the synergistic, mutually catalytic relationship between old and new new media can be easily missed when focusing on the revolutionary impact of new new media. In the case of blogging, for example, investigative reporting from old print media fuels much of the reporting and commentary on new and new new media such as *The Huffington Post* and *Daily Kos* (see chapter 11, "Blogging," for more). And successful television series beginning with *Lost* have vigorously enlisted the viral Internet for promotion. In the case of the "cybergenic" candidate, most of the political video clips that appear on the Web, embedded from YouTube or directly from news sites such as MSNBC.com, originated on traditional cable television.

This means that a candidate must look good on television to look good on the Web. No matter how good I may look in a television appearance, thanks to expert lighting, I am not going to look like George Clooney. Similarly, Obama's YouTube superiority over McCain in 2008 flowed from Obama's looking and sounding better on television. For all the magic and power of YouTube, it cannot make a new new media silk purse out of a TV sow's ear.

The relationship of new and old media, of new new media to the preexisting real world, is one of the main areas of focus in this book. The gist, politically, is that success in new new media is not in itself enough—or is not really success unless it is aided and abetted by older media, and reflected in the world offline.

YouTube Undeniability and Democracy

At the opposite end of the professional production spectrum, we have YouTube clips not taken from a television talk show or news show and not even created by non-network producers such as Ben Relles. We have clips taken via cellphone, smart phone, or other lightweight, handheld video cameras that could be in the hands of…well, anyone.

And though the producers of such clips taken on the fly can be anonymous or completely unknown, the subjects of the videos could be the same politicians and celebrities we see on traditional television.

Senator George Allen (R-VA), for whatever reason, called on a questioner at a public event on August 15, 2006, and referred to him as "Macaca." The term is a racial epithet in some parts of the world. Allen denied that he uttered the term; he said he had no recollection of saying it. YouTube knew better. A clip of George Allen saying "Macaca" was up for all the world to see—which they did, one by one, hundreds of thousands of times (more than 625,000 views as of the beginning of 2012). Allen lost his bid for reelection to the Senate that year and, along with it, his position as a likely contender for the Republican presidential nomination in 2008. *Rolling Stone* aptly titled an article, shortly after the incident, "The First YouTube Election: George Allen and 'Macaca'." The subtitle was "George Allen: Digital Foot in Twenty-First Century Mouth" (Dickinson, 2006).

Michael Richards, the comedian who played Kramer on *Seinfeld*, also discovered that cellphone videos and their dissemination on the Web were no laughing matter. Richards' response to a heckler at the Laugh Factory in West Hollywood on November 16, 2006, was to refer to the heckler as a "nigger"—six times (TMZ staff, 2006). Richards later apologized but will always be something more—and worse—than a funnyman in the public eye.

Jonathan Alter (then of *Newsweek*), on Keith Olbermann's *Countdown* on MSNBC on June 9, 2008, captured this facet of the YouTube revolution early on—what it means for politicians, and, by extension, anyone in the public arena. In 2000, Alter said, a videotape of a politician talking would be in some vault in some network backroom somewhere, after its airing on television. (This was the case in 2004, as well.) But by 2008 and thereafter, anything a politician said could be up in the bright, unblinking lights of YouTube minutes later, out of the custody and control of both the network and the politician.

Alter was talking about John McCain's claim that he had never commented on the media's impact on politics and elections—a claim refuted by McCain's statement just a few days earlier that the media had been unfair to Hillary Clinton in her race for the Democratic nomination. "The media often overlooked how compassionately she spoke to the concerns and dreams of millions of Americans" McCain had declared (2008), in a speech widely available on YouTube.

And a politician's words not only can be posted on YouTube a few minutes after they have been spoken, but they also can stay on YouTube for years—in effect, forever. Words in a YouTube video clip are not only undeniable, they are indelible. The lights are not only bright and unblinking but permanent. They and any video can be removed from YouTube, but the lights do not burn out on their own. Unlike a television broadcast, which must be recorded via TiVo or DVR to last beyond the moment, the YouTube video is inherently in the longevity zone.

The political consequences of this indelibility pertain not only to live events such as George Allen's, but also to appearances on television that show up on YouTube.

Republican 2008 vice presidential candidate Sarah Palin's response on the *CBS Evening News* to Katie Couric about what newspapers Palin read—she could not name a single one—was first broadcast on September 30, 2008. It soon was on YouTube, where it had received nearly 2 million views by November 2008 (more than 2.5 million as of January 2012). It is impossible to ever know what precise impact this had on the election results in 2008, but it certainly could not have helped the Republicans. In the Republican presidential primary campaign of 2011–2012, the repeated surge and collapse of some half a dozen candidates—Michele Bachmann, Rick Perry, Herman Cain, Newt Gingrich, Rick Santorum—was no doubt fueled by video clips of embarrassing, damaging statements on YouTube. Rick Perry's November 2011 infamous "oops" moment, for example—when he could not name in a televised debate the three federal cabinet departments he wanted to abolish—was still enjoying a brisk viewership in early 2012, with more than half a million cumulative views on several video clips.

Anything recorded via any audiovisual device is a candidate for universal and long-lasting dissemination on YouTube—and that includes not only what politicians and other celebrities are saying now but also what anyone said or sang or otherwise communicated since the invention of motion pictures in the 1880s and the phonograph in 1877, if a motion picture or a recording was made of that communication. YouTube now (January 2012) has recordings of U.S. presidents Benjamin Harrison (1888–1892), Grover Cleveland (second term, 1892–1896), and William McKinley (1896–1901). (See the upcoming section, "'My Guitar Gently Weeps' Through the Ages," for more on YouTube immortality.)

YouTube Usurps Television as a Herald of Public Events

By all accounts, including mine (e.g., Sullivan, 2008; see Suellentrop, 2008, for a summary of blog reviews; Levinson, "Superb Speeches by Bill Clinton and John Kerry," 2008), 2004 Democratic nominee for president John Kerry gave one of the best speeches of the 2008 Democratic Convention in Denver, and probably the best speech of his life, on August 27, 2008. Unaccountably, the speech was carried in its entirety on none of the three major all-news cable television networks. Instead, MSNBC, CNN, and Fox News went for their own talking heads. As Andrew Sullivan aptly noted, "Cable believed their pundits were more interesting than this speech. They made the wrong call."

Or perhaps we can indeed account for why the cable television networks cut Kerry. Driven by the need to attract a maximum of viewers, required in turn to attract a maximum amount of revenue from advertisers, the program directors at the networks probably figured that John Kerry, not known as an electrifying speaker, might well lead viewers to other channels with more scintillating talking-head programming. Or, the networks at least thought that Chris Matthews, Wolf Blitzer, and Brit Hume—on MSNBC, CNN, and Fox News, respectively—would bore fewer viewers than Kerry.

C-SPAN and PBS, not beholden to advertisers, did broadcast John Kerry's speech. My wife and I had C-SPAN on as an inset on our television screen—we were watching MSNBC—and we switched to get an idea of what Kerry was saying. We kept our television on C-SPAN for the rest of Kerry's speech.

Noncommercial television thus saved TV as an instant herald for John Kerry. Beyond that, the speech was posted on YouTube within an hour. It attracted thousands of viewers in a few hours (more than 170,000 views by January 2012). Television increasingly counts only in the immediate run—in the short, medium, and long runs, YouTube has become the medium of record.

The relationship of YouTube to television in the coverage of public events complements the relationship of blogging to newspapers and helps pinpoint the position of new new media in our culture. Blogging provides commentary far faster than the op-eds of any printed newspaper. YouTube provides audiovisual records of events on television that would otherwise be gone the instant they concluded—or, in the case of John Kerry's 2008 speech, incompletely broadcast or not at all. Television, of course, can replay parts or all of any programming, but such replays are not accessible 24 hours a day, from most places in the world, as is any video on YouTube. Anything on television can be captured on TiVo or DVR, but those records are private, not publicly accessible. The new new media herald of events is thus faster in the case of blogging and more reliable in the case of YouTube than their old media counterparts. For the time being and near future, newspapers will continue because they do not require batteries to read, and television because it is still often an effortlessly accessible first word. But the better heralds of new new media are likely to continue to supplant and replace newspapers and television, especially as old and newer media—newspapers, blogs, television, YouTube videos—are all available on the same smart phone or tablet screen, which makes moving between the old and newer medium, between television and YouTube, that much easier.

YouTube Is Not Only Omni-Accessible and Free to Viewers—It's Also Free to Producers

Barack Obama paid $5 million for a 30-minute address (Sinderbrand & Wells, 2008), carried by most of the major television networks, a week before the presidential election of 2008. Some 33 million people saw his address (Gold, 2008), so the money was well spent.

But YouTube charges nothing for placement of videos on its site. As Joe Trippi remarked, Obama "can do a half-hour YouTube address every Saturday, addressing millions. The networks would never give the president that much television time each week, but the press is still going to have to cover what he says on YouTube" (Fouhy, 2008). A presidential candidate would certainly not get 30 minutes free of charge every Saturday to talk to the nation via network television, but Trippi astutely observes that likely neither would a president. Broadcast media have become more protective of income earned from their rented time in the 21st century than back in the first part of the 20th, when FDR delivered 30 "fireside chats" to the American public in prime time via radio from 1933 to 1944 (Dunlop, 1951).

Trippi, author of *The Revolution Will Not Be Televised: Democracy, the Internet, and the Overthrow of Everything* (2004), first came to America's attention as the manager of Howard Dean's unsuccessful campaign for the Democratic nomination for president in 2004. Trippi chronicles and assesses the Dean campaign in his book. Dean became known as the "Internet candidate," and Trippi was the Internet mastermind, but new new media back in 2004 were not what they were in 2008 and 2012. Blogging was thriving in 2004, but Facebook was in its infancy and YouTube and Twitter were still a year or two away.

Obama as the New FDR in New New Media as Well as the New New Deal?

The November 24, 2008, cover of *Time* magazine depicted Barack Obama as the new FDR—the then president-elect in specs, gray suit and hat, sitting in a car, cigarette jutting jauntily upward—and was captioned "The New New Deal."

The comparison, of course, was to FDR and Obama both first taking office in the throes of financial crises and catastrophe, and to Obama's plans for public works projects—"infrastructure" in 21st-century parlance—to help Americans get back to work and lay the foundations for more efficient commerce, just as FDR did in the Great Depression of the 1930s.

But the announcement—a day after the *Time* cover became public on November 13, 2008—that Obama's radio address on November 15 would also be made available on YouTube showed that Obama was trying to be the new FDR not only in New Deal economic terms but also in the employment of the newest media to communicate to the American people.

Roosevelt's "fireside chats" had used the new medium of his day, radio, to communicate directly to the American people, as no president had ever done before. Roosevelt and his advisers understood the advantages of new radio, which allowed anyone talking through it, including the president, to sound and seem as if he were talking directly to Americans, in their living rooms, bedrooms, or in whatever room their radio was situated. The effect was powerful, unprecedented, profound. My parents, who grew up in the Great Depression, often told me how they regarded Roosevelt as almost a kind of father—which makes sense, for whose deep voice would otherwise be talking to you in the inner sanctums of your home, if the economy and then the war were making you feel almost as helpless as a child? When World War II came, my parents, in their late teens and early 20s, felt especially comforted by Roosevelt's voice. They felt that, as long as FDR was talking to them and all Americans, the country would be okay. (See Levinson, 1997, *The Soft Edge* for more on radio and FDR.)

Americans stopped listening to radio that way in the 1950s, when television became the predominant political broadcast medium, and radio became a vehicle of rock 'n' roll. By 1960, people who saw the Kennedy-Nixon debates on television thought Kennedy won, in contrast to those who heard the debates on radio, as we considered previously. Unfortunately for Nixon, 87 percent of American households had televisions in their homes by 1960 (Roark et al., 2007). And by the election and its aftermath in 2008, YouTube was replacing television as the predominant political audiovisual medium—though, as discussed in the "Cybergenic" section, this by no means indicated that television had become unimportant in politics. To the contrary, a lot of what is on YouTube comes from television.

Obama's YouTube addresses, however, certainly did not have the same success as FDR's fireside chats in the 1930s and '40s—certainly not as of early 2012 for Obama, when his prospects for reelection were by no means assured. Roosevelt was the first four-term American president (and the last, due to the term limits set in the 22nd Amendment to the Constitution); Obama, in contrast, as of early 2012, is just in his first term and on a popularity roller coaster in the polls. The reasons for FDR's and Obama's different receptions surely reside in more than the media—for example, the de facto current need for majorities of 60 in the Senate making passage of new legislation more difficult than in the 1930s—but YouTube, for its part, may not be as comforting to viewers in the 21st century as radio was to its listeners in the 1930s. In place of the voice in the home, the fatherly reassurance that radio conveyed for FDR, YouTube plays to people on the move, in a peripatetic society in which everything, including the words of the president and the Congress, is subject to high levels of distrust. If new new media facilitated Occupy Wall Street and the resurgence of direct democracy, then the flip side of that, what comes along with it, is a bounding dissatisfaction with elected officials of all parties. Indeed, not only has YouTube played a major role in bringing the world an ongoing eyewitness record of Occupy Wall Street, but the need that YouTube unleashed to see these events as they're happening led to real-time video new new media such as UStream (founded in 2007), which exceed YouTube in being on the literal cutting edge of news (see chapter 14 for more).

Amateur YouTube Stars and Producers

Because YouTube is fed by anyone with a video camera or camera phone, the people in the video—the subject of the clip—can just as easily be unknown as famous. The amateur or unknown YouTube producer can point the camera at himself or herself, friends, the general public, or celebrities (if they're close at hand) with almost equal facility.

Kony 2012—a 30-minute documentary about the depredations of Ugandan Joseph Kony—became the fastest-growing video in the history of YouTube in March 2012, with more than 75 million views in its first week. Although the movie's director Jason Russell had some prior professional experience—he sold a script for a dance movie to Steven Spielberg, to help finance *Kony 2012* (Greene, 2012)—he certainly was not known to many people prior to 2012. The documentary has what have become some of the standard winning ingredients for a YouTube video, including Russell's five-year old son, and a call to action to make Kony and his villainy infamous (see Vamburkar, 2012, for a critique, and Levinson, 2012, "In Defense," for defense of the movie).

As of April 2012, Justin Bieber's "Baby" had the most all-time views on YouTube—more than 725 million—and *Kony 2012* more than 85 million. "Charlie bit my finger—again!" was in sixth place (formerly in first place), with more than 440 million views (see MacManus, 2012, for the history). What "Baby" and "Charlie" both have in common is their stars were discovered on YouTube—Bieber by his would-be manager in 2008, and Charlie and his older brother by their parents, who put up their video in 2007. Bieber went on to become a pop icon in the music world beyond YouTube, while Charlie and his family continue to hold forth only on YouTube. Comparing the numbers of viewers for both YouTube stars to television, the 2012 Super Bowl was the most watched broadcast in TV history, attracting 111.3 million viewers, which means the two total amateurs (baby Charlie and his slightly older brother) have attracted almost four times the number of viewers of the most watched show ever on television, and amateur-turned-professional singer Bieber has six times as many viewers as the Super Bowl on his lead video. (But in a good example of old and new new media synergy, the Super Bowl also set a record for greatest number of tweets per second, or TPS, for an English-language event—10,245—see Horn, 2012, for details.) Of course, the Super Bowl broadcast was live, over several hours, while the YouTube views accrued over several years. So the comparison of YouTube and television viewers is not completely equivalent, although it nonetheless shows that YouTube and television are both in the same huge audience ballpark, and you need not be a superstar to play in it. The extraordinary success of then-unknown-vocalist Susan Boyle in April 2009, first appearing on television's *Britain's Got Talent*, but with video clips receiving more than 100 million views on YouTube within a month after, provides another example both of the power of YouTube in contrast to television and the symbiotic relationship of these two media. Boyle was brought to public prominence by both television and YouTube.

Meanwhile, Chris Crocker, a total unknown when he first uploaded his video in 2007, had attained more than 42 million views for his hilarious "Leave Britney Alone" clip as of January 2012. His video is in effect an amateur/celebrity hybrid, with the producer or creator an amateur prior to the making of the video, but the subject already a big star (Britney Spears). "Obama Girl" would be another example (Ben Relles, little-known producer, about Barack Obama).

"Food Fight" provides a more purebred example of how lack of previous fame is no impediment to success on YouTube—much like Charlie and his brother, though a little more artistic. The YouTube description tells us that the video presents a short history of wars since World War II from the American perspective, as seen through the best- known foods of the warring nations. It was produced, written, and animated by Stefan Nadelman, at the time also a complete unknown, as the Dylan line goes. And, indeed, nothing about the animated video was well known beforehand—no stars, no voices, just animated. It was uploaded to YouTube in February 2008, had attained more than 3.6 million views by February 2009, and twice that amount, more than 7 million views, by February 2012. How could such a video, however superb, but with such utter lack of celebrity status, attract millions of viewers? I first saw "Food Fight" when a friend and colleague at Fordham University—Professor

Lance Strate, who was also a "Friend" on Myspace—placed it in a comment he entered on my Myspace profile. Such nonprofessional promotion, which now typifies Facebook and Twitter, can be every bit as effective as a multimillion-dollar publicity campaign. Indeed, most public relations and publicity firms these days spend a lot of money in attempts to simulate such word-of-mouth, in-the-street marketing, a/k/a social media promotion.

This is best known as viral marketing, and it is the unpredictable, wildly successful promotional engine of the new new media age. "Charlie Bit My Finger—Again!" and "Food Fight" are archetypal examples of the unadulterated viral video on YouTube.

Viral Videos

Viral marketing, viral videos—viral any product or activity relating to popular culture—operates via one person who loves a song or video or whatever on the Web or elsewhere letting another person know of this enjoyment. When millions of people let millions of other people know about such a video, it can become enormously popular—as much as or more so than a video promoted by old-media advertising and publicity.

Once called "word of mouth," "viral" is something more, because digital word of mouth can reach anyone, anywhere in the world, and millions of people, instantly, in contrast to old-fashioned spoken word of mouth, which can reach only the person right next to you or, in the days of just landline telephone, at the other end of your phone connection (nowadays, cellphones and smart phones, especially when texting, are part of viral communication).

But why "viral"? In the biological world in which we and our physical bodies reside, a virus spreads by hitching a ride on or infecting a host cell; every time that host cell reproduces, the new cell takes a piece of the virus along with it. The viral video does much the same, by infecting or hitching a ride in the mind of every viewer who may see it. When these minds have access to new new media, where they can talk about, link, and even edit the video, the viral dissemination can become epidemic. Whether in the world of biology or popular culture, the virus or viral video sells itself.

Richard Dawkins was the first to apply this viral metaphor to human mentality in his discussion of "memes" in his 1991 essay "Viruses of the Mind." Human beings become hosts—happy, unhappy, conscious, or otherwise—of ideas. And the words all humans speak, and the books and articles that authors, reporters, and now bloggers write, and the links to videos and whatever anyone puts on Facebook and Twitter, then proceed to spread these ideas, these "memes," to other people, just as viruses disseminate their genetic materials from cell to cell, and just as DNA perpetuates itself through the reproduction of living organisms. Dawkins is here picking up on Samuel Butler's famous observation (1878) that a chicken is just an egg's way of producing more eggs—in Dawkins' schema, living organisms are machinery used by DNA to make more DNA. Dawkins first presented this perspective on DNA in his 1976 breakthrough book, *The Selfish Gene*, some 15 years prior to his equation of memes or infectious ideas with biological viruses. We could now say that DNA, viruses, memes, and viral videos all operate on the same hijack-the-host basis—to the general betterment of the host with DNA, detriment of the host with biological viruses, and either betterment or detriment depending on the specific meme or viral video.

Prior to Dawkins' "Viruses of the Mind," and well before the advent of the Web as a major fact of life, the virus analogy became prominent in the computer age in the popular designation of certain kinds of destructive computer programs as "computer viruses." (Dawkins prominently acknowledged and built upon the computer virus metaphor in his 1991 paper.) Attached to a computer program or code that did, or was purported to do, something useful—something the computer owner desired—the virus, once set loose on the computer, would erase files and do all manner of things that interfered with the user's work, to the point of shutting down the computer. This virus analogy obviously has a lot in common with the biological virus (more than does the virus metaphor in viral marketing), because both biological and computer viruses can result in the breakdown of their hosts—illness and possible death in humans and animals, uselessness and incapacity of computers.

The migration of the analogy to popular culture memes, however, resulted in "virus" not necessarily signifying anything bad. A viral video, after all, may be instructive and humorous—as is "Food Fight"—with no damage done to any of the hosts. (As an aside, the very growth and expansion of the use of the adjective "viral" has been viral, and not at all in a bad way, because the term indeed helps us understand how YouTube, new new media, and popular culture in general increasingly work together in the 21st century.)

Nonetheless, an abuse does occur on YouTube in which videos of beatings and other mistreatment of people and animals are uploaded for the perverse satisfaction of their creators and the perverse enjoyment of some viewers.

Viral Videos Gone Bad

The inevitable drawback of all open systems, the trade-off for the democratic benefits of all new new media, is that open systems can admit bad eggs. In the case of Wikipedia, which we will look at in chapter 13, the damage done by disruptive writer/editors is to the words in Wikipedia—its online articles. Such despoiling is easily discovered, removed, or otherwise remedied.

A video portraying a beating, or "beat down," can be easily removed from YouTube. But because real people are being beaten, the damage is to far more than information, and removal of the offending video cannot reverse or undo the beating or other depredation. The one upside of the ubiquitous video in such cases is that there is a permanent record of the crime, which makes it easier for the offenders to be brought to justice. But YouTube is nonetheless open to the question: Did the culture it created, in which anyone can be a star given the right (i.e., massively attractive) viral video, provide too easy an invitation to mentally unbalanced or ethically vacant people?

This is a question that arises whenever people as a whole are empowered by a new technology. The new device rarely creates the appetite for the evil deed. I recall kids in my schoolyard, alas, being beaten up by what the teachers called "toughs" back in the 1950s (when I was a student, not yet a teacher). Would people who toss babies across rooms (see O'Brien, 2008) and puppies over cliffs (see Wortham, 2008), just so they can be videotaped and see themselves on YouTube, not be likely to do similar things in the absence of YouTube?

We will examine the beat downs and other abuses conducted via or on behalf of YouTube and other new new media in more detail in chapter 15, "The Dark Side of New New Media." For now, we might well consider *Salon*'s Farhad Manjoo's (2008) thought that "the idea that the Web has desensitized kids to beatings and that MySpace has given rise to teen brutality is extremely dubious....despite high-profile news stories, we've got no evidence that that's the case—that bullying, fighting, or generalized teen angst has worsened during the MySpace era. Also, doesn't it seem just as plausible that headline-making incidents like this could deter, rather than provoke, violence in kids?"

Manjoo's last point suggests that kids with any brains will see that a beating that features them as the beaters, on YouTube, will provide both legal evidence against them and continuing shame in the future. Whether this would restrain all potential abusers eager for publicity, we don't know, but we can nonetheless assume that they would probably sooner or later do something deplorable, with or without YouTube, and YouTube in general contributes a lot more to the public good than to its undermining. We will continue to consider some of those beneficial effects in this chapter, but we should not lose sight of the abuses, and always stay on the lookout for ways to reduce or remove them, while maintaining and increasing the benefits.

The YouTube Revolution in Popular Culture

It was Harold Innis (1951), one of Marshall McLuhan's inspirations, who first wrote about how all media either space-bind or time-bind—that is, make communication easier across space or distance (as in the case of written documents carried across Roman roads), across time (as in the case of hieroglyphics carved on walls), or both (books produced by the printing press). As McLuhan (1962, McLuhan, 1964) noticed, new technologies in the 19th and 20th centuries continued to facilitate these kinds of "extensions," usually either across space or time, primarily, not both. The telegraph and telephone were space-binding extensions, while the photograph and phonograph were time-binding.

Here in our 21st century, all new new media are both space-binding and time-binding, due to the speed (across space) and retrievability (across time) of any information conveyed on the Web. But YouTube, especially, does both, par excellence.

A few years ago, I was watching a DVD of Martin Scorsese's 2005 documentary about Bob Dylan, *No Direction Home*. The movie has a clip of Dylan and Joan Baez performing Dylan's "With God on Our Side" at the Newport Folk Festival in July 1963. Baez takes Dylan by the hand out onto the stage, and they start singing.

After the movie, I searched on Baez and "With God on Our Side" on YouTube and found her complete rendition of the song in Stockholm, Sweden, in 1966. I embedded the YouTube video on my website, InfiniteRegress.tv, and commended it to people running for president—one line in the song in particular, "If God's on our side, He'll stop the next war."

There are as many examples of such discoveries as there are videos with music performances on YouTube, which has turned every computer, smart phone, and tablet screen into on-demand television at your 24-hour disposal—or, as Innis or McLuhan might have put it, had they lived to see this age, an easily accessible window across space and time.

Roy Orbison's Guitar

The Traveling Wilburys were—in my opinion and that of many critics and fans (e.g., Gill, 2007)—the best rock supergroup ever to have existed. Bob Dylan, George Harrison, Jeff Lynne, Tom Petty, and Roy Orbison recorded under that name from 1988 to 1990. Their best-known songs were "Handle with Care" and "End of the Line."

Roy Orbison died at the age of 52 in December 1988. When the time came to record a video of "End of the Line," the Wilburys put Orbison's rocking guitar in a rocking chair in the part of the song starting at 1 minute 44 seconds, where Orbison carried the lead. You also can see the rocking guitar at the very end of "End of the Line." (You can read all about this in the Wikipedia entry on the Traveling Wilburys.)

You can see the video and this moving tribute to Orbison any time you like on YouTube—in your home, office, or any place you happen to be with a smart phone or tablet.

YouTube, in other words, has robbed death of some of its meaning—at least insofar as it pertains to popular culture. The end of the line for audiovisual popular culture has become immortality on YouTube.

When I heard the news on February 11, 2012, that Whitney Houston had died, the first thing I did was watch her performance of "I Will Always Love You" from *The Bodyguard* (1992)—on YouTube. Millions of other people had done the same in the preceding years, and who knows how many million more will do this in the future. I did the same for The Monkees' "Daydream Believer," when news of Davy Jones's death broke on February 29, 2012 (see also Levinson, 2012, "Why The Monkees Are Important").

"My Guitar Gently Weeps" Through the Ages

Roy Orbison's is not the only immortal guitar on YouTube. George Harrison (1943–2001), another member of the Traveling Wilburys who is no longer with us, also has a guitar that plays across YouTube, in a way that brings home another one of YouTube's signature characteristics: presentation of numerous, slightly different takes of the same real-life event or numerous versions of the same song or creative work.

Slightly different takes of the same event can come from numerous people in a live audience with camera phones and other handheld vid-cams. Numerous renditions of the same song can also come from recordings of different performances throughout the decades.

YouTube has at least a dozen versions of George Harrison's "While My Guitar Gently Weeps," beginning with Harrison's performance at his 1971 Concert for Bangladesh, which also features Eric Clapton on guitar, and proceeding through the years to Eric Clapton and Paul McCartney's rendition of the song at the 2002 Memorial Concert for George, and the 2004 performance (my favorite) by Tom Petty and Jeff Lynne, with incandescent guitar work by Prince, when Harrison was posthumously inducted into the Rock 'n' Roll Hall of Fame for his solo work.

We see Harrison progressing through 20 years in these videos, Clapton through 30 years, with the song poignantly surviving its author. We see blurry videos with unclear sound taken by "bootleggers" at concerts, and we see top-of-the-line clips made for television broadcast. We see a de facto library, hear a record album through history, which we can add to or subtract from at any time, including—if perchance we happened to have recorded it—even adding a video clip of our own making.

We see, in short, the essence of YouTube and new new media.

We can also see on YouTube about 10 renditions of George Harrison's "All Things Must Pass," including one sung by Paul McCartney after Harrison's death. (My favorite, however—McCartney's performance at the Memorial Concert for George held at the Royal Albert Hall in London on November 29, 2002, one year after George's death—was gone from YouTube when I looked in November 2008. Indeed, when I looked at my list of more than 100 musical "Favorites" on YouTube in early 2012, seven had been removed, including videos by the Rolling Stones, David Bowie, and Langhorne Slim. The reason was copyright violation, which we will examine in the "YouTube's Achilles' Heel" section later in this chapter.)

"All Things Must Pass" is about the fleeting quality of all things, undesirable as well as desirable facts of life, bad as well as good states of being.

All things must pass. But it is tempting to now add to Harrison's perceptive lyric: except for performances lost in the night, now captured on video and added to what may well be the bright eternity of YouTube. For although YouTube itself, as it is currently configured, may well come to pass or be transformed or subsumed into something different, there is no reason to suppose that videos currently on YouTube, especially those of groups such as the Beatles and the Traveling Wilburys, or any great contemporary artist, will not be included in such post-YouTube media. And even when a video is removed from YouTube, it can be restored, and that removal cannot possibly erase the video already downloaded to users' computers, tablets, and smart phones. (See, however, Amazon's removal of George Orwell's *1984* from Kindles in 2009, discussed in chapter 13.)

YouTube Retrieves MTV

"Video Killed the Radio Star," the U.K. New Wave group The Buggles sang to everyone in 1979, heralding the success of music videos on MTV in the 1980s and being the very first video played on MTV when it began in 1981.

Here is what really happened:

To begin with, the enormous and rapid dissemination of television sets in the 1950s was thought by many observers to spell the end of radio. (A famous *New Yorker* cover in 1955, Perry Barlow's "Another Radio to the Attic," shows a radio languishing next to a crank-up Victrola in a dusty corner, as if it were an artifact from some long-ago era. Carl Rose's 1951 *New Yorker* cartoon similarly depicts a little girl and her mother in the attic, with the little girl pointing to a radio and asking, "What's that, Mama?") Television had co-opted radio's original and highly successful network programming of soap operas, serials, and news.

But radio did not fade away; it instead thrived and became the most profitable medium, dollar spent for dollar earned. Radio did this by playing rock 'n' roll records, supplied free of charge by record companies and sometimes even with payments (which the U.S. government soon investigated and prosecuted, calling this "payola"). And radio capitalized on the capacity of all acoustic media to be listened to when doing other things—in the case of radio, when driving, getting up in the morning, and so forth. Thus rock 'n' roll and multitasking propelled Top 40 radio in the 1950s and '60s, and FM radio in the 1960s and '70s (see Levinson, 1997, for details).

The debut of MTV in the early 1980s indeed diverted some of the limelight from radio to the television screen. But MTV hardly "killed" radio or the radio star, and by the mid-1990s, CDs and, even more important, MP3s were tipping the scale of attention and prominence in the popular culture back to acoustic media.

This was the situation when YouTube opened its virtual doors in 2005. But the music videos easily available on YouTube, from decades past to the present, have given the video a new, expanded lease on life in the popular culture.

In sum: video didn't kill the radio star in the first place. But YouTube has made the music video even more of a major player than it was on MTV in the 1980s—an example of a new new medium (YouTube) supplanting a newish old medium (MTV or cable television).

Will YouTube Put iTunes Out of Business?

As we have seen, new new media compete not only with old media but with new media on the Web, or media on the Web that charge for their information, operate via strict editorial control, and employ other procedures of old, mass media.

How long can iTunes, which as of January 2012 charges 69 cents, 99 cents, or $1.29 per song, survive YouTube's free competition? iTunes, Amazon.com, and newspapers online such as *The New York Times* and *The Wall Street Journal* that charge for subscriptions are classic examples of "new" in contrast to "new new" media. Old media exist offline. New media exist online but retain old media ways of doing business. Some new media retain more old ways than others. iTunes charges (but not for podcasts) and has strict editorial control over what appears on its pages. *The Huffington Post*, which can be considered about halfway between new and new new media, is free but still wields strict old media gatekeeping, or editorial control.

New new media coexist with new media online but dispense with all old media confinements of payment and editorial control.

iTunes is still not without its advantages in comparison to YouTube—mainly in the great number of songs it offers and their easy organization. More than 10 billion tracks had been downloaded from iTunes as of February 2010. The quality of the music for sale on iTunes is likely better than the sound of most, but not all, YouTube videos, but as high-quality videos become more prevalent on YouTube, this difference is likely to vanish. Further, the accessibility of YouTube and videos on iPhones (and iPads) makes them competitive with MP3s played on iPods—ironic, because Apple is the maker of both iPhones and iPods, which means Apple succeeds whatever way the new new media cookie crumbles. But the pace of media evolution is so fast that it cannot help but generate competition even among products of different divisions of the same company.

Perhaps such concerns are what led iTunes to say in October 2008 that it might shut itself down if artists and record producers received higher royalties for sale of their songs on iTunes (Ahmed, 2008). The Copyright Royalty Board in Washington, D.C., was convinced by iTunes and supported its refusal to raise royalties from 9 to 16 cents per download (Frith, 2008).

But, again, Apple would have won in any case. If iTunes went out of business, Apple would still be doing well with its iPhones and iPads and their YouTube access. Meanwhile, iTunes continues to grow, as evidenced by the Beatles' catalog finally coming online at the end of 2010.

YouTube Refutes Lewis Mumford and Turns the Videoclip into a Transcript

Lewis Mumford (1895–1990) typified the attitude of many critics of television when he compared watching it with being in a state of "mass psychosis" in his Mumford, 1970 *The Pentagon of Power* (p. 294). Mumford's objection to television was that it provided no sense of past or future, allowing viewers no way to look back or skip ahead when they were watching a television series or news show, as readers easily could when reading a book or newspaper. VCR technology began to give viewers some control over the past and future in television as early as 1976. DVR and TiVo technologies have greatly expanded that control by allowing users to program the recording of episodes weeks in advance.

But YouTube ratchets up this viewer control a significant step by allowing people to watch what is on YouTube not only at any time but also from any place, if the viewer happens to have a smart phone or other portable, Internet-accessing device at hand. Via the combination of YouTube and mobile media, the audiovisual image is at last as controllable by the viewer as pages in a book are to a reader. (See my *Cellphone: The Story of the World's Most Mobile Medium*, 2004, for a history and current impact of mobility in media.) Mumford's hyperbole was incorrect in the first place. But YouTube has decisively consigned it to the attic of bygone intellectual error.

YouTube has made the online video as accessible and "readable" to the viewer as a written transcript online or in hand. Just as the reader of a written transcript can stop, go back, browse forward, or read a section again, so can the viewer of a YouTube video do the same with the moving images on the screen. From the point of view of the new new media user, there is indeed no significant difference between an online transcript and video, other than that one must be literate to read the transcript. We can make the following analogy: a transcript or book or newspaper in hand is to VCRs and DVDs as a transcript or book online is to a video on YouTube and other online video sites. The goal or target of all new new media—or, in Aristotle's terms, their "final cause"—is to make their worldwide contents as accessible as a book in hand.

Tim Russert, 1950–2008

YouTube has also made the immediate past unforgettable and universally retrievable. Tim Russert, *Meet the Press* moderator and NBC Washington News Chief, died unexpectedly on June 13, 2008. The story was covered all that day and most of the weekend on three all-news cable networks in the United States—MSNBC, CNN, and Fox News. YouTube played a different role, with more than 500 clips of Tim Russert added in the first 24 hours after his death. Tom Brokaw's report of Russert's death had more than 700,000 views nearly four years later.

The YouTube contribution underscores another significant difference between new media (cable television) and new new media (YouTube). Although CNN International is available in many parts of the world, it appropriately moved on to other stories in the days following Russert's death (MSNBC and Fox have much less international reach). In contrast, the YouTube clips of Russert were instantly available everywhere in the world and will continue to be instantly available for years to come—or, as indicated previously regarding the music videos of Roy Orbison and George Harrison, in principle, forever. Unless the videos violate copyright.

YouTube's Achilles' Heel: Copyright

The following has happened to many a blogger: You write a nice post about a favorite song or a musical performance—as, in fact, I did, in June 2008, about Paul McCartney's rendition of George Harrison's "All Things Must Pass" at the 2002 Royal Albert Hall Memorial Concert—and flesh it out with a video of the performance, via an embed from YouTube. It looks and sounds great. You put links to your post on Twitter, Facebook, Reddit, and all the appropriate places. You receive complimentary comments. But a few months later, you also receive an email from a disappointed reader, who got a message that the video is "no longer available."

You check on your blog site, and then on YouTube, and, sure enough, you find that the video has been taken down from YouTube, because it violated its "terms of service"—or, in plainer English, some person or corporation told YouTube that the video violated its copyright. The hand of old media copyright enforcement, withered but not without power, has pulled the rug and the fun out from under your new new media blog creation. Or, to try another appendage metaphor, you have just encountered YouTube's Achilles' heel: copyright enforcement.

YouTube's one flaw is that, despite the potential immortality of every video on its site, there is no guarantee that any given video clip available today will be there tomorrow, or even five minutes from now. The immortality is the default condition, which can be deliberately broken at any time. This means there is no guarantee that any links to video elsewhere on the Web, and embeds of the video, will continue to work.

The Internet, on the one hand, has gone a long way to achieving even more stability and even permanency than paper—what I call "reliable locatability" (see Levinson, "The Book on the Book," 1998; Levinson, *Cellphone*, 2004; and Levinson, "The Secret Riches," 2007)—via "permalinks." But even permalinked text and videos can be taken down, and YouTube's vulnerability to copyright enforcement, in addition to the person who put up a video in the first place deciding to remove it for whatever reason, is a significant, retrograde old media step backward. The great asset of YouTube and new new media, which is that anyone can become a producer, finds its limitation in the reverse effect that stems from the same power, and makes every producer a potential deleter.

There is software readily available that allows users to download videos—not just link to or embed them—with the result that these users can then put the videos up on their own Web pages, without recourse to YouTube or other video storage and dissemination sites such as Blip.tv, Metacafe, and Vimeo.

But this might well be a copyright violation, also. And though the violation might never be discovered, its possibility keeps us on one of the prime battle lines of old and new media, on the one hand, and new new media on the other: the battle line of copyright.

Copyright—literally, the right to copy—started as a royal prerogative in Europe, after the introduction of the printing press in the middle of the 15th century. Monarchs gave printers the right to make copies and thereby controlled the output of written information in their realms. But in 1710, Parliament in England enacted the Statute of Anne, which made copyright a right to be claimed by authors and protected on behalf of authors by the government (see Kaplan, 1966; Levinson, 1997).

This is where copyright resides today. It protects the author's interests in three ways. The owner of the copyright determines who, if anyone, can (1) make copies of the work, (2) make money from copies of the work, or (3) use portions of the work in new creations, not of the original creator's making.

Details in the practice of copyright are complex and have evolved. At the beginning of the 20th century, authors had to formally claim copyright. By the end of the 20th century, copyright was accepted as a right belonging to authors, inherent in the authorship of the work (registration of copyright with the government makes enforcement of copyright easier but is not required for an author's assertion of copyright). A hundred years ago, the term of a copyright in the United States was 28 years, with one renewal possible. It is currently for the lifetime of the author plus 75 years. (The Berne Convention, of which the United States and 163 other nations are signatories, provides copyright protection for the life of the author plus 50 years. Signatories are free to provide longer protection.) "Fair Use" is a custom supported in U.S. courts of law, which allows inclusion of small portions of work for educational and similar uses, without obtaining the approval of the copyright holder. But all rights deriving from the copyright can be assigned, or bought and sold.

Someone who embeds on his or her Web site a YouTube video of someone else's creation likely has none of the preceding copyright factors in mind. The burgeoning millions of embeds on the Web—done without any attention to the copyrights that YouTube boilerplate says must be observed and adhered to—speak loudly of the reality that the traditional old media mold of copyright is irrevocably broken in the new new media age.

The controversy over SOPA—the Stop Online Piracy Act, introduced in the U.S. House of Representatives in October 2011, and shelved in January 2012 after online protests, including a one-day shutdown of Wikipedia and Reddit (see Levinson, "Is Wikipedia Wrong?" 2012)—is indicative of the rough sailing copyright faces ahead. Proponents of the bill wanted to prevent theft of intellectual property online—movies, music, the very content of YouTube. But the strong provisions of the bill would have held not only the uploaders of the pirated content responsible, but also the online systems such as YouTube on which the content was made available.

Unsurprisingly, Hollywood studios were the most vociferous supporters of the bill. But online sites—YouTube, Facebook, Twitter, Wikipedia, the prime movers of new new media—correctly pointed out that policing their sites for pirated content would cripple their operation. And supporters of the First Amendment, including me, noted that SOPA would violate the provision that says Congress can make "no law...abridging the freedom of speech, or of the press." (The Communications Decency Act was struck down by the Supreme Court in 1997, as noted earlier in this chapter.)

But is copyright completely shattered, or are some parts worth preserving and applying, if possible, to YouTube and new new media? The fundamental right to control who can make copies seems lost, and that is likely for the best. But the copyright holder's right to share in any income generated from the work—and, indeed, to determine whether another person or corporation can make money from the work—seems a reasonable right to preserve. Further, because income is more easily tracked than placement of embeds on a Web page, this commercial aspect of copyright is not impossible or even very difficult to enforce.

Plagiarism is also worthy of prevention and punishment. In its worst forms, the plagiarist takes work created by someone else and not only passes it off as his or her own but seeks to make income from it. Here the Web is not the plagiarist's best friend. The universal access that makes everything available to everyone on the Web means that, sooner or later, someone familiar with the original work will come across the plagiarist's version and report the plagiarism to the original author or current copyright holder.

The bottom line is that dissemination of copies of a work, whether an MP3 of a recording or a YouTube clip of a video, is impossible to prevent in the realm of new new media, and probably should not be prevented, unless money is made from the dissemination or the work is plagiarized (disguising the original author's creation of the work), in which case the creator should be paid and/or the dissemination should be stopped, if possible.

In practical terms, the Recording Industry Association of America's (RIAA's) attempt to prevent dissemination of MP3s purely for the purpose of sharing and not for making money will not succeed in the long run (see Marder, 2007, and Levinson, 2007, "RIAA's Monstrous Legacy," for discussions of how the RIAA has alienated segments of the music-loving public). Neither will the Associated Press (AP) succeed in its attempt to require payment for posting of quotes from its articles in the free blogosphere (see Liza, 2008). As for the future of copyright, it will likely evolve to something closer to the "Creative Commons," in which the creator specifies what kinds of rights are given to the world at large—for example, right to copy but not commercialize (see creativecommons.org).

"Net neutrality" and "open source" systems are consistent with this post-Gutenberg, post-Marconi—or post-old media—approach to intellectual property. Net neutrality wants the digital architecture or operating systems and widgets of the Web to be entirely usable by any personal computer system, including nonproprietary, noncommercial systems, or those that may access the Web with programs other than Microsoft's or Apple's, or not protected by copyright and patent. Open-source systems permit anyone to see the code that makes a Web page work the way it does. The viewer can then capture and use this code to create new pages. Both net neutrality and open source approaches, which have yet to be universally realized and implemented, give the amateur, nonprofessional Web builder and programmer—that is, everyone—the same producer possibilities that new new media bestow to all readers, listeners, and viewers. Or we could say that net neutrality and open sourcing are to the structure or architecture of new new media as YouTube and everything else we are considering in this book are to the content of new new media, and the production and reception of this content.

Comments as Verifiers on YouTube: The Fleetwoods

As is the case with all new new media, the open invitation to everyone to upload video clips to YouTube means that some of the information that accompanies these videos—the brief descriptions of what is on the little screens, even the titles—could be wrong, intentionally or accidentally. Text and video comments, which can be written or uploaded by anyone (if the original video uploader allows this option), provide a mechanism for correction of such errors, just as text comments do in blogging.

Consider the case of The Fleetwoods. The California trio had two hugely successful No. 1 records in the 1950s, "Come Softly to Me" and "Mr. Blue," which featured mellow vocals and beautiful harmonies. The group was unusual in its membership, consisting of one male and two female singers: Gary Troxel, Gretchen Christopher, and Barbara Ellis. YouTube has a fine, vintage video of the group performing "Come Softly to Me" on *American Bandstand* in 1959. (I actually remember seeing that, with Dick Clark's introduction and all, when I was a kid.)

YouTube also has half a dozen other videos of The Fleetwoods, including performances in August 2007 on a PBS special and in November 2007 in Las Vegas. But, on closer inspection, these two performances are not quite by the original Fleetwoods. Gary Troxel is still singing a mellow lead in the PBS performance but with two other women. And Gretchen Christopher is the only original member of the group performing in Las Vegas.

But how would someone watching these video clips know this? Not from the titles or descriptions, which give only the name of the group, song, and venues. Fortunately, the comments entered by savvy viewers provided the clarifying details.

Of course, there is no guarantee that all or any comments for any video with misleading information will provide accurate corrections. But their capacity to do so—to draw upon the general wisdom of the millions of YouTube viewers—is an example of the self-corrective quality of new new media, which we will see in even greater prominence in Wikipedia, to be examined in chapter 13.

YouTube also added an "annotation" option in 2008, which allows uploaders of videos, at any time, to insert brief phrases of text (annotations) into the video. These can also help clarify who and what is seen in the video.

The Pope's Channel

January 2009 brought the news that "Pope Benedict XVI has launched his own dedicated channel on the popular video sharing website, YouTube" (BBC, 2009). A subsequent Associated Press article (Winfield, 2009) observed that, "The pontiff joins President Barack Obama, who launched an official White House channel on his inauguration day, as well as Queen Elizabeth, who went online with her royal YouTube channel in December 2007." The Vatican Channel, as it is officially called, had more than 1300 videos and 36,000 subscribers as of January 2012.

According to Winfield, the Vatican's embracing of what we are calling new new media is by no means free of proviso and controversy. On the one hand, "In his annual message for the World Day of Communication, Benedict praised as a 'gift to humanity' the benefits of social networking sites such as Facebook and MySpace in forging friendships and understanding." On the other hand, the pontiff "also warned that virtual socializing had its risks, saying 'obsessive' online networking could isolate people from real social interaction and broaden the digital divide by further marginalizing people." Pope Benedict reiterated and expanded this dialectic analysis in 2012—this time, about Twitter—observing that "in concise phrases, often no longer than a verse from the Bible, profound thoughts can be communicated, as long as those taking part in the conversation do not neglect to cultivate their own inner lives" (quoted in Golijan, 2012).

As we saw previously in "Viral Videos Gone Bad" and will see in more detail in chapter 15, "The Dark Side of New New Media," social media certainly have their dangers, ranging from cyberstalking and cyberbullying to even use by terrorists. But the concern about social media taking the place of real-life interactions and isolating people from in-person contact and their own deeper lives has been raised not only about new and new new media but as far back as motion pictures early in the 20th century (McKeever, 1910) and is the basis of concern about "bookworms," or people who spend too much time reading books and not enough in the "real," flesh-and-blood world (see Levinson, 2003, for more on the relationship of virtual and physical interactions). Not only is there no evidence of any such deleterious effect, but the use of Twitter and other new new media to bring together people in small and large groups for the Arab Spring and Occupy Wall Street in 2011 also refutes the proposition that social media get in the way of real-life meetings and interactions, or distract from pursuit of profound concerns. The Arab Spring and Occupy Wall Street similarly refute the notion of a burgeoning "digital divide," in which socioeconomic lower-income groups are locked out of the online process. YouTube, Facebook, Twitter, Wikipedia, and all new new media are, after all, free, and most are available via any kind of computer or smart phone, including older, less expensive models.

The Roman Catholic Church, indeed, has given a mixed reception to the new media of the day at least as far back as the introduction of print in Europe in the 1450s. Although writing was regarded as the "Apostolate of the Pen," the printed word was held suspect by some Church fathers as a debasement of the written manuscript, in which the hand that wrote was thought to be guided by the soul (see Eisenstein, 1979, for more). The dependence of the Protestant Reformation in 1519 on the printed Bible—Luther urged people to read the Bible for themselves, which would not have been possible without mass-produced printed Bibles—ironically substantiated the Church's concern about printing (see Levinson, 1997), but the Jesuit Counter Reformation was quick to recognize the pedagogic and propagandistic value of print. In the second part of the 20th century, the Church was once again a little slow to recognize the power of television, but the Vatican II Council from 1962–1965 rectified that. Like the Jesuit endorsement of print and the Vatican II's appreciation of one-way electronic mass media, Pope Benedict's YouTube channel demonstrates that, despite the Church's unwarranted misgivings, it is correct that in order to effectively disseminate its teachings in the 21st century, the Church needs to utilize the new new media of our day—in the case of YouTube, the ability to view a video message any time of day, from any place in the world, whenever one desires.

YouTube as International Information Liberator

Just as YouTube in America is available both to heads of state and to people on the street, as both consumers and producers, so, too, is YouTube internationally available to more than the Queen of England and the Pope.

Yulia Golobokova, my former student, is in her late 20s now. She was born in the Soviet Union and is presently a citizen of Russia. In December 2008—the last meeting of my fall 2008 graduate class "Media Research Methods" at Fordham University—Yulia presented a 10-minute summary of her final project, a proposal for research into some aspect of media or communication. Her topic was YouTube. Among the important points she made, many of which I introduced to the class and have discussed in this chapter, the one that struck me the most was this: YouTube, Yulia said, enabled her to find out what was going on in the world, find out the truth, when she was living in Moscow. Unlike television in her country, YouTube is not controlled by her government.

The beauty of YouTube is that it is not controlled by any government—neither Russian or American. I already knew that, and it is easy to take for granted, but the value of YouTube—and, indeed, of all new new media—to the world at large was brought home to me and became more than a theoretical point with a student from Russia standing up in my class and talking about it.

I first met Yulia in September 2008 when she walked into my office, a few days before our first class, and introduced herself. She said how happy she was to meet me and that I looked and sounded just as she had expected.

"How is that?" I asked, wondering how and why she might have some preconception of what I looked and sounded like.

"I've seen your videos in Moscow, lots of times, on YouTube," Yulia replied. In the realm of new new media, there is no difference between a computer screen in New York and in Moscow—they are equidistant on YouTube.

Of course, governments can attempt to ban YouTube, as Pakistan did for at least two hours in February 2008 because of "anti-Islamic content" (Malkin, 2008). The ban apparently caused worldwide problems with YouTube service, showing that the system is far from invulnerable and indeed is interconnected with and dependent on all kinds of other systems and servers and hence potentially weak or vulnerable links, as is the case with all new new media. Pakistan lifted the ban when informed that its "erroneous Internet protocols" had caused problems outside of Pakistan.

Fortunately, attempts of dictatorial governments to regulate media have had a poor record of success, as Nazi Germany found out with the "White Rose" anti-Nazi photocopiers (Dumbach & Newborn, 1986) and the Soviet Union discovered with its "samizdat videos" in the 1980s (Levinson, 1992). See the timeline in chapter 12 in the "Iran" section for the complete record of totalitarian regimes versus revolutionary media in the 20th and 21st centuries.

Resistance to authorities, whether in government or media, has never been easier in our age of YouTube and new new media. In chapter 13, we will look at how Wikipedia has overthrown the tyranny of the expert, at least insofar as the information and wisdom we expect to find in an encyclopedia.

Chapter Eleven

Blogging

**B**loggers are often referred to as "citizen journalists," to underline the fact that a blogger need not be a professional journalist to write and publish about the news. But the adjective "citizen" is still insufficient to convey the scope of liberation that blogging has bestowed upon us. The truth is that one need not be a citizen of this or any particular country, one need not be an adult, one need not have any attribute other than being able to read and write in order to blog.

Consider, for example, the following, and bear in mind that, although I am a professor of communication and media studies, I have no professional expertise in politics. I am just a citizen. But, even if I were not...

It was past one in the morning on May 7, 2008. Ninety-nine percent of the vote had finally come in from the Democratic presidential primary in Indiana. Hillary Clinton had won by just 2 percent. A few hours earlier, Barack Obama had won big in North Carolina. I wrote a blog post saying Barack Obama would be the Democratic nominee for president.

I posted it not only on InfiniteRegress.tv—my television review and politics blog—but on my Myspace blog as well. I put up links to it on Facebook and Digg. My blog on Amazon automatically posted it via a "feed." A link to my post also automatically appeared on Twitter.

My various "stat counters" reported that thousands of people had read my blog within an hour of its posting.

Just a few years earlier, the only possible recipient of my thoughts about such a decisive political development, moments after it had occurred in the middle of the night, would have been my wife. We could have talked about the results in

Indiana. I could also have written about them and sent this to any number of online magazines, but my words would not have been automatically posted. Gatekeepers—otherwise known as editors, likely not at work until the next morning—would have needed to approve them.

From the beginning of the human species, from the very first time that two people spoke, speech has been as easy to produce as to consume. We switch effortlessly from hearing to talking. But speech lacked permanence, and we invented writing to safeguard what our memories might lose. The written word was also almost as easy to produce as to consume—writing well is more difficult than being able to read, but to be literate was and is to be able to write as well as read. As long as the written words remained personal, individual, and not mass-produced, the process of writing—at least writing something, however brief—was as widespread as reading.

The printing press changed all of that. It opened many doors. It made Bibles, reports of Columbus's voyages, and scientific treatises readily available to millions of readers. But it ended the equality of consumers and producers, and radically altered the one-to-one ratio in which just about every reader was also a writer. A sliver of the population contributes what goes into books, newspapers, and magazines.

And now blogging has in turn changed and reversed all of that. Although there are still more readers than writers of blogs, any reader can become a writer, either by commenting on someone else's blog or, with just a little more effort, by starting a blog of one's own. More than 165 million blogs were being written in 2011.

Although speaking is easier than writing, publishing of writing in digital form—online—requires less production than online publishing of audio or audiovisual clips of spoken words. In fact, publication of a written blog requires no production at all beyond the writing and initial posting of the writing. "Web-logging" has been known by the name "blogging" since 1997 (McCullagh & Broache, 2007; but see also Katie Hafner's 1999 *New York Times* review of Heather Anne Halpert's *Lemonyellow.com*, identified as an "on-line intellectual diary"). It has roots in the digital age in "computer conferencing" and message boards that go back at least 15 years prior (Levinson, 1997), and thus became the first big player in the new new media revolution.

A Thumbnail History of Electronic Writing

Writing always had some advantages over speaking as a mode of human expression. Not only was writing permanent, in contrast to the instantly fleeting quality of speech, but writing also allowed the sender greater control of the message. An angry, very happy, or extremely sad speaker can find it difficult to disguise those emotions in speech. But the same emotions can make no appearance at all in a written document, unless the writer chooses to make those feelings plain. This is one reason texting surpassed speaking on cellphones in the hands of people under 45 around the world (Nielsen Mobile report, discussed by Finin, 2008).

But after the enormous boost given to the dissemination of the written word by the printing press, the progress of writing in the evolution of media was slow. The telegraph in the 1830s gave the written word the capacity to be sent anywhere in the world—or anywhere connected by wires and cables—instantly. But the requirement of a telegraph operator to make this happen, as well as someone to deliver the telegram, not only worked against the immediacy of this electronic communication but also made it far more impersonal than written letters. It was one thing to declare your love in a letter and quite another to utter those words to a telegraph operator for transmission to the intended recipient.

The telegraph, however, revolutionized news delivery by allowing reporters to file stories instantly with their newspapers. Baron Julius von Reuter started his news service with carrier pigeons, which could convey news more quickly than via boats across the English Channel. But the baron's news agency soon came to rely on the telegraph. Its successful descendant was bought by the Thomson Company for $15.8 billion in 2008 (Associated Press, 2008).

Blogging takes the dissemination of news and opinion one big step beyond the telegraph by allowing "reporters"—that is, people, everyone—to file their stories instantly not with their newspapers but on their blogs and, therein, with the world at large. And because blogs are under the personal editorship of the writer, they can be about anything the writer pleases—unlike newspapers and magazines, where professional editors—not writers—usually decide the subject of the stories.

This personalization or "de-professionalization" of communication is one of the signal characteristics of new new media. It was not until the deployment of the fax in the 1980s, and the advent of email around the same time, that the writer finally reclaimed privacy and control over the written word. But the fax was primarily for one-to-one communication—much like the telegraph. And even emails sent to groups were less than a drop in the bucket in the reach of mass media such as newspapers. Blogging combines the best of both—the personal control of email and the long reach of mass media.

Blogging About Anything, Forever

The personal control that the writer has over his or her blog means that the blog can be about any subject, not just news. On the evening of May 29, 2008, my blog received 20,000 "hits" on a page (views of the page) I had written the year before, about the previous season's finale of *Lost* (Season 3 finale: "Through the Looking Glass"). This development, something that happens on blogs all the time, highlights two significant characteristics of blogging, in particular, and new new media, in general. The first is that anyone can blog about anything—I'm a professor and an author, not a professional television critic. The second is that the impact of a blog post, including when it will have its maximum impact, is unpredictable. My blog post about *Lost* received thousands of online visits shortly after it was written in 2007, but these were less than half of the visits or hits it surprisingly received on that one day a year later in 2008.

Permanence is one of the most revolutionary aspects of new new media and characterizes all new new media—as we saw with YouTube in chapter 10—not just blogging. One of the prime characteristics of old electronic media, such as radio and television, was their fleeting quality. Like the in-person spoken word, the word on radio and television was gone the instant after it was spoken. This evanescence led Lewis Mumford (1970, p. 294) to critique the viewers of television as in a "state of mass psychosis" in which "man" is confined to a "present time-cage that cuts him off from both his past and his future." Mumford apparently was not aware of the professional video recorders and "portapak" video cameras that were already giving television some permanence in 1970 (see Levinson, 1997, for more of my critique of Mumford), but he certainly was not wrong that the electronic media of his day offered information that was far less permanent than that conveyed by print. The first wave of new, digital media—the Web of the mid-1990s—began to invest its communications with more permanence. But until the use of "permalinks" became widespread, a development that awaited the rise of blogging in the first years of the 21st century, items on the Web lacked anything remotely like the "reliable locatability" of words on pages of books on shelves discussed in chapter 13 (see also Levinson, 1998; Levinson, *Cellphone*, 2004; and Levinson, "The Secret Riches," 2007, for more).

Although blog pages still lack the reliable locatability of books—it is easier for a blogger to remove a post, or her or his entire blog, than it is to write a new post—their instant availability to anyone, anywhere, with a connection to the Internet may in one way give them a greater net durability (pun intended), a durability to more people, than any book. If a text is available online for 10 years to millions of people, is it more or less durable to the culture than 1000 books available for 100 years on library shelves? Indeed, it may well be that the ease of making permalinks, along with the sheer number of people who can easily access them, will make the contents of blogs more permanent, in the long run, than printed books—even though, in the short run, printed books are still the best bet for durability.

The blog post is thus not only immediate and universally accessible, but, like the YouTube video, the blog post can last forever. Indeed, whether photograph, video, or text, once it is committed to the Web, it is not only easily deletable on a given page but in principle all but impossible to delete everywhere. This is because anyone can make a copy and post the item to his or her blog or Web page. And once a photograph, video, or text has been downloaded to a device held in your hand, it is beyond the capacity of any system on the Web to erase (unless its text is on an Amazon Kindle). The immediacy of new new media and the ease of erasing or preventing access to its contents can disguise this kind of permanence through dissemination and give the impression that everything posted on the Web is easy come, easy go. But, in fact, the potential indelibility of anything posted online may be, literally, its most enduring characteristic.

We might also say that the sovereignty that the blogger has over his or her blog—the freedom from foreign gatekeepers ("foreign" being anyone other than the blogger)—finds its limit not only in the larger system on which the blog resides (Blogspot, Wordpress, whatever—see the upcoming section on blogging platforms), but in the ability of anyone to copy whatever is in the blog, for saving or dissemination.

Comment Moderation

The blogger's sovereignty also relates to gatekeeping in a different way: Although the blogger is not subject to anyone else's gatekeeping, the blogger becomes a gatekeeper in deciding whether to allow comments by others on the blog and, if so, how to moderate them.

The pros and cons of gatekeeping or moderating comments on one's blog are straightforward. Moderating comments, rather than allowing them to be posted automatically, allows the blogger to keep disruptive comments out of the blog. But such moderation also slows the pace of the blog. Unless the blogger is online every minute of the day, an excellent comment, which could spark further excellent comments, could be left waiting for approval.

Is the protection of the blog from undesirable comments worth such a potential slowing and even stifling of worthwhile conversation? It depends on what the blogger and the larger world of readers deem undesirable. Certainly we can see why even strong disagreement with a blogger's political positions, or analysis of a television show, should not be barred from the blog. Indeed, a blogger can usually use such criticisms as a springboard for elaboration of the blogger's initial opinion. "But don't you think mega-funding of candidates is undermining our democracy?" a comment could ask. "No, I do not," the blogger could respond and go on to explain how people can separate truth from falsity regardless of who pays for the message.

But this is all a matter of the blogger's judgment. A comment deemed disruptive by one blogger might be deemed conducive to valuable, multiple discussions by another blogger. Or a given blogger might want no comments at all, preferring the blog to be a one-way rather than an interactive mode of communication.

Bloggers can also install a CAPTCHA system ("Completely Automated Public Turing test to tell Computers and Humans Apart"), which requires commenters to answer a computer-generated question (for example, reproduce a blurry sequence of numbers and letters) designed to distinguish human commenters from automated spam. A CAPTCHA, of course, will not get in the way of a human being bent on entering a nasty or disruptive comment in a blog.

In general, bloggers who want to encourage comments might keep in mind the following principle: Only block or remove comments if you believe they will discourage other comments from you and your readers. A blog without comments is like a flightless bird: The blog may make important contributions or bring satisfaction to its writer, but it will lack one of the signature social characteristics of new new media—interaction with the audience. (But see the discussion of Kathy Sierra in the "Online Gossiping and Cyberbullying" section of chapter 15, "The Dark Side of New New Media," for what can happen when comments become abusive. And see Kennedy, 2012, for the *New Haven Independent* decision to do away with commenting, because it had "skidded to the nasty edges and run off the rails.")

Commenting as the Ubiquitous Greek Chorus

As easy as blogging is, writing a comment in someone else's blog, or any online forum, is even easier. All the commenter needs to do is enter the comment in a blog that already exists. Indeed, entering a comment on someone else's blog can be a very effective way of promoting your own blog. If your comment is about an issue that you are blogging about and you sign your comment—that is, your comment is not anonymous (see the "Anonymity in Blogging" section later in this chapter)—then readers of your comment can easily find your blog. You can encourage this discovery of your blog by including a link to it in your comment, but some bloggers may see this as use of their blog for promotion of other blogs and lodge an objection (either by entering a comment that says "please don't use my blog to promote yours" or by removing your comment—see "Further Tensions Between New New Media and Older Forms" later in this chapter for details).

As a blogger, I welcome comments with links—as long as the comments and links are relevant to the discussion at hand and not spam for gold sold at low prices. Because, whatever the motivation of the commenter, comments that are not spam serve to further what Comenius centuries ago called "The Great Didactic" (1649/1896).

Given that blog entries on new media systems such as *Entertainment Weekly* or *USA Today* regularly draw hundreds of comments—and on new new media amateur blogs (such as mine) anywhere from none to a few to occasionally hundreds of comments per entry—the comment is clearly the most frequent form of sustained written discourse in the new new media world. Comments on active Facebook and YouTube pages can number in the thousands, and are part of this commenting culture. (My 2006 debate with Jack Thompson about violence in video games, put on YouTube in 2007, had more than 3700 comments as of February 2012.)

At their best, comments serve not only as a voice of the people but as conveyors of truth and correction to blog posts, videos, and any item on the Web. In this capacity, commenting epitomizes the democratic alternative to expert-driven information that is one of the hallmarks of new new media, and has been developed to a fine art on Wikipedia (see chapter 13). At their worst, comments can be vehicles for trolls to grab attention and can mar or derail an online conversation (see chapter 15 for more). In between, comments are the ubiquitous Greek chorus of the new new media world.

"Is it a fact—or have I dreamed it—that, by means of electricity, the world of matter has become a great nerve, vibrating thousands of miles in a breathless point in time?" Nathaniel Hawthorne's character Clifford asks about the telegraph in *The House of the Seven Gables* (1851/1962, p. 239). It was indeed a fact back then. But not as much as when Marshall McLuhan talked about the "global village" in *The Gutenberg Galaxy* in 1962. And by no means as much as now, when Hawthorne's and McLuhan's visions have achieved their fullest realization in the hundreds of millions of comments on Facebook, YouTube, and 165 million blogs worldwide at any instant.

Comments as Correctors

I try to get my reviews of television shows posted on my *Infinite Regress* blog within a few minutes of the conclusion of the show's episode on television, which serves to maximize the number of people who will read my review.

But such a tight schedule does not always make for a review that is perfectly factual. I make it a point to mention the names of actors and actresses, if they play important roles in a show I am reviewing, but sometimes these may not be available online, either on the show's website or on IMDB (Internet Movie Database).

On October 12, 2007, I reviewed the 12th episode of the first season of AMC's *Mad Men* on my blog. It was an excellent episode, and I mentioned in my review that "my favorite sex/romantic scene in this show was Harry (Isaac Asimov!) (played by Rich Sommer) and that secretary (played by xxxx)." The "Harry" was Harry Crane, who, in my opinion at least, looks a lot like science fiction author Isaac Asimov did in the 1950s and 1960s. (You can see their two photographs side by side at my "Interview with Rich Sommer," 2007.)

But to return to comments as correctors, the reason I wrote "played by xxxx" in the preceding paragraph is that, in my original blog post, I listed the wrong actress. I had looked at IMDB and every site of relevance I could find on the Web. I could find no actress credited with playing beside Rich Sommer on the couch. So I then pored over whatever photos I could find of actresses who played secretaries on *Mad Men* and came up with the wrong actress as having played "that secretary."

The first I learned of my mistake was via a comment in my blog, written about 30 minutes after I posted my review. It read, "Hey, Paul. I read your reviews every week. Thanks for the kind words, and for helping to get the word out. We really appreciate it! An important correction: Hildy is played by Julie McNiven. She deserves full credit for her amazing work!"

And the comment had been entered by none other than Rich Sommer!

We exchanged emails after that, and I interviewed Rich on my *Light On Light Through* podcast by the end of the month.

But, aside from the coolness of blogging about an actor and then being contacted by him on the blog—something that has happened to me more than once and is a good example of the equalization of new new media, in which famous and not-so-famous people can more easily be in touch—the comment by Rich Sommer, with a correction of my misidentification of the actress in his scene, spotlights the important role that comments can serve as correctors in blogging.

The whole world, in principle, is not only reading what you write when you blog but is waiting there as a potential safety net and source of correction for any mistakes you might make. These readers are much like the reader/editors on Wikipedia, except reader/commenters on blogs are likely a more diffuse community, larger but less intent on finding and correcting errors.

Of course, not all comments are helpful, and some might be hostile. But the correction of your review by the very subject of your review, within half an hour of its posting, is something new under the sun of media, unless your review was delivered on a live television broadcast, and the subject of the review happened to have your phone number.

As for Rich Sommer's helpful correction (his comment is still on the page), I changed the wrong name to Julie McNiven as soon as I finished reading his comment, and taking in the larger significance of hearing from a celebrity.

Myspace Message from Stringer Bell of *The Wire*

Everyone is a fan of someone, usually more than one actor, actress, singer, musician, or author. As exciting as it was to hear from Rich Sommer after blogging about him, his was not the most extraordinary and unexpected comment I received from an actor, or from a member of an actor's family, after blogging about the actor. In addition to Rich Sommer, I heard from Len Cariou's wife (via a comment still on the page) after I had blogged in 2007 about how much I had enjoyed his performance in two seasons of *Brotherhood* on Showtime (the character died at the end of the second season) and from the father of Aaron Hart (via email), one of two actors who played Don Draper's little boy in the second season of *Mad Men* in the summer of 2008. But as fortunate as I was with *Mad Men*—hearing from two actors or relatives of actors on the series—and as much as I enjoyed both *Mad Men* and *Brotherhood* (and still enjoy *Mad Men*; *Brotherhood* ended its run in 2008), neither, in my view, achieved the extraordinary quality of *The Wire*, which ran for five seasons on HBO, from 2002 to 2008.

Paramount among *The Wire*'s characters, dominating every scene he was in for the first three seasons (his tenure on *The Wire*) was Stringer Bell, second in command of the drug operation under investigation by the police. An attendee of night classes in economics, a copy of Adam Smith's 1776 *The Wealth of Nations* on his shelf, and as ready to kill if necessary as to worry about inflation, Stringer Bell was no ordinary ghetto drug chief.

In August 2006, when the only blog I was writing was the very occasional *Twice Upon a Rhyme* on Myspace (named after my 1972 album of the same name), I wrote a piece about *The Wire*. The little knowledge I had then of blog promotion led me to post a link and brief summary of the blog post on HBO's "Community" forum about *The Wire*.

A few months later, in the wee hours of a day in late October, I was quickly reading through a batch of "Friend" requests on Myspace. It was late. I was tired. I was not thinking at all about *The Wire*, and although the name Idris Elba seemed familiar enough for me to accept his Friend request without looking at his page, I went on quickly to the other Friend requests and promptly forgot about Idris's— until I received a message from Idris Elba about a week later, in which he told me that he'd read my comments about his acting on *The Wire* a while earlier, thanked me for my support, noted my long involvement in the music business and wondered what I thought of his music. He added that he'd be buying my latest book, *The Plot to Save Socrates*, because it was the sort of novel he liked to read.

I liked his music, especially his hip-hop version of "Johnny Was," so much so that I played it on a special episode of my *Light On Light Through* podcast, "*The Wire* Without Stringer," on November 4, 2006. I received another message on Myspace from Idris Elba a few days later in which he thanked me for dedicating an entire podcast to his work, appreciated my scholarly analysis of his acting and music and what made his character Stringer Bell so compelling, and indicated that his music came from the same place as his acting, except his music was his own script.

(This message is currently posted on the right-hand column of my *Light On Light Through* podcast page.)

In the realm of new new media that we all inhabit, it is that easy for someone, anyone, watching television, with computer, now tablet or smart phone, at hand, to strike up a relationship with the star of that television show.

Changing the Words in Your Blog—After Publication

The blogger's authority over the blog pertains not only to the comments but also to the blog post itself, not only before it is posted on the blog but also for as long as it remains on the blog, which could be forever after.

Writing used to be the archetypically immutable medium. Writing with ink or whatever chemical or dye on papyrus, parchment, or paper gave those words life as long as the papyrus, parchment, or paper survived. The words could be crossed out or obliterated, of course, but the obliteration was still observable. Ink could fade, but rarely to the point of being totally illegible. Even erasing the marks of a pencil on paper leaves signs of the erasure.

The printing press heightened this immutability. Under pressure from the Roman Catholic Church, Galileo recanted his views that the Earth revolved around the sun. But the thousands of copies of books expressing his original opinion were not changed with the recantation. The Church won a Pyrrhic victory, and the Scientific Revolution continued (see Levinson, 1997, for more).

That happened in the first decades of the 1600s. This immutability of published writing was still very much in effect at the end of the 19th century, at the end of the Victorian age of printed literacy, when Oscar Wilde famously is supposed to have observed about the process of authoring that "books are never finished, they are merely abandoned" (the quote more likely originates a little later, however, with French poet Paul Valéry in 1933 and is about creating art or writing poetry). But whether of book, poem, or painting, the abandonment was as real as a loved one moving out of the home. Once published, a book or a newspaper article was beyond being changed by the author, except via means of a new edition of a book (as you are reading now of *New New Media*) or an editor willing to publish an amending note by the reporter in the newspaper, neither of which were likely. But that was to radically change with the advent of "word processing" and then online publishing by the end of the next century (see Levinson, 1997). And in our 21st-century age of new new media, bloggers may be seen to have the reverse problem: The easy revision of a blog means it is never really finished and all but impossible to abandon if the blog is on a site under the blogger's control.

Here is how that came to be: In the last two decades of the 1900s, word processing for the first time in history gave writers the capacity to change their written words with no telltale evidence of the original. Spelling errors could be corrected in an email prior to sending and ideas could be sharpened in manuscripts with no one other than the writer the wiser.

But email and manuscripts submitted to editors were by and large one-on-one communications. Once a manuscript was printed and published, it was as immutable in the 1980s as were the words wedded to the paper of Galileo's books in the 1600s.

Blogging made the publication as easy to alter as the initial writing. The most innocuous result is that spelling errors are easily correctable, as are missing words. There is no downside to such correction, nothing nefarious. But what about the capacity of any blogger to easily change the material wording and meaning of a blog post after it has been published?

If no one or few people have seen the original, such alterations pose no problem. But what if many people have read the original and commented on it, in whatever media available?

On the one hand, changing a text already extensively commented on can certainly generate confusion. What is Reader "C" to make of a blog post and comment in which Blogger "A" quietly changed the wording of the blog to reflect and remedy a critique made by Commenter "B"? One way Blogger "A" can eliminate any ensuing confusion is to speak up about the change—that is, put a postscript in the blog post, appropriately dated, that explains that a change was made in response to a comment made by Commenter "B." But what if the blogger neglects or decides not to do that?

On the other hand, the greater the number of people who have read and commented on a text, the more difficult for the author to surreptitiously alter the text and pretend the altered text was in the blog post all along. The audience for the initial text thus serves as protection against the changing of the text for purposes of deception, just as the same audience can be a safety net for the blogger by pointing out errors in the blog that can be corrected. (Wikipedia, as we will see in chapter 13, deals with this problem in a more efficient way, providing an easily accessible transcript of every edit made to an article.)

The social group as a guarantor of truth or, at the very least, accuracy, is a check-and-balance that works to the benefit of all new new media and their users.

Long-Range Blogging and Linking

The duration of blog posts for months, in some cases years, after their posting allows for another kind of self-promotion, in which the blogger keeps abreast of comments about his or her post in other blogs on the Web and adjusts the links in the original post to take advantage of these new comments.

Here is an example: In August 2007, I wrote a short item in one of my blogs with four pieces of advice to would-be writers. The item drew many readers (see "Gauging the Readership of Your Blog," later in this chapter, for how bloggers can keep track on a daily or even more immediate basis of the number of readers). A few months earlier, I had begun a podcast—*Ask Lev*—with brief, 3–5-minute bits of advice to writers. At some point a few months after my August 2007 posting, I got an email from a reader saying he was trying to locate my "My Four Rules: The Best

You Can Do to Make It as a Writer" blog post but could not find it and instead had discovered my *Ask Lev* podcast, which had answered his questions.

The first improvement of my August 2007 "Four Rules" then occurred to me: put a link in that post to the *Ask Lev* podcast, because readers of the post would be likely to find the podcast of interest. Of course, that could and should have occurred to me when I first wrote the post. But the infinite perfectibility of any blog allowed me to recover and to put in this link months later.

The story continues: In December 2007, I interviewed Dr. Stanley Schmidt, editor of *Analog Magazine of Science Fiction and Fact* (the leading science fiction magazine), for my *Light On Light Through* podcast. That interview drew many listeners, including those on *Analog*'s online site, AnalogSF.com, where it became a topic of conversation. I, of course, kept a happy eye on these online discussions and noticed in October 2008 that someone said one of the best parts of the interview was the advice it gave to writers who wanted to get published in *Analog*. This immediately set off another insert-a-link bell, and I proceeded to put a link to the August 2007 "Four Rules" blog post in the text accompanying my podcast interview with Stan Schmidt.

You can see where this is going: Once you begin to look at not just your blog but the whole Web as your oyster for blog promotion, you have entered a realm in which your words not only do not deteriorate but also can improve with time, as you draw ever more readers from different places to your blog. The key is that, although blogging is usually a solitary process, its promotion is inherently social and thrives on the easy linking of the Web.

Of course, if you are not interested in large numbers of readers, or any readers at all, you can always make your blog private and admit only those readers who meet your criteria. This would deprive your blog of many of the social advantages of new new media, but the preeminent principle is nonetheless that the blogger has complete control over his or her online work and its dissemination (aside from the organization that owns the blog platform).

Usually, the blog will be the continuing creation of an individual. But sometimes the very blog writing itself can be a group activity.

Group Blogging

Entries or articles on Wikipedia are edited by everyone, which is also an option for any blogger who might want to open one or more blog posts to other authors. Such group blogging is a good example of readers literally becoming writers of the very text they are reading.

Writing has traditionally been and usually is an individual effort, in contrast to talking, which usually entails two or more people (it could be argued that talking to yourself is not really talking because no interpersonal communication takes place unless someone overhears you, in which case you are no longer talking only to yourself). The advent of group blogging thus can be seen as a further erosion of the difference between writing and talking, which began when word processing made correction of the written word almost as easy as the spoken and in some ways more effective, because the digitally corrected written word can leave no trace of the original, in contrast to the listener's memory of a spoken error.

But group writing has at least one disadvantage: Unlike a spoken conversation, in which each voice is identifiable as belonging to a separate person (even if we do not know who that person is), nothing in the written word intrinsically connects it to any author. Wikipedia, again, addresses this problem by providing detailed "histories" of every article, in which every edit is clearly identified. Group blogs are usually less sophisticated and often do nothing more than list everyone who has written or edited a given post.

The main benefit of group writing of blogs is that it can increase the sum total of expertise brought to the blog. For example, in December 2008, I started a blog entitled *Educated Tastes* about food, drink, restaurants, recipes, and groceries. Because my expertise in food pertains mostly to consumption, I had a choice of either leaving recipes out of the mix or bringing another writer on board who knew how to cook and write about it. Because my wife excels in both, I invited her to join the blog as a writer.

Whether blogwriting or songwriting or scriptwriting, the same calculus of collaboration applies. If such collaboration adds more to the project than any frustration you might feel from sharing your creative control, then it is worth trying.

Monetizing Your Blog

The commercial essence of the Web has always been that it's free—"only suckers pay for content," as David Carr aptly observed about what succeeds most on the Web in *The New York Times*, back in 2005. That still holds true, and more so than ever, with flourishing, free sites such as *The Huffington Post*, even though newspapers such as *The New York Times* have begun to put much of their content—formerly available for free on the Web—behind "pay walls" to offset loss of income from declining paper sales (literally newspapers on paper) and loss of advertising (see the discussion later in this chapter). But a site being available for free—whether *The Huffington Post* or your own blog—does not mean that you cannot earn money from your blogging.

You can make money from any blog or online site in five general ways:

1. Google AdSense is the grandparent of revenue-making by individuals (you and me) on the Web. You sign up, get "code" to put on your blog, and you're in business. Text, image, and/or video ads, the size and subject and placement of your choosing, appear on your blog. The work required to set this up is easy and less demanding than the writing of most blog posts.

That is the good news. The not-so-good news is that you won't make much money—not enough to retire on or earn a living from and not even enough in a month to buy a decent dinner in New York. An average of 500 to 1000 visitors a day is likely to earn you no more than about $10 per month from Google AdSense, which pays on clicks and impressions, meaning you get paid for the number of people who click on the ads (clicks) or view them (impressions). As is the case with many online ad services, Google AdSense only pays you when your ads have earned a set minimum amount of revenue—in the case of AdSense, $100.

You will likely find that ads about certain topics—usually those that relate in some way to the subjects of your blog posts—attract more clicks on your blog than ads that have nothing to do with the subject of your blog. AdSense automatically runs ads, when available, that relate to the subjects of your posts. Unfortunately, this selection process is keyed only to the subject and can miss the tone or opinion of your blog post. A post on my blog that criticized John McCain in the 2008 presidential campaign attracted Google ads in support of McCain. The same happened with Mitt Romney in 2012. If such ads are not acceptable to the anti-Republican blogger, Google AdSense provides a means of filtering out any ads on specified unwanted subjects. But unless this is done when the ad code is first created, an unwelcome ad can nonetheless appear on the blog. The code, however, can be revised at any time. If I hadn't been so busy, I would have put in filters for ads that went contrary to my political views before I blogged on the subjects. Blogging takes more than compelling writing to make money in a way that stays true to the goals of your blog. It requires careful tending, much like a garden, to limit the likelihood and impact of weeds—that is, ads you don't want to see on your blog.

You might find that video and image ads attract more clicks than text ads. Placement of the ads can also increase your revenue. A text ad at the top of a blog can generate far more hits than attractive image and video ads in the sidebar. But ads placed at the top of the blog give the blog a more commercial look than ads placed in the sidebar. The blogger thus has a choice: Which is more important, appearance of the blog or income earned? Of course, if you want your blog to look as commercial as possible, then your course of action is clear.

The key point in all cases is that you have complete control over the kinds of ads (text, image, video) and where on your blog they are placed, as well as some control over the subject of the ads. You can learn via experiment which combinations look best and which produce the most revenue.

2. Amazon Associates has a different approach. You place ads for Amazon's books and other products on your blog page and get paid a percentage every time someone clicks on the ads and buys something from Amazon. The percentage, as of January 2012, starts at 4 percent for the first 6 sales, increases to 6 percent when sales number 7 or more, increases to 6.5 percent when there are 33 or more sales, and so forth. As an author, I find it valuable to have numerous Amazon ads on my blogs for my own books. But the more general guiding principle for this kind of monetization is not that you need to be an author of books sold on Amazon but a blogger willing to do the little research required to see which books on Amazon relate to subjects of your blog posts.

For example, in a review of an episode of *Lost* in its fourth season, in which time travel played a major role, I not only placed Amazon ads for my own time travel novel, *The Plot to Save Socrates*, but also for such time travel classics as Isaac Asimov's *The End of Eternity* and Robert Heinlein's *The Door into Summer*.

Because Amazon sells much more than books, you can use its Associate services to sell a wide range of products on your site. For example, if you have a blog about food, you could put Amazon ads for foodstuffs, beverages, cutlery, and the like on your blog.

CafePress operates in a somewhat similar way. You design a logo, which can be placed on coffee mugs, T-shirts, and so forth. You place an ad for the item on your blog. CafePress produces an item every time one is ordered—publishing on demand—at no cost to you. CafePress sets its price, and you can add whatever you like, above that price, for your commission. If your logo is some sort of advertising for your blog, you earn not only a commission but also good publicity for every sale.

Unlike Amazon, however, you either need sufficient talent to design an attractive logo for CafePress or will have to hire or persuade someone to design it for you. In contrast, Amazon supplies images of the book covers and all of its products in the ads for your blog.

3. In the case of Google AdSense and Amazon Associates, nothing is changed in the writing of your blogs—the ads are placed at the bottom, the sides, the top, or in the middle (if you prefer) of your text; it's your choice. PayPerPost, one of several different such operations, offers another kind of approach to making money from your blog: You are paid to write posts on given subjects.

PayPerPost pays anywhere from $5 to $500 or more for blog posts requested by its clients. Your payment depends mainly upon the popularity of your blog—how many readers the advertiser can expect will see your post about the advertiser's subject.

The great advantage of this kind of blog monetization is the money you see in hand from your blog posts. Leading earners on PayPerPost since its inception in 2006 have received more than $10,000 per year for their written-to-order blog posts. It's relatively easy to see hundreds of dollars of income in a year—more than the Google AdSense revenue indicated earlier.

The disadvantage is you may be tempted to write about subjects you otherwise might not want to write about in your blog. This can undermine one of the crucial benefits of new new media and blogging: writing whatever you want, with no gatekeepers to approve or disapprove of your output. The fine line to be walked is writing reviews of products you already know about and like. But this could be difficult: Would you pass up $500 to write a positive post about a product you thought was just okay, not great?

The principle of being honest with your readers can also come into conflict under this kind of monetized blogging. PayPerPost insists as standard operating procedure that all of its assigned posts have a clearly displayed notice that the blog post was purchased or written for hire. As a further safeguard, PayPerPost also requires all participating bloggers to publish at least one nonhired post for every purchased post, which further makes clear to the reader which posts were hired. But several other "blog for money" organizations want otherwise—reasoning, probably correctly, that readers would take the post more seriously if they thought the post came from the blogger's mind and heart and not the advertiser's paycheck. Indeed, even

PayPerPost offers a few of these "nondisclosure" opportunities, with the proviso that it did not endorse the approach but would be willing to serve as broker if that is what the advertiser and the blogger both wanted.

Another, related problem can arise from the general topic of the blog post. Favorably reviewing a movie you already saw and liked, or even expected that you would like, is one thing. But what about accepting PayPerPost blogging assignments for political or social issues, in which the assignment requires you to write on behalf of the issue or candidate? Even if you support the issue, and even with the PayPerPost disclosure advisory on assigned posts and no advisory on everything else, taking on such political assignments can cast doubt among your readers that you mean what you say in your nonhired posts. If you want your readers to be 100 percent certain that the political analyses they read on your blog are 100 percent yours, the safest course of action may be to avoid doing any PayPerPost or hired blog posts on political and social subjects. (See also "Bloggers and Lobbyists," later in this chapter.)

4. You can put a PayPal donation widget—a digital money tip jar—either on your overall blog or on any specific blog post. PayPal is in effect an online banking service, which receives payments from other PayPal accounts, as well as traditional credit cards, and makes payments to other PayPal accounts. PayPal account holders can transfer funds from PayPal to their traditional bank accounts.

How much money can a PayPal donation button generate on a blog? Shaun Farrell's 2007 podiobook of my 1999 novel *The Silk Code* provides an instructive example. A podiobook is an audiobook available free, online, in weekly installments, from Podiobook.com. *The Silk Code* podiobook placed in the top 20 of podiobooks downloaded in 2007 (its exact placement in the top 20 was not revealed). More than a thousand people downloaded all or part of the novel. Farrell received about $100 in the PayPal donation box on his blog page.

But a podiobook is not a typical blog. Because a podiobook appeals to an audience that might otherwise purchase an audiobook, donations to the author (and, in Farrell's case, the narrator) make some sense. In contrast, authors of written blogs tell me they are lucky to receive even a few dollars a year from their tip jars.

5. A fifth way of making money from one's blog draws upon the oldest form of advertising and predates new new media by centuries: You can accept and place ads on your blog, paid for directly by the advertiser. You can make far more money than via Google AdSense—you can charge whatever the market for blog ads will bear, based on the number of people who read your blog—but the price you pay for not going through the Google AdSense middleman is you have to find the advertisers, or they have to find you.

This kind of advertising goes back to the advent of newspapers in the 1500s, 1600s, and 1700s—they were called "pamphlets" back then—and developed as follows: Originally, printers were funded and supported by the monarchs of Europe, and especially fortunate printers were designated "royal presses." But monarchs expected printers to publish stories favorable to the monarchs, and eventually some printers began to chafe under this arrangement.

Merchants with ships laden with goods from the New World provided a way out and indeed a solution that provided the economic basis of democracy. Merchants paid printers to run announcements of their products, what we today call "ads." Other than printing these announcements, the presses could print whatever else they pleased. Printers thereby gained the economic freedom to break free of royal purse strings and political reins. This worked best first in England and then America, which enacted the First Amendment to ensure that the government, even in a democracy, could never control the press. (As I detail in my "The Flouting of the First Amendment," 2005, the First Amendment has not always been adhered to in America; see the "First Amendment" section later in this chapter. See also *The Soft Edge*, Levinson, 1997, for more on the advent of advertising and its political consequences.)

The advertising symbiosis, however—merchants get publicity, printers get money, both are beneficiaries—became a bedrock of American media and continued in the age of radio and television, which went a big step further than newspapers by providing content free of charge to their listeners and viewers. Consumers paid for the receiving equipment—radio or television set—but received the content free. Radio and television stations and networks made money by attracting consumers of the free programming and then selling airtime, or exposure to the audience numbers, to sponsors. The free blog, though it is written like a newspaper article, is therefore more like the traditional broadcast media in terms of being free. And, although one of the hallmarks of new new media content is that it costs the consumer nothing, this characteristic began not with new new media but with older broadcast media. Ironically, although free radio and television continue to be major players in our lives, "teens and young adults cut their radio-listening time in half as they became infatuated with the Internet, cellphones and video games" in the past decade (Lieberman, 2011, who also notes a small "renaissance" for radio in 2009–2011), and the number of network television viewers has been declining on and off for almost two decades, with paid cable and free new new media drawing away audiences (Associated Press, 2008; see also Hibberd, 2011, for TV ownership declining in 2011–2012).

In all such classic cases of paid advertising, the ad is paid for on a cost-per-thousand basis—that is, how many thousands of people will see or hear the ad. Television programs live or die depending on the number of their viewers, as reported by the Nielsen ratings. These ratings are based on statistically valid samples of the total television-viewing public. In contrast, the new new medium of blogging on the Web offers direct counts, not samples, of blog visitors (see "Gauging the Readership of Your Blog," later in this chapter).

But the blog, as we learned earlier, also offers ways not available in print or broadcast media to earn income from an ad—there is no way to click on an ad heard on radio, or seen on television or in a newspaper, unless we're experiencing those old media on the Web. Online ads also can provide knowledge of where the purchase of an online product or service originated by showing the clicked link that resulted in a purchase. This is a much more precise and efficient method of tracking the source of sales than providing a code seen on television when ordering a product by phone, and facilitates the Amazon method of payment, in which the blogger is paid a percentage of the sale.

Television, radio, and newspapers, then, charge for their ads based solely on how many people can be expected to see or hear the ad (the cost-per-thousand, or CPM, formula). In contrast, although blog ads that come directly from advertisers can also work on such a CPM basis, the blogger can also be paid based on the number of clicks and actual purchases resulting from an ad. When payments are made based on number of impressions, or CPM, methods of gauging the readership of one's blog are crucial (see "Gauging," later in this chapter).

These five ways of earning money from your blog—Google AdSense, Amazon ads, PayPerPost, PayPal donations, and direct ad purchases—all pertain to blogs completely under the blogger's control. In the "Blogging for Others" section later in this chapter, we will consider the opportunities for remuneration when you blog for someone else. But, first, let's consider in a little more detail the degree to which any way of monetizing your blog may be incompatible with the communicative and democratizing ideals of blogging.

Is Monetization Incompatible with the Ideals of Blogging?

Not everyone in the blogosphere is happy about the monetization possibilities of blogging. Jeff Jarvis, creator of *Entertainment Weekly* and the well-known *BuzzMachine* blog, put the "problem" he saw with the PayPerPost model as follows: "The advertisers are trying to buy a blogger's voice, and once they've bought it they own it" (Friedman, 2007).

David Sirota, then a senior fellow at the Campaign for America's Future, saw a different kind of harm arising from advertising in blogging. Criticizing a report that Jonathan Martin gave on Politico.com about President-elect Obama's December 7, 2008, appearance on *Meet the Press*—that Obama was "backing off" (Martin's phrase) his campaign pledges on taxes and Iraq—Sirota concluded with the following: "I'm not linking to [Martin's] story because the entire reason the *Politico* made up this outrageous lie is to get people to link to the story and build up traffic which it then uses to attract ad revenue" (Sirota, 2008).

Jarvis, then, sees money as putting literal words in bloggers' mouths—or via their fingers in their blogs—while Sirota sees the desire to increase the number of readers, to increase advertising revenue, as leading to the writing of blogs of "outrageous lies."

Both concerns may be warranted. But let's try to put the pursuit of money by the press in historical context. Why and how did advertising as a source of income for the press arise in the first place? And what damage, if any, has resulted to a free press from this?

As we saw in the previous section, the press adopted advertising in the first place as a means of freeing the press from economic and thus political reliance on the monarchies of Europe. And as far as we know, the press has had but three sources of income, as have media in general, in history.

One income source is government support, which has always translated into government control of the media. Whether Pravda in the Soviet Union or the BBC in Britain or the royal press hundreds of years earlier in that country under Henry VIII, government financing of the press has always made the press an organ of government. In a totalitarian society, this hardly matters, because the government controls everything anyway. In a democracy, government control of the press can undermine the democracy, because it can obstruct the press from being a critic of the government and reporting to the people what the government might be doing wrong. During the Falklands War, to cite just one example, the British government controlled and censored the BBC's reporting on that war (see Levinson, 1997, for details). Indeed, one of the reasons that democracy was able to arise and flourish in England is that printers were able to break free of royal control. Thomas Jefferson, James Madison, and James Monroe understood the crucial role of a free press in a democratic society, which is why they insisted on the First Amendment to our Constitution and its guarantee of a press unfettered by governmental fiat.

A second source of income for media is the purchase or rental of the media by the public. Sales of newspapers, magazines, books, DVDs, CDs, and movie theater tickets (a form of rental) have worked well for many media. But they have not worked very well for newspapers, especially in recent years. *The New York Times* thus loses money on every paper it sells, and *The Village Voice* (a New York progressive, counterculture weekly) dispensed with its price per copy altogether and has been distributed at no charge for the past decade. Newspapers do this because they want to keep their number of readers as high as possible, to attract advertising revenue.

Furthermore, or maybe first of all, to charge for reading a blog would cut far more deeply against the ideal of blogging, and new new media in general, as available to the public for free, than would advertising if needed to keep the blog free. *The New York Times* online went behind a pay wall, but, again, a newspaper online is not a blog or a new new medium for many reasons, so charging for online access is just a continuation of another old medium characteristic. Organizations such as Media Pass allow for easy creation of pay walls, but its clients, including Social Toddlers and Wizzard Media, are online businesses selling know-how, not blogs.

Which brings us to the third source of income for media for the past hundreds of years: advertising. In a Platonically ideal world, perhaps we would not need it— not for blogging or older media such as newspapers and magazines. Independently wealthy bloggers with the best of motives would write just the truth as they saw it and would not contaminate it in either reality or appearance by taking any money for their work. But we do not live in such an ideal realm—in our world, bloggers and people in all media need to eat. I love teaching, but I do not usually do it for no payment, because I do have to pay my mortgage and electricity bills.

And what, specifically, is the evidence of damage done to blogging, either by the PayPerPost approach or the pursuit of advertising? Sirota's post is titled "Politico's Jayson Blair" after the infamous *New York Times* reporter who made up stories and plagiarized (Levinson, "Interview about Jayson Blair," 2003)—and unintentionally brings home a telling point: The "newspaper of record," *The New York Times*, was plagued by "outrageous lies" on its pages by Jayson Blair. Was that because it, too, was pursuing advertising revenue?

The more likely explanation is that there is no cause and effect between advertising and faulty reporting, which arises from the frailties of all human beings, including reporters (though see Nissenson, 2007, for Dorothy Schiff, *New York Post* publisher, killing a story in 1976 because her advertisers objected to it). Nor is there any evidence that PayPerPost blogging has deluded the public with lies. If a post is clearly identified as written to someone else's specification, right before and after posts that are clearly written only to the blogger's specifications, the reader is no more likely to perceive the paid-for post as the blogger's "voice" than the reader of a newspaper is to confuse an ad with the paper's editorial opinion, even though both kinds of confusion do happen.

Photos on Blogs and Photoblogs: Photobucket, Instagram, Flickr, Pinterest

Ads on blogs come in text, images, and video. Amazon ads have images of the books for sale, and Google AdSense offers options for text, image, or video ads, as discussed previously. But images and videos also can be placed on blogs just to make the blogs more interesting, colorful, and spiffy—to illustrate blog posts or just attract viewers—with no ad revenue earned from them.

Many blog platforms (such as Blogspot, see "Different Blogging Platforms" later in this chapter) allow the writer to upload images and videos directly to the blog. In the case of videos, they also can easily be embedded by code available from YouTube and other video sites.

Photobucket is an example of a free site that hosts images. HTML code is generated for every hosted image and can be edited to change the size and placement of the image on your blog. You can align images to the left or right, and the text will wrap around them. Links can also be easily placed in the image code, so that when readers click on the images, they will be taken to the page on the Web in the link. This is the way Amazon and Google image ads work.

Instagram, a relative newcomer (launched in October 2010) initially designed to facilitate photosharing on iPhones and iPads, was purchased by Facebook for one billion dollars in April 2012. The dot.com boom lives in new new media.

Flickr not only hosts images but also works, in effect, as a photographic blog, or a photographic equivalent of YouTube, which attracts viewers to its site, as well as provides content embeddable on blogs. Photobucket and Instagram can be used that way, too. Twitpic and yfrog, as mentioned in chapter 12, are image hosts especially designed to work quickly with Twitter, but their hosted images can also be put on blogs.

Pinterest allows easy capture of any image on the Web, including an image of a video, which then appears on your profile board or pinboard, for repinning and comment by other Pinterest users. Pinterest images can also be uploaded from your computer, embedded on your blog, and tweeted about and placed on Facebook pages via links. Techcrunch named Pinterest "best new start-up of 2011" (Constine, 2012; see also *MarketingProfs*, 2012) and the site had an Alexa rank of #88 in February 2012. Bianca Bosker, writing in *The Huffington Post* (2012), attributes Pinterest's success to its refreshing focus on items (images we like) rather than the burden of reporting on what we are doing (Twitter, Facebook, Foursquare), or a push back against the tide of new new media. If so, Pinterest especially bears further watching (and see Ferraro, 2012, for a critique).

Widgets are a way that blog posts, videos, and links of any kind can easily be integrated into a blog or Web page. As distinct from a "button," which usually links to just one other site, a widget is designed to offer numerous connections. Facebook and Twitter, for example, supply "buttons" or "badges," which allow readers to connect to a specified profile. Amazon supplies widgets, which allow readers to connect to numerous pages on its site.

Widgets are supplied not only by companies such as Amazon to help readers of your blog or Web site see Amazon's products (for which purchases you will be paid a percentage, if you are monetizing your blog) but also by networks and organizations that are not selling anything. Twitter offers not only buttons but also widgets that allow your readers to see the tweets of specified people, including you or only you, or everyone on Twitter. In all cases, the widgets are supplied for free. They, in effect, act as little building blocks of the Web, apps appearing on your page with a bundle of connections to other websites.

One of the distinguishing characteristics of widgets in contrast to static links is that the links in widgets change, or are "dynamic," based on the purpose of the widget. Amazon has widgets for its products that provide updating links to those products based on the content of blog posts on the same page. For example, if I post a review about *Dexter*, the Showtime television series, my Amazon widget will display the *Dexter* novels and DVDs of earlier seasons. Google AdSense ads work in the same way. Twitter's widgets are constantly updated to show the most recent tweets. I also sometimes have a "Politics" widget on my blog from an organization called "Widget Box," which takes yet a third approach, displaying headlines with links for the most popular—meaning, most read—political posts on blogs in the "Politics" division of the Widget Box network (divisions exist for television, science, and other categories). Widget Box also provides a widget that lists the posts in your blog with updates; this can be very useful if you have more than one blog and want to attract readers back and forth and, of course, if you can get friends to put your widget on their blogs and Web pages. Blogging platforms such as Blogspot also provide numerous widgets, including one—much like the Twitter widget—that lists and links to the most recent posts of other blogs, which you have entered into your "blogroll."

Note that blogs listed in any Widget Box widget may display Google AdSense or any kind of ads, even if your blog does not. If for some reason you are not only allergic to making money but also to aiding any kind of income generation on the Web, you need to take special care in choosing your widgets.

Gauging New New Media Impact: Statcounter, Alexa, Klout

Unless you blog purely for the pleasure of seeing your writing on a Web page—which is certainly one motivating factor for most writers—you will be interested in how many people are reading your words, and in other statistics that measure the popularity of your blog.

Services such as Statcounter and SiteMeter provide details on the number of people who visit your blog, including raw number of visitors, what pages they read, where the visitors come from (what countries, what Web sites, and so forth), how long they stay on your blog, and where they go when they leave your blog (what exit links they click). The basic services are free, with paying options that provide analyses of larger groups of visitors.

Technorati has been measuring the popularity of blogs in a different way since 2002: how many other blogs have linked to your blog. Further, Technorati, in turn, keeps track of the linkages of all blogs that link to yours. Being linked to 10 blogs with 500 links each is more impressive than being linked to 100 blogs with 5 links each. In the first case, many more readers are likely to see your blog.

Alexa takes another, complementary approach, ranking blogs according to a formula based on number of readers, links, and rates of growth. Google PageRank does something similar but over longer periods of time. Both systems are secretive about the precise "algorithms" they use to determine the rankings, to discourage unscrupulous bloggers and Web site developers from manipulating or "gaming" the data to achieve higher rankings.

Such "gaming" is something we will encounter in other systems that measure popularity or base their listings on popularity. Reddit and Digg put articles, images, and videos on their front pages based on the number of up or down votes ("Diggs" and "Buries" on Digg) that submissions might receive from readers. This makes such systems especially prone to gaming, as users attempt to inflate the positive numbers by marshalling votes on behalf of given articles.

Klout, a newcomer to new new media measurement (September 2009) with 100 million users by the end of 2011, measures the popularity or impact not of blogs but of bloggers, and their "influence" on Twitter, Facebook, Google+, YouTube, Foursquare, LinkedIn, Flickr, Tumblr (see next section), and Last.fm (a music listening site). Influence is gauged by number of re-tweets, comments on blogs, Facebook, Google+, YouTube, and the like. Users with high Klout scores receive "perks" (I've received perks ranging from a free Subway sandwich to a discount on Leftlane gloves). Because Klout keeps track of so many different systems, it is more difficult to game.

Different Blogging Platforms

My InfiniteRegress.tv blog uses Google's "Blogspot," or "Blogger," platform (launched independently of Google in 1999). In addition to the virtue of being free, it offers a big assortment of blog templates (which determine what the blog looks like—colors, positioning of blog posts and sidebars, for example) or allows you to import and therein design your own template. The Blogspot platform also offers extensive control over comments, including notification of new comments and various moderator tools such as CAPTCHAs. Blogspot also allows multiple blogs by the same or multiple authors, all at no charge.

A key feature of Blogspot—perhaps the most important—is that bloggers have access to the underlying HTML code that determines the look and feel of the blog and allows easy insertion of stat counters and widgets, as discussed in previous sections.

Wordpress (launched 2003) is most like Blogspot, in that it offers a wide variety of features and is free. Amazon and other websites also offer free blog space to their users but with no access to the HTML code and far less control over the blog in general.

At the other end of the spectrum, some platforms offer features equivalent to Blogspot but are not free. Typepad (launched in 2003) charges anywhere from $8.95 (basic service) to $29.95 (premium service) per month. Its main advantage over Blogspot is a more distinctive look (assuming you like that look), and it comes packaged with sophisticated stat counters and other features. Movable Type (launched in 2001) is free for noncommercial use (no ads on your site, and you do not use it to make money); it otherwise costs hundreds of dollars per year. The LiveJournal (launched in 1999) basic blogging account is free but offers "paid" accounts at $19.95 per year. (Typepad, Movable Type, and LiveJournal are all owned by Six Apart.)

Tumblr (launched 2007) and Posterous (launched 2008, sold to Twitter in 2012) are more recent, free platforms, which feature easier integration of videos, images, and anything on the Web with a URL. Tumblr in particular caters to short blog posts, making it a form of microblogging halfway between Twitter and Blogspot, and faster to post to than Blogspot on a smart phone.

In the end, if money is no object, your choice of blog platform will likely be most determined by what you find most attractive or consonant with your image of your blog's purpose. For a cheapskate and on occasion long-winded writer like me, the free cost of Blogspot is irresistible. And I do like its general appearance and the powers I have to sculpt and control the blog. But if you prefer the short burst but want a platform with posts less ephemeral and a little longer than Twitter, go for Tumblr. Or go for both Blogspot and Tumblr, and have them link to one another.

Are Bloggers Entitled to the Same First Amendment Protection as Old-Media Journalists?

Blogging can be serious business, not only in the money that can be made and the ethical issues involved, which we have examined previously, but in its political and social impact and its relationship to older media ranging from newspapers to television. We turn in this section and the remainder of this chapter to a consideration of some of these issues, starting with the question of whether bloggers are protected from government interference under the First Amendment.

The Supreme Court generally sided with newspapers and print media on First Amendment and freedom of the press issues in the 20th century. In *The New York Times* v. Sullivan (1964), the Court severely limited the degree to which the press could be sued for defamation and libel; in *The New York Times* v. the United States (1971), the Court stopped the Nixon administration's attempt to shut down publication of the Pentagon Papers (see Tedford, 1985, for a detailed discussion of these and the other First Amendment cases mentioned in this chapter; see also Levinson, "The Flouting of the First Amendment," 2005).

Broadcast journalism, the other old-media part of the press, has not fared as well. The Fairness Doctrine, introduced by the Federal Communications Commission in 1949, required broadcasters to give balanced coverage to controversial issues. In Red Lion Broadcasting v. Federal Communications Commission (1969), the Supreme Court upheld that doctrine, on the grounds that broadcast stations are necessarily scarce in comparison to print media—only a limited number of stations can fit on the broadcast spectrum, in contrast to no natural or technological limit on the number of newspaper publishers. The FCC decided to abandon the Fairness Doctrine in 1987. But in the interim, on an issue relating more to social satire than journalism, the Supreme Court ruled in Federal Communications Commission v. Pacifica Foundation (1979) that the FCC had a right to tell radio stations not to broadcast comedian George Carlin's "Seven Dirty Words" routine (the reason in this case was that listeners could tune in and accidentally hear such objectionable broadcasts, unlike a deliberate decision to buy a copy of *Playboy*).

New media—or the appearance of old media such as newspapers on the Web— received a major endorsement by the Supreme Court in Reno v. American Civil Liberties Union (1997), in which the Communications Decency Act and Attorney General Janet Reno's attempt to use it to punish Joe Shea for publication of "indecent" language (critical of Congress for passing this law) in an online magazine were struck down as a violation of the First Amendment's protection of the press (see Levinson, 1997, for more). The decision in effect held that an online magazine was more like a newspaper than a radio or television broadcast.

And what of new new media—such as blogging?

Here a battle began and is still being waged over government coercion of the press in an area that may be a bit beyond First Amendment territory: shield laws, which protect journalists from being forced to reveal their sources to prosecutors and courts and do not address the right to publish, per se. The Supreme Court held in Branzburg v. Hayes (1972) that the First Amendment did not give journalists the right to refuse to testify or reveal sources, but Congress and the courts could enact legislation that gave journalists that privilege. Shield law supporters argue that, without such protection, journalists would be unable to do their jobs, because their sources could not rely on any pledge a journalist made to not reveal his or her sources in a story. I agree and was quoted in *USA Today* about *New York Times* reporter Judith Miller's 2005 imprisonment for failing to reveal her sources in the Valerie Plame CIA leak investigation: "It is wrong to jail a reporter for protecting sources, including flawed reporters" (Levinson, quoted in Johnson, 2005). Miller quoted my comment in the opening statement of her testimony to the U.S. Senate Judiciary Committee, Hearing on Reporters' Shield Legislation, on October 19, 2005.

At that time, there was no federal shield law—there still is none—which is why federal prosecutor Patrick Fitzgerald was able to get a judge to put Miller behind bars. Forty states and the District of Columbia currently (as of 2011) have shield laws, but do they—should they—protect bloggers or journalists who blog? Judith Miller reported on the *Fox News Watch* (2008) that, for the first time, more online journalists than print journalists had been arrested around the world in 2008.

The imprisonment of video blogger Josh Wolf in San Francisco in 2006–2007 shows that, for some people, the very phrase "journalists who blog" is a contradiction. Wolf was videotaping a protest in San Francisco in July 2005 about the G-8 Summit taking place then in Scotland. He sold some of his video to local television stations and posted other clips on his blog. A police officer, ironically named Peter Shields, was assaulted at another part of the demonstration, not videotaped by Wolf, and suffered a fractured skull. Wolf was asked by authorities to turn over his videotapes. He refused and was thrown in jail. Commented U.S. Attorney Kevin Ryan in a court filing, "[Wolf] was simply a person with a video camera who happened to record some public events"; U.S. District Judge William Alsup, apparently agreeing, described Wolf as an "alleged journalist." Wolf's attorney, First Amendment advocate Martin Garbus, thought otherwise and indicated, "I would define a journalist as someone who brings news to the public" (see Kurtz, 2007).

Wolf was released in April 2007, after eight months in prison, when prosecutors withdrew their insistence that Wolf had to testify. I concur completely with Garbus and was pleased to produce several blog posts and one podcast (Levinson, "Free Josh Wolf," 2007) as well as a letter to the federal prosecutors on Wolf's behalf. But he nonetheless was deprived of his freedom for eight months.

One way of looking at this case, and the more general issue of whether bloggers are bona fide journalists, is how to best apply Marshall McLuhan's famous aphorism that "the medium is the message" (1964). Applied superficially, we might well conclude, as Prosecutor Ryan did, that the medium of blogging is different from the media of print and broadcasting, as it indeed is, and different enough to negate or not allow journalists in its online ranks. A more accurate analysis, however, would note that there are media within media—that journalism, a form of communication, is a medium that can be presented via other media, such as newspapers, radio, TV broadcasts, and written and video blogs (see Levinson, 1999, for more on media within media). As Garbus observed, the medium or practice of journalism is the bringing of "news to the public." Wolf was clearly working in that medium, within the larger packaging of video blogging.

Wolf's case was likely complicated by the fact that he was not only a blogger but also a nontraditional blogger, in that he was using video rather than text as his medium (media within media: journalism via video via blog). Text blogging, which is what we have been looking at in this chapter, has significant differences from video blogging, including that the text can be written and uploaded and therein disseminated at least a little more quickly, with less technical requirement or savvy than required for videos. But Garbus's definition of what makes a journalist indicates that the capacity for journalism is not among such differences.

Wolf's release might have been a sign that the world of law enforcement was becoming aware of the role of new new media in journalism. But it was Wolf's arrest, instead, that would prove to be a harbinger of massive police mistreatment of citizen journalists six years later, with not only arrests but beatings of reporters using the tools of new new media to tell the world about Occupy Wall Street.

Citizen Journalists, the First Amendment, and Occupy Wall Street

In one sense, the police response to Occupy Wall Street across the United States in the Fall of 2011 was an equal-opportunity abuser of the First Amendment rights of all journalists across the media spectrum: journalists for old media, new media, and new new media, that is, video streaming and tweeting. In New York City, Mayor Michael Bloomberg kept all of the press, including local TV news helicopters, away from his eviction of the protesters from Zuccotti Park on November 15, 2011. Reporters on the ground were shoved and worse. A reporter for the *New York Post*—the 13th oldest continually published newspaper in the United States, founded in 1801 (you can't get much more old media than that), and a politically conservative paper—was put in a choke hold. A journalist working for National Public Radio (NPR) was detained by police (see Stelter & Baker, 2011, for details). Justifiably outraged over this mistreatment of their own, establishment media delivered a letter of complaint to Mayor Bloomberg, written by *The New York Times*, and signed, among others, by the Associated Press, *New York Post, Daily News,* Thomson Reuters, Dow Jones & Company, and WABC, WCBS, and WNBC local TV news stations (Stelter, 2011). The New York Police Department responded a week later, with a directive read in precincts that police should not interfere with journalists doing their jobs (Associated Press, 2011).

But that was just part of the story. In one of the other parts, police mistreatment of reporters covering Occupy Wall Street continued, with Mayor Bloomberg defending such conduct. In another part, new new media journalists endured worse and more extensive mistreatment by police than did traditional media reporters, even as tweeted-about videos and text reports got the news out to the world when traditional media were handcuffed (figuratively and literally). As Stelter and Baker pointed out, as a result of the police muzzling of traditional reporters, "much of the early video of the police operation was from the vantage point of the protesters. Videos that were live-streamed on the Web and uploaded to YouTube were picked up by television networks."

And the NYPD responded. *The Huffington Post* (Mirkinson, 2011) provided an account of small-press and new new media reporters hit by police with nightsticks, shoved against walls, slammed against barricades, and arrested. The victims were reporters for such sites as *The Daily Caller* and *DNAinfo*—likely unfamiliar to most readers of *The New York Times*, but well known to people who get their news via smart phones and tablets.

According to the preceding accounts, the reporters for the older and newer media mistreated by police had clearly visible credentials. But there were also many others with no credentials, because they were affiliated with no organization at all, but were recording and tweeting out the truth for all to see, anyway. We will encounter some of these ultimate citizen journalists and their work in chapter 14, "Politics and New New Media." For now, we can say that the work begun by Josh Wolf—insisting that anyone practicing journalism be protected by the First Amendment, professional affiliation or not—still has a long way to go.

Bloggers and Lobbyists

Another kind of First Amendment blogging issue surfaced in Washington state in December 2008 (*Fox Report with Shepard Smith*), where its Public Disclosure Commission began looking at whether bloggers who are paid to write posts endorsing specific positions are, in effect, lobbyists and therefore subject to the regulations that govern lobbyists (these amount to always disclosing that you are a paid lobbyist).

Horsesass.com blogger David Goldstein argued on the Fox segment that bloggers are entitled to First Amendment protection from any disclosures to the government, including whether they are paid for their blogs and who is paying them. But advertising and lobbying are already under substantial governmental regulation, which insists on full disclosure for lobbyists and truth in advertising for commercials on television, radio, the press, and, indeed, anywhere. In the political sphere, the McCain–Feingold Act (2002) placed limits on campaign financing, including prohibition of ads paid for by corporations and unions, but this restriction was struck down by the Supreme Court as a violation of the First Amendment in Citizens United v. Federal Election Commission (2010).

Before addressing the question of whether bloggers who are hired to write posts endorsing political positions are entitled to First Amendment protections given to the press, we first should ask: Are the lobbying laws and restrictions on advertising themselves in violation of the First Amendment, as the Citizens United decision held about corporate and union ads on behalf of political candidates?

The question regarding advertising and governmental insistence on truth is the easiest to answer, because advertising is clearly a form or part of business, which is itself regulated in numerous ways by the government. False advertising is surely a kind of fraud in business and therefore not really in the same arena as reporting and commenting on public policy or any other subject—which is the job of the press, whether new new media blogs or old media newspapers. Regulation of lobbying is a different issue, part of the goal of making politics in our democracy "transparent," as in obliging candidates for office to reveal their financial contributors. But I am not sure, even aside from blogging, that any government monitoring of election contributions is in the best interests of our democracy. An argument could be made that the best policy is for the government to keep its hands and scrutiny totally off election financing, because such supervision could lead to a party in power taking actions that support its continuing dominance. For that reason, I think the Citizens United decision is a step in the right direction.

But even if, for the sake of argument, we agreed that lobbyist financing should always be made public, there is still the question of whether a blogger being paid to write in favor of a candidate, official, or political position is in effect a lobbyist. A lobbyist usually works on an interpersonal basis, via meetings with the targets of the lobbying (lawmakers and so forth) to convince, cajole, and pressure the targets to vote or act in favor of or against a certain piece of legislation, or to take a certain position on a package or wide range of bills revolving around a central issue, such as global warming. Although production of press releases may well be part of such efforts, the text is just a component of the campaign.

In contrast, a blog post, whether hired or created on the blogger's initiative, exists in its own right on a blog page. A lobbyist may well link to it, reprint it, or include it in campaign materials, but if we are talking about a blog post, and not a press release, the text also has a life of its own. Although it obviously has characteristics in common with advertising and should be identified as a purchased post (as discussed previously in "Monetizing Your Blog"), I would argue that government insistence that the blogger reveal all circumstances of the purchase goes too far and does violate the blogger's First Amendment rights. The publisher paid an advance and pays royalties to me for *New New Media*. Newspapers pay reporters salaries. The name of the publisher is on the title page of this book, and the name of any newspaper is clear to any reader. But other than the IRS getting notified of this income for tax purposes, no one would dream of saying the government has a right to know the specific financial arrangements between my publisher and me, or between a newspaper and its reporters. A blogger being paid to write on behalf of a political cause or candidate should be entitled to the same business privacy. And as for the public being misled to think that a blog post is the blogger's when it is really a purchased opinion, what does it matter whose opinion the post really is? Should not the opinion be assessed on the basis of what the opinion says, not who said it? (See, again, Richards, 1929.)

Anonymity in Blogging

Although bloggers should not be compelled by government to reveal the circumstances of a blog post's creation, good form nonetheless suggests that a blogger should let readers know when a post is hired. This question of what should and should not be revealed about how and why a blog post is written relates to a larger question of anonymity, or whether a blogger (or commenter) should write under his or her real name.

Anonymity is antithetical to journalism; most reporters and documentarians, including Josh Wolf, are all too happy to have their names associated with their work, and, indeed, in old media such as newspapers, a byline is rightly considered crucial in building a career.

But *The New York Times* (Glater, 2008) reported a case in which a district attorney in the Bronx subpoenaed a text blog about New York politics, titled "Room 8," to reveal or help prosecutors discover the identities of several anonymous bloggers. As was the outcome with the Josh Wolf case, the DA's office withdrew the request—this time under threat of a lawsuit by the blog over violation of its First Amendment rights.

The great advantage of anonymous blogging, of course, is that it maximizes the freedom of bloggers to speak or post their minds without fear of reprisal from supervisors, bosses, voters, friends, and family. Anonymous blogging goes even further in this direction than blogging under a pseudonym or a nickname unrelated to the blogger's real name—all anonymous blog posts literally have the same "anonymous" attribution, which defeats any attempt to identify a series of blog posts as the work of a single person, obviously apparent when a post is signed by a pseudonym, even though the real name of the blogger is not known.

Posting without revealing one's identity has a long history on the Web and online communication. When my wife Tina Vozick and I founded Connected Education in the mid-1980s—a nonprofit organization that offered courses for academic credit, completely online, in cooperation with the New School and other land-based institutions of higher education (see Levinson, 1985, 1997)—one of the first things I discussed with a colleague, Peter Haratonik at the New School for Social Research, was whether we should allow anonymous comments in the Connect Ed Café, an online forum for casual discussion. Anonymous comments by students in their online classes were ruled out from the beginning, but we thought that perhaps discussion in the Café would benefit from the opportunity of anonymity by those who wanted it. In the end, we decided against it; people don't like talking to people with "bags over their heads," as Haratonik put it.

But anonymity, and/or pretending to be someone you are not, has evolved into many other uses in blogging and new new media, including not only the capacity to make controversial posts without worry of reprisal but also disruptive, cyberbullying, and cyberstalking comments without revealing one's identity (see chapter 15). Used for such purposes, anonymity serves as a coward's mask for reprehensible behavior.

In an entirely different kind of disruptive application, anonymous and pseudonymous accounts can be employed to boost the popularity of a blog post or anything with a URL on the Web. All the booster needs to do is create multiple accounts. This rears its head on Wikipedia, as we will see in chapter 13, where "sock-puppets," or accounts created by users to buttress their arguments, can short-circuit or bias attempts to build a consensus among online editors. Anonymous and pseudonymous accounts also aid and abet voting stories up and down on Reddit and Digg.

There may also be a personal disadvantage to both anonymous and pseudonymous blogging for the blogger, in addition to the professional problem of not building your reputation as a writer. I often joke that I would never write under a pseudonym, because I want the girl who sat next to me in seventh grade, and didn't pay much attention to me, to see the error of her ways when she walks into a bookstore—or, nowadays, if she's reading on the Web. The general principle here is that anonymous writing will not assist your quest for fame, if that is what you seek.

Anonymity is obviously easier in text media than audiovisual media, where disguising of voices and images takes a little work, and any muffling of sound or image is obvious. Indeed, anonymous comments are an option on most blogs, although the moderator can block anonymous comments. If a blogger wants to encourage discussion, blocking or removal of a comment merely because it is anonymous may be counterproductive. As a rough, anecdotal statistic of the popularity of anonymous comments on blogs, more than one of four comments on my *Infinite Regress* blog are anonymous.

WikiLeaks and Anonymous

WikiLeaks—founded in 2006, and with no connection to Wikipedia—is technically neither a blog nor a new new medium, but an online publisher of secret and classified documents submitted to it by anonymous sources ("classified" means classified by government as not available for public scrutiny). Venerable media such as *The New York Times*, *The Guardian* (UK), *Le Monde* (France), *El Pais* (Spain), and *Der Spiegel* (Germany) have partnered with WikiLeaks in publishing the documents.

The release of U.S. State Department cables by WikiLeaks and its old media partners in November 2010 provoked a U.S. Department of Justice criminal investigation of WikiLeaks—ongoing as of February 2012—and brought to the front burner questions of whether WikiLeaks was entitled to First Amendment protections. Few disputed that *The New York Times* was—as made clear in the Pentagon Papers case (New York Times Co. v. United States, 1971)—but opponents of WikiLeaks argued that it was not a bona fide organ of journalism, much like the arguments against blogging as journalism.

First Amendment advocates once again begged to differ. I told *The Christian Science Monitor* in February 2011 that the WikiLeaks release of U.S. State Department communiques was akin to the Pentagon Papers, "which was a very important moment in our history because it showed how our government had manipulated the truth and lied to the American people" (Levinson, quoted in Goodale, 2011).

Some supporters of WikiLeaks went beyond words. Anonymous—a group of anonymous "hactivist" groups and individuals who use the name Anonymous—hacked Paypal and old-line credit card companies (Mastercard and Visa) in December 2010, in retaliation for their freezing of WikiLeaks accounts. Arrests soon ensued in England and Holland, and the FBI issued search warrants in the United States but made no arrests. Significantly, although Anonymous was and is anonymous, the founder of WikiLeaks, Julian Assange, is well known. Bradley Manning, a soldier in the U.S. Army, was arrested in March 2010 on suspicion of supplying WikiLeaks with classified information. As of February 2012, he has been set to stand for court-martial.

To be clear, hacking for the sake of disruption, as Anonymous did in protest of the credit card company actions against WikiLeaks, is by no stretch a form of journalism, and therefore not deserving of First Amendment protection. But I would argue that the actions of WikiLeaks and Manning certainly are, in the same way that Daniel Ellsberg's release of the Pentagon Papers and its publication in *The New York Times* and *The Washington Post* was deemed worthy of First Amendment protection by the U.S. Supreme Court.

And since its actions on behalf of WikiLeaks, Anonymous has gone on to do work that certainly is journalism, including video coverage of and trenchant commentary about the Arab Spring and Occupy Wall Street, to which we will return in chapter 14.

Blogging for Others

Although blogging on your own blog is the newest new media use of blogging—that is, the specific kind of blogging that most captures the qualities of new new media and its differences from older media—numerous blogs on the Web permit, invite, and consist of posts written by people who are not the blog's owner. The crucial difference between writing for these kinds of blogs and your own blog, of course, is that you have far less control over how what you write is published on the blogs of others. In its most extreme form, this kind of gatekeeping can decide whether your post will be published. The applicant blogger is in such cases no different from a freelance writer or reporter submitting a story to an online newspaper. But even when the publication of anything you submit is assured, writing for the blogs of others may leave decisions in the hands of others about where on the blog page your post is placed, in what category, and so forth. The blogger may also be deprived of the ability to edit the post after it has been published, remove or moderate comments, keep track of the number of readers, and earn advertising revenue from the blog post. These and other specific limitations of blogging for others differ from blog to blog.

The great advantage of blogging for sites other than yours is that these sites may well have enormously greater numbers of readers than does your blog. *Daily Kos*, for example, had some 5 million readers on Election Day 2008, and averaged hundreds of thousands of visits on weekdays in 2010. Compare those numbers with the readership of *The Wall Street Journal*, the highest circulation (in paper) newspaper in the United States with 2.1 million readers a day in 2010, and *USA Today* with 1.8 million per day, and you can get an idea of the power of the most successful blogs to attract large numbers of readers. (The most readers I've ever had on *Infinite Regress* on a given day was 20,000 for the Season 3 finale of *Lost*, a year after the review was first posted.)

Daily Kos started in 2002, which makes it one of the oldest of the new new media. It publishes "diaries" submitted by registered users (registration is free and open to everyone). Such blog posts cannot be submitted more than once a day. They are listed briefly on the front page—unless they are "Recommended" by *Daily Kos* editors, in which case they are listed on the front page longer—or, even better, "Front Paged" by the editors, in which case the blog post is actually published on the front page (this happened to me just once, out of about 50 submissions, "Take It from a College Prof: Obama's 'Missing' Paper Is Another Conservative Red Herring," 2008). The writer can edit the diary after publication, but there is a public indication that the diary has been edited. Other registered users can make comments—diaries on the front page often get hundreds of comments—but the writer has no power to eliminate, reject, or otherwise moderate the comments. The writer, however, is free to join in such discussions and respond to comments. Diaries can be recommended by readers. Comments can be rated (a form of recommendation), and writers can also post a special comment titled "Tip Jar," which readers can rate and therein show additional approval and appreciation of the diary.

These features of blogging on *Daily Kos* provide an excellent example of a mixture of new new media and new media (or top-down, expert-driven, editorially controlled approaches of older print media applied on the Web). Another of *Daily Kos*'s new new media characteristics is that it permits cross-posting, or publishing pieces that have already been published on other blogs, including your own. Not so *Blogcritics* (founded in 2002, acquired by Technorati in 2008), which insists on first publication of all submissions. It adopted this policy in 2007, as a way of maintaining its readership. Google usually puts the earliest publication of a blog at the top of its search results.

Neither *Daily Kos* nor *Blogcritics* pay the writers who post blogs on their sites. But some blog sites do. This, obviously, can add a powerful incentive for writing for the blogs of others. Payment can generally come in one of two ways: payment for publication of the story (either on a per-word or per-story basis) or payment from ad revenues earned from your stories' publication. *Internet Evolution* is an example of a blog site that pays in the first way. *Open Salon* employs the second method. Guess which kind of payment is most likely to provide the most income?

The answer should be apparent in the "Monetizing Your Blog" section. Advertising on blogs generates negligible payment unless your daily readership is in the many thousands. *Open Salon* allows its bloggers to earn ad income directly from Google AdSense. My *Infinite Regress* posts are automatically relayed to my *Open Salon* blog, where they earn about 10–20 percent of the advertising revenue generated on *Infinite Regress*.

In summary, it is worth noting the obvious: All blogs under the control of someone other than you not only can refuse to publish a given piece by you, but also can fire you if you are a regular blogger, or ban you from the blog. *Daily Kos* banned Lee Stranahan in August 2008 (Stranahan, 2008) for cross-posting a piece he had written for *The Huffington Post*, urging John Edwards to tell the truth about his affair first reported in the *National Enquirer*. Stranahan's banning took place before Edwards admitted to the affair, but the truth or falsity of Stranahan's or anyone's post is not the issue that concerns us here. The lesson of Stranahan's banning is that any blog other than your own, regardless of how progressive and writer-driven, can still exercise old-style media control any old time it pleases.

Daily Kos, in terms of the ultimate control it exercises over its pages, is thus no different from *The New York Times*. Given that *Daily Kos* publishes "diaries" written by readers—or, at least in principle, anyone—we can reasonably designate it an example of new new media, in contrast to *The New York Times,* which is an archetypal old medium in journalism (not really "all the news that's fit to print" but "all the news that we the editors of *The New York Times* deem fit to print"), with articles written by assigned, professional reporters, even when published on the new medium of the Web.

But *Daily Kos* is nonetheless very much on the old side of the new new media continuum, if only because of its power to ban any blogger. In a truer or full-fledged new new medium, which arises any time anyone writes a blog under his or her control, the blogger may retire or refrain from blogging but cannot be fired or banned.

Of course, a blogging platform—Google's Blogspot or Six Apart's Typepad or Moveable Type—could refuse for whatever reason to provide or sell a platform to a given blogger. But such refusals seem closer to a telephone company refusing to provide service to a given customer—because of the customer's poor credit, for example—than an editor of a blog banning one of its writers.

Changing the World with Your Blog

As in everything we do in life, we may have different motives for publishing our blogs—and often more than one motive. These could include the joy of writing and having other people read what you write, making money, and changing the world—influencing something real in the world, in politics or science or whatever area—by the words on your blog. Words, after all, can be very powerful. And the power of a blog is unique in comparison to older forms of writing, in that the writing, as we have seen, can be instantly published, which means that anyone, including powerful, important, and famous people, can read it. A significant limitation, however, is that readers, whether famous, important, powerful or not, are not likely to know about a blogger's writing, are not likely to look for it, and are not likely to pay much attention to it if they stumble on it, unless the blogger already possesses some of these qualities—that is, the blogger is powerful, important, famous. Nonetheless, when all factors are taken into the equation, the unknown blogger still has a much better chance of being read by the powerful and famous than the unknown writer in older media, mainly because those older, unknown writers had little chance of being published in the first place.

How do you know if someone important is reading your blog? Stat counters can tell you the IPs—Internet locations—and geographic locations of your readers. These may include the company or school in which their computer is located but not likely their names. Ultimately, the only completely reliable way of knowing who, specifically, has read your blog is when readers comment, link, or refer to your blog in their own blog, or speak or write about your blog in other media.

Rich Sommer's comment on my blog about *Mad Men,* discussed previously, would be a case of someone more famous than I not only reading but also communicating to me and the world on my blog. But the world did not change as a result of this. And, indeed, television reviews are not all that likely to have a big impact on the world.

Political blogs, of course, are different in their potential impact. I have no idea if Barack Obama or any of his close advisers or anyone significant in politics has ever read any of my blog posts, let alone been influenced by them.

But on the early afternoon of September 24, 2008, I published a piece titled "Obama Should Reject McCain's Call to Postpone Friday Debate" on *Infinite Regress* and cross-posted to *Open Salon* and several other sites. This was my response to John McCain's announcement that he was putting his campaign on hold, so he could go to Washington to deal with the financial crisis, and his request to Barack Obama to join him in postponing their first scheduled debate of the 2008 Presidential election.

I "advised" Obama that postponing the debate would be a big mistake, that the financial crisis called for an affirmation of the democratic process, including a continuation of the campaigns and the scheduled debates, not suspending or delaying them.

I was soon pleased to post the following on my blogs:

> BREAKING NEWS: 4:47 p.m.: Obama just said that he thinks the debates should go on—that this is precisely a time when the American people need to see what he and McCain would do as President. Good!

And, at 6:00 p.m., Joan Walsh, then editor-in-chief of *Salon* and blogger on *Open Salon*, posted the following comment on my blog:

> Paul Levinson speaks, Obama listens! I just blogged on this, too!

Did Obama or any of his advisers actually read my blog? Were they influenced by it? Probably not. Obama's team was far more likely to have read and been influenced by the blog of Joan Walsh, who was not only chief editor of *Salon* back then but also a frequent guest on Chris Matthews' *Hardball* and other news shows on MSNBC. (She is still a frequent guest on MSNBC shows, and is now—in January 2012—editor-at-large at *Salon*.)

But I included this true story of my blogging in this book because it highlights the potential of any post, anywhere on the Web, to be read by a presidential candidate or even the president. And this, too, is one of the hallmarks of new new media: You sit at your computer and type your words, and those words can tip the world in a better direction, or at least the direction you think best. You can be a major editor, a college professor, or a sophomore in college or high school.

A Town Supervisor and His Blog

Paul Feiner, who since 1991 has been town supervisor of Greenburgh, New York (an elected two-year term, in Westchester County, a little north of New York City), is explicit about his reliance on blogging. When I was a guest on his weekly "Greenburgh Report" radio show on WVOX on January 9, 2009, Feiner explained that he finds comments made on his own public blog to be helpful, even crucial, in staying informed of what his constituents are thinking.

Feiner even recognizes the benefits—and drawbacks—of anonymous commenting. "I let people write anonymously on the blog," Feiner told me, even though such commenters can be "very nasty" and "make up stuff." Feiner appreciates the dividends of this: "I'm able to get a sense from my blog [of] what some of the issues and controversies are going to be well before they hit a Town Board meeting…because sometimes people can say what's really on their mind in a blog.…If I hadn't had a blog or used the Internet or just relied on newspapers, I would never know what people are saying, not in my presence."

In other words, for officials and political leaders such as Paul Feiner who perceive the advantages of new new media in governing, we might say that "foreblogged" is forewarned or "fore-informed."

"Bloggers in Pajamas"

The political impact of blogging, however, has not been applauded by everyone. Back in September 2004, Jonathan Klein, a former CBS News executive, defended Dan Rather's *60 Minutes* segment about George W. Bush's lack of National Guard service during the Vietnam War, by observing on Fox News that "You couldn't have a starker contrast between the multiple layers of checks and balances [at *60 Minutes*] and a guy sitting in his living room in his pajamas writing" (quoted by Fund, 2004). Klein, who would soon be appointed CNN/USA Network president, was attacking the conservative bloggers who were attacking Rather and CBS. And, although I thought then and now that CBS and Rather were right to run that story (see Levinson, "Interview by Joe Scarborough about Dan Rather," 2005, and Levinson, "Good For Dan Rather," 2007), I certainly did not agree with Klein's myopic "analysis" of blogging, nor with his confidence in the "multiple layers of checks and balances" in mass media journalism. Jayson Blair's several years of fictitious and plagiarized reporting for *The New York Times* had already been exposed. And given the power and reach of the Internet even then, and the way all kinds of information could become available in all sorts of unexpected ways, it struck me that pajamas and living rooms were no impediments to the pursuit and publication of truth.

That is obviously much more the case today, in a world in which tweets from private and public places, by people at all levels of professionalism, provide a constant flow of news. But the "bloggers in pajamas" meme lives on, not only as a justifiably defiant comment on Klein's 2004 statement and any like-minded old-media worshipers still among us—and in the names of successful online news venues (for example, *Pajamas Media*) and well-read independent blogs such as *The Pajama Pundit*—but also in the thinking of conservatives such as Sarah Palin, unsuccessful Republican candidate for vice president in 2008.

Palin, shortly after losing the election, told Greta Van Susteren on Fox News that a lot of the media's negative stories about her were due to their reporting on the basis of "some blogger, probably sitting there in their parents' basement, wearing pajamas, blogging some kind of gossip, or a lie" (Palin, 2008). Palin not only demoted the blogger in pajamas from guy to kid, from living room to basement, but also later switched the focus of her concern from pajamas and parents' basements to anonymity in blogging, asking John Ziegler in the segment of his *Media Malpractice* documentary put on YouTube in January 2009, "When did we start accepting as hard news sources bloggers—anonymous bloggers especially? It's a sad state of affairs in the world of the media today—mainstream media especially, if they're going to be relying on anonymous bloggers for their hard news information. Very scary." (See also Kurtz, 2009.)

In Klein's slight defense, in 2004, new new media were much newer than they are now. *The Huffington Post*, YouTube, and Twitter did not yet even exist, and Facebook was just a few months old. Palin's attack in 2008 was thus more unwarranted than Klein's.

But Palin's contempt for new new media is nonetheless shared by many in the older media themselves. Or as "John Connor," lead character in Fox's *Terminator: The Sarah Connor Chronicles,* sarcastically observed in the 13th episode of its second season (2008): "We all know how reliable bloggers are." That bloggers were mentioned at all on a television series about fictional characters is an indication of how important blogging had become in our lives and culture. But the fact they were cited with disdain shows the degree to which so many people in our real world did then and still do distrust them.

Not coincidentally, Facebook took a lashing in the 10th episode of the same season of *The Sarah Connor Chronicles* (2008), a few weeks earlier, when "Riley," John's girlfriend, lambasted her adoptive family and their obliviousness to the real dangers that awaited them with a remark that all they care about is looking at their "Facebook pages." Meanwhile, over on the premiere of the fifth season of *Weeds* on Showtime in 2009, "Celia Hodes" observed that a Facebook account "would be a waste of time." And "Margene Heffman" on the sixth episode of HBO's third season of *Big Love* in 2009 bad-mouthed yet another new new medium, apologizing that some of the information she had obtained about a Mormon pioneer "may not be right—I got it off Wikipedia."

In incurring this disfavor among some politicians and people who write fiction for older media, new new media continue a tradition that in one way or another afflicted the advent of many nascent media in their time, including the telegraph, motion pictures, and television. *The London Times* delayed printing the news it received about Abraham Lincoln's assassination, because the news was received via telegraph. Motion pictures were considered a "primary school for criminals" early in the 20th century (thus wrote McKeever, 1910). And, first, television and, more recently, video games have been blamed for violence in the real world, on the basis of no reliable evidence, or at best a misunderstanding of correlation (A and B happen together) and causation (A causes B to happen). Just for good measure, television also has been blamed for a reduction in literacy, even though a survey taken in 1978, in the same town in Indiana as in 1944, showed no decline in literacy at all, and book sales have risen through the past 50 years of television. (See Levinson, 1997, for details on the initially distrusting reception of telegraph and motion pictures, the continuing attacks on television, and the status of book sales in the 20th century; Maeroff, 1979, for the Indiana literacy study; and Levinson, 2006, for the confusion of correlation with causation in the "evidence" attempting to link violent video games to violence in the real world.)

The telegraph was replaced in the 20th century by the telephone and, ultimately, by fax and email. But motion pictures and television did just fine, even though the screens on which movies and television shows are viewed are increasingly on smart phones and tablets, the same screens on which blogs are read.

And there are those in old media who see blogging as neither bogeyman nor panacea but subject to the same events that threaten to undermine old and new media, and all of society. Or, as Neil Young put it in his 2009 "Fork in the Road" song, in part about the economic crisis: "Keep on blogging, till the power goes out, your battery's dead, twist and shout."

Blogging cannot in itself cure what ails our society. (No communication can.) Blogging certainly cannot solve economic crises or make peace in the world. But it beats the alternative of saying nothing, and it goes a lot further than saying a word to the person next to you or relying entirely on professional reporters and commentators to say it for you.

Further Tensions Between New New Media and Older Forms

As we have seen and will see throughout this book, media rarely live just in harmony. In fact, media throughout history have both cooperated and competed for our attention and our patronage in a struggle for survival that Charles Darwin would have recognized. The only difference is that, in the Darwinian evolution of media, we humans make the natural selections, or decide which media survive (Levinson, 1979).

The competition between new new and older media is therefore no surprise, and it plays out in the disdain and misunderstanding of new new media by people working in and through older kinds of media, as we saw in the previous section. Another clear example can be found in the attitudes of official television blogs— message boards set up by television networks for discussion, that is, promotion, of their shows—to the posting of comments with links to other blogs. Over the past years, both as promotion for my own blog and as a low-key experiment, I have posted comments on Fox, NBC, CBS, ABC, AMC, TNT, HBO, and Showtime television series pages and blogs. These comments were all signed by me and contained links to my reviews of these same television shows on my own *Infinite Regress* blog.

Moderators from some of these sites occasionally moved or removed my comments, and the Fox *Sarah Connor Chronicles* blog removed my account—that is, blocked me from its blog completely. As of January 2012, all Fox TV official blogs are closed with the following notice—"Our FOX.com community is currently under construction"—but for many years the Fox TV sites advised that "The only links that are allowed are ones to articles about the show, cast, etc., in the mainstream media, or the official sites of the cast. Links to fan sites, personal sites, competing sites, commercial sites, links to download sites, jpgs, MP3s, etc., are not allowed."

In terms of the tensions between new new and older media we have been tracing, we might more accurately put the preceding policy as follows: "The only links allowed on our new media site, about the old medium of television we are promoting, are links to other new media or official sites such as those in the old, mainstream media or official, professional sites about the show, cast, etc. Links to new new media fan sites, personal sites, competing sites, etc., are not allowed."

The hundreds of millions of new new media users show that these media are already part of the "mainstream," but even if those numbers were smaller, a moment's reflection shows how destructive Fox's restrictions were to the purpose of the Fox blogs, which presumably was to promote the television programs. Although links to "unofficial" blogs in comments posted on official blogs may indeed draw readers from the official blogs to the unofficial blogs, the readers of the unofficial blogs are still reading discussions of the television program that is the subject of the official blog.

The phrase "competing sites" in the original statement of the rules shows, in particular, just how illogical and counterproductive this policy is. What is a "competing site"? Is not any site that posts blogs and reviews of the same television series a site not in competition with but in support of the same goal as the official site? A blog site not allied with any television series—such as BuddyTV—might at least have a logical point in forbidding links to other sites, because what these sites want is not necessarily an increase of viewers of any television show but an increase in readers of their site. So might television recap and review sites affiliated with major networks—such as TV.com (CBS) and *Television Without Pity* (NBC)—at least insofar as links to reviews about television series on other networks. I would still disagree with such a strategy—because I think the profusion of links raises all boats in the blogosphere, or all blogs—but I could at least see its logic. (Of the three blogs mentioned, only *Television Without Pity*—perhaps apropos its name—has a tradition of zealously removing links and banning writers for posting them.)

Conceivably, the official blog moderators do not actually read any blog posts with links to other sites and do not click on the external links posted in the official blogs, and as a result assume the external links are nothing more than spam, with no connection to the television show. But, in that case, the old media top-down approach of deciding what gets published, rather than letting all readers become writers and publishers, is still to blame.

For highly successful television shows, such self-destructive actions—or inoculations against the very advantages of viral marketing and promotion—likely will not have much ill effect on the popularity of the shows. But as we move into a world that increasingly expects unfettered participation of viewers—one of the hallmarks of new new media—the difference between a show that gains a reliable audience and a show that does not may well reside in how fully the online discussion boards divest themselves of old media habits. (It may be worth noting, in this context, that *The Sarah Connor Chronicles* was not renewed by Fox for a third season.)

The misunderstanding of new new media by older forms manifests itself in other ways. As *Mad Men*, the AMC television series about early 1960s advertising executives, gained popularity and notice in the first part of 2008, people with names of characters from the show—"Don Draper," "Peggy Olson"—began tweeting. Myspace had for years hosted accounts of users with names ranging from Socrates to Jack Bauer (hero of Fox television's *24*). These, like the Twitter names, are a form of role-playing that people enjoy, and which therefore help promote the show. AMC at first did not see it that way and filed a copyright violation notice that forced Twitter to take down the accounts. Fortunately for all concerned, AMC's ad agency had more new new media savvy than AMC and talked it into backing off (Terdiman, 2008). Don (with 16,000 followers), Peggy (21,000 followers), and the gang are happily tweeting, at least as of January 2012, and *Mad Men* has won numerous Emmys.

The Associated Press and bloggers have been embroiled in a different kind of copyright conflict. AP regularly files "take down" notices to bloggers who extensively quote AP articles without permission and payment. (AP—which as we saw in the "Occupy Wall Street" section joined *The New York Times* and other traditional media in protesting NYPD mistreatment of the press—is a news agency or wire service like Reuters, which sells news reports and stories to newspapers and broadcast media. It has roots going back to 1846 and the advent of the telegraph and is the only surviving international news service headquartered in the United States.) Bloggers retaliated by threatening to boycott AP (Liza, 2008). So far, neither side has annihilated the other, but the battle continues, with AP suing an aggregate online news site, Meltwater, for violation of copyright in 2012, on the grounds that Meltwater charges for access to its service (Ellis, 2012). Copyright continues to be a major bone of contention between old and newer media, as we also saw in chapter 10 regarding YouTube.

But it would also be a mistake to conclude that old media and their practitioners have nothing of value to teach or impart to new new media. We turn now to hardline, investigative reporting, at the opposite end of the journalistic spectrum from the commentary that thus far has been the mainstay of blogging.

The Need for Old-Media Reporting in an Age of New New Media Journalism

Marshall McLuhan astutely observed back in 1977 that "the Xerox makes everyone a publisher"—but, like his recognition in 1962 that electronic media were turning the world into a "global village," his observation about the Xerox machine was more a prediction, based on a powerful trend he noticed, than a depiction of how the media and the world of that day actually were.

It would take the rise of new new media in general, and the internationally interactive participants they created, for the global village to be fully realized (see the Arab Spring in chapter 14, and my *Digital McLuhan*, 1999). For the global village of the 1960s was neither global (television was a national medium) nor interactive like the residents of a village (television viewers across a nation could not talk to each other, except in very small groups).

As for photocopying creating publishers, almost all of the output of such machines, even today, is also for very small numbers of readers. That limited kind of publishing would finally be surpassed—and in a way that rivaled older publication of newspapers and magazines—only with the advent of blogging, as we have seen in this chapter.

And what of the older vehicles of journalism—*The New York Times*, *The Washington Post*, *The Wall Street Journal*, and other paper press? Their numbers have been declining, in circulation, number of different newspapers, and the size of the newspaper operations that have survived (Perez-Pena, 2008). *The New York Times*'s paper circulation continued to decline in 2010–11, though it is still around a million. These older media have to some extent migrated to the Web. *The New York Times*'s website gets 30 million visitors per day—the most of any online newspaper, twice that of *The Huffington Post*—and has had financial success with its pay wall (charging for online content) along with staunch criticism (see Levinson, 2011; Chittum, 2011). See "themediaisdying," 2009, on Twitter for hourly or more frequent reports about cutbacks, layoffs, and closings in old media. (The title gives cause to think that grammar may be dying, too—"media" is plural for "medium.")

But whatever the ultimate fate of the paper press, there remains, as of April 2012, a crucial resource in older media that newer media such as *Daily Kos*, *The Huffington Post*, and *Politico* have yet to fully re-create for themselves, and thus continue to seek from old media. As Jeff Jarvis noted in an NPR interview back in 2008 about "How Will Investigative Stories Fare in an Era of Layoffs and Slashed Newsroom Budgets?": "Bloggers rely on the resource that mainstream media put into this....The whole business is still in trouble and investigative journalism is in peril...." But David Wood's winning of a Pulitzer Prize in 2012 for his stories in *The Huffington Post* about wounded veterans is a big, promising step in the right direction. As Amy Chozick (2012) observed in *The New York Times*, which won two Pulitzer Prizes in 2012, "the awards to *Politico* and *The Huffington Post* reflect the emerging power of Web-based journalism as it competes with legacy newspapers." (*Politico*'s Pulitzer was for an editorial cartoon.)

Ironically, *Daily Kos* and new new media blogging first achieved prominence as important media of journalism in the aftermath of the failure of old media journalists to report the absence of weapons of mass destruction in Iraq and in general to supply sufficient criticism in reporting the buildup to that war. (*Daily Kos* began in 2002; *The Huffington Post* in 2005.) One could say, cynically, that new new media would do well to field their own investigative reporters, who could not do much worse than the old media professionals on the crucial issue of going to war (see Reilly in Hunter, 2009, for a similar point). That might be all well and good, but given that new new media may not have their own extensive investigative teams fully in place, where would investigative journalism come from, if the older media ceased to exist?

Citizen journalism, as indicated in the "Occupy Wall Street" section, is part of the answer, but the good news from the history and evolution of media is that new media rarely replace, utterly, their ancestors. For every hieroglyphic or silent movie that did not make it into the future—because it could not survive the competition of alphabetic writing in the case of hieroglyphics or talkies in the case of silent movies—hundreds of media, large and small, have taken the path of radio (which amply survived the advent of television) and still photography (which easily survived the rise of motion pictures).

The key, as I alluded to earlier when I said that humans decide the survival of media—and I explain in *Human Replay: A Theory of the Evolution of Media* (1979) and *The Soft Edge: A Natural History and Future of the Information Revolution* (1997)—is that media survive if they uniquely satisfy a human communication need. Radio survives in an age of television because it caters to our need to sometimes hear one thing when seeing something else. Imagine driving down the highway and watching television; if you were the driver, you would not get very far. In addition, the world grows dark every night but never really silent, and our eyes close but not our ears, making hearing without seeing—radio—a quite natural and comfortable kind of communication. In contrast, seeing without hearing does not really exist in our natural perception, and this spelled the end of silent movies when talkies came along.

Words on newspaper pages still have their advantages. They are inexpensive in comparison to the cost of any electronic device and its data charges, and easily disposable. As long as such advantages continue in contrast to words on a screen, old media newspapers will survive in some form, which, one hopes, includes some number of investigative journalists. And if and when that advantage fades, presumably most exclusively online newspapers by then will be generating enough steady income to field their own investigative reporters.

Old Media and New New Media Symbiosis: Easter Eggs for *Lost* and *Fringe*

As indicated earlier in this book, not everything in the natural, Darwinian world is competition. Organisms also live in mutually beneficial relations, as do bacteria in our digestive system, which help us digest our food, as we give them a nice warm place to live. Bees eat pollen, which helps plants reproduce, as the bees carry some pollen from one plant to another. And we humans also benefit, doubly, because we like both honey and flowers.

The old medium of television clearly benefits from publicity given to its shows by the new new medium of blogging; the new new medium of blogging benefits from television or any medium that gives bloggers something to write about. News blogs benefit from the work of old print media investigative journalists, while old print and broadcast news media draw upon opinions and analyses expressed in tweets and blogs. And old media such as television shows and newspapers advertise extensively on blogs, just as blogs such as *Television Without Pity* show up on Bravo Television in our living rooms (both are owned by NBC), and Twitter comments appear at the bottom of cable news programs such as *The Dylan Ratigan*

Show and *The Ed Show* on MSNBC (see chapter 12 for more on Twitter/TV news anchor integration).

The symbiotic or mutually catalytic relationship of old and new new media is thus undeniable and vibrant. And although conflicts can get in the way of such cooperation—as when an official television blog prevents links to reviews on other blogs—there are also cases in which television deliberately works new new media into its programming and promotion.

The virtual "game" of Second Life—in which users appear as avatars—figured in a *CSI* television episode in 2007, in which characters from the television show pursued an investigation in Second Life and entered there as characters (Riley, 2007). *Lost* tried something even more ambitious, setting up a real website for "Oceanic Airlines"—the fictitious airline which flew the lost flight that started the show—on which users could look for "additional" flights. *Lost*, as well as one of J. J. Abrams' more recent shows, *Fringe*, offer "Easter eggs," or clues on the Web, which fans can then find to gain special insight into the ongoing stories on television.

As *Fringe* Executive Producer Jeff Pinkner told *TV Guide*'s Mickey O'Connor in an online interview (2008), "There are many Easter eggs, several of which have yet to be discovered by anybody—either on the show or out there on the Internet. There's a clue in every episode that tells you what the next episode will be about."

So *Lost* and *Fringe* deliberately seeded the Internet with clues to enhance the viewers' enjoyment of the show, not just by giving them valuable information but also by making the viewers more than viewers, turning them into researchers, and in effect much more active participants in the unfolding fiction of the show. And, to complete the cycle, some of these viewers who were transformed into researchers were so inspired that they blogged about the show. And the cycle continues in the university classroom. Sarah Clarke Stuart's Spring 2009 "The Infinite Narrative: Intertextuality, New Media and the Digital Communities of *Lost*" course at the University of North Florida, for example, used blogs about *Lost* (see Stuart, 2009; Aasen, 2009).

But the symbiotic qualities of new new media go beyond their relationship to older media, online and offline.

Chapter Twelve

Twitter

Would you like everyone in the world to know what movie you just saw or are going to see, what you really think of your teacher or boss or president, what you just ate for lunch or intend to eat, whether it's sunny or raining, or the police are pepper spraying the people next to you—any and all of those things, and more, whatever you might want the world to know—just a second or so after you had the thought or experience and the idea to broadcast it to the world? Twitter makes it easy for you to do all of that.

You can disseminate whatever information you please, to whatever portion of the world you like, as long as the people in that portion have accounts on Twitter. That would be more than 300 million people in the world at large as of 2011, up from some 30 million in May 2009, with Twitter growing faster at that time than any other social medium (Schonfeld, 2009), and the first tweet from outer space on May 12, 2009 (Van Grove, 2009). Twitter was still the fastest growing medium in 2011, second only to Facebook in total number of users (Bennett, 2011).

Further, the fact that you can do that from your smart phone, iPad, or any other mobile Web-connecting device at hand means that your access to the world, and its access to you, is as much a part of you, as close at hand, as your hand itself. This pertains to all new new media, but the simplicity of posting and reading on Twitter makes it almost as fluid as speech, and even more subject to impulse because it can be done silently, with no one nearby who can overhear and thus inhibit what you might want to say.

Concerned about your privacy? Worried that this ease of access will give unwanted eyes access to you and your thoughts? Like all online systems, you can tweet under a pseudonym or assumed identity. You can even adopt the name of a television character. Or you can choose not to tweet at all.

On the other hand, if you welcome publicity and need it for your profession, you can tweet engagingly under your real name. Don Lemon of CNN, Tamron Hall of MSNBC, and *Meet the Press* anchor David Gregory were actively using Twitter as early as the beginning of 2009. Now just about every television news anchor and commentator has a Twitter account. They work tweets they receive into their television news shows, in another example of old and new new media cooperation. Accounts of celebrities, politicians, and other high-profile users have blue verification check marks next to their account names—signifying that Barack Obama's account is really Barack Obama's and not someone else's using his name. A "beta" procedure in which any user could apply to have his or her account verified was discontinued in 2011 by Twitter, which now (2012) advises users to verify their accounts by linking to their blogs or official websites.

Ashton Kutcher (more than 9 million followers in January 2012) and Barack Obama (nearly 12 million) have Twitter accounts—though Obama's tweets, authorized by him, are mostly not his own, in contrast to Kutcher's. "This account is run by #Obama2012 campaign staff," the President's Twitter Profile truthfully advises, "Tweets from the President are signed -bo." Obama held the first presidential press conference on Twitter in July 2011 (Olander, 2011), but the tweeted questions presented to the president were "curated" rather than randomly selected, which weakened the democratic new new media potential of the event (see Levinson, 2011, "First Presidential Twitter press conference"; and the discussion of YouTube presidential debates in chapter 10). The pope will have his own Twitter account, the Vatican announced in February 2012, explaining that "though he may not always write the tweets, he will approve each one" (Chansanchai, 2012; see also "The Pope's Channel" in chapter 10 for the Vatican analysis of the pros and cons of new new media).

Tweeting was once called "microblogging"—long ago and far away, it seems, but that was only three years ago, in 2009—which, come to think of it, is indeed long ago and far away given the speed-of-light pace of new new media evolution. Today, tweeting is mostly just known, irrevocably and irreversibly, as tweeting.

Welcome, then, to this burgeoning world of tweeting, or the publication and dissemination online of a line or two about yourself, or anything you might like to say, personally, professionally, or politically, anytime you please. Twitter is no longer the new kid on the media block, started as a project by Odeo podcasting people Jack Dorsey, Noah Glass, Biz Stone, and Evan Williams in March 2006. It grew so fast in just the first half of 2009—Twitter had a total of only about 6 million users in February 2009, in contrast to 30 million by May of that year—that an article in the February 8, 2009, issue of *New York* magazine (Leitch, 2009) advised, "If you're the last person in the world to not know what Twitter is, here's a simple explanation." By June 15, 2009, Twitter needed no introduction. It was, to nobody's surprise, the cover story of *Time* magazine (Johnson, 2009).

But as both articles go on to explain and we will detail in this chapter, there is much that is complex and profound about tweeting—even more so in 2012 than 2009.

The Epitome of Immediacy

Instant publication—whether of text, images, sounds, or videos—is one of the hallmarks of new new media. But the hallmarks are not distributed in new new media equally.

You can raise a phone and take a photo or grab a video, which is usually easier than any kind of writing. But editing a video is usually not as easy as editing text, and uploading it to an online site and publishing it can take much longer than writing, especially with the processing time required for lengthy videos. Further, because writing directly online to a blog or a page or a site is as easy or easier than writing offline, in contrast to photos and even the briefest videos, which need to be taken offline and uploaded, getting written words online is also a little easier than doing the same for photographs and videos.

The upshot, when all aspects of creation and publishing online are taken into account, is that text is easier to disseminate than photos and videos. And a line or so of text—140 characters is the limit on Twitter—moves the fastest of all. If you're an author who agonizes over every word, this very short form could take a long time to write. I was once asked to write a 200-character blurb—not 200 words, but 200 characters—about one of my novels for the Science Fiction Book Club, and it took about 15 minutes for me to write. That was because I wanted every word, and therefore every letter or character, to count—every word to attract potential readers to my novel. If all I was writing about was how much I enjoyed the slice of pizza I just bought on Fordham Road, or even what I thought, in a phrase, about First Amendment rights being violated, or about the president's latest speech, I could dash off that line in a few seconds with no problem.

All thoughts originate in the mind—or, if you want to be less metaphysical, in the brain. One kind of synapse or neurological pathway delivers the thought to our vocal apparatus when we speak. Another kind of synapse gets the thought to our fingers, with which we write or type. Presumably these two synapses or pathways to personal communication are the same length—the thought travels at the same speed to tongue or finger.

Prior to the advent of electronic media, immediacy of thought conveyed to the tongue only reached as far as anyone within hearing distance. Immediacy of thought conveyed to the finger was even more limited: It ended with the finger, because for anyone else to read what had been written, the parchment, papyrus, or paper had to be passed from hand to hand. Although this nonelectronic "digital" transmission—digital as in finger to finger—could happen quickly, it was slower than the speed of sound. Thus, speech had the edge over writing in immediacy. (See Levinson, *Digital McLuhan*, 1999, for handwriting as a form of "digital," or finger, communication.)

Electricity travels at the speed of light, which means that any message encoded and committed to electronic delivery—whether voice or written word—can be sent anywhere in the world instantly. Electricity travels at 186,000 miles per second, and the world is about 24,000 miles around at the equator. However, this did not mean that such messages would be received—heard or read—by any human being instantly. Equipment at the receiving end, whether turning on a television or walking to a ringing telephone, added seconds at the very least to the ultimate reception of information transmitted at the speed of light.

More than any other old, new, or even new new medium, Twitter's revolution is that it makes the sending and receiving of its brief messages nearly as instant as their conception and writing. Twitter is faster than blogging, because its tweets are shorter than blog posts. Twitter is faster than Foursquare, which consumes crucial seconds or more in verifying your location for the check-in. Twitter's one-liners can be created, sent, and received with the flick of a finger. Writing when tweeted has thus become as easy and effortless to communicate over vast distances as speech has always been to people within earshot.

Further, the messages conveyed via Twitter are readable by anyone who wishes to "follow" your tweets on the system—that is the default—or they can be sent to specific groups or just one person. This means that Twitter is not only the most immediate written medium in history, but it is also the most integrated combination of interpersonal and mass communication.

Interpersonal + Mass Communication = Twitter

The preceding title is about 45 characters, so it easily could have been sent via Twitter. And it would have been sent in ways that combine these two great branches of communication.

One of the basic lessons of communication is that it comes in two kinds. Interpersonal communication consists of one person sending a message to another person, in which the second person can easily switch from being a receiver to a sender. Examples would be in-person and video face-to-face communication, written correspondence, IMing on computers, and talking and texting on the phone. Mass communication consists of one person or source sending a message to many people at the same time, with these many receivers not having the capacity to become senders. Examples would be wall carvings, books, newspapers, motion pictures, radio, television, and Web pages and blogs that allow no comments. Interpersonal is thus pinpoint and two-way, whereas mass communication is broad (hence the word "broadcast," from the widespread or broad casting of seeds in planting) and one-way.

Sometimes people mistakenly say that interpersonal is nontechnological in contrast to mass media, which must be high-tech or at least use industrial technology such as a printing press. But talking on the telephone is an example of interpersonal communication that is technological, and a poster on a wall or writing on a blackboard is an almost no-tech, or very low-tech, kind of mass communication.

Apropos of blackboards, the classroom is one of few communication settings that can and does easily switch between mass and interpersonal communication. When I lecture in a class, the students are receivers of mass communication, or my message to many people. But as soon as a student asks a question and I answer, she and I are communicating interpersonally—while for the rest of the class, who continue as listeners, the communication is still mass communication. When I finish answering the first student's question and call on another student, the first student moves back into the mass communication audience, as the second student and I now engage in interpersonal communication.

Twitter takes the classroom to a global level. Although it is not without precedent in digital media—chat rooms and private IMs also swing between mass and interpersonal communication—Twitter is a chat room, classroom, or gathering that goes on 24 hours a day, 7 days a week. And although the messages on Twitter can certainly be educational, it is the communication structure of the classroom, not its content, that is catapulted into a worldwide conversation on Twitter.

Twitter expands the classroom communication structure in a second way, making group-to-individual communication as easy as individual-to-group (teacher-to-class). Groups of all sizes and purposes send out tweets—old media giants such as Fox News and CNN, which offer real-time tickers or updates of news stories; political campaigns for president and all manner of elected offices; and groups devoted to a particular cause or social purpose, such as TwitterMoms, which helped mobilize opposition to Facebook's ban on photos of breastfeeding. Messages of 140 characters on such subjects, with links to bigger content in blogs, videos, and traditional news media on the Web, reach tweeters on the same smart phones, tablets, and laptops on which they see tweets such as "Just got to my dentist's office. Ugh!"

Tweets also allow effortless broadcasting of professional and personal information, such as this text from Karl Rove on February 14, 2009: "Back in Washington. Working on the book this weekend. Tune in to Fox News tomorrow AM. I'll be on Chris Wallace's 100 Day Special." Indeed, links to all of my blog posts and podcasts show up on my Twitter account and are seen by my 4700 (as of January 2012) "Followers," as are tweets about my TV and radio appearances and interviews in the old-media press, and off-the-cuff comments about baseball games and snowstorms.

The automatic sending to Twitter (via applications or "apps") of links to anything and everything on the Web, or anything and everything with a URL—blog posts, videos, news stories, the full gamut of new and new new media—and the instantly subsequent, automatic relay of these tweets (if the tweeter enables this) to Facebook, LinkedIn, Squidoo, Reverbnation, and "meta" or "aggregate" new new systems such as FriendFeed ("meta" because their content consists of links from Twitter, Facebook, YouTube, and other new new media activity) constitute a self-perpetuating, not entirely planned, expanding network that has much in common with living organisms and evolutionary systems (see Levinson, 1979 and 1997, for more on the organic evolution of media).

Twitter as Smart T-Shirt or Jewelry

But when Twitter functions as a statement of feeling—"I'm so bored in this class" or "I'm feeling really good tonight, don't know why"—Twitter is working as a kind of virtual apparel or jewelry. It becomes something we "wear" or send out to the world, like a dark hat or a bright necklace, to indicate our emotional disposition.

When messages on Twitter get more specific, such as "I just voted for Obama" or "I just voted for Romney," they move metaphorically from jewelry to campaign pins or T-shirts with messages. Back in 1970, when the personal computer revolution was more than a decade away, Gary Gumpert wrote about "the rise of mini-comm." He was talking about how people could "broadcast" their own personal messages, or messages tailored to their views and feelings, via words printed on their T-shirts, sweatshirts, and other clothing. As in all new new media improvements in the written realm, personal and political messages in the digital age via updates on Twitter do the "mini-comm" one big series of steps better, by allowing any words to be "printed" or published worldwide instantly, retweeted or RT'd by receivers to their Followers, and then revised or changed a split second later, with a new "tweet," if the writer so desires.

Messages on T-shirts, of course, can be commercial—promoting a given product—as well as political or personal. Twitter messages have similar diversity and can range far beyond reports of emotional states, political candidates, and public demonstrations. Furthermore, because such messages are all received on media already connected to the Web, Twitter messages are well suited for creating buzz about items and activities that live on the Web, with handy URLs or links.

URLs are a frequent component of Twitter messages sent by major news media such as Fox News and *The New York Times* with links to breaking stories on their pages. In that function, Twitter becomes a type of wire service, like AP or Reuters. "Followers" receive these messages but do not usually reply. In those communications, Twitter is working as a mass rather than an interpersonal medium, though receivers of those messages can certainly communicate among themselves via Twitter.

Twitter allows one-way Followers in which A gets all of B's tweets, but B does not get tweets from A, and mutual Followers in which A and B each see all of the other's tweets. One-way Followers are the equivalent of Subscribers on Facebook, and mutual Followers are the equivalent of Friends. Mutual Followers can send each other private messages (DMs or "direct messages"), unseen by anyone else on Twitter, in addition to public tweets directed at one another that everyone on Twitter can see. (Rep. Anthony Weiner thought he was sending a DM but instead sent a public or "mass media" message with sexually suggestive content to a Follower. See "The Other Congressman Who Tweeted Too Much," in an upcoming section, for what ensued.)

When Twitter works as a form of one-to-one interpersonal communication, it operates not only as a kind of jewelry but a neo-telegraph. Or, as I told Ken Hudson in our November 2007 interview in Second Life, "the telegraph was much like microblogging." The telegraph also was indeed much like tweeting—not in the speed of delivery, but the succinctness of its telegrams, for which senders were charged per word.

Bloggers not only can send out links to their blog posts via Twitter, but also can automate this dissemination via free services such as TwitterFeed. In the second half of 2011, approximately 15 percent of all readers of my *Infinite Regress* blog arrived via links to my pages sent out automatically on Twitter (three times as many as the 5 percent in the second half of 2008). To return to the jewelry and T-shirt analogy, then, Twitter messages range from store-bought (news from CNN) to handmade (a link to a blog post by any individual). As is the case with all new new media, older media are not really obliterated but rather are subsumed and furthered on Twitter.

Google+, Twitter, Facebook, and Pownce

Thus far, less than a decade into the age of new new media—if we count this age as not fully starting until the arrival of Twitter in 2006—the main victims of new new media have been not old, off-line media but new new media themselves. Yes, newspapers have shut down (we will discuss the decline of newspapers in chapter 11, "Blogging"), but most printed newspapers continue in some diminished form. In contrast, new new media disappear from the Web with regularity, distressing or exhilarating, depending on your perspective. Since the publication of the first edition of this book, Odeo the podcasting host has gone, as have Aardvark the real-time expertise service, Adjix the Twitter-link shortener with embedded advertisements, and Google Buzz, which lasted about a year (2010–2011).

Pownce, developed by the Digg design team, was Twitter's only, and much smaller, competitor from 2007 through December 2008, when it closed shop. Its main advantage in comparison to Twitter was that files—images, music, and video—could be sent along with the messages, in contrast to Twitter, which sent just links. The Pownce receiver thus was saved the step of clicking on the link and could immediately enjoy the sights and sounds.

This advantage was not enough to save Pownce, but it is one of the main features that at first distinguished Google+ from Twitter. With the failure of Google Buzz—which was little more than another form of Twitter—already written on the wall by June 2011, Google launched Google+. It had more than 60 million users by the end of 2011, was adding more than half a million new users per day, and expected to reach 400 million users by the end of 2012—exceeding Twitter's 300+ million at the beginning of 2012, assuming that number doesn't grow by at least 33% (Guynn, 2011). (But see also Ferraro, 2012, "Google+ Defenses," for some weaknesses in Google+'s growth.)

Google+'s success is no doubt a result of it being not just a Twitter lookalike, but also an amalgam of Twitter and Facebook. Google+ has "Circles," the equivalent of Facebook Groups, but with much easier means of information targeting. A link posted on Google+ can be sent out to the entire public of Google+ users, or to specific Circles—for example, "media theory," "science fiction," "music," and "former students," in my case. These links give more of the original text or article or blog post than is available on Twitter, and there is no 140-character limit on the accompanying message or caption. Videos and photos are now embeddable in both tweets and Facebook status bars, and easily viewable on Twitter and Facebook without having to leave the sites, but Google+ has a more seamless interface with YouTube, which is also owned by Google. Like Facebook, Google+ has Profile Pages for its users, as well as Pages for books and businesses (see Bodnar, 2011, for a detailed, comprehensive analysis and comparison of Twitter, Facebook, and Google+ features).

As in all aspects of the new new media universe, there is increasing convergence of systems. Google+ was created with full knowledge of Twitter and Facebook (and the failure of Google Buzz). Facebook's constant alteration of its architecture cannot help but take into account successful new features on Google+. Twitter has updated its system as well, making it easier to see who has made your tweet a "Favorite" (much like the + in Google+, and the "Like" on Facebook), who has retweeted your tweet (the equivalent of "Share" on Google+ and Facebook), and replied or responded to your tweets ("comments" on Google+ and Facebook). These three "newer" new new media are inevitably becoming more similar.

Will they eventually totally merge into one system—whatever its name—that combines the most successful characteristics of all three? Perhaps, eventually. In the meantime, Google+ clearly has the most immediate potential for growth—given its 60-million size—but Twitter remains the scrappy upstart, given its secondary position to Facebook, and the fact that it is not owned by a digital behemoth like Google.

Twitter Dangers: The Congressman Who Tweeted Too Much

The dangers of telling the world what you are doing via tweets should be obvious, especially if what you are doing is provocative and you are in a vulnerable, publicly accessible place. You might think that this applies to chatterbox—or, better, tweet-erbox—kids, and it does. But consider the series of tweets sent by Rep. Peter Hoekstra (R-Michigan), on February 6, 2009: "Just landed in Baghdad..." And, later, "Moved into green zone by helicopter Iraqi flag now over palace. Headed to new US embassy Appears calmer less chaotic than previous here" (Donnelly, 2009). Hoekstra, a member of the House Intelligence Committee, had fallen prey to a dangerous illusion that has accompanied online communication since the 1980s—dangerous, in Hoekstra's case, because let's say a terrorist anywhere in the world had read his tweet, and forwarded it to people on the ground in a position to attack Hoekstra's party. The illusion comes from mistaking the screen in front of you—whether a computer on your desk in the 1980s or a BlackBerry in your hand today—as a personal device upon which you can record your thoughts, be they private, angry, whatever, for delivery only to the person or people you had in mind. After all, the device in the 1980s was called a "personal computer." Tweets can be even more misleading because you might think that they can be seen only by your Followers. Your tweets are indeed seen by your Followers but also can be seen by everyone else on Twitter, unless you chose to "protect" your Profile and make your tweets available only to your approved Followers and not to the Twitter world at large—which, as we've seen, now (in early 2012) numbers 300 million and counting. As an indication of how intrinsically public and global almost all Twitter activity is, less than 1 percent of Twitter users have "protected" or shielded their accounts (Shapiro, 2011).

In Hoekstra's enthusiasm for the new new medium, then, he neglected to check out all of its features and control mechanisms. This was an understandable, albeit potentially deadly, error. Adults become children—usually in the best sense of the word—when we encounter and adopt a new mode of communication, especially one such as Twitter, which with a few keystrokes can open new vistas for our personal and professional lives. It might also be worth noting that the average age of Twitter users, according to an unscientific, sample survey conducted via Twitter in February 2009, was 37 (Weist, 2009; see also the scientific sample survey by Heil & Piskorski, 2009, and its findings of 90 percent of all tweets by the 10 percent most active users, "an average man is almost twice more likely to follow another man than a woman," and other demographics of interest). New new media in general, including Twitter as one of its leading cutting edges in particular, are not just for kids anymore, and have not been for at least five years.

The Other Congressman Who Tweeted Too Much

Indeed, tweeting too much is a bipartisan hazard. Anthony Weiner, D-NY, Member of the House of Representatives until June, 2011, tweeted too much in a very different way—sending a sexually suggestive photo to a Twitter Follower (a 21-year-old woman not his wife). Weiner used yfrog, which, like Twitpic, stores photos for easy sharing through Twitter. His tweet was intended to be private (a "direct message"), but Weiner mistakenly sent it out via public message to his Follower. He quickly removed the tweet after it had been posted, but the damage was done—the tweet was seen by a conservative tweeter, who clicked on the link, saw the photo on yfrog, and promptly forwarded what he had found to Andrew Breitbart's popular blog (Breitbart.com—Alexa rank #3574). Weiner at first claimed his Twitter account had been hacked, but when additional photos, some sexually explicit, came to light, Weiner apologized, for lying as well as for sending the photos, and resigned (Weiner transcript, 2011).

Why would a congressman, someone in national public office and therefore the public eye, do such a private thing in such a public venue? The answer, as with Representative Hoekstra, was that, at the time of the tweeting, the tweeter didn't feel or realize that what he was doing was potentially very public—or, in Weiner's case, public at all. As with Facebook pages and all forms of communication with a screen right in front of you, on desk, lap, or in your hand, which no one who is in your physical proximity can see, Twitter engenders the deception that what you are communicating is entirely between you and the intended receiver or receivers. But unlike Las Vegas, nothing that happens via new new media stays in the new new media system in which it happens—or, if it does, that's just coincidence, because the deeper reality is that whatever happens online is intrinsically and pervasively connected to all other media and therefore all people in the world. Putting something online in any fashion is giving it the potential of being up in bright lights on Times Square, with cameras from every news operation in the world on it.

Yuri Wright, a promising high school football player with big college prospects, learned this lesson in January 2012, when his crude sexually explicit and racially charged tweets attracted public attention. As Andy Staples aptly put it in *Sports Illustrated* (Staples, 2012), "in most football locker rooms, the words recruit Yuri Wright used on Twitter tend to pepper casual conversation between teammates—provided no coaches are around." But on Twitter, not only coaches but also everyone and their grandparents are around, and Wright was expelled from Don Bosco Prep for his tweets.

High school student Emma Thompson's tweet heard 'round the world—or at least, around most of the United States—had a happier ending in November 2011. She tweeted that Kansas Governor Sam Brownback "sucked," with the hashtag "#heblowsalot." Brownback's staff took umbrage and contacted Thompson's high school administrators, who directed her to write a letter of apology to Brownback. She refused. Fortunately, Brownback, unlike the high school's administrators, apparently understood the First Amendment, and apologized to Thompson for his staff's overzealousness (Madison, 2011). This incident nonetheless brings home the same unavoidable lesson as in the Hoekstra, Weiner, and Wright episodes: Anything tweeted, whatever the intentions of the tweeter, can in principle be seen by anyone and everyone, including the last people in the world the tweeter would want to see it.

Far worse dangers of new new media, however, come not from their mistaken use but their savvy employment by people bent on bad deeds. In chapter 15, "The Dark Side of New New Media," we will consider the deliberate use of Twitter by terrorists.

But Twitter has also been a powerful enabler of democratic expression.

Twitter vs. the Mullahs in Iran

People took to the streets in protest about what they saw as the fraudulent presidential election in Iran in June 2009. This is an old story in dictatorial regimes—people protesting in public squares—and often has dashed hopes for democracy, as was the case in Tiananmen Square in China in 1989 (see Levinson, *Cellphone*, 2004, for more). But people and democracy had new tools at their disposal in 2009.

The Supreme Leader of Iran, who supported the reelection of Mahmoud Ahmadinejad, moved with like-minded mullahs to ban reporting of the growing objections to the election, the call for a new one, and the fact that protesters were being beaten and killed. The news blackout worked for eyewitness reporting by traditional, centralized media, such as broadcast facilities, and for professional journalists, who were easy enough to identify and expel or otherwise prevent from directly reporting on events. But YouTube, Facebook, and, most prominently, Twitter were not as easy to stop or even control in 2009 Iran.

Internet and cellphone service were intermittently restricted and partially shut down in Iran. However, cutting off all tweets and uploads of videos to YouTube would have required all Internet and cellphone service to be severed in that country, which its authorities were wary of doing, because that would have had ill effects for Iranian business and other essential exchanges of information. The result left protesters and citizen reporters with pipelines for their tweets and videos, which people outside Iran could also use to send tweets back into Iran via "proxies" that appeared legitimate to the authorities.

At the same time, of course, Iranian authorities could and apparently did use Twitter to send out misleading information. When I was asked on an interview on KNX Radio broadcasting from Los Angeles on June 16, 2009, how anyone could know if tweets coming out of Iran were true or disinformation, I replied that the aggregate of tweeters, just like the many reader/editors on Wikipedia, provided some checks and balances on the accuracy of the information (Levinson, 2009, "New New Media vs. the Mullahs"). And, indeed, tweets suspected of being planted by the government were identified and denounced on Twitter (see Grossman, 2009).

The protest in Iran did not succeed in 2009. The mullahs and Ahmadinejad are still in power as of January 2012. But it is worth noting that a new medium of the late 1970s, the audio cassette, was instrumental in the Iranian revolution of 1979 (Zunes, 2009), cellphones helped organize the successful Second People Power Revolution in the Philippines in 2001 (see Rheingold, 2003; Popkin, 2009), and the U.S. State Department thought Twitter was so crucial in the early days of the 2009 protest in Iran that it asked Twitter to delay a scheduled shutdown for maintenance until a time when most of Iran was likely asleep (Grossman, 2009).

The new new media techniques first used in Iran in 2009 had greater success in the Arab Spring of 2011 and after—ridding Tunisia and Egypt of their dictators, and Libya (with military assistance from the United States and Europe) as well. These same techniques also facilitated Occupy Wall Street across the United States and much of the world beginning in the Fall of 2011. We will consider these profound political developments in chapter 14, "Politics and New New Media."

Here is the timeline of some of the major clashes of newly invented media with governmental authority in the 20th and 21st centuries. Newly invented media are intrinsically difficult for governments to control, because they are usually too recent for people in government to fully understand. Further, even before the Internet and new new (social) media, the devices and systems listed in the following timeline were conducive to individual creation of messages, unlike mass media of similar vintage, in particular radio and television.

1942–43:	The White Rose uses photocopying to tell the truth to Germans about the Nazi government. Fails to dislodge the Nazis.
1979:	Audio cassettes of Ayatollah Khomeini distributed in Iran. Succeeds in fomenting successful revolution against Shah.

1980s:	Samizdat video in the Soviet Union criticizes Soviet government. May have helped pave the way for Gorbachev's perestroika and glasnost, and end of Soviet rule.
1989:	Email gets word out to the world about Tiananmen Square protests. Fails to dislodge Chinese government.
2001:	Cellphones help mobilize peaceful opposition to President Estrada in Philippines. The Second People Power Revolution succeeds.
2009:	Twitter and YouTube get word out to the world about Iranian opposition to reported election outcome. Fails to dislodge the Iranian government.
2010–ongoing:	Twitter, Facebook, and YouTube help mobilize opposition to governments in Tunisia and Egypt, and help get word out to the world about these developments. Dictators are dislodged in peaceful revolutions. The Arab Spring spreads to Libya (regime overthrown via military force) and Yemen (prime minister resigns), and to Bahrain and Syria, with results inconclusive as of January 2012. Arab Spring protests in 12 other countries (see Wikipedia, "The Arab Spring," for current statuses).
2011–ongoing:	Twitter, Facebook, and YouTube help facilitate protests in the United States, which soon spread around the world, known as Occupy Wall Street. Results inconclusive as of January 2012.

McLuhan as Microblogger

The short form of Twitter is not only a politically efficient and socially cool necessity; it had already been developed, long before Twitter, into a well-known literary form. Marshall McLuhan died on the last day of 1980—not only years before there was tweeting and blogging but a few years before email and more than a decade before easily accessible Web pages. But McLuhan was microblogging or tweeting in one of his most important books, *The Gutenberg Galaxy* (McLuhan, 1962), with chapter titles or "glosses" such as "Schizophrenia may be a necessary consequence of literacy" and "The new electronic interdependence recreates the world in the image of a global village." There were 107 such "tweets" in that book.

I first recognized the digital format of McLuhan's writing two decades prior to Twitter. In 1986, I wrote a piece for the *IEEE Transactions of Professional Communications* entitled "Marshall McLuhan and Computer Conferencing," in which I suggested that the pithy, aphoristic bursts that characterized his writing—his great works from the 1960s consisted of chapters often not more than a page or two in length—were actually a form of Web writing ("computer conferencing"), or what we today call blog posts, decades before the Web and online communication had emerged.

Fast-forward 21 years....I was browsing through a Twitter page, a few months after I had joined in the summer of 2007, and realized that the tweets bore a strong resemblance to the titles of those short chapters in McLuhan's books. If the contents of his chapters were blog posts, a page or two of thoughts, with no necessary connection between one chapter and the next, no fixed order, then the titles of those chapters were tweets, or an arresting phrase or two, at most. McLuhan's chapter "glosses," in other words, were tweets before their time (Levinson, "McLuhan," 2007)—fixed on paper, not floating on the screen. Of course, titles such as "Nobody ever made a grammatical error in a non-literate society" in *The Gutenberg Galaxy* were far more meaningful than most of the tweets on Twitter. So McLuhan's titles not only presaged Twitter, they also presaged the best that Twitter could be. (And to complete the transformation, there are now several Twitter accounts under McLuhan's name that tweet his aphorisms.)

But how did the real Marshall McLuhan manage to see the digital age? It was not that he had access to some sort of crystal ball that provided glimpses of the future. McLuhan owned no fantastical Prester John speculum that breached time. It was rather that McLuhan's mind worked in a way that our digital age, and new new media in particular, have captured and projected onto our screens and lives. If new new media express how human beings always wanted to communicate, all along, but could not, because our ancestors and parents lacked the technological sophistication (see my "anthropotropic" theory of media evolution for more; Levinson, 1979, 1997), then McLuhan understood and was in touch with this way of communicating, decades before it came to be. He wrote not about his age but ours, in a style that worked best not with the print media of his day but the new new media of our current time.

This, in turn, suggests that such a short form of writing was always part of our human capability, but, with the exception of graffiti and the telegram, our culture and education until the present served to limit or rule it out. McLuhan was able to break through those limits, and the short form is now becoming the norm in texting, IMing, status reporting, and tweeting.

The resurgence of the short—Shakespeare got it, when he wrote "brevity is the soul of wit"—also points to a more general historical dynamic between old and new new media. Retrieval of earlier communication forms by new technologies is an important part of McLuhan's media theory and was most developed in his "tetrad," or four-part model of what he referred to as media "effects." Every newly introduced medium "amplifies" aspects of our communication (radio, for example, amplifies sound across distance), "obsolesces" a currently widespread form (radio took the place of some reading), "retrieves" an earlier form (radio brought back the spoken word), and eventually reverses or "flips" into something else (radio becomes audiovisual television). *Digital McLuhan* (Levinson, 1999) provides more details and examples of tetrads, but, regarding Twitter, we could say it amplifies the short written phrase; obsolesces long blogs and phone calls; retrieves graffiti, telegrams, poetic phrases, and McLuhan's writing; and flips into...well, that's yet to be seen.

But maybe we already have a glimpse of one of the new new media forms that Twitter is engendering or flipping into. Robert K. Blechman's *Executive Severance* (2012), described by the author as a "twitstery," is a novel written entirely on Twitter, once a day, one tweet at a time. Whereas Amazon, a new medium, engendered the Kindle (another kind of new medium with digital content in traditional book form), Twitter the new new medium has engendered a genuinely new kind of novel, one that could not have existed before Twitter. The novel created in tweets on Twitter completes the cycle started by McLuhan, who wrote in tweets before Twitter was born.

But most of Twitter plays not off fiction but the real world in which you and I exist.

Chapter Thirteen

Wikipedia

We come from a tradition in which knowledge has to be vouched for, authorized, and approved by experts before it is allowed to reach us. Whether clerics or professors or newspaper editors, the effect is the same: Knowledge must be vouchsafed and deemed acceptable by professionals, before it reaches the eyes and ears of people in the world at large. Of course, all kinds of knowledge, information, facts, and falsities can be seen, heard, or discovered by anyone and everyone. But our tradition, common to both Western and Eastern and all cultures in between, with roots deep in the ancient world, requires that knowledge have the imprimatur, or seal of expert approval, to be considered worthy of study and further dissemination.

Before we scoff at this vetting, we should understand its logic. It is as easy to create and disseminate a falsehood as it is a truth. We might be flooded by such falsehoods, were gatekeepers not carefully regulating what can reach us.

On the other hand, is not our very rationality in the business of separating truths from falsehoods, lies, and distortions, and recognizing truth in the crowded field? Certainly John Milton thought so. In his *Areopagetica*, published in 1644, Milton argued that truth and falsity must be allowed to confront each other without restrictions in the marketplace of ideas. Milton was confident that truth would be recognized, unless censorship accidentally or otherwise kept some truth from entering this contest and thereby warped the results. Thomas Jefferson wholeheartedly agreed, which is why he and like-minded Founding Fathers from Virginia insisted on the First Amendment to our Constitution: "Congress shall make no law…abridging freedom of speech, or of the press." (See also Percival, 2012, for a brief on the power of rationality.)

Boards of experts that determined what went into encyclopedias prior to Wikipedia were certainly not governmental censors or in any way in violation of the First Amendment. But they nonetheless embodied and practiced a kind of censorship, or gatekeeping, that prevented the people at large from determining the truth or falsity of a factual statement, or the more complex question of its relative importance.

Wikipedia, which was brought online in January 2001 by Jimmy Wales and Larry Sanger—Wales continues to play a predominant role in Wikipedia's administration—and by January 2012 had nearly 4 million articles written in English (out of 20 million in 283 different language editions), overthrew that reign by philosopher-king experts. None of those articles was written by an appointed expert—or, if experts wrote the articles, the knowledge embodied in their Wikipedia writing, not their official expertise, was what decided whether those articles survived.

Pickles and Pericles

Almost anyone can write and edit entries on Wikipedia (the "almost" refers to people who have been banned, which will be discussed in detail in "All Wikipedians Are Equal, but Some Are More Equal Than Others" later in this chapter). Age, education, location, gender—none of this makes a difference, or is supposed to make a difference, on Wikipedia. Even intention to help with the writing of an entry, or the opposite intention—to destroy it—makes no difference, at first. Hence, entries on Wikipedia are teeming with the work of pranksters—deliberately introduced errors. These are quickly corrected by readers/editors (readers and editors are the same on Wikipedia). Indeed, there is an ever-waging war on Wikipedia, between those who attempt to make and keep entries truthful and those who seek for whatever reason to disrupt this process.

My favorite example, because it is so trivial yet instructive, comes from a few years ago, when a synopsis for an entry on Pericles made the front page of Wikipedia (the front page is controlled by administrators—see "All Wikipedians Are Equal"). In the first line of the entry, an alternate spelling of Pericles—Perikles—was given. When I logged on to that page, I immediately noticed that Perikles had been changed to Pickles by some anonymous vandal. I changed Pickles back to Perikles (in those days, I absent-mindedly did not even always use my account on Wikipedia—I was also an anonymous user, with just an IP, or numerical Internet address). Another vandal (or at least someone with a different IP address from the first vandal) soon changed Perikles to Pickles, and this pickle fight went on with various combatants for at least a few hours.

Of course, far more serious battles of this sort are being waged daily, even hourly, on Wikipedia concerning character assassinations of public figures and celebrities, calumnies (to use that great 18th-century term), and other misleading information posted about political candidates. Barack Obama being falsely described as a Muslim was among the most common of misrepresentations on Wikipedia in 2008. In all cases, trivial and profound, the dynamics are the same: Armies of light, or immune systems, or good cops—whatever metaphor appeals to you—fight armies of darkness, or infection to Wikipedia, or marauders of the truth.

The medical analogy might work best to underscore the difference between expert-driven, gate-kept encyclopedias such as the venerable *Britannica* and mass-intelligence-driven encyclopedias such as Wikipedia. In an expert-driven system, the only people who can write are those who have been certified as free from mental maliciousness or other incapacity. In the people-driven system, because anyone can write, all readers/editors serve as antibodies to correct infection—false information—introduced by harmful germs.

But the battlefield on Wikipedia is even more complicated.

Inclusionists vs. Exclusionists: Battle Between Wikipedian Heroes

Life would be simpler if battles between heroes and villains were the only kind that afflicted our world. But, in fact, battles—or at least disagreements—often break out in the ranks of defenders of the truth.

On Wikipedia, a battle is waged constantly between two kinds of readers/editors, who are both trying to make the online encyclopedia the best it can be. Both do their utmost to root out vandalism wherever they see it. But their battle is not primarily about vandalism but about what kind of truthful information should be allowed on Wikipedia. Their battlefield is thus not about truth but about relevance and worthiness to be included in an encyclopedia.

As their names suggest—names proudly touted by the two factions themselves—the "exclusionists," or deletionists, want to limit the entries on Wikipedia, while the "inclusionists" want to keep and expand entries. But there is a lot of room between no entries at all (which, of course, the exclusionists do not want) and anything truthful that anyone writes about anything, however unimportant (which, of course, the inclusionists do not really want, either). And there are subtleties and variations within the groups. "Deletionists" focus on removing complete articles deemed unworthy for an encyclopedia, while "exclusionists" are more concerned about removing irrelevant or unimportant sections of otherwise acceptable articles. "Mergists" are a school of deletionists who want to merge two or more articles into one, because some of the articles are deemed insufficient in importance to stand on their own or merit their own article. If these groups sound to you almost like religious or political factions, you would be right. Except the subject matter need not be political or religious and can indeed be any topic. What makes these factions seem religious or political is not the subject of their focus on Wikipedia but the intensity and specificity of their editing philosophies.

Expert-driven encyclopedias such as *Britannica*, which ended its printed edition in 2012 (the last printed edition was in 2010), were exclusionist, and, given the limitations of print on paper, had no choice but to be. After all, would anyone purchase an encyclopedia of 1,000 or 10,000 volumes? The *Encyclopedia Britannica* thus not only restricted the number of new entries but also removed or reduced the length of older entries that its editors deemed less relevant. (I pointed out in the preface of my novel *The Plot to Save Socrates*, 2006, the value of having access to a *Britannica* from the mid-1950s or earlier—entries on ancient history were shortened in the mid-1950s to make room for the enormous growth of scientific knowledge such as DNA in that era.) The *Britannica*'s digital editions survive the demise of the printed edition, but follow the same selective editorial policies (see Pepitone, 2012).

Inclusionists point out that an online encyclopedia labors under no such draconian paper master.

Among the most frequently debated issues between exclusionists and inclusionists on Wikipedia is the "notability" of possible subjects of articles—is the person, current or historical, important enough to warrant a Wikipedia entry? Among the many guiding principles used by editor/readers in making such decisions is one that holds that "notability is not inherited." For example, you will find no entry on Francine Descartes, daughter of the great philosopher. But a major entry, of course, is found on Wikipedia for John Stuart Mill, son of James Mill, who was also an important philosopher and has a Wikipedia article (though James Mill was not as significant in impact as his son). The point here is that John Stuart Mill would have merited an entry even if his father had been an unknown stable hand.

Incidentally, you or any reader can post an entry on Francine Descartes on Wikipedia any time you like. It would likely be put up for immediate deletion, however. (See "All Wikipedians Are Equal, but Some Are More Equal Than Others," later in this chapter, for much more on the process of deletion on Wikipedia.)

The "notability is not inherited" principle is not at all controversial or difficult to apply in the cases of Francine Descartes and John Stuart Mill. But it can be and has been highly contentious in many other cases.

Consider, for example, the article for Lolo Soetoro, Barack Obama's Indonesian stepfather. The brief history of the man, as it relates to Obama, is that Barack Obama's mother, Ann Dunham, married Soetoro after she and Obama's biological father (Barack Obama the elder) were divorced. Barack Obama the future U.S. president lived in Indonesia for four years, from ages six to ten. He returned without his mother or Soetoro to Hawaii, where he lived with his grandparents and completed his secondary education through high school.

So does Lolo Soetoro warrant a Wikipedia entry? "Notability is not inherited"—whether forward to descendants or backward to ancestors—would suggest not, but the question became contentious in the 2008 American presidential campaign, for reasons having little to do with traditional exclusionist/inclusionist debating points. Obama supporters on Wikipedia thought readers/editors in favor of a Soetoro entry wanted it as a way of drawing attention to Obama's Muslim upbringing in Indonesia and thereby painting him as an un-American candidate. This led some readers/editors who were usually inclusionists to oppose the article—that is, delete it, merge it, or redirect it (for example, to an article about Ann Dunham).

The Lolo Soetoro article was at first removed from Wikipedia, with searches for it redirected to a more general "Family of Barack Obama" article, which contains a section on Soetoro. (Technically, then, the article was not deleted but merged into the "Family" article.) But the Soetoro article was reinstated in June 2008 and survived at least one additional attempt to remove and merge it. (See Wellman, 2008, for a detailed account of the Wikipedia battles over the Soetoro article. My wife, Tina Vozick, who edits on Wikipedia as "Tvoz," was a "mergist" in these discussions, departing from her usual "inclusionist" perspective.)

A nonpolitical example of what exclusionists and inclusionists argue about on Wikipedia is the "category" about "Fictional Jews." A category on Wikipedia is a link that can pull together diverse articles. The category links appear at the bottom of articles and all together on compilation pages that display the titles of the articles, or the names of the subjects. Not all categories are controversial. "Fictional private investigators," for example, is accepted by exclusionists and appears on pages for Sherlock Holmes, Hercule Poirot, Sam Spade, Mike Hammer, and the like. This was not the case for "Fictional Jews," which once appeared on pages ranging from Shakespeare's Shylock, James Joyce's Leopold Bloom, *Law and Order*'s John Munch, and my barely known character Dr. Phil D'Amato. The category was removed in March 2008, but brought back to life in April 2010 after considerable discussion. (An article called "List of fictional Jews," however, continued without interruption. A "list" is a less dynamic component of Wikipedia than a category—the listed items do not appear at the bottom of articles about the people or items in the list.)

Aside from the easy come, easy go lesson about "categories" on Wikipedia— or maybe "difficult" would be a better adjective—the "fictional characters" story provides a textbook case of the ongoing inclusionist/exclusionist debate. On the exclusionist side, clearly, such a category has nothing essential—nothing not already available in the subject entries themselves, whether about Shylock, Bloom, or others. But on the inclusionist side, the category provided another way of accessing the information, another method of linking and learning. And because the storage and bandwidth capacities of Wikipedia are in effect infinite in comparison to words printed on paper, what harm was ever done by including such a category? Perhaps the exclusionists were concerned about ethnic stereotyping.

Neutrality of Editors and Conflicts of Interest

As the author of novels and short stories in which Phil D'Amato appears as a character (for example, *The Silk Code*, 1999), I have a professional interest in wanting any category in which he appears to continue on Wikipedia. I actually first found out about the "Fictional Jews" category after it had been deleted and did not take part in any of the subsequent online discussions pro or con, because the ideal editor on Wikipedia is supposed to be a reader who has no vested interest in the article or page he or she is writing or editing. This means the editor has nothing to gain or lose financially, personally, or professionally from the words on the page. Friedrich

Engels, the Wikipedia guidelines on conflict of interest (COI) helpfully inform us, would not be the best person to edit an entry on Karl Marx.

But day-to-day, more current situations on Wikipedia may not be as clear-cut. Should someone who supports Obama refrain from editing pages about him and his work, or should Obama supporters, if they are known, be called out by other editors or warned by Wikipedia administrators not to edit Obama's pages? If this seems extreme to you, as it does to me, would you feel the same way if pages about Mitt Romney or Ron Paul were at issue? And staying in the political realm, but moving up the ladder of possible conflict of interest, what about a Democratic Party precinct captain? What about David Axelrod (a senior White House adviser) or Howard Dean (former Democratic National Committee chairman)? What about Michelle Obama? Should she be editing President Obama's Wikipedia page?

The last three people would seem, ipso facto, to be courting conflict of interest if they edited any Wikipedia pages in which Obama was the subject. But would it be fair for them to be banned from such editing?

Joe de Santis, Newt Gingrich's Communications Director in the 2012 presidential primary campaigns, in fact did substantial editing under his real name on Gingrich's Wikipedia pages in 2011–2012. He was alerted to the conflict-of-interest rules, stopped editing, and confined his contribution to comments in the "Talk," pages, where editors publicly discuss their work. Was any harm done to Wikipedia or the body politic?

In the end, the only objective way to enforce neutrality in Wikipedia entries might well be to limit the appraisal to the words on the page and not to the person who wrote them. As literary critic I. A. Richards warned us way back in 1929, the intentions of the writer are often inscrutable and have no real connection to the impact of the text. All that should count in analysis and criticism of a text, Richards wrote, is the text itself.

Furthermore, this problem of looking at the identity of the editor and assessing his or her neutrality is exacerbated on Wikipedia by the ease of creating pseudonymous accounts.

Identity Problems

Authenticity of users (readers, writers, and commenters) is a problem everywhere in the worlds of new and new new media, where setting up a false identity is as easy as creating an email account on Gmail or Yahoo, under any name you choose, and then using it as the verifier on Facebook, Twitter, here, there, and everywhere.

But the problem is especially vexing on Wikipedia, because it initially operates via consensus achieved in online discussions of readers/editors ("initially" meaning before a problem might be passed on to and reviewed by administrators, for discussion of which, see "All Wikipedians Are Equal, but Some Are More Equal Than Others" later in this chapter). Wikipedians even have a name for accounts created by individuals solely or mainly for the purpose of bringing additional support for their positions into consensus discussions: "sock puppets."

Creating accounts on Wikipedia is actually easier than on Facebook and most online systems; verification via email to an already-existing Gmail or other address is not currently required. Indeed, editors can work on Wikipedia with no Wikipedia account, in which case they are identified by their IPs. Wikipedia is in the business of encouraging and maximizing participation. As in all things participatory and democratic, the process works better with more participants.

But this ease of creating accounts also has the result of making sock puppetry easy to pursue. And a clever creator of sock puppets can be difficult to identify. The bogus accounts can be created on different computers, with different IPs, and can lie dormant for months or get involved in Wikipedia discussions that have nothing to do with the sock puppeteer's real motives. When the sock puppet eventually springs into action and begins writing on behalf of articles near and dear to him or her, urging their retention or deletion in any debates that may ensue, there is no reason for anyone to think that this reader/editor has a vested interest in the article. Used in its most intelligent and effective forms, the sock puppet is thus the new new media equivalent of a sleeper cell. A sharp-eyed participant in the discussion may suspect something amiss, especially if the sock puppet writes in a style that is in some way idiosyncratic, but such suspicions can be difficult to prove when based solely on similarities in writing style.

An interesting back formation from the sock puppet, which is actually very different, is the so-called "meat puppet"—or a real account, created by a real person, for the purpose of supporting a friend's or associate's project on Wikipedia. The problem with equating sock puppets and meat puppets, however, is that the motive of any living human can be unclear. If I come to the aid of a friend in a discussion about whether to delete or keep an article about whatever on Wikipedia, who other than I can know for sure whether I really support my friend's position, and would have had the same opinion if my friend did not exist, or whether I don't care at all about this issue and entered the online discussion only at my friend's behest? Or perhaps the truth is that I spoke up in the discussion because of a mix of the two factors: I believe in the issue but wrote what I wrote because my friend encouraged me.

Issues such as sock puppets versus meat puppets, and the difficulty of identifying and protecting against them, show that online life is by no means immune to the complexities and complications of real life. The two are both subject to vandals and troublemakers, who may be more or less difficult to deal with online. The saving grace of anything destructive online, however, is that it can in itself cause no physical damage in the real world—no damage, that is, unless we act on it or allow its misinformation to guide our actions in the real world. This is the case whether we are dealing with cyberbullies on Facebook or vandals of knowledge on Wikipedia. And we can add to that, as a cause for this real-world concern, a report that the U.S. government contracted for "software which could create multiple fake social media profiles to manipulate and sway public opinion on controversial issues" (Storm, 2011). It seems that sock puppets are not just for Wikipedia any more.

All Wikipedians Are Equal, but Some Are More Equal Than Others

Wikipedia is the most thoroughgoing, consistently user-driven system on the Internet. It is the pick of the new new media litter, at least insofar as its primary, revolutionary characteristic of allowing consumers to become producers. It is the closest to direct democracy in the actual operation of a major online system. But although all readers can indeed be editors of Wikipedia, a preliminary survey reported that 90 percent of Wikipedia edits were made by the top 15 percent of the most active Wikipedia editors (working paper by Mikolaj Jan Piskorski and Andreea Gorbatai, cited in Heil & Piskorski, 2009). This is an intrinsic shortcoming of all democratic processes, in which opportunity to participate (as in voting) only partially equates to actual participation. And although editors usually decide via discussion and consensus whether an article, or part of an article, is worthy of Wikipedia, what happens when editors cannot decide? Or what happens when an editor acts as a vandal or creates sock puppets to support his or her position? Or what happens when an entry is so controversial that it is rife with constant deletions and reinstatements to the extent that it changes back and forth every few minutes?

Enter the Wikipedia administrators, who are nominated and chosen by a public discussion and consensus of editors (an editor may nominate any other editor, including oneself). A special super kind of administrator—a "bureaucrat," also chosen by community consensus—determines if consensus has been reached in favor of promoting the editor to administrator and, if so, bestows the promotion. A few administrators also act as "checkusers"—they are given the authority to see the IPs of named or account-holding readers/editors (see "Transparency on Wikipedia Pages," later in this chapter).

One of the two prime powers of administrators is blocking the accounts of errant editors. Vandalism is one way to be errant but so is violation of the "three-revert" rule, which insists that no editor can revert changes—reinstate after something is deleted, delete after something is reinstated, and so forth—more than three times in 24 hours on a given page or entry. Administrators have the power to block an editor's account after fewer than three reversions, but three is the stated and usually followed number.

An account can be blocked for an hour, a day, a week, a month, or indefinitely. The blocked editor can appeal, and any other administrator can reverse the decision of the blocking administrator or reduce the sentence (the duration of the block). However, because part of the purpose of blocking is to reduce or defuse so-called "edit wars"—two editors undoing each other's work—administrators try not to initiate a similar war of their own by repeatedly blocking and unblocking editors (which constitutes a "wheel war," in Wikipedian parlance).

The second major power of administrators is "protecting" a page or entry—preventing any reader/editor other than an administrator from making further edits. As with blocking of accounts, the protection can be for any length of time, and any administrator can unprotect a page or open it for renewed editing. So "wheel wars," or administrators reversing one another's actions, are a pitfall to be avoided here, too.

The daily main or front page of Wikipedia, which contains a "featured article" (a synopsis of a longer article) selected by a single, specially appointed administrator, is always "read-only," or incapable of being edited by anyone other than an administrator. On that always-protected page, Wikipedia becomes perilously close to the organizing structure of the front page of *The New York Times*. In this straightforward method, Wikipedia gains reliability at the expense of its democratic process. All that readers/editors and even other administrators can do is make suggestions about what "Today's Featured Article" should be. And all that readers/editors can do about errors is point them out, so an administrator can correct them.

Protection of other pages, however, can be an especially tricky business. Let's say, for example, that on a given day, two groups of editors (reader/writers) with sincere, diametrically opposing political viewpoints, are busy "correcting" and "uncorrecting" a political candidate's page. This is not about straight-up vandalism, which can be corrected as many times as necessary (an important exception to the three-revert rule is that it does not apply to correction of obvious falsehoods and the work of vandals, but the falsehoods have to be obvious). But in a politically motivated edit war, where the page receives thousands of views an hour, the stakes can be much higher than in run-of-the-mill Perikles/pickles vandalism. An administrator who comes upon this battle might decide to protect the page, to give the warring editors a little time to cool off. But for this period of time, no one other than another administrator would be able to edit the page—thus depriving Wikipedia of its main mechanism of error correction. What if the administrator, either accidentally or otherwise, left an interpretation in the protected page, not because it was agreed by consensus that the interpretation was best, but because it most suited the administrator's political perspective? Thousands or more readers would see this interpretation on the page. Pages for Barack Obama, John McCain, Joe Biden, and Sarah Palin were indeed briefly protected on October 30, 2008, as edit wars and racist attacks escalated five days prior to that year's election. Rick Santorum's page was fully protected for almost three days in February 2012, over an edit war concerning contraception. The full protection, originally decreed for three full days, was changed to "semi-protection" after editors objected to the full protection (see Levinson, 2012, "Rick Santorum," for details).

In practice, full protection of pages for politicians or any subject is infrequent on Wikipedia—and the front page, always protected, is an obvious one-of-a-kind special case. But pages can also be semi-protected, or blocked from anonymous and new account edits (new account defined as more recent than four days and having made fewer than ten edits on Wikipedia), and this is a much more common practice. Obama's page has been intermittently semi-protected since 2007. (See Vargas, 2007, for discussion of vandalism on Obama's Wikipedia page.) Semi-protection is usually deployed to stop drive-by vandalism, which is far more common than political spinning. But even semi-protection ties at least one of Wikipedia's hands behind its back—the hand of anonymous and new accounts for correcting errors. Editors not blocked by semi-protection will, of course, be able to correct errors, but the pool of error correctors is still reduced.

But Wikipedia does have at least one additional, built-in defense against vandals.

Transparency on Wikipedia Pages

A major feature of Wikipedia that puts even the most diligent vandal at a disadvantage is the complete history of edits easily available on every page or entry. This means that any and all changes, additions, and deletions, profound and trivial, can be seen on the screen by any reader/editor. A vandal may seek to disguise an important piece of dirty work by bundling it with a lot of obvious vandalism, and a revision, helpful or destructive, may be missed by a casual reader of the History page, but every single revision is nonetheless listed. Wikipedia also shows what every page looked like before and after the edit.

The transparent History pages on Wikipedia make it radically different from most blogs on the Web, which at most indicate if and when a page has been edited, or, as in the case of Google's Blogspot (of which my *Infinite Regress* blog is an example), give no indication that a page has been edited at all. Facebook's Timeline provides a record of everything the user has done on Facebook, but the user can easily hide any actions from public view or remove them totally. Given that a page on Wikipedia can be edited by a myriad of people, in contrast to only the blogger being able to edit his or her blog, and only the account holder (user) on Facebook, this hypertransparency of editing history on Wikipedia makes sense.

This level of transparency on Wikipedia, however, pertains to pages or articles and not to readers/editors. As indicated earlier, one need not have an account to edit on Wikipedia, in which case, you are identified by your IP. An IP is unique to your computer connection to the Internet. If you take your laptop to a friend's house and log on via wi-fi available there, you will be using his or her IP. (Mobile media such as smart phones and tablets have their own IPs.) IPs are thus not a foolproof way of identifying a particular reader/editor.

If you register for an account (free) on Wikipedia, you are thereafter identified by your account name, not your IP. But this allows individuals to register for any number of accounts and serves as the basis for sock puppetry (though an individual may want to have more than one account for non-nefarious purposes). Only specially appointed administrators —"checkusers"—have the ability to see the IP of any given account, as mentioned earlier. These can be helpful in rooting out sock puppets, though the recalcitrant puppeteer can resort to different IPs for the puppets—for example, in libraries, Apple stores, schools, and indeed any wi-fi hot spot such as Starbucks, Panera Bread, or a hotel lobby.

Wikipedia vs. *Britannica*

So, with all of these potentials for error and safeguards, with the battles waging on Wikipedia between vandals and editors, between editors and editors, between editors and administrators, and sometimes between administrators and administrators—all for the purpose of making sure that the articles on Wikipedia contain only accurate and relevant information—how does Wikipedia fare as an accurate source of information? An error is easier to identify than an irrelevance. If Wikipedia's reader-written, constantly in-flux pages were as free from error as, say, the distinguished, expert-written pages of the *Encyclopedia Britannica*, that would tell us something very important about how the democratic antibodies of a new new media book of knowledge compare with the strict gatekeeping of our older, trusted reference sources.

The correct answer is that Wikipedia seems to be holding its own against the *Encyclopedia Britannica*—a remarkable accomplishment—but the jury is still not entirely in. *Nature*—one of the two leading science magazines in the world (along with *Science*)—reported the results of a study it conducted in 2005, in which experts examined 42 articles each from Wikipedia and the *Britannica* online edition (Giles, 2005). The experts found an average of four inaccuracies per Wikipedia article and three per *Britannica* article—in other words, not much of a difference at all. This result was widely publicized (for example, Associated Press, 2005) but drew an outraged objection from *Britannica*, which alleged that *Nature*'s investigators were the ones who got their facts wrong and, in other cases, offered mere opinion not expert judgment (Orlowski, 2006). *Britannica* called upon *Nature* to retract its report. *Nature* (2006) replied with a lengthy explanation of its methods and findings and concluded, "We do not intend to retract our article." Three years later, *Nature* stood by its 2005 findings (Giles, 2008).

The clearest lesson of these dueling experts may be that expert opinion is not as reliable as it holds itself out to be—either *Nature* was in error, or *Britannica* erred in its criticism of *Nature*, or both—which in itself provides another strong argument in favor of encyclopedia by democracy on Wikipedia, or what *Nature*'s study suggests works as well as encyclopedia by expert, oligarchic decree. (See also Messer-Kruse, 2012, for the travails of a recognized expert trying to edit on Wikipedia—or another example of conflict between the expert and the democratic editing cultures.)

Old vs. New New Media in Reporting the Death of Tim Russert

Wikipedia competes not only with old media encyclopedias but also with old media news reporting in newspapers, radio, and television. When *Meet the Press* moderator Tim Russert died unexpectedly, shortly after 2:20 p.m. on June 13, 2008, NBC and other traditional news media understandably waited until relatives were notified before informing the general public. That occurred at 3:30 p.m., when Tom Brokaw broke into the afternoon programming on NBC, CNBC, and MSNBC and announced Russert's death. ABC, CBS, CNN, and Fox News all waited for Brokaw's announcement to broadcast their own announcements and reports.

Wikipedia did not. According to a *New York Times* June 23, 2008, account of the events of June 13 (Cohen, 2008), Russert's page on Wikipedia was updated at 3:01 p.m. to reflect Russert's death. (You can see this in the history of Russert's page on Wikipedia.) Also according to *The New York Times*, the person who made the change on Wikipedia was "a junior-level employee" of Internet Broadcasting Services—an organization that supplies information to local NBC-TV stations and other companies—who was subsequently fired. (*The New York Times* put the story of Russert's death on its own Web site five minutes before Brokaw's announcement.)

The difference between Wikipedia's and television's treatment of the Russert story highlights the radical departure of new new media from the way old and new media operate. In the case of NBC and all the broadcast and cable media, an executive—a gatekeeping editor of some sort—made the call as to when the story would be aired. This is the procedure for any and every story we see on broadcast and cable TV, hear on the radio, or read in the newspaper. In contrast, no one in the employ of Wikipedia made such a decision, because that is not the way Wikipedia works. (The Wikimedia Foundation and lawyers who work for Wikipedia do not make initial publishing decisions.) An employee of a company totally unrelated to Wikipedia updated Russert's page. Anyone could have done that—you or I. Or we might have put up a completely false story about Russert or anyone.

It is not that Wikipedia has no standards for what is published in its online encyclopedia. It does, but the standards are applied, again, by you, me, anyone who happens to read an article. One of Wikipedia's primary standards is that facts need confirmation in other media before they stand on Wikipedia. Because no confirmation existed at 3:01 p.m. of Russert's death, the update announcing it on Russert's page was deleted 10 minutes later (according to *The New York Times*, by someone using another Internet Broadcasting Services computer). And, soon after, it of course was reinstated.

But would any new reader/editor know about this or any of the other many guidelines for articles on Wikipedia? Extensive, detailed descriptions, explications, and summaries of standards are posted on Wikipedia, and these are accessible in numerous ways (for example, see "Category: Wikipedia behavioral guidelines"). As is the case with any democracy, it can work only if citizens have easy, reliable access to its laws. As is also the case in any democracy, the laws or guidelines are constantly debated and refined.

Wikipedia Wrongly Reports the "Deaths" of Ted Kennedy and Robert Byrd

Indeed, the egregiously wrong Wikipedia report of Ted Kennedy's and Robert Byrd's "deaths" on Inauguration Day, 2009, led Jimmy Wales to urge a new level of editorial review, in which "trusted editors" would need to approve all biographical entries by new and anonymous editors (see Pershing, 2009; Kells, 2009). In reality, Ted Kennedy had a seizure and was taken out of the post-inauguration luncheon by medics. Byrd, age 91 at the time, was apprehensive and decided to leave the luncheon as well. Kennedy recovered, and Byrd was not really ill in the first place, but in the initial confusion, Wikipedia listed both senators as deceased. (Ted Kennedy died eight months later, and Robert Byrd the following year.)

Whether by accident or vandalism, such erroneous posts call into question the reliability of Wikipedia. They were removed within five minutes—a testament to the correcting power of numerous readers/editors—but numerous readers nonetheless saw the incorrect reports. Instating a layer of editorial review would certainly help with this problem, but it would also undermine Wikipedia's fundamental policy that anyone can write and edit and publish on its pages. Several proposals (including Wales's) addressing this issue have long been under discussion on Wikipedia. (Wikipedia in Germany already has such a review policy in place—for all articles, whatever the subject. See Wales, 2009, for preliminary details. And see also Perez-Pena, 2009, for how Wales and Wikipedia administrators kept news of a kidnapping off Wikipedia to help enable the victim's eventual escape.)

Encyclopedia or Newspaper?

The immediate announcement of Tim Russert's death on Wikipedia—and the erroneous reports about Kennedy and Byrd—raises another contentious issue: Is Wikipedia an encyclopedia or a newspaper? Publishing news as quickly as possible is, after all, what a newspaper does. But Wikipedia and newspapers are not the same.

News media, in general, are supposed to report events that are true and significant in some sense, and as soon as possible. Certainly an encyclopedia subscribes to the first two—everything in it should be true and significant—but instead of speed, an encyclopedia presumably wants to publish information that has some kind of enduring relevance. And the very definition of enduring means it cannot cohabit with immediate, unless one wants to take a leap of faith and predict or assume that an event that occurred yesterday will be of interest to general readers 10 years later.

Sometimes such predictions are easy to make with confidence: Regardless of who wins an election for president of the United States, we can rest assured that the results of that election will continue to be of at least some historical importance. But what about the unexpected death of a prominent news moderator such as Tim Russert?

In the days following Russert's death in June 2008, not only was his already-existing page on Wikipedia updated hundreds of times, but additional pages also were put up, with reactions to his death by famous people and other information. Was Wikipedia working as an encyclopedia or a newspaper with such entries?

Newspapers, of course, report not only immediate and breaking news but also publish follow-up and retrospective stories as well. To the extent that enduring Wikipedia articles are as well researched as stories in newspapers—assuming that the newspapers have researched their stories—then the Wikipedia article becomes less distinguishable from a follow-up newspaper story. Ironically, Wikipedia guidelines require stories to be sourced, and although no firm ranking of sources (which sources are preferable to others) is insisted on or provided, old media newspapers are held in higher regard as sources than blog posts, and world-renowned newspapers such as *The New York Times* are preferable to high school newspapers (see Wikipedia, 2012, "Identifying Reliable Sources," for more). This provides yet another example of the interdependence and love/hate relationship of old and new new media.

In the end, the dominant principle in determining whether Wikipedia is an encyclopedia or a newspaper or both is that Wikipedia editors and administrators really have little say in how the rest of the world sees and uses Wikipedia. If readers use Wikipedia as they would a newspaper—a more up-to-date version of *The New York Times*—then how can Wikipedians stop that?

This, once again, is a cardinal principle of new new media: Not only do consumers become producers, but consumers—not necessarily the same consumers but all consumers, in general—always determine how the new new medium is used. This gives a new meaning to the concept of user: not just one who consumes or uses a medium but, in that very use, helps determine what that medium is. John Dewey (1925), the American philosopher who argued that truth is best perceived and reached through real use and experience, not preexisting thought and analysis, would have approved.

Does Wikipedia Make Libraries Unnecessary?

If Wikipedia is not quite yet, but may be becoming, a kind of newspaper, how does the online encyclopedia, which in principle has an infinite number of articles, compare with book and brick libraries?

Colin Powell, Secretary of State in George W. Bush's first administration (2001–2005), was an early appreciator of Wikipedia. He told Fareed Zakaria on Zakaria's CNN *GPS* program in December 2008 that, when he arrived at the State Department in 2001, he advised everyone to "get rid of all the books in your office. You don't need them anymore, as long as you have a couple of search engines and Wikipedia. And then I challenged my people to try to keep up with Wikipedia in terms of changes in countries."

Powell—whatever history may say about his presentation to the United Nations, prior to the Iraq War in 2003, that Saddam Hussein had weapons of mass destruction when it turned out later he apparently did not—was alert to something significant about Wikipedia and its advantages over older media, and alert to this very early. Books on the shelf suffer from an utter inability to be corrected or updated. All print media, in which words are wedded to paper, are similarly unchangeable and no different in this crucial respect from hieroglyphics carved into a pyramid (see Levinson, 1997, for more).

Newspapers do the best they can in this rigid realm by putting out new editions daily—they did this even more often prior to the triumph of electronic media in the mid-20th century—and offering follow-ups and updates on stories, as well as corrections. But unlike last year's books, last month's newspapers are far more likely to stuff packing boxes than provide missing information.

Books in libraries, then—and even online or digitally delivered—carry the burden for reference media. But like the facts in printed encyclopedias, the information in such books and libraries may well be out of date, as Colin Powell noted back in 2001.

That's the argument in favor of Wikipedia over books in libraries. Yet Powell went a little too far when he said we "don't need" books anymore, whether in the State Department or the world at large, and such a statement still goes too far in 2012.

Wikipedia has two disadvantages in comparison with libraries in 2012. The first is that it no doubt does not have some information available in books, whether about international politics and geography or any subject. But this is a classic example of what I call a "caterpillar criticism" (Levinson, 1988)—assessing a medium's incapacity at a given time as if it were permanent, rather than a work in progress, just as we might note that one problem with a caterpillar as an insect is that it cannot fly. There is no reason to think that, in ensuing years, knowledge will exist in any book on any shelf that will not be on Wikipedia. Indeed, Colin Powell's advice about not needing books, though still not correct today, is more correct now in 2012 than it was in 2001. And we can expect it to become more correct every year, every day, every hour.

But Wikipedia suffers from a second disadvantage in comparison with books, which is far more chronic, with no solution presently in sight. As we considered in chapter 10 about YouTube, anything online, anything dependent on a link to a URL for retrieval, lacks what I call the "reliable locatability" of books. If you are currently reading these words on page 77—or the words on any page of this book, page 33, 63, any page—and the book consists of bound pages, those words will be there, on the same exact pages, tomorrow, next year, even a hundred or more years from now if you put the book in a safe place. The act of just putting the book on a shelf is usually enough to ensure that the words will be there for you the next time you look for them, in the exact same place in the book on the page. But anything on the Web, even a site totally under your control, does not have this reliability—you could decide to close the site at any time. Even e-books downloaded to your Kindle do not have this reliability, as Amazon's removal of George Orwell's *1984* from Kindles around the United States in 2009, over concern about copyright, demonstrates. Ironically, Orwell's book is about the total information control of a future nightmare society, a society consistent with Amazon's action (see Levinson, 2009, for more).

The exception to the expectation of reliable locatability in paper books would be a real bookworm that ate some pages, or some other unforeseen cause of damage to the pages of the book. Even a book on a shelf (see Petroski, 1999, for the history and impact of bookshelves) could be destroyed, the page may be torn out or obliterated, and this means reliable locatability is not an absolute guarantee that the text will survive in place. But the wedding of printed words to paper is permanent, and this means that their readers can have a much greater assurance than with anything on the Web, or any device like the Kindle that receives text from the Web, that the words and images will be where expected, remembered, noted, or cited for future reference.

Wikipedia, to be sure, is probably the most reliably locatable source of information on the Web. Its myriad readers/editors take great care to make sure any changes in links to articles are automatically redirected, often from more than one path or alternate spelling of a name or title of an article. And, as indicated previously in the chapter, Wikipedia maintains complete and accessible histories of every change or edit made on any of its pages. But the system is still not perfect. For example, an article that is completely deleted may be available only to Wikipedia administrators and not the general reading/editing public. And the sheer ease with which anything can be deleted online, if someone with the necessary access wants something gone, makes even the most secure online entry less secure than any old book. In fact, Wikipedia recognizes the inherent evanescence of Web sources in comparison with books and other old media sources by putting in its Web citations at the bottom of articles not just the date of the cited Web page's creation but also the date it was last checked by a Wikipedia editor to make sure it was still online at the indicated URL. For the same reason, I noted in the Bibliography to this book that the links supplied were good as of February 2012.

The bottom line is that a paper book on a shelf is more reliable—more likely to be there when we need it—than even the most dependable site on the Web: Wikipedia. On January 18, 2012, Wikipedia went dark for a day—shut itself off—in protest of SOPA (Stop Online Piracy Act), then under consideration by the U.S. Congress. The cause was just—SOPA was yet another proposed violation of the First Amendment (see Levinson, 2012)—but the lesson of the voluntary shutdown is disquieting for those who value and yearn for more reliable locatability on the Internet. No decision by any institution, whether reached by consensus as on Wikipedia or traditional corporate fiat as on Amazon, could possibly make the paper book in your bookcase go dark. The deepest decisions regarding the new new media are not in the hands of the users on whom the new new media bestow unprecedented powers. These decisions, including whether the medium lives or dies, whether it is on or off for just a day, remain in the hands of the media themselves (and potentially the government). In this regard, new new media are no different from the oldest media in our midst.

The future of old-fashioned books and libraries thus seems under no near, total jeopardy from Wikipedia and other new new media, though we can expect the offline media to play a decreasing reference role in our lives. (In the realm of entertainment, Netflix has been offering an increasing number of movies and television shows streaming on its website, rather than DVDs in the mail.) And, although books have been banned and burned throughout history, the practical impossibility of rounding up all copies of a book, once printed and distributed, makes them invulnerable to complete banning by government, commercial, or religious directive.

That's not the case for anything online, including Wikipedia, as we will see for yet another reason in our concluding section of this chapter.

The United Kingdom vs. Wikipedia

An encyclopedia is about the last kind of text one would expect to be banned—the very word "encyclopedia" breathes something stodgy—especially in the United Kingdom, where the *Encyclopedia Britannica* was first published, in Scotland in the 1770s. On the other hand, encyclopedias have been politically troublesome to some regimes, but this was not the problem that Wikipedia encountered in the United Kingdom in December 2008 (Kirk, 2008).

It was an album cover posted on Wikipedia—*Virgin Killer* by The Scorpions, from 1976—that attracted the concern of the U.K.'s Internet Watch Foundation (IWF), which put the album on its blacklist due to the image of a nude young girl on its cover (the genital area, however, cannot be clearly seen, due to a cracked-glass effect in the image). The IWF is not affiliated with the U.K. government, but British Internet providers, whom the government expects to maintain standards of decency, take the blacklist very seriously. The result: Some 95 percent of British Internet users were blocked from Wikipedia for three days until the IWF lifted the ban (Raphael, 2008; Collins, 2008). That's right: British Internet users were blocked from all of Wikipedia on account of one album cover. Although the intent was to block the offending page, "The initial move last Friday by the IWF, which acts as a watchdog...for Internet content visible in the U.K. meant that some people could not see any pages on Wikipedia at all, while others were unable to edit pages on the user-generated encyclopedia" (Arthur, 2008).

As with Pakistan's ban of YouTube for several hours in February 2008, the blocking of Wikipedia in the United Kingdom over a questionable page highlights again the deep vulnerability in new new media—the stark reality that, for all the power they put in our hands, they are fundamentally not in our control. Although new new media may be outside the scope of the FCC (Federal Communications Commission) or other governmental supervision in the United States—for now—they are subject to control and banning in other parts of the world. In the case of Wikipedia, this can be especially destructive, because every reader unable to access Wikipedia is also an editor, unable to write or work to reach consensus in editorial discussions, which are the lifeblood of the online encyclopedia. (Collins, 2008, reported that the ban "left millions of Britons unable to make edits on the Wikipedia site.") And the interconnectedness of everything in new new media—in the case of Wikipedia, of all of its pages to one another—meant that the banning of a single page took the whole encyclopedia offline and beyond access to everyone attempting to access it via the Internet in the country where the ban was in effect. This is equivalent to putting a padlock on an entire bookstore or library, just to keep one book out of the public's hands.

Indeed, in the case of the Pakistani ban, not only was that country affected but so was access to YouTube around the world. Not just the bookstore was boarded up; bookstores around the world were behind the shutters, too.

Presumably, digital surgical techniques sooner or later will be able to take out just the offending page, or remove from public access what the censor considers a tumor, rather than shutting down a whole, vital new new media organ. But the fundamental problem remains: The current architecture of new new media and their conduits makes them all too easy to ban by central authorities. A glaring irony of new new media is that the digital engineering that makes them the most democratizing media in human history also gives governments and other authorities more power to ban them than the Catholic Church ever had over Galileo's books nearly 400 years ago.

The problem with the global village, from the perspective of combating censorship, is that the entire globe can be censored just by boarding up a few of the vendors of free information on Main Street. Had SOPA and its potential for government shutdown of Internet sites in the United States been enacted into law, the interconnected nervous system of the entire world would have been in jeopardy.

Chapter Fourteen

Politics and New New Media

Eric Schmidt, currently Executive Chairman and then also CEO of Google, immediately agreed with Arianna Huffington—founder of The Huffington Post—when she said Barack Obama won the presidency in 2008 because of the Internet. Schmidt was a guest on The Rachel Maddow Show on MSNBC, where Huffington was filling in for Maddow, on November 17, 2008, 13 days after Election Day.

Since then, new new media have played important roles in the rise of the Tea Party and the midterm 2010 election in the United States, and in the Arab Spring around the world, where Twitter, YouTube, and Facebook continue to play a vital role. New new media have also been a mainstay in Occupy Wall Street protests here in the United States and abroad, and are a major part of the strategies of both the Democratic and Republican Parties in the 2012 presidential election underway in the United States as of this writing.

Barack Obama, New New Media, and the 2008 Election

The perspective of *New New Media*, of course, is that Huffington and Schmidt were completely right. Blogging, the oldest of the new new media, was well established in 2004. But Facebook, Twitter, and YouTube did not even exist then. Howard Dean, the Internet candidate in 2004, lost in the primaries. Barack

Obama, the Internet candidate in 2008, won the primaries and the general election. Although many other factors no doubt played a role, that comparison is as clear an indication of media influence as Nixon doing better than JFK among radio listeners in their 1960 debates, JFK doing better than Nixon among TV viewers of those same debates, more people watching the debates than hearing them on television, and JFK winning the election.

How might new new media, had they then existed, have helped Howard Dean in 2004? The "Dean scream"—given by the candidate in a speech to his Iowa supporters after coming in third in the state's 2004 caucuses—is widely said to be the beginning of his undoing. The so-called scream was replayed extensively on television, with sage, sarcastic commentary from news anchors and experts. What if YouTube had been online then, and the clip with the scream had been uploaded there, for all to see, without the cable news commentary? You can see it now—search on YouTube for "Dean Scream" (2004)—does it seem that bad to you?

New new media encourage people to think for themselves. In the 2008 election, they also encouraged people to act—do more than support and eventually vote for a candidate—to actually work for a candidate.

I volunteered for Eugene McCarthy's presidential campaign and his effort to stop the war in Vietnam in 1968. That was the last time I had worked for any national candidate until 2008, when I registered at mybarackobama.com. I occasionally posted a blog on that site and from time to time logged on to keep apprised of various campaign developments. But for two days prior to Election Day 2008 and on Election Day itself, I logged on to do something else. My wife also logged on—the last time she had worked for a national candidate had been when we'd worked together for Eugene McCarthy.

The site provided names and phone numbers of Obama supporters. You could locate supporters in many states via a map on the site. We chose Pennsylvania, because the McCain campaign had been saying it was its "last stand"—that is, a state crucial to any chance of a John McCain victory, which we wanted to thwart.

It took about an hour for each of us to call about 50 different Obama supporters. We each encountered some wrong numbers and left voicemail for many people who were not at home. But we each managed to speak to dozens of supporters, from Philadelphia to the other side of the state—all from the convenience of our living room, a little north of New York City. After each phone call, we filled out a brief form on the site, where we indicated if we had made contact and noted the result—if the supporter was still planning on voting for Obama, or if he or she knew where the polling place was located, for example. Then we proceeded to do the same for Ohio, another crucial state.

Keith Goodman of the Obama campaign sent out the following email two days after the election, to everyone who had made calls for Obama: "I wanted to thank you for helping us make an astounding 1,053,791 calls on Election Day. I know it wasn't easy, and many of you kept calling long after you were tired and your voice had grown hoarse, but your calls to get our supporters out to the polls helped tip the scales in key battleground states like Florida and Ohio. Together we did it!"

New new media, as we have seen, change readers into writers all the time. In making those million calls on behalf of Obama's selection, readers and writers on mybarackobama .com had been briefly transformed into active campaign workers.

New New Media VP Announcement Misstep

Before we go too far down the misty road of hindsight that Obama did everything right, at least regarding new new media in the 2008 campaign, we need to note that his campaign was not infallible in its use of new new media. The single biggest misstep was likely its announcement in July 2008 that it intended to let the world know about Obama's choice of vice presidential running mate only via email to people on Obama's list of contributors. This was an attempt to reward his supporters by giving them a special preview, to the explicit initial exclusion of media such as television, radio, and newspapers—or the old media press.

This announcement was ill-advised for at least two reasons. First, there were, obviously, many members of the traditional press on this email list, and they could easily have transmitted Obama's choice to their old media channels instantly. Second, the previewing of anything to be done on new new media, any new new media strategy, runs contrary to the viral new new media principle of making the event seem as if it happened spontaneously, not via high-level, top-down strategy (see Levinson, "Announcing Obama's Choice Through Email Not Good Idea," 2008). As it was, word of Obama's choice of Joe Biden first broke on the old medium of CNN—and the much-heralded email announcement actually came hours later, when it was anticlimactic and no longer breaking news.

Inauguration and After on the Internet

CNN reported a four-fold increase in the number of live-streamed videos viewed on Barack Obama's January 20, 2009, Inauguration Day, in comparison to Election Day November 4, 2008, viewing—some 21.3 million in a nine-hour period through midafternoon on Inauguration Day versus 5.3 million all day on Election Day. *The New York Times* also reported that "Internet traffic in the United States hit a record peak at the start of President Obama's speech as people watched, read about and commented on the inauguration, according to Bill Woodcock, the research director at the Packet Clearing House, a nonprofit organization that analyzes online traffic" (Vance, 2009, which also provides details on CNN video viewing; Internet traffic and viewing of online videos surpassed Obama's for the Michael Jackson memorial in July 2009, see Hibberd, 2009).

It was no surprise that a lot of this traffic and viewing got stalled, as the Web and its carriers struggled to meet the demand. But such problems are healthy growing pains and the best stimulus for improving the hardware infrastructure on which all new new media depend.

Obama's new administration took control of whitehouse.gov—the official Presidential website—right after the noon hour of the Inauguration. The change not only in president but approach is a textbook example of the difference between new and new new media. Under the George W. Bush administration (2001–2009), the site provided information—in the words of one observer, mainly "links to press releases, speeches, and propaganda documents" (Manjoo, 2009). The new rendition of the site was no less propagandistic but promised to be more interactive. Its first blog post, on January 20, 2009, proclaimed that "One significant addition to whitehouse.gov reflects a campaign promise from the President: we will publish all non-emergency legislation to the website for five days, and allow the public to review and comment before the President signs it." That pledge, however, was already broken for 10 out of 11 pieces of legislation by April 2009 (Harper, 2009; see also Maddow, 2012, for an equivalent list of promises broken by Republicans in the House of Representatives in the 2011–2012 congressional term). Like all things new new media, interactivity and transparency in governance is better just done than promised.

There is also an argument that, in a democracy, elected officials should do what they think best—follow their intellects and their consciences—and let the people demonstrate their approval or not in the next election. ("A leader's relevant decision makers should be his heart and mind, not his political consultants and Gallup poll readouts," as Messerli, 2006, observes.) In our day and age of constant consultation of polls, this ideal, to the extent that it was ever held, has been mostly abandoned. New new media may well have the effect, for better or worse, of pushing that principle ever further out of play. They certainly have facilitated, as we will see later in this chapter (in the Occupy Wall Street section), a rise of direct democracy, which challenges the effectiveness of all representative democracy, Democratic or Republican, here in the United States and around the world.

The President and the BlackBerry

Not everyone in the new administration of 2009 was happy about new new media. The story broke 11 days after the election that prospects did not look good for Barack Obama to continue personally sending and receiving email once he got into the White House (Zeleny, 2008). The problem of hacking into the president's email was raised, as well as the Presidential Records Act, which requires all presidential communications to be eventually available for public review.

I blogged at the time that I thought depriving the president of email, especially in this day and age, was a bad idea (Levinson, "Keeping Obama with His Email," 2008).

The "President and the BlackBerry" turned out to be a story in four parts, with a happy ending:

1. Surely a system could be devised that would automatically record all email that the president sends and receives. Come to think of it, isn't that what happens on every Gmail or any email account anyway?

More important, should not a president be able to communicate in whatever way is most effective for him or her? A person in such a position, who is comfortable with current technology, needs to be able to devote maximum attention to thinking and communication, without having to be handicapped by using old-fashioned paper, telephone, and other systems. Email has grown astronomically in the past decade for good reason: It has all the advantages of writing—permanence—and yet it is as immediate as speech. Plus, it is global and easily searchable. (See Levinson, 1997, for more on the evolution and advantages of email.)

And then there is the question of mindset: Should not a president be able, if at all possible, to continue to use a communications system with which he or she is already very comfortable and accustomed?

This raises an issue fundamental to the evolution and adoption of all media. As we begin and continue to employ any new—or new new—medium, we come to rely on it as we would our eyes, ears, mouths, and fingers. As Marshall McLuhan (1964) famously put it, media act as our "extensions"—as surrogates for the communicating parts of our bodies and brains.

Taking email away from anyone so accustomed to using it would thus be the equivalent of a psychological amputation. The president should be the last person we would want to undergo such draconian and counterproductive treatment.

2. Barack Obama himself offered a very new-new-media–savvy argument in favor of keeping his BlackBerry—short for unfiltered email contact with the world—in an interview as president-elect with Barbara Walters on November 26, 2008. "I'm negotiating to figure out how can I get information from outside of the 10 or 12 people who surround my office in the White House," Obama told Walters. "Because one of the worst things I think that could happen to a president is losing touch with what people are going through day to day" (Obama, November 26, 2008). In a January 7, 2009, interview with John Harwood on CNBC-TV, Obama said the same thing, adding, in Charlton Heston-and-gun fashion, that "they would have to pry" the BlackBerry out of his hands. In other words, at the same time as the president-elect was assembling not just a team of rivals but a team of the best experts in foreign and domestic policy he could find, he was also fighting to keep his lines of communication at least somewhat open to the world at large of non-experts—or open to the logic of blogging, Wikipedia, Twitter, and the revolution of non-expert opinion—which is the democratizing hallmark of new new media ("every consumer a producer"). Actually, a better name for such "non-experts" would be "non-appointed experts," because the public at large was not likely to have the president's BlackBerry phone number or his email address—but, presumably, some experts outside the appointed ranks might well know how to contact the president, and making that easier and more direct is certainly a step in the right, democratizing direction. In addition, that same device would enable the president to reach out himself, not just receive advice.

Or, as Mike Allen, chief political correspondent for Politico.com, told Norah O'Donnell on MSNBC on November 26, 2008, "people [read: appointed experts] are reluctant to tell the truth to their boss…let alone a president of the United States." Whether president of the United States or town supervisor—like Paul Feiner— who, as we saw in chapter 11, relies on anonymous comments in his blog to keep informed—our leaders and representatives can all benefit from new new media connections to people outside the realm of appointed advisers.

3. Norah O'Donnell reported on MSNBC on January 18, 2009, two days before Obama's inauguration, that the "lawyers" had informed Obama and his team that they would be able to keep their BlackBerrys but not their instant messaging. The lawyers thought that IMing could make "embarrassing" messages available to hackers. If the concern, however, was salty language, such as that spoken by then White House Chief of Staff Rahm Emanuel, the cat was already well out of the bag (see rahmfacts. com for many examples).

4. And on January 21, 2009, Marc Ambinder reported in *The Atlantic* online that "Obama Will Get His BlackBerry," albeit with "a super-encryption package," but nonetheless for "routine and personal messages." An excellent example of human beings—in this case, the president—running our technologies, rather than letting concerns about their possible problems run us.

Off and Running

So the new administration in 2009 was off and running on all new new media cylinders. As we saw in earlier chapters, the president would go on to have an active Twitter account and regularly post YouTube videos. But as Obama successfully struggled against the forces of legal caution and inertia to keep his BlackBerry, his staff discovered upon moving into the White House that its telecom was stuck in a "technological dark ages" (Kornblut, 2009; Patterson, 2009), with no Facebook or Twitter, not even Gmail.

Law has always been among the slowest elements of society to embrace new media. Verbal contracts were considered more binding than written documents until the printing press standardized writing. Digital contracts have been a problem for decades, with questions arising over what constitutes a valid and binding signature if it is not produced by pen on paper (see Wright and Winn, 1998, for some early details).

But law sooner or later does catch up to technology, as do most people in politics. By February 2009, new new media were breaking out all over, especially in political circles. Republicans tweeted during meetings with President Obama (Goddard, 2009). John McCain, no longer a presidential candidate but still a Republican senator from Arizona, had a busy Twitter account. The stage was set for a Republican resurgence, buoyed by new new media and the Tea Party, that swept Republicans into an overwhelming majority in the House of Representatives.

The Tea Party and Twitter in 2010

Ron Paul's success on Digg and other new new media in 2007–2008 did not translate into votes in primary elections. But the online support was real—not, for the most part, the result of gaming new new media, as the older media wrongly supposed—and in 2009 this was transformed into hundreds of Tea Party demonstrations across America, most in protest of tax policy and Obama's proposed health care law.

Twitter was a key facilitator of these protests (see Nationwide Tea Party Coalition, 2010). By the November 2010 midterm national election, not only Twitter but the whole array of new new media helped propel Tea Party candidates—that is, Republicans with Tea Party views and support—into office.

In Massachusetts, for example, where Democratic hero and icon Ted Kennedy's U.S. Senate seat was up for special election due to his death the summer before, Republican Tea Party candidate Scott Brown "had a more effective strategy of using social networking tools including Facebook, Twitter, and YouTube to promote his campaign and connect with supporters" than did his Democratic opponent Martha Coakley (Emerging Media Research Council study, reported by Davis, 2010). Among the differences in new new media engagement as of January 2010:

> *Facebook Fans*: Brown (70,800), Coakley (13,529)
>
> *YouTube Video Views*: Brown (578,271), Coakley (51,173)
>
> *Twitter Followers*: Brown (9,679), Coakley (3,385)

Among politicians already in office, another study cited in the same article "found that Republican lawmakers are taking advantage of the Twitterverse significantly more than their Democratic counterparts. In the House, GOP lawmakers send out 529% more tweets than Democrats."

Brown soon joined them in the Senate, beating Coakley 52 to 47 percent in the usually Democratic state. He was the first Republican to be elected to the U.S. Senate in Massachusetts in almost 40 years (the previous Republican was Edward Brooke, elected in 1972).

When the November 2010 midterm national election came around, in which all members of the House of Representatives were up for election, the Republicans made good their Twitter advantage, and took control of the House with a majority of 241 to 192 for the January 2011–December 2012 session. Sixty-six members of the Republican majority formed the Tea Party Caucus. Obama's health care plan and the repeal of the "don't ask don't tell" policy in favor of equality for gays in the military had already been passed by Congress and signed into law by the president. But those would be the last pieces of major, pathbreaking legislation Obama and the Democrats would get through Congress in the first three years of his presidency. The new new media revolution that had facilitated Barack Obama's election in 2008 had now done the same for his opponents.

Is this giving too much credit to new new media? Consider this: In the national election of 2000 for the House of Representatives (before new new media) Democrats received 47 percent and Republicans 47.3 percent of the popular vote. In the election of 2004 (still before YouTube and Twitter, and with Facebook in its infancy), Democrats received 46.6 percent and Republicans 49.2 percent. In the House election of 2008, with Barack Obama and therefore the Democrats having the new new media advantage, Democrats received 53.2 percent and Republicans 42.5 percent in a near landslide victory. But just two years later in 2010, with Republicans clearly more in command of new new media than the Democrats, the landslide was all but completely reversed, with the Republicans getting 51.6 percent over the Democrats' 44.5 percent.

New new media have proven to be equal opportunity providers of political advantage.

The Arab Spring and Media Determinism

The year 2010 would have one more political revolution in part indebted to new new media—actually not one but three revolutions and more than a dozen other major and minor protests, beginning in 2010 but resulting in new governments in the three revolutions in 2011, and happening not in the United States but the Arab world—hence, the Arab Spring.

Indeed, the unsuccessful "Green Revolution" in Iran in 2009 can be seen as the beginning of the Arab Spring, even though Iran is not an Arab nation. So significant did the U.S. State Department view Twitter to be in getting word out to the world about that protest, that it asked Twitter to cancel a systemwide maintenance shutdown that had been planned for a night expected to be crucial in Tehran (see chapter 12).

The protests that began in Tunisia on December 18, 2010—considered the official commencement of the Arab Spring—had better results. The regime was overthrown on January 14, 2011, including the dissolution of its police, and a Constituent Assembly was elected on October 23, 2011. Although opinions differ on the precise significance of Twitter and YouTube in facilitating the successful revolution, most observers agree that they played important roles in coordinating actions on the ground and getting real-time reports out to the world (Ingram, 2011).

No one doubts the role of Facebook and Twitter in the Egyptian revolution that began January 25, 2011, and resulted in the resignation of Hosni Mubarak on February 11. Wael Ghonim's anti-Mubarak Facebook page was a trigger and rallying point for the revolution. "This revolution started online," he told CNN, "this revolution started on Facebook." Protesters held up signs in Arabic thanking Facebook and Twitter after Mubarak's departure (Evangelista, 2011; see also Levinson, "Marshall McLuhan, North Africa, and Social Media," 2011).

But the success in Egypt turned out to be shorter-lived than in Tunisia. Protesters were back in the streets a year later, outraged that nothing had really changed with Mubarak gone. The Egyptian military "threw Mubarak under the bus, then got back to business as usual," an American colleague who lives in Cairo told me, explaining that their domestic policies hadn't changed at all.

The revolution in Libya, which began February 15, 2011, was worse in process but better in results than Egypt's. Not only were new new media not enough, but neither were the protesters in the streets in Libya—Muammar Gaddafi's overthrow on August 23 and death on October 20, 2011, required massive NATO military intervention by air, and 25,000–30,000 lives lost (in contrast to 226 in Tunisia and 846 in Egypt; see The Arab Spring, Wikipedia, for details on these and the other Arab Spring protests, including in Syria, where, as of March 2012, the government and the protesters were locked in conflict). The better result in Libya is that, unlike in Egypt, there is apparently a thorough rebuilding of the government taking place.

The question of just how significant were and are the new new media in these uprisings can be better assessed by bearing in mind a distinction made by the concepts of "hard" versus "soft" determinism. In hard determinism, A is all that is necessary to cause B. If A spills a pail of water over B's head, that is all that is necessary for B to get wet (this is also known in science as a "sufficient" condition). But the relationship between, say, an elevator and a skyscraper is different. You couldn't have a skyscraper without an elevator or some sort of automatic lifting device, but you also need steel girders and other kinds of construction technology for skyscrapers to be built and to work. The elevator, in other words, is a necessary condition, not a sufficient condition for the skyscraper, and we call this kind of relationship "soft" determinism. When media are said to be responsible for a development in society, we're talking about soft determinism. This is what McLuhan had in mind when he wrote that there would have been no Hitler without radio, and no JFK elected as president in 1960 without television (McLuhan, 1964), and what I and others mean when we say there would have been no Arab Spring without new new media (see Levinson, 1997, for more on hard versus soft media determinism). It also was what NBC correspondent Harry Smith was thinking when he said of "The Revolution of the White Snow"—the Russian version of the Arab Spring, also known as "The White Revolution," ongoing since the summer of 2011—that "if no Facebook, there's no revolution" (Smith, 2012).

This cause-and-effect between new new media and freedom around the world is what makes Twitter's announcement in January 2012 that it now had the capacity to "withhold content from users in a specific country" so surprising and disquieting. Twitter mentioned the banning of "pro-Nazi content" in France and Germany as a policy it would like to accommodate, but, as Jon Bershad pointed out in *Mediaite* (2012), what if Twitter for whatever reason shut off the tweets of people struggling for freedom in the Middle East or anywhere in the world? In contrast, Google redirected its search engine from China to Hong Kong in 2010, rather than allowing searches on its system to be subject to Chinese censorship (Drummond, 2010).

Twitter did indicate that the rest of the world would be able to see the censored tweets, but the "freedom to connect"—Jerry Edling's (2011) apt description of the necessity of new new media for political freedom in today's world—applies to getting the message out not only to the world at large but also among the people struggling for freedom themselves.

The same applies to Occupy Wall Street.

Occupy Wall Street and the Resurgence of Direct Democracy

The first inkling I had that the Arab Spring would have ramifications that went beyond the Arab world, and would lead to protests not against dictators but elected leaders in representative democracies, was when I was in Barcelona in May 2011, to give a lecture at the McLuhan Centenary Conference at the Centre de Cultura Contemporània. My wife and I, strolling on the Rambla a few blocks from the Centre, saw protests about the economic conditions—Spain, like most of Europe and democracies in the West, was in the grip of the current recession. Later that evening, we asked Cristina Miranda de Almeida, one of the conference organizers, what the protesters wanted—a change in government? Were they campaigning for an opposition party? Not really, we were told. The protesters just wanted to call attention to unfair economic policies.

The Indignatos in Spain mounted protests throughout the country, gathering supporters and reporting to the world via Twitter and Facebook. It didn't take too long—July 13, 2011—for the Adbusters Media Foundation in Canada to propose a peaceful protest about the destructive effects of corporate greed, to take place on Wall Street, the symbolic and in many ways literal capital of capitalism and its corporate abuses (Berkowitz, 2011).

And that protest started two months later, in September 2011. As the Occupations continued, several things became increasingly clear:

1. The old media were misunderstanding the movement. I was asked on a panel on Fox-NY TV on October 27, 2011, why Occupy Wall Street had not come out with a list of demands. I explained that the need for a headline, for a lead story, was a characteristic of old media, and that media such as Twitter and Facebook, unhindered by space and time restrictions (limited pages in newspapers, limited minutes in newscasts), could present a more realistic multiplicity of demands. In the case of Occupy Wall Street, these ranged from ending usurious bank rates for students who needed extensions for repayment of their loans to helping people with mortgages underwater (owing more on their mortgage than their property was currently worth).

2. The police were abrogating the First Amendment rights of people to peaceably assemble, and the First Amendment rights of the press in all of its forms to report on Occupy Wall Street (see chapter 11 for more on this).

3. Occupy Wall Street was not interested in fielding candidates for the 2012 election (see Seltzer, 2012, for more)—making OWS, in this respect, very different from the Tea Party. (See also Aldous, 2011, for a comparison of OWS and Tea Party Twitter behavior—Tea Party tweets were fewer in number and less frequent than their OWS counterparts, but Tea Partiers were more likely to follow each other's accounts, making them a more "tightly knit" de facto group than OWS on Twitter.)

This point about elections, I think, gets at the most fundamental truth about Occupy Wall Street, and fuels the others. Occupy Wall Street is not particularly interested in the 2012 election, because it is at its core a protest against elections and representative democracy itself. As Adbusters' Kalle Lasn, quoted at the top of Wikipedia's Occupy Wall Street article, puts it: "When the financial meltdown happened, there was a feeling that, 'Wow, things are going to change. Obama is going to pass all kinds of laws, and we are going to have a different kind of banking system, and we are going to take these financial fraudsters and bring them to justice.' There was a feeling like, 'Hey, we just elected a guy who may actually do this'" (Eifling, 2011). And when that didn't happen, and the inspiration of the Arab Spring and the Indignatos did, Occupy Wall Street was born. (See Hazen, Lohan, and Parramore, 2011, for detailed analysis of the beginnings of Occupy Wall Street; see also Levinson, 2011, "Occupy Wall Street Chronicles"; and see also Lawson, 2012, for a list of scholarly articles investigating "Social Media and Protest," including The Arab Spring and Occupy Wall Street.)

It is not surprising that the old media did not and still do not understand Occupy Wall Street—the press was the right hand of the representative democracy that arose in the Renaissance and then in America. But the freedom of press insisted upon in the First Amendment was not to protect the representative democracy in America, and not even the press—it was to protect the people, whom Jefferson, Madison, and Monroe correctly saw as always on the edge of endangerment by the government the people had elected. When the police pepper spray peaceful demonstrators, as they did in California, or rough up both demonstrators and the press, as they did in New York City, they are the very agents of representative democracy Jefferson and his colleagues most feared. In this crucial area, the interests of the Tea Party in respecting the Constitution and Occupy Wall Street in bypassing representative government to address the damages wrought by greed are one and the same.

But how far away are we actually from bills being debated and voted upon by citizens via Facebook and Twitter instead of elected representatives and senators in Congress? On the one hand, the new new media, as we have seen throughout this book, allow for far more input by individuals than older media controlled by editors and producers. On the other hand, the new new media, as we also have seen, are ultimately controlled by people beyond the user's control—by the owners of Facebook, Twitter, YouTube, and the rest. This would make the new new media, as they currently are, ultimately unsuitable as vehicles of direct democracy. What might eventually be required is a Facebook-like system run by the government, and specifically designed to maximize discussion and voting (see Straus, 1991, 2001, for thoughts on direct democracy via the Web, prior to Facebook and new new media). But any governmental system—like the current voting system itself, vested, as per the Constitution, in the states—has problems of its own.

Iceland made forays into direct democracy facilitated by new new media in 2011, with a new constitution written with citizen input via Facebook and YouTube and a "direct democracy website" that allows citizens to easily communicate with their MPs (representatives) on proposed legislation (IceNews, 2011). But as Sorin Adam Matei (2011) pointed out, the final decisions regarding the new constitution were reached not via consensus as on Wikipedia but by executive fiat—or in the same way that voters got to have their questions posed to candidates in the first YouTube debates on CNN in the United States in 2008 (the questions were selected from voter submissions by CNN—see chapter 10).

Here in the United States, the Americans Elect organization is seeking to have candidates chosen on the Internet on the ballot in every state in the 2012 election (they have candidates in 30 states as of January 2012—see Heilemann, 2012, for details). This would direct-democratize the primary electoral process—certainly a good first step—but not the general election nor the actual workings of government, as in Iceland.

Meanwhile, new new media themselves are almost daily evolving to more directly democratic, less top-down structures. I interviewed Tim Pool, who has live streamed much of the Occupy Wall Street protest in New York (Timcast on UStream), in one of my classes at Fordham University in January, 2012 (see also Levinson, 2012, "Timcast"). He pointed out that the best way to report to the public via video is via live streaming—not in edited clips that we see in the old television media. But Pool's view that "we've got to get rid of the idea of editing" applies to YouTube, as well, which is neither live nor usually even a recording of an unedited video stream. Whether edited by a traditional media producer or the individual with the video camera in a phone, the result is an adulterated presentation of what actually happened in front of the camera.

But live streaming is still a long way from replacing or even competing with YouTube, which had more than 500 million users in 2011 in comparison to UStream's 2 million. In the U.S. presidential election of 2012, YouTube will undoubtedly be the big new new media video player, and representative democracy the electoral mainspring.

The U.S. Election of 2012

Mitt Romney all but wrapped up the 2012 Republican nomination for president in April 2012. Prior to that, however, there was serious speculation that the 2012 Republican nominating convention might be "brokered"—that is, not enough delegates would be chosen in support of any candidate in the primaries to give that candidate enough delegate votes to win the nomination on the first ballot in the convention. Prior to 2012, the last time a Republican convention had been brokered was 1940.

Thomas Dewey received 49.9 percent of the vote in the 1940 Republican primaries, but the nomination went to Wendell Willkie, whose supporters used radio—the new medium in those days—to create and convey the impression of surging support at the convention (Gizzi, 2012; see also Peters, 2005). Romney in many ways was the antithesis of a new new media candidate. He outspent his rivals in the primaries on mass media advertising by 10 to 1, and offered a stream of gaffes—calling attention to his wealth—that were fodder for Twitter and YouTube, and worked against him in the 2012 primaries. But he nonetheless was on his way to securing the Republican presidential nomination at the end of April 2012.

What does this tell us about the role of new new media in 2012 American politics? Romney was certainly not the choice of anyone with any sympathies for Occupy Wall Street, nor was he favored by even the Tea Party. The only conclusion is that the role of new new media in the 2012 Republican primaries was not decisive.

But neither was it negligible. Orrin Hatch, Republican senator from Utah, failed to win enough votes in the primary in that state to avoid a run-off election—the first one in his career in the Senate since 1976. His opponent was a Tea Party candidate.

Hatch went on to win the run-off election, but his Republican colleague Dick Lugar of Indiana—also in the Senate since 1976—was not so fortunate. He was trounced by his Tea Party favored opponent in the primaries, and became the first six-term senator to lose a primary battle since 1952.

Meanwhile, Occupy Wall Street, though yet to have major political impact in 2012, achieved a significant victory in May: A citizen photojournalist arrested during an OWS demonstration in New York City on New Year's Day 2012 for blocking traffic was found not guilty in Manhattan Criminal Court. The key piece of evidence in this acquittal of Alexander Arbuckle and triumph of the First Amendment was UStream video provided by none other than Tim Pool (Robbins, 2012). As has been the case since Rodney King in 1991, the video camera in the hands of a citizen serves as an effective check on abuse of official power.

At least two things now seem clear regarding the general presidential election in the Fall of 2012. The Republicans will continue to make as much good use of new new media as they did in 2010, and did not in 2008. And older media, especially cable television and talk radio, will continue to have an impact. The revolution in new new media is now bestowing equal opportunities for Democrats and Republicans, progressives and conservatives, Obama and Romney—and indeed people affiliated with no political party—as Facebook, Twitter, YouTube, and even newer media continue not to preempt but transform and work right alongside older media in our political world, and in all aspects of our lives.

Chapter Fifteen

The Dark Side of New New Media

I have for decades been delivering a lecture to my classes, and at conferences and symposia, titled "Guns, Knives, and Pillows." The lecture seeks to answer the question of whether some technologies are inherently good or bad in their use and impact on people.

I start with guns—they kill and wound people and are implements of crime. Indeed, they help make some violent crimes possible. So the gun is bad, right? It is a weapon that we would be better off without. But what if someone uses a gun as a weapon to stop or prevent a crime? Or not as a weapon against humans at all but as a way of getting food? Or as a technology of sport? Or, again as a weapon, but to defend our nation against violent attack? These cases make it clear that, although we might argue that the world as a whole would be better off without guns, we cannot consider them only or exclusively devices of evil.

Okay, then, what about the other side—can we think of a technology that is consistently, solely good? Is there a device with no ill effects? How about a pillow? It is soft, comfortable, and helps us sleep. So far, so good. But a pillow can also be used to murder someone via suffocation. This means that the pillow can be used to accomplish something that is not so good. Just as the gun cannot be considered solely a "bad" technology, neither can the pillow be considered solely good. Guns and pillows are actually a lot alike, in that they can each be used for good or bad.

Perhaps the problem is that we are looking at weak examples. How about stronger, more powerful technologies? Nuclear energy, atomic power, started off with a pretty bad reputation—atom bombs and nuclear weapons. Even that, however, had a morally ambiguous component; historians are still arguing about whether President Harry Truman was right to drop the atom bomb, twice, on Japan. On the one hand, it soon brought the world, in the Cold War that followed, to the brink of atomic destruction. And it killed many innocent civilians in Japan. On the other hand, the Japanese government was insisting on continuing the war, which would have meant the death of some additional number of American soldiers, had the bomb not been dropped. And Japan did attack the United States to start the war in the first place, not vice versa. Further, in addition to those ethical controversies, nuclear energy has been put to indisputably good use as a source of energy to generate electrical power and in medicine via radiation therapy. Nuclear energy thus turns out to be like guns and pillows, too, with both good and bad results for humanity.

Can we think about any stronger example of a good technology? How about medicine, which, based on its understanding of microbes and viruses, cures or reduces the damage of illness? Unfortunately, that same technology can and has been turned into a weapon arguably as dangerous as nuclear weapons—germ warfare. This indeed was used in World War I and by Saddam Hussein against Iran and his own people in Iraq, but even Adolf Hitler, fearing it could be used against German troops, refrained from using it in World War II. So medical technology ends up in the same category as guns, pillows, and nuclear energy: All can be used for good and bad purposes.

All technologies, indeed, are best described, in their capacity for good or bad, as knives. A knife can be used to cut food, which is good, and to stab an innocent person, which is bad. The determining factor in whether the knife—or whatever the technology—is used for good or bad turns out not to be the technology but the human being or group of humans using the technology.

In this chapter, we look at how the knives of new new media, which up until this point we have examined mostly with an eye to their advantages, can be used in the wrong hands for bad. Unfortunately, but not surprisingly, the evidence is that they can. We thus consider how the very advantages of new new media, when understood by people with evil intentions, can be used to hurt us.

Pre-New New Media Abuses: Bullying, Flaming, and Trolling

Some misuses and abuses of Web life predate new new media and were already part of the older new media constellation from which new new media arose.

Email, as is the case with any kind of communication, can be used to harass and cyberbully. Lori Drew used Myspace's message system to send the deceptive "the world would be better off without you" note, but it could just as easily have been sent via any email. And, indeed, email is used to convey all manner of spam and scams, ranging from easy ways to increase your sexual assets; to offers to entrust millions of dollars in your safekeeping by some desperate widow on the other side of the world, in order to get your bank account information; to messages urging you to immediately log on to your PayPal account, designed to get you to unknowingly give up your password to someone who would clean out your account.

Confidence games, of course, predate the Internet. There were probably Cro-Magnons who charmed the prehistorically naïve out of their best shells and furs. But the absence of a face and voice in email has long made it especially well-suited for all kinds of swindles.

Bullying was probably going on in Cro-Magnon circles as well—it certainly has long been a distressing feature of our schoolyards. Faceless, voiceless names on the Web have made bullying easier to mete out, too.

But bullying in a schoolyard or any physical place is usually more dangerous than cyberbullying, because physical intimidation is involved and can escalate into a "beat down." And, as we saw in chapter 10, YouTube, unfortunately, has given physical bullies an additional inducement, by providing a worldwide audience for uploaded videos of the beatings. Victoria Lindsay, a 16-year-old girl in Lakeland, Florida, was hospitalized in March 2008 after receiving a severe beating from six teenage girls, who videotaped it and told police they were responding to "trash" that the victim had posted about them on Myspace. "Police say the teens planned to post the video on YouTube," Rich Phillips reported on CNN.com (2008). He noted that "the idea of girls administering a vicious beating so they can post the video online may seem shocking, but it's becoming an increasingly common scenario, according to experts and news reports." The suspects were offered plea bargains in November 2008 (Geary, 2008).

The new new medium of YouTube thus can act as an accelerant for the ancient abuse of physical bullying. But it can also act to diminish additional bullying, after the video is posted on YouTube. The one drawback of bullying in person—disadvantage for the bullies, benefit for potential and actual victims and the world at large—is that the bullies can usually be clearly identified. This, obviously, does not stop bullies who want to see themselves on YouTube, but it does help police catch them (and, as Manjoo, 2008, suggests, potential bullies could even be deterred by the thought that the police might see them on a YouTube video made by some onlooker—see chapter 10 for more on such possible remedial effects of YouTube). Physical bullying, cyberbullying, flaming, and all such abuses flourish in anonymity.

Flaming goes back to the very origin of online communication in the 1980s; I noticed it in the first online class I taught for the Western Behavioral Sciences Institute in September 1984. The students were CEOs in business and public service, along with several Army generals, and we all used Kaypro II CP/M computers and 300 to 1200 bps modems to communicate. In this case, people did use their real names—we had met several months earlier in an in-person seminar, and the lack of pseudonymic cover likely restrained the flaming. But it was there, nonetheless, in comments entered late at night, when one student would be far harsher in criticism of another student than these business and public service executives had ever been as in-person students years earlier, or as business executives at the time of the online course. I realized back then that the synapse between anger and the expression of it was a lot shorter and quicker when it went to fingers over a keyboard than to tongues in in-person conversation (see Levinson, 1997; and Strate et al., 2003; and Barnes, 2012; for more).

The synapse only gets shorter and more grievous when real names and identities are unknown. Here is a user's assessment of the flaming she witnessed of another user on a popular conspiracy theory site in November 2008: "You hide your mediocrity and spew your rancor from behind your anonymity and attack/accuse/berate someone who could surely tear your ass up if he were similarly cloaked." This analysis of flaming accords double importance to the incendiary nature of anonymity: It emboldens the flamers yet restrains the victim (who is not "similarly cloaked") from responding in kind. And this makes perfect, unfortunate sense. Although the flamers and targets are both beyond in-person, physical range, and the flamers are encouraged by that distance to give vent to their anger or grievance, the target, using his or her real name, takes heightened care in commenting and responding, because those comments will leave a record directly traceable to the real-life commenter.

Trolling, which also goes back to the origins of online communication in the 1980s, is usually anonymous for much the same reason. But users can troll under their real names as well, as when a political troller writes comments for the purpose of inflaming and angering those with different or opposite political opinions. On my blog posts in support of Barack Obama in the 2008 presidential campaign, I encountered in the comments section many Republican or conservative trollers who were proud to use their real names.

But what constitutes a comment made by a troll versus a comment made by someone with a genuinely different opinion, political or otherwise? Sometimes it is difficult to tell the difference, but the defining characteristic of a troll's comment is that it is intended to evoke an angry reaction, not dialogue. "Obama will work with those who share his Islamic terrorist religion to destroy the United States" is what a troll's comment looks like. (Mattathias Schwartz notes in "The Trolls Among Us," 2008, that a troll has long been defined as "someone who intentionally disrupts online communities.") In contrast, "Obamacare will seriously damage heath care in America, and put the nation in further debt" could well be an example of a point made in a continuing dialogue.

Genuine attempts at dialogue invite rational response—or a reply that employs some kind of logic or offers evidence in support of its view—and this suggests a strategy to combat trolling. "Do not feed the troll" is the advice offered by many an online discussant in an attempt to silence or mute a disruptive commenter. Because the goal of the troller is to disrupt an online conversation by directing attention away from the conversation and toward the troll, starving the troll for attention makes sense. (See Sternberg, 2012, for more on trolling, especially its history in the 1990s.)

Ironically, flaming can arise from a genuine attempt at dialogue, when one or more people in the conversation lose their temper. In contrast, trolling is a deliberate attempt to extinguish a dialogue. Trollers may be more incorrigible than flamers, whom I have seen apologize and sometimes leave an online forum completely after regretting their initiation and pursuit of a flame. Nonetheless, the Pew Research

Center found that "negative behavior, such as trolling, seems to remain an admissible exception to at least 85% of SNS [social network site] users" (Northendom, 2012)—that is, trolling, when it occurs, does not disrupt a satisfactory new new media experience for at least 85 percent of users.

Online Gossiping and Cyberbullying

Online gossiping also has roots in earlier digital and offline media but brings us more fully into the realm of social new new media. Cyberbullying, which usually entails a group of online users "ganging up" on another user and talking "trash" or otherwise ridiculing and embarrassing the target, feeds on online gossip and can be fanned by flaming. (The Lori Drew/Megan Meier case is not really an example of cyberbullying, even though it was extensively reported as cyberbullying in the media, which is why I have used the term in connection with that case in this book and online. But it is, rather, an example of cyberstalking—by an adult of a teenager. See the "Cyberstalking" section.)

Online gossiping has colorful roots in newspapers, which reach back at least as far as Walter Winchell in the 1920s. As in all things new new media, the difference between Walter Winchell's columns in the *New York Daily Graphic* (and later in the *New York Mirror*) and online gossip leading to cyberbullying is that Winchell, Ed Sullivan, and Louella Parsons dished gossip about celebrities, whereas online gossip is often about the kid sitting next to you in class. JuicyCampus.com, in operation from 2007 to 2009, bragged that its "posts are totally, 100% anonymous" and inveighed its users to "give us the juice"—that is, juicy tidbits about people on campus, which may or may not be true. When I logged on to the site in 2008, I found this on the front page about a student at a major university: "really loose girl." Searching on another university, I found this gossip from a few days earlier: "What do you think about this girl? I heard she has a tattoo of a pussy cat right below her panty line." Forty-three percent of the seven people who voted on this entry agreed that it was true.

Online gossiping hardens into cyberbullying when the nasty messages are directed at the target, so the target sees them, and the people sending the messages work intentionally or unintentionally not as disparate individuals but as a group. I-Safe (2009) reported for the 2003–2004 school year that "42% of kids have been bullied while online," a figure that held constant through 2007–2008, with the National Crime Prevention Center indicating that "40% of all teenagers with Internet access have reported being bullied online" during that year (Cyberbully Alert, 2008). Ryan Halligan, age 13, committed suicide in October 2003 after a combination of in-person and instant-message bullying (Associated Press, 2007). Because Myspace did not go online until August 2003, and Facebook not until February 2004, the stability of the 40 percent number between 2003–2004 and 2007–2008 suggests that Myspace and Facebook inherited cyberbullying from earlier social media such as instant messaging and chat rooms. Indeed, I-Safe indicated with its 2004 survey that "savvy students are using Instant Messaging, e-mails, chat rooms and websites they create to humiliate a peer." By 2008, Cyberbully Alert included Myspace: "Chat rooms, MySpace, email, instant messaging and other online tools have all helped create the cyber bullying epidemic." The epidemic would soon spread to other new new media.

Phoebe Prince, 15 years old, committed suicide in January 2010, after cyberbullying so relentless that taunting comments were left on her Facebook page even after her death (James, 2010). By September 2010, Twitter and video streaming had enabled cyberbullying that led to another suicide—of 18-year-old Rutgers University freshman Tyler Clementi—whose gay sexual encounter was secretly captured on video and publicly streamed and tweeted about (Pitts, 2010). Clementi's roommate Dharun Ravi was tried and found guilty of invasion of privacy and bias intimidation (Allen & Ali, 2012).

The remedies advised by I-Safe are the same as those for traditional schoolyard bullying: A victim should let school officials and/or parents or a trusted adult know about the bullying and contact the police if physical harm is threatened—with the additional advice, especially appropriate for targets of cyberbullying, to block the bullies' online accounts and keep copies of all harassing messages. But in Tyler Clementi's case, there wasn't really enough time for that—the damage was done the instant the video was streamed. The immediacy of the new new media world, which is such an advantage in so much that it does, also is an advantage to those who wield it for ill.

One of the goals of responding to cyberbullying is to stop it before it escalates into cyberstalking, which can take the abuse out of the virtual schoolyard, into someplace more dangerous. Kathy Sierra received harassing comments on her *Creating Passionate Users* blog, initially ranging from "banal putdowns to crude sexual garbage," which then turned violent, with posts such as "...i hope someone slits your throat...." (Walsh, 2007). Sierra stopped writing her blog, "cancelled all speaking engagements," and added that "I am afraid to leave my yard" (BBC, 2007). *Creating Passionate Users* continues as a comment-only public record of Sierra's earlier blogging (Sierra, 2007). Her case serves as a disquieting example not only of the dregs of humanity who bully but that cyberbullying can target adults and professionals and veer into a kind of cyberstalking that makes the victim afraid to leave her own yard.

Cyberstalking

If cyberbullying is usually a group activity, cyberstalking is usually solitary, just as is stalking by a psycho or some other kind of obsessed or maladjusted individual in the real world. The essence of cyberstalking is persistent, unwanted online monitoring or contact of the target, to the point of obsession (see Netlingo, 2009). And just as stalking in the real world can be much more dangerous than traditional schoolyard bullying, so can cyberstalking have a worse impact than cyberbullying. Lori Drew in effect stalked Megan Meier—first with feigned affection, then a vicious comment—and Megan Meier took her own life. More common examples of cyberstalking entail a stalker with real, unrequited affection or obsession for the target. A U.S. Bureau of Justice Statistics advisory in 2009 reported that "3.4 million persons identified themselves as victims of stalking during a 12-month period in 2005 and 2006." Further, "more than one in four stalking victims reported that some form of cyberstalking was used, such as email (83 percent of all cyberstalking victims) or instant messaging (35 percent)." Myspace and Facebook were still but a year or two old when those people fell prey to cyberstalking. As with cyberbullying, cyberstalking has migrated from IMing and chat rooms to the specific, highly publicized venues of social media.

"Enhancing Child Safety & Online Technologies: Final Report" (Internet Safety Technical Task Force, 2008)—a task force of which Facebook, Myspace, Linden Labs (Second Life), Google, Yahoo, and 25 other major cyberplayers were members—highlights the conduciveness of social media for cyberstalking: "Contrary to popular assumptions, posting personally identifying information does not appear to increase risk in and of itself. Rather, risk is associated with interactive behavior" (p. 20). The recourse for targets of cyberstalking is the same as for victims of cyberbullying: Let responsible, trusted people know, including police, if any physical threats are made.

Foursquare, unfortunately, can provide an ideal tool for those who want to take their cyberstalking to the real world. So does Google Earth, in a different way. Many an address typed into the system yields a photograph literally of a nearby house on a street, replete with yard signs and cars parked in the driveway. The house being close by and not the address itself is a security precaution, as is the photograph being a few years old, but the camera angle can be shifted to actually show your house, which means that the whole world can see whether your lawn was mowed. And a stalker who knows what car you drive can easily see right where you live.

And Google maps can also be used by terrorists.

Tweeting and Terrorism

Let's begin by looking at how new new media can assist not terrorists but the combating of terrorists and the reporting of terrorism and its aftermaths in the real world.

New new media helped, and even played a crucial role, in the initial reporting of the Mumbai massacre on November 26, 2008. Adrian Finnigan on CNN International early the next day described how he had heard on his Facebook account from a friend in Mumbai, with word that he was okay and details on what he was seeing. James Winston, a Facebook "Friend," IM'd me on November 28, 2008, that his "best friend just moved to Mumbai a couple of weeks ago. He lives about two miles from the Taj Hotel. Facebook let me know he was safe." Meanwhile, Finnigan also reported that Twitter was buzzing with brief messages from people near the hotels that were under attack in Mumbai.

John Ribeiro (2008) provided similar news that the "Micro-blogging site Twitter is also being used to pass on information, or to just express feelings about the terrorist attack, and sometimes about the inadequate coverage of the crises by some Indian TV channels"—more evidence of new new media providing a dimension not available via old broadcast media—in this case, providing direct, personal information about a terrorist massacre. Just as students had sent email from the Tiananmen Square massacre of 1989, letting the world and the mass media know what was happening, so did Twitter and Facebook in 2008 provide much-needed windows onto what had happened in Mumbai.

At times during the three-day crisis, the old media of television provided no coverage at all. On the final night of November 28, 2008, as the Taj Mahal Hotel still burned and Indian commandos were readying their final assault, MSNBC ran canned programming—its "Doc Bloc" with unrelated footage several years old— and Fox interspersed its coverage of Mumbai with reruns of *The O'Reilly Factor* and Greta Van Susteren's *On the Record*. Only CNN provided live, continuing coverage (see my "MSNBC Runs Canned 'Doc Bloc,'" November 28, 2008, for further details). Fortunately, people interested in learning what was happening in Mumbai could consult Twitter, where updates were posted more often than once a minute from onlookers in Mumbai.

Some of the tweets I noticed, just seconds apart in the early morning, New York time, of November 28, 2008, follow: "Indian officials are big on bulllshit, weak on results"; "What guns are our commandos using???"; "100 trapped at Trident"; "this whole thing stinks, our govt have left us as sitting ducks, throw UPA [political party in power in India] out"; and "Japan had terrorist strike in past, China is blessed to have neighbors like us, we are not that fortunate." Twitter advised that 216 new tweets on this subject had arrived in the 30 seconds it took me to capture the preceding tweets. Of course, there is no guarantee that those blurbs all came from Mumbai—though Twitter would have had a record of the IP addresses, if the source of the tweets needed confirmation.

But no system is perfect. As Stephanie Busari pointed out on CNN.com/asia (2008), "Someone tweets a news headline, their friends see it and retweet, prompting an endless circle of recycled information" on Twitter.

Twitter would go on to play a crucial role in what can be perceived to be the beginning of the Arab Spring—with the U.S. State Department asking Twitter not to go down as scheduled for a few hours of maintenance during the unsuccessful Green Revolution in Iran in 2009. We explored this and the use of Twitter in democratizing other countries in further detail in chapter 14 (see also chapter 12), and Twitter's January 2012 announcement that it might censor tweets in some countries.

But Twitter, to return to the evil use of new new media that is the subject of this chapter, can also be an effective tool in the hands of terrorists. Busari notes that "it was suggested via Twitter that terrorists were using the medium to gain information about what Indian security forces were doing." And this does not address the possibility, even the likelihood, that Twitter and other social new new media could have been used by the terrorists in the planning of their attacks.

Indeed, a U.S. Army report of October 16, 2008, expresses the concern that Twitter "could theoretically be combined with targeting" by terrorists (Musil, 2008). The Army report does not point out, however, that Twitter offers no digital communication that could not already be accomplished by group email, IMs, and chat rooms. But Twitter and its facility for rapidly creating de facto groups of "Followers" undeniably makes the mobilization and deployment of any group easier—including groups of terrorists. The upside for civilization is not only that law enforcement and security can similarly tweet, but also, in the event that Twitter is used by terrorists or criminals, Twitter would have a record of those communications, for subsequent pursuit and conviction of the terrorists.

New new media thus can be employed for abusive social activities ranging from virtual school bullying to worldwide terrorism. We look next at how new new media can abet a more conventional kind of crime.

The Craigslist Bank Heist

Almost sounds like the name of a movie, doesn't it? But it's real, and, even if Craig's didn't quite rob the bank, it was used to hire "a dozen unsuspecting decoys" (see King5.com, 2008) to help the real bank robber get away in a heist that took place on September 30, 2008, at a Bank of America branch in Monroe, Washington.

Now, my wife and I have used Craigslist to do good things. Not long after the bank heist was reported, we used Craig's to purchase a nice La-Z-Boy loveseat for $75. But like the knives of all media, the no-cost ads sell just about anything people want to buy and sell, including not only loveseats but also (until not too long ago) prostitutes (see Lambert, 2007; Abelson, 2009) and, in the case of the Bank of America in Monroe, accomplices in a bank robbery.

The robber's plan was quite ingenious. Have a dozen people, dressed just like you, standing in front of the bank. This little flashmob would dilute the value of what eyewitnesses told the police. "I came across the ad that was for a prevailing wage job for $28.50 an hour," one of the decoys explained to King5.com. He was instructed to wear a "yellow vest, safety goggles, a respirator mask…and, if possible, a blue shirt"—the same outfit as the robber, who made good his escape through a nearby creek.

He was, however, arrested a few weeks later—DNA did him in (see Cheng, 2008, for details). I guess this shows that biological code is still more powerful than digital code. Or, as my character, NYPD forensic detective Dr. Phil D'Amato, says in my 1999 science fiction novel, *The Silk Code,* "DNA is the ultimate dossier" (quoted in Gerald Jonas's *New York Times* review, 1999).

It's fun to take a break in this dark chapter with such an amusing, true story. But the unyielding, grim reality is that the criminal use of new new media can serve up death and destruction. The accused "Craigslist Killer" Philip Markoff, arrested in April 2009 on charges of murdering a masseuse obtained through Craigslist, brings home once again the perilous, frightening side of new new media. Yet, as Leslie Harris (2009) noted, "What if the criminal in question had lured his victims using newspaper classifieds? Would we be calling this the *Boston Globe Killer*?" Her apt point is that killers trolling the media for victims are hardly an invention or unique consequence of new social media. Still, their abuses, whether unique or in common with older media, must be studied, understood, and protected against, where possible. Markoff, for his part, committed suicide in 2010 before his case could come to trial.

Spam

We come near the end of this tour of the dark side to the least destructive but most prevalent despoilers of online systems: conveyors of spam, not just in email but also in blog comments. In its most common new new media form—comments about gold jewelry or something else utterly irrelevant to the subject of the blog post—spam is like an online mosquito bite, digital graffiti, which distracts from the reading of the blog and may annoy the reader but otherwise does no harm.

Indeed, the main ill effect of spam is the extra work it imposes on bloggers and Web administrators who want to eliminate it, and the impediment that protective measures installed by bloggers can have upon nonspamming commenters. As we saw in Chapter 11, CAPTCHAs are a common defense against spammers, but these make legitimate commenters go through an additional hoop to enter their comments. A blogger interested in a no-holds-barred political discussion might choose to leave a blog unmoderated, to encourage immediate entry of comments and rapid response, but this would also leave the blog open to spam having no connection to the blog.

Facebook, Twitter, and all social media suffer from similar annoyances. Spam tweets with a link to a page selling a usually dubious product or service can be sent to anyone's account. Twitter allows reporting of such spam, which automatically removes the spamming tweet and blocks the spammer. Facebook allows users to be tagged, which means their names can be associated with any text, image, or video. The taggee can remove the tag, or hide or delete the item from his or her timeline. Facebook privacy settings allow selection of who can tag you—"Friends," family, everyone—but using this option could result in not being tagged when you might want that. Myspace has long been vulnerable to unwanted comments on the member's profile comment section—these can be removed as well as marked as spam. YouTube has similar options for comment pages on videos, including the uploader choosing not to allow comments at all.

One vulnerability that spammers have on these systems, but not when they post spam on individual blogs not situated on some central social system, is that Facebook and the rest can and do cancel the accounts of spammers. New accounts can be created easily enough, but the spammer is at least slowed down a little.

"Blog spam" is a phrase that applies to something a little different from the just-noted spam. In general, "blog spam" is a derogatory assessment of the worth of a blog post, and it sometimes refers to a blog post whose only goal—as least as perceived by the person who calls it "blog spam"—is to lure readers for the purpose of earning Google AdSense revenue, or clicking on some other ad or link associated with the blog. Digg has yet an additional usage of the "blog spam" appellation, which refers to a news article that has taken a story from a previously posted article, with an eye toward drawing readers to the new post. This might also be called plagiarism, except the new post might even give credit to the earlier source of the story.

Stepping back a little and looking at new new media as part of the larger constellation of all human communication, we can see that spam is just the digital equivalent of noise, or the most common example of noise (in media theory, any interference with communication), that afflicts all media. In the case of older media such as newspapers, noise occurs every time the newspaper prints something that is false. Noise can occur when the ink smears or when we get distortion on our television screens (see Levinson, 1988, for more on the Shannon-Weaver model of communication, and noise). Similar kinds of noise can occur with false information on blogs and Wikipedia, or when any online system or laptop or smart phone encounters technical difficulties. But the power that new new media gives all consumers to become producers creates a new kind of noise—a noise deliberately created and posted by a user.

In the old media world, and indeed in the physical world as well, noise has long been recognized as never totally reducible or capable of elimination. You introduce a new system for improving storage and transmission of music—MP3s—and this creates new intellectual property problems. Every remedy for one kind of noise opens up the system for a new kind of noise. As a form of new new media noise, spam is likely also impossible to eliminate entirely, at least not without incurring a new form of new new media noise. Fortunately, the price of spam on blogs is usually not too high to pay.

Or, put otherwise, one form of noise that new new media are especially not likely to eliminate, or even effectively control, is the digital trespass of spam—because, to truly and effectively eliminate spam, the new new medium would have to be so heavily controlled as to no longer be a new new medium. (See also chapter 13, Wikipedia, for intrinsic new new media capabilities of identifying and removing noise.)

Old Media Overreaction to New New Abuses: The Library vs. the Blogger

We have been tracing throughout this book the antagonism (as well as the mutual dependence) of various old media to new new media—antagonism that looks at new new media as unworthy competition and alternatives to old media. Press and broadcast media critiques of bloggers—not the content of given blogs, which is fair game, but the process of blogging itself—are the seminal example. Denunciations of "bloggers in pajamas" discussed in chapter 11 are indicative of the ridicule and scapegoating, going beyond rational criticism, that bloggers have been subjected to. New new media have not been above wielding similar attacks on themselves, as when Facebook banned photos of women nursing their babies.

But the underlying tension is greatest between old and new new media, and it comes to the surface whenever any real wrongdoing on or by new new media is involved. Cyberbullying and cyberstalking are justifiably big stories in all news media—old, new, and new new—because they can lead to real life-and-death situations, and therefore need to be known by everyone. But the tension also erupts when there is no real wrongdoing in the new new media, only the incorrect perception of it.

Twanna A. Hines writes in "I'm a Writer, Not a Child Pornographer" (2008) that she showed up for "a hard day's work" with her laptop at the Mid-Manhattan branch of the New York Public Library, where she liked to do her writing, to find that access to her blog had been banned. The reason? She writes in her blog about "dating, sex and relationships…about men who wear thongs, technology, and sex." The library advisory indicated that sites that depict obscenity, child abuse, and materials "harmful to minors" could be blocked.

None of these were depicted on Hines's site, and, indeed, after someone else contacted the library and complained that access to her site was blocked, the library removed the block. But what does the fact that her site had been blocked at all say about the role of libraries in our new new media world?

A frequent critique of personal computers, going back to the 1980s (see Levinson, 1997), is that people who spend time on them are cutting themselves off from "real life"—that is, in-person, interactions with other human beings. This argument might claim today, for example, that shopping in a Barnes and Noble would be better or healthier than buying books on Amazon, because in a Barnes and Noble you deal with real people, not pixels. Facebook would be seen as exacerbating this perceived problem, by offering digital social alternatives for a variety of in-person interactions. And as we saw in chapter 10 in the Vatican's statement accompanying the Pope's YouTube channel, the Vatican has indeed expressed this concern about social media.

Looking at the case of Hines in this context of virtual versus in-person interactions, we can see that she sought to be out among real people, in a public library, when she was practicing her new new media craft of blogging. And this made the New York Public Library uncomfortable, because of the content of her blog. To be clear, she was not using a library computer, just its wi-fi Internet connection. If we agreed with the library that the materials on Hines's blog were not suitable for children, was there no better method to protect them from the site? Rather than blocking out everyone else, including the author herself, perhaps the library could have required some special code to access such sites, one given only to people showing proof of age.

One hopes that libraries will use these kinds of solutions in the future. But in the present age of misunderstanding and suspicion of new new media, including not only by old media but also their repositories in venerable institutions of free societies such as libraries, the simple banning or blocking of the new new media access is, unfortunately, the easy remedy.

Twanna Hines says she continues to love the New York Public Library and quotes T. S. Eliot that "the very existence of libraries affords the best evidence that we may yet have hope for the future of man." That future will be a little better assured when libraries show a little better comprehension of media that are increasingly rivaling and supplanting the books on their shelves as the library's intellectual stock and trade.

As with going out to the movies rather than watching television, or dining in a restaurant rather than at home, the eventual future of libraries will reside in providing places that offer social advantages not found at home, along with all the informative avenues available at home, to lure people out of their homes with their laptops. But to the degree that all of the world's books may someday be available for free via smart phones and tablets, the library will be any place we can sit comfortably and read, be it café or park bench.

Credits

Index